Real Essentialism

Real Essentialism defends the metaphysical position that everything in the world has an essence or nature that fixes its identity. Although a traditional view in philosophy, defended most famously by Aristotle, scepticism about and hostility to the notion of essence in modern and contemporary philosophy are a commonplace. Recent work in logic and philosophy of language has given essentialism a new life, but *Real Essentialism* argues that it has still not been given the contemporary defence it requires. It sets out a full theory of essence and applies it to such questions as the nature of species, the nature of life and the essence of the person.

David S. Oderberg is Professor of Philosophy at the University of Reading. He has published many books and articles in metaphysics, philosophical logic, ethics, philosophy of religion, and other subjects.

Routledge Studies in Contemporary Philosophy

Real Essentialism

David S. Oderberg

Routledge
Taylor & Francis Group

NEW YORK AND LONDON

First published 2007
by Routledge
270 Madison Avenue, New York, NY 10016

Simultaneously published in the UK
by Routledge
2 Park Square, Milton Park, Abingdon, Oxon OX14 4RN

Routledge is an imprint of the Taylor & Francis Group, an informa business

Transferred to Digital Printing 2008

Typeset in Times New Roman by
Taylor & Francis Books

Library of Congress Cataloging in Publication Data
Oderberg, David S.
  Real essentialism / David S. Oderberg.
    p. cm. – (Routledge studies in contemporary philosophy ; 11)
  Includes bibliographical references and index.
  1. Essentialism (Philosophy) I. Title. II. Series.
  B105.E65O43 2007
  111'.1–dc22
    2007010357

British Library Cataloguing in Publication Data
A catalogue record for this book is available from the British Library

ISBN13: 978-0-415-32364-2 (hbk)
ISBN13: 978-0-203-35675-3 (ebk)

Contents

List of illustrations

Figures

Preface

The following study is an exercise in traditional metaphysics. By 'traditional' I mean, somewhat tendentiously, to qualify that method of thinking and those doctrines which, despite occasional interludes and conflicting interpretations, embodied the prevalent school of philosophy for nearly two thousand years. That is the school of Aristotelianism and its followers, in particular St Thomas Aquinas and the Thomists, who dominated philosophy throughout the medieval period, and whose ideas continued to exercise influence despite the advent of Cartesianism, the Scientific Revolution of the seventeenth and eighteenth centuries, and the ascendancy of empiricism in anglophone philosophy. Its influence even lingered on into the nineteenth and early twentieth centuries, to be found especially in the domain of logic but also in metaphysics itself.

Nevertheless, the decline of traditional philosophy, and of traditional metaphysics in particular, was assured by the movements mentioned above, the death sentence having already been pronounced by the nominalism and scepticism of late Scholasticism in the fifteenth century. The aim of *Real Essentialism* is to rehabilitate some of the core ideas of Aristotelian metaphysics in a contemporary context devoid of the minutiae of historical exposition and textual exegesis (though quite a bit of this will be found in the notes to each chapter). If traditional metaphysics is to have a future – and I believe it assuredly does – then it must not allow itself to be bogged down in interpretative niceties. Instead, it must show itself to be a living system and method for doing philosophy. Its concepts must be deployed to tackle fundamental problems, including those that occupy contemporary thought. And it must shake itself free of the time-worn rhetoric that has, for several centuries, been used to vilify it in the absence of argument at worst, and, at best, by virtue of a highly defective understanding of just what the concepts and theses of neo-Aristotelianism actually mean.

At the heart of traditional metaphysics is the thesis that everything has a real essence – an objective metaphysical principle determining its definition and classification. Such principles are not mere creatures of language or convention; rather, they belong to the very constitution of reality. Needless to say, no book can discuss the essence of everything there is. What I aim to do is to set out the core theory of real essentialism and apply it to some selected categories of object. Central to the core theory – which is about substances, a kind of entity that has only fairly recently seen metaphysicians taking it seriously again after centuries of empiricist neglect – is the revival of one of the most reviled of the traditional doctrines, namely the doctrine of substantial forms. The vast majority of professional philosophers (let alone students) do not even know what the doctrine is; still less are they able to discuss it with any insight. And by those who do know, the doctrine is assumed to have been utterly discredited by Descartes and the empiricists. Nothing is further from the truth: for not only are substantial forms defensible – they are necessary to metaphysics, especially to any position that takes essence seriously. Hence, as I argue in Chapter 1, expanding on the theme throughout the rest of the book, the welcome contemporary revival of essentialist thinking fails adequately to explain essence if it does not use the ideas and conceptual tools of traditional metaphysics, not least the doctrine of substantial forms.

In Chapters 2 and 3 I address the most common anti-essentialist arguments, such as are to be found in empiricism, in Quine, Wittgenstein, Popper and elsewhere. None of them stands up to scrutiny, however popular they may be. One common criticism is that essences are unknowable, a mysterious posit that plays no role in scientific thinking, something underlying all phenomena but forever inaccessible to observation. This sort of objection betrays a serious misunderstanding of how essences are knowable and is symptomatic of the scientism that pervades even the most robustly metaphysical thinking in current philosophy. An important aim of this book is to undermine scientism and thereby to restore to metaphysics some of the methodological autonomy it has long lost – and not regained even among the most committed of contemporary metaphysicians.

In Chapters 4–7 I set out the complete theory of which substantial forms are but a part, namely hylemorphism. The term has come a little into vogue recently (especially among that growing number of philosophers who have come to be known as 'analytical Thomists'), but there has as yet been no statement of just what hylemorphism amounts to in all its detail and ramifications. Those who use the term will likely blanch at what they must be committed to if they are to count themselves as genuine hylemorphists, but this is a bullet they must bite or else refrain from using the term. The doctrine of substantial forms is but one part of a system of logically related concepts, principles, and distinctions; to lose one is to lose them all. Form and matter; species and genus; dichotomous classification; act and potency; properties and accidents; even the dreaded doctrine of prime matter – these are all part and parcel of the hylemorphic system, and together they provide a coherent and eminently plausible framework for understanding the essences of things. In Chapters 6 and 7 I apply the system to topics such as artefacts, powers, laws of nature, origins and constitution, showing how we must deploy the traditional machinery to fit such issues into an overall essentialist theory.

In many ways, Chapters 8–10 are the most controversial. It is one thing to set out a metaphysical system and quite another to use it to encroach upon the hallowed domain of natural science. Even the most autonomous minded of contemporary metaphysicians hesitate long and hard before venturing to suggest that metaphysics can correct the supposed deliverances of science. Such hesitation, more often downright refusal, is doubly misguided. First, it ignores the metaphysical presuppositions that litter scientific thinking. Second, it is itself born of the contemporary scientistic view of the world, according to which philosophy can only ever have a 'bookkeeping' role in respect of science. The philosopher must keep the house of science neat and tidy – no contradictions, no fallacies, and maybe even a few suggestions as to how to make sense of the phenomena – but the philosopher may not raise the possibility of structural or design flaws. There can be no intrusion upon the phenomena themselves. The metaphysician is free to say, 'If this happened, then you can interpret it like that'; but it is almost unthinkable that he should say, 'According to sound metaphysical principles, it could not have happened like that – even if I cannot tell you how it did happen.'

The last three chapters pay no heed to scientism. They not only show how traditional essentialism should be applied to concrete problems – the essence of life, the essence of species in biology, and the essence of the human person – but provide arguments that explicitly encroach upon terrain normally reserved for natural science. For, according to the traditional view, metaphysics is not the handmaid of science; rather, it is *itself* a science – indeed the queen of the sciences. Whether a given metaphysical argument works is one thing, but whether the metaphysician is ever free to say, 'However it happened, it could not have been like *that*', is another. I hope that at least some of the arguments in the last three chapters do show that the metaphysician's role in helping us to understand reality is far wider, and far deeper, than even the most 'hard-headed' of realist metaphysicians currently dare to allow.

David S. Oderberg
Reading, August 2007

Acknowledgements

Much of the preliminary research for this book was undertaken during 2003–4 when I held a Leverhulme Trust Research Fellowship. I am grateful to the Trust for its generosity and its continued support for academics working in all fields no matter how abstract. I would also like to thank the University of Reading, whose Research Endowment Trust Fund and sabbatical scheme gave me the freedom to continue my research on this project.

I would like to thank the University of Notre Dame Press for permission to use material from my paper 'Hylomorphism and Individuation', published in J. Haldane (ed.) *Mind, Metaphysics, and Value in the Thomistic and Analytical Traditions* (2002); also Cambridge University Press and Ellen Paul, Fred Miller and Jeffrey Paul for permission to use material from my paper 'Hylemorphic Dualism', published in *Social Philosophy and Policy*, Vol. 22, No. 2 (Summer 2005) and in Paul, Miller and Paul (eds) *Personal Identity* (2005).

I am also grateful to the following people, who read various parts of the draft material for the book and provided many helpful comments: George Englebretsen, Edward Feser, James Franklin, Peter Hacker, Joel Katzav, Joseph LaPorte, Jonathan Lowe, and Fred Sommers. I am also grateful to Stephen Braude, John Cottingham, John Haldane, David Jehle and Eduardo Ortiz for their feedback on the paper that formed the basis of Chapter 10. Thanks go also to my graduate students, including Philip Rees, Zhiheng Tang and Eileen Walker, for helpful comments on various portions of the book. And a final thank-you to Fiona Woollard for her proofreading of the entire typescript, which saved me from many errors.

Needless to say, it should not be inferred that any of the people who have commented on any parts of the draft of this book agree with any of the theses defended in it.

Rem tene, verba sequentur
(Grasp the thing and the words will follow)
Cato the Elder (234–149 BC)

1 Contemporary essentialism and real essentialism

1.1 Against modalism: possible worlds

That there are at least some things in the world that have essences is a proposition to which more philosophers are prepared to subscribe than there once were. This is due almost exclusively to the growth of what might be called modal thinking – or *modalism* – in the light of the development of formal modal logic in the second half of the twentieth century.

The development of modal logic went hand in hand with the development of modal semantics, which it is standard to give in terms of the theory of possible worlds. The semantics naturally gave rise to speculation on just how we should understand possible worlds, with positions ranging from strongly anti-realist to strongly realist. Yet, whatever the position, most philosophers have come to believe that thinking about possible worlds can give us some insight into whether or not objects have essences.

The famous work of Saul Kripke and Hilary Putnam in the 1970s sparked a resurgence of essentialist thinking, and was based firmly on an understanding of meaning that relied heavily on the concepts of modality and possible worlds. In one way or another, Kripke–Putnam style reflection has supposedly allowed many to see that water is essentially H_2O; that tigers are essentially animals; that heat is essentially molecular motion; that material objects could not have been originally constituted differently from how they were in fact originally constituted; that maybe certain material objects could not have a wholly different constitution at any time from the one they actually have; that an animal could not have originated from a different sperm and egg to the ones it actually originated from; perhaps that the mind is not necessarily identical with the brain (and hence, according to Kripke's well-known view, not actually identical with the brain); and so on.

Whether or not any of these propositions is true is not the present concern. (I will say more about such claims and many similar ones throughout this book.) Rather, what is of concern is that anyone should think that modalism can tell us anything – at least anything of any metaphysical significance – in the first place. There are serious problems with the very idea of appealing to possible worlds to tell us anything about essences.

Some of them derive from the use of possible worlds itself, and I do not propose to add to the already voluminous discussion of which theory of possible worlds, if any, is correct.[1] We should, though, note a few issues that undermine appeal to the concept of possible worlds in trying to gain some metaphysical insight into modality in general and essence in particular. First there is the following worry: any realist theory of possible worlds will be circular in its attempt to illuminate modality, for there has to be some criterion of what counts as a *possible* world; there are by definition no *impossible* worlds. But then we have to have a prior conception of modality before we can use possible worlds to explain modality. Why, as Scott Shalkowski (1994) asks, are the pencils in my drawer not possible worlds either collectively or individually? David Lewis replies that they 'bear no interesting relation to our common modal notions' and do not have the 'right constituents' to serve as truthmakers for modal statements (Shalkowski 1994: 679).[2] Yet this is to state the obvious. The question is why it is so, and the answer is that we already possess a prior grasp of modal notions sufficient to rule out pencils as possible worlds. But this means the realist theory of possible worlds is circular: it cannot be used to explain or analyse modality if we already have to understand modality (at least to some fairly robust degree) before we can even give the theory.

Secondly, even if the realist could get around the circularity problem, say by postulating possible worlds as primitive existents, as a modal *given* – rather than as entities for which we have to have modality-involving criteria – he would end up merely relocating the analysandum. Instead of having to understand the modal properties of objects *within* a world, we will have to come to terms with the modal properties of the worlds themselves. What is it for the *worlds* to have the modal properties they do (at the very least being possible, and perhaps also necessary)? We are still faced with unanalysed modality, only it has moved somewhere else. Now there may, as realists believe, be net theoretical benefits to be gained from explaining the modality of individuals within worlds in terms of the worlds themselves, but unless one is wedded, implausibly, to a cost–benefit approach to metaphysics, this will not be satisfactory. We want to know why objects have the modal properties they do. To answer that this is (at least in part) because worlds have the modal properties they do is only to push the problem from one place in the rug to another.

Thirdly, all possible worlds theories stare in the face the problem of irrelevance. Kripke famously stated the objection that when we say that Humphrey might have won the election, we are talking about *Humphrey*, not some counterpart (Kripke 1980: 45). It is irrelevant to what Humphrey might have done that in some other world some other individual (albeit very similar to Humphrey) does something, no matter how similar what he does is to what Humphrey himself might have done. Lewis replies obscurely that the other world, with its Humphrey counterpart, 'represents' our Humphrey as winning – '[s]omehow, perhaps by containing suitable constituents or perhaps by magic' (Lewis 1986: 196). Yet this is beside the point: I could represent Humphrey as winning by painting a picture of him doing so, or writing a screenplay. The problem is how what is going on in another world – especially in a world causally isolated and spatio-temporally disjoint from ours, as it is in Lewis's theory – could have any bearing whatsoever on what might have happened to Humphrey. Lewis is well known for attacking 'magical ersatzism', the view that possible worlds are simple abstract entities. Yet if any theory contains a hefty dose of magic, his does.

The problem of irrelevance undermines not only Lewis's theory. Whether possible worlds are understood as abstract natures (Stalnaker 1976), possible states of affairs (Plantinga 1974), 'world books' (Adams 1974), or some other kind of real but abstract entity, the question arises as to how what is true of that kind of thing can have any bearing on the modal properties of a concrete material object such as a man, a mouse or a mountain. For example, according to Plantinga every possible world w is a maximal or 'super' state of affairs to which there corresponds one and only one 'super-proposition' S – the union of some set of propositions with the set of all of their consequences. Worlds are correlated with superpropositions (or 'books', as he also calls them) in the following way: w obtains if and only if every member of S is true (Plantinga 1970). Now it is true that Socrates is essentially not a number. For Plantinga this is true if and only if every world containing Socrateity contains the non-numberhood of the thing that possesses Socrateity, which in turn is true if and only if every book containing the proposition that Socrates exists entails the proposition that Socrates is not a number.

Now leaving aside for the moment the issue of individual essences or haecceities (about which I shall say a little in Chapter 5.4) and also the question-begging use of the modal concept of entailment, the problem is what bearing either states of affairs or books has on the essential non-numberhood of Socrates. Formulations involving either of them do not give the *meaning* of the statement that Socrates is essentially not a number, because the latter proposition is about *Socrates*, not about either non-actual states of affairs or books. But does either kind of formulation give the *truth conditions* of such a statement? It depends on what one means by 'truth conditions'. In whatever sense possible worlds may be said to exist, of course 'Socrates is essentially not a number' is true if and only if every world (for Plantinga, maximal state of affairs) containing Socrates (or Socrateity) contains the non-numberhood of Socrates (or of the individual possessing Socrateity). It would be inconsistent to hold that Socrates was essentially a non-number but that there *was* some world in which Socrates was a number. In this sense the appeal to worlds (or books) provides truth conditions: it tells us what is the case if and only if Socrates is essentially a non-number. But it does not tell us what *makes it true* that Socrates is essentially not a number. Plantinga and other realists may think it does, but again they would be guilty of irrelevance, and of confusing the *consequences* of

Socrates's having the essence he does with the *constituents* of that essence, which belong to the individual person of Socrates. It is because of what Socrates *is* that, if there are possible worlds, then in every possible world in which he exists he is essentially not a number. But what he is by virtue of which this is true of him has no more to do with how things are in a possible world than his being snub-nosed has anything to do with what is going on in the Himalayas.

If the appeal to real possible worlds changes the subject from the possessors of essences to the situations in which those possessors exist, then the appeal to modal fictionalism or other anti-realist devices fares no better. No appeal to fictional discourse can explain why a real entity like Socrates has the essence he does – why he is essentially a man but essentially not a mouse. If talk about possible worlds is akin to talk about fictional characters in a novel but the modal truths they illustrate are still literally true, then the fictional discourse is a mere heuristic by-product of literal modal truths that remain to be explained. If the fictionalist takes modal truths *themselves* to be not literally true, then he has given up on real modality (and hence real essence) altogether, and should be classed together with other modal sceptics and anti-essentialists (on whom see Chapter 2). If the anti-realist takes appeal to possible worlds in the revelation of modal truth to be a akin to using a calculator or an abacus to uncover arithmetical truth, then one can question how useful the heuristic device may be (nowhere near as useful as a calculator, to be sure); but there will be no question of such a device having any explanatory or analytical force in giving flesh to the concept of essence. (For more on modal fictionalism, see Rosen 1990.)

Modalism is characterized in part by its reliance on possible worlds theory, or perhaps more accurately by its reliance on intuitions about possible worlds with a certain amount of theory to clothe the intuitions. It is also characterized by the modal approach to meaning, specifically via rigid designator theory. According to Gyula Klima, contemporary essentialism just *is* the thesis that 'some common terms are rigid designators' (Klima 2002: 175). This approach was driven by the work of Kripke and Putnam (Putnam 1970, 1973, 1975a; Kripke 1980) and has had enormous influence on essentialist thinking ever since. The basic ideas are too well known to require restating here: what is relevant for our purposes is the central thought that one can approach essence by considering language, in particular whether a term functions as a designator of the same thing in all possible worlds in which it exists. It is via this consideration that Kripke, for instance, argues that heat is essentially molecular motion (Kripke 1980: 131ff.). Scientists have discovered that heat is identical with a certain kind of molecular motion (more precisely, mean molecular kinetic energy). But since 'heat' and 'molecular motion' are rigid designators, their identity must be necessary if it obtains at all. Putnam approaches the matter in a similar way, but more in terms of indexicals such as 'this' (as in 'this stuff') guaranteeing sameness of extension for a term such as 'water' across possible worlds.

The problem with the rigid designator approach to essentialism is that it is shot through with essentialist assumptions from the beginning. First, the necessity of identity is built into the very conception of a rigid designator: if '*a*' designates *a* in the actual world, then we know trivially that the conjunction '"*a*" designates *a* and "*a*" designates *a*' is true, i.e. we know that '*a* = *a*' is true, in other words that *a* = *a* in the actual world. But since a rigid designator designates the same object in every world (in which the object exists), we know that '*a* = *a*' is true in every world, in other words that *a* = *a* in every world, i.e. that, necessarily, *a* is identical with itself. The same applies for distinct rigid designators '*a*' and '*b*' that designate the same object *a* (i.e. *b*) in the actual world. Hence the necessity of identity is part of the very concept of a rigid designator, and the necessity of identity is a fundamental – indeed *the* fundamental – truth of contemporary essentialism. (The point is a familiar one; see, e.g., Mellor 1977: 75–6.) To the reply that it is a metaphysical truth but not an *essentialist* one, or that it is only 'trivially' essentialist in some innocuous sense, I claim that its apparent insubstantiality must not be confused with its real import. It is not simply that identity is the relation that everything necessarily bears to itself and nothing else,[3] but that the necessity of identity carries the appearance of triviality. This is because it is in fact the eviscerated contemporary essentialist form of a foundational real essentialist truth to the effect that every object has its own nature – a matter to which I will return in Chapter 5.

Secondly, even if one were to argue that this objection confuses constitution with consequence – that the thesis of the necessity of identity is a consequence of rigid designator theory, albeit an immediate one, but not itself part of the theory – this will not help the contemporary essentialist. For even if one were to present the necessity of identity as an inference from necessary self-identity and Leibniz's Law[4] (as Kripke 1971 does), one would still have to presuppose Leibniz's Law as a *de re* necessary truth, i.e. a necessary truth about objects, not a mere *de dicto* necessary proposition, and one would also have to assume the necessity of self-identity. Now, it is true that the necessity of identity is not really (as opposed to logically) distinct from the necessity of self-identity, in which case the presentation of the proof in this form is merely circular anyway.[5] But, leaving that aside, Leibniz's Law is also an essentialist truth: no object can, at the same time and in the same respect, lack the qualities it possesses. And this itself is but a species of the law of non-contradiction, viz. that nothing can both be and not-be at the same time and in the same respect.[6] Note at this point that a retreat to the 'formal mode', reformulating the argument as one concerning substitutivity and referential transparency, is no more than a kind of anti-metaphysical escapism: if one takes refuge in language one will never get to *any* essentialist truths at all (except, perhaps, concerning language).

Thirdly, as Nathan Salmon has shown, Kripke's own purported essentialist derivations presuppose even more substantial essentialist truths (if the preceding are not thought substantial enough). For example, in trying to prove the necessity of origin – specifically the necessity of original constitution – Kripke has to presuppose the *sufficiency* of origin for a thing's identity (Salmon 1979; 1981: 196ff.). The same applies to Putnam, who, as part of his argument that water is essentially H_2O, has to presuppose that no liquid substance could have a chemical structure different from the one it actually has (Salmon 1981: 176ff.). More generally, the problem is one of accounting for rigid designation itself. The standard way of determining whether a term is a rigid designator is by consideration of how it behaves in modal contexts – 'Aristotle' is not equivalent to a definite description such as 'the tutor of Alexander the Great, etc.' because Aristotle might not have tutored Alexander, and so on. But in order to know how a term behaves in modal contexts we have already to know certain modal truths about its referent. We know that Aristotle might not have been the tutor of Alexander because we know this is not part of his *essence*. If Twin Earth thought experiments concerning 'water' are correct, that is because we know that 'water' designates a thing with a certain essential structure. If Kripke is right about mind–brain identity, this is because we know that 'pain' designates a certain kind of feeling with an essential phenomenological quality. No mere reflection on semantics can tell us how a term behaves unless we have a criterion for separating correct from incorrect behaviour. In the case of rigid designators, the criterion has to be *independent* access to metaphysical truths. This is what the so-called 'problem of transworld identity' amounts to.

In the case of ordinary knowledge of common or garden objects, knowledge, however tacit, that a term is a rigid designator presupposes knowledge that things have essences as well as knowledge of what some of those essences are. The same also applies to scientific knowledge. Kripke and Putnam help themselves, quite reasonably, to scientific findings such as that heat is molecular motion and that water is H_2O. But to what *exactly* are they helping themselves? For a start, it is a putative *identity*: heat is identical to molecular motion and water is identical to H_2O. The contemporary essentialist does not help himself to the discovery that there is, say, a mere *correlation* between the presence of water and the presence of H_2O, or that having the structure of H_2O is a mere accidental characteristic of water. What has been discovered (assuming the science to be correct for present purposes) is that water has a certain *nature* – it is a substance whose very being is that of something with a certain chemical structure. Put another way, what scientists have discovered is that water belongs to a certain *kind* whose identity is given by the chemical composition of its members: it is this sort of consideration that gives Twin Earth cases any of the metaphysical purchase they have, and that underlies reflection on the semantic behaviour of rigid designators. (Needless to say, if water is *not* a kind, and water is not necessarily H_2O, then contemporary essentialists will be wrong, but not for any reasons that could be uncovered merely by reflecting on semantics rather than metaphysics.)

1.2 Against modalism: Fine's critique

The critique of modalism goes further and deeper than what has been said so far. In two important papers, Kit Fine has undermined the very thinking at the heart of contemporary essentialism (Fine 1994a, 1995a). He asserts that

> the contemporary assimilation of essence to modality is fundamentally misguided and that, as a consequence, the corresponding conception of metaphysics should be given up ... the notion of essence which is of central importance to the metaphysics of identity is not to be understood in modal terms or even to be regarded as extensionally equivalent to a modal notion.
>
> (Fine 1994a: 3)

Fine's objections stem from a rejection of the basic modal criterion of essence, namely that an object x has a property essentially if and only if it has it necessarily, i.e. in all worlds (in which it exists). He does not deny the necessity of the criterion, namely that objects that have properties essentially have them necessarily; but he denies its sufficiency. For example, modalism implies that Socrates essentially belongs to the singleton set containing him, but there is nothing in the *nature* or *essence* of a person that requires that he belong to one set or another – and more crucially, perhaps, even that there *be* any sets. On the other hand, even though singleton Socrates also contains Socrates necessarily, it does so *essentially* since it is part of the nature of the singleton set containing Socrates that it contain Socrates, given that the very identity of a set is determined by its members. Hence there is modal symmetry between the cases of singleton Socrates's containing Socrates and Socrates's belonging to the singleton – yet there is an asymmetry in terms of essence.

Another example Fine gives is of Socrates's being necessarily distinct from the Eiffel Tower, even though there is nothing in his nature that connects him to the Eiffel Tower. Yet although Fine is correct in one sense in raising these sorts of cases, he is not in another. For being necessarily distinct from the Eiffel Tower and necessarily belonging to the singleton are what we might call *virtual parts* of Socrates's essence, since his essence – being a rational animal – virtually contains the categories of *being a material object*[7] and *being an entity of some sort or other*,[8] to which necessary distinctness and necessary singleton membership apply, respectively, as parts of *these* essences formally stated.[9] That is to say, it is not part of the essence of *Socrates* formally stated that he be necessarily distinct from the Eiffel Tower: the formal statement of a thing's essence is the statement of its definition, of *what it is*. Hence even individuals have definitions: Socrates is defined as a human being, it is what he is, and so he has exactly the same definition as Plato and King Henry VIII. (It is a further question as to *which* human being he is, which is not a question of definition but of identification.)

Nevertheless, it is still part of Socrates's essence in the *virtual* sense that he is both a material object and an entity of some sort or other (a *being*), where: being F is a virtual part of the essence G of an object x if and only if x's being G logically presupposes x's being F.[10] Socrates is a rational animal; being a rational animal logically presupposes being a material object; hence being a material object is a virtual part of his essence, and we can truly say that he is essentially a material object *by virtue of* being essentially a rational animal. The same goes for his being an entity of some sort or other. Now I would argue that it is part of the formally stated essence of all material objects that they have necessary distinctness from one another. One might not frame the definition in quite those words, thinking instead of a material object as a single thing made of matter or some such, but implicit in any such definition are the concepts of necessary self-identity and necessary distinctness from all other material objects. Since we can very plausibly regard being necessarily distinct from everything apart from itself as part of *what it is* to be a material object, and since it is a virtual part of Socrates's essence to be a material object,[11] it is virtually a part of his essence to be necessarily distinct from the Eiffel Tower. Does this make his essence undesirably relational? No, because his being necessarily distinct from the Eiffel Tower is not a truth about Socrates that is really, as opposed to merely conceptually, distinct from the *intrinsic* characterization of him as a material object[12] whose necessary distinctness from all other material objects is part of its essence. This explains the fact that before the Eiffel Tower exists Socrates's essence is no different from what it is after the tower comes into being, and that when it ceases to be, Socrates does not lose part of his essence.

Although this is more controversial (because of the controversial nature of set theory itself), I would also argue that it is a virtual part of Socrates's essence to be a member of the singleton. This is because to think of something as an object of some kind or other is to think of it as an individual, a unit of being and no more. And singleton set membership is part of what it is to be a unit of being. It is a necessary way of thinking of individuals that is conceptually prior to the formalism of set theory and its various axiomatizations, and on which these are built. A unit of being is, as it were, in a class apart from everything else, and to describe it as belonging to a singleton set is just a way of formalizing this basic ontological thought. Hence I would argue that being a member of the singleton is, in a virtual sense, part of what it is to be Socrates because part of what it is, in a virtual sense, to be Socrates is to be something or other.

Set-theoretical speculations aside, what Fine has drawn attention to is that the modal criterion is not fine-grained enough to distinguish between the grounds on which different objects have the essential properties they do. If we confine ourselves to the formal statement of the essence of a thing – where by formal is meant the explicit statement, by means of genus and species, of the thing's nature such that it distinguishes the thing from every other thing with a different nature – then we do indeed have a modal asymmetry between Socrates and singleton Socrates. The modal criterion cannot tell us by virtue of *what* a thing has the necessary features it has, and therefore it does not 'carve reality at the joints', to use the familiar metaphor. The modalist will no doubt reply that he can add various criteria or restrictions that ensure Socrates and his singleton are not put into the same kind, hence that there is an explanation of their modal asymmetry. After all, there are plenty of necessary features the former has that the latter lacks (such as possessing mammalian characteristics) and vice versa (such as being an abstract object). But the reply is that introducing restrictions, say on the similarity relation across possible worlds, makes the real essentialist's point for him: mere attention to modality does not make the sorts of distinction that partition the world into the distinct real natures of things. To introduce such restrictions is to presuppose that we have a grasp of real natures (however imperfect and incomplete, about which more in Chapter 3 and elsewhere) for which the modal criterion cannot account.

The same point applies to another of Fine's examples. He asserts that 'it is not part of Socrates' essence that there be infinitely many prime numbers or that the abstract world of numbers, sets, or what have you, be just as it is', even though it is necessarily true of Socrates that if he exists there are infinitely many prime numbers (Fine 1994a: 5). Now the short way with this objection, for the modalist, would be to deny the following as a genuine property: *being an x such that if x exists there are infinitely many primes* (or some other mathematical truth).[13] The real essentialist has alternative responses here. A controversial if interesting reply is to insist that the above alleged property really is a property of Socrates for the following reason: it is a necessary feature of Socrates, just as it is a necessary feature of any object, that there are numbers at all; and it is a necessary feature of numbers that there are infinitely many primes among them; hence it is a necessary feature of Socrates, albeit indirect or non-immediate, that there are infinitely many primes. The argument relies on two claims. The first is that the existence of numbers depends on the existence of things that are not numbers. This is the Aristotelian (hence anti-Platonist, but *not* therefore nominalist) account of number that should be congenial to the real essentialist. Without things that are not numbers there would be no numbers, since numbers are *abstractions* from the existence of things. (See further Chapter 6.) It will not be a feature of Socrates *qua* human being, or *qua* rational animal, that there are numbers, but a feature of him *qua* object. Hence, following the above account, it would be a virtual part of his essence that he is an object and so a virtually essential feature of him that there are numbers. If he did not exist but something else did, say a rock, then it would be a virtually essential feature of the rock that there were numbers (only one object being needed to abstract the entire number series).[14] If both Socrates and a rock existed, it would be a virtually essential feature of them both individually and jointly that there were numbers; and so on for any objects whatsoever.[15]

The second claim needed to support the argument is that *being a necessary feature of x that there is y* is a transitive relation. Consider: it is a necessary feature of colour that there be light; it is a necessary feature of light that there be a source of light; so it is a necessary feature of colour that there be a source of light.[16] It is a necessary feature of angles that there be sides; it is a necessary feature of sides that there be lengths; so it is a necessary feature of angles that there be lengths. These sorts of case are not obviously incorrect as far as they go, though there may be counterexamples. The real essentialist would be unwise to stake his life on the principle's being true, but if it is he could say that it is a necessary feature of Socrates that there are infinitely many primes. He could then explain that modalism again fails to account for what it is about Socrates – in this case, being essentially an object – that guarantees the existence of infinitely many primes.

Nevertheless, the modalist could well insist with the full force of incredulity that even if certain things necessarily exist because Socrates exists, these facts of existence are in no wise facts or features *of Socrates*. The real essentialist might bow to the incredulity and offer an alternative response to that just proposed – by pointing to other features that satisfy Fine's objection. It is a necessary feature of Socrates that if he is a giraffe, then he is a quadruped and of Fido that if he is a man, then he is mortal; and of both that if they are identical to the number seven, then they are prime; and so on. Even if the antecedents are necessarily false the conditionals are true and, it seems, true of Socrates, Fido and both of them respectively. What if the antecedents are incoherent? Then consider that it is a necessary feature of Socrates that if he is eight feet tall, then his height is equal to an even number: the antecedent is only contingently false and the feature is still true of him. Needless to say, David Armstrong would reject conditional universals for the same reasons he rejects disjunctive and negative universals, in particular that they lack causal efficacy (Armstrong 1978b: 19–29; 1989a: 82–4); hence he would reject the very idea that *being hard if identical to a rock* was a genuine feature of anything, not even of rocks. But it is by no means clear that features of abstract objects such as numbers enter into causal relations either, and even if we restrict ourselves to objects that *could* enter into causal relations, it is no part of real essentialism that features of things be acknowledged only insofar as the demands of science require it. In any case, if conditional properties such as those mentioned above are indeed features of Socrates, then modalism cannot tell us why or how it is so: it merely recognizes that such features are necessary without being able to enter further into the kind of metaphysical analysis that explains why objects have the necessary features they do.

If, says Fine, the modalist claims that an object is essentially *F* if it is *F* in every world in which it exists, then Socrates exists in every world in which he exists – but he does not essentially exist. The point is good, but Fine's accompanying one less so: Socrates has parents in every world in which he exists, but it is not part of his nature to have parents (Fine 1994a: 6). For it is part of the nature of animals to have parents, and Socrates is an animal. Does this mean an animal couldn't just spring into existence without natural parents (maybe from a rock?) or be zapped into existence, Adam-and-Eve-like, without parents? Or that it couldn't, say, be synthesized in a lab? I will discuss such scenarios in Chapters 7 and 8, but the first two cases do not invalidate the point: for them to obtain would require some sort of miracle. To say that Socrates's nature requires that he have parents is *not* to exclude his miraculously springing fully formed from a running stream. The metaphysical impossibility of his not having parents must be taken to mean that *in the natural order of things* he must have parents. (For more about laws of nature and the natural order of things, see Chapter 6.) This should be distinguished from metaphysical impossibility in the absolute sense: for instance, that nothing can come into existence wholly uncaused is metaphysically impossible in the absolute sense – not even by a 'miracle' could it happen.[17] Socrates's nature is of a kind of thing that comes into existence via a biological generative process, whether or not the process involves some degree of human artifice beyond or instead of normal sexual procreation. Moreover, since Socrates might spring into existence without parents – or so I claim – it is not the case that he has parents in every world in which he exists. Hence both conjuncts of Fine's assertion are false.

Fine goes on to assert that no alternative modal criterion of essence can be found, because 'it seems to be possible to agree on all of the modal facts and yet disagree on the essentialist facts. But if any modal criterion of essence were correct, such a situation would be impossible' (Fine 1994a: 8). Fine's own example concerning minds, bodies and persons is somewhat obscure (Fine 1994a: 8), but the point can be made with a different one, thus showing that modal agreement can co-exist with disagreement about natures. Two philosophers might agree that necessarily if there is a dog, then there is a certain structure S of dog-parts, and that necessarily if there is S, then there is a dog. But one of them might insist that it is of the essence of a dog just to be a certain structure of dog-parts, while the other might insist on the reverse – that S exists *because* there is a dog, i.e. it is of the essence of S to be the structure of a dog. They would agree on the modal facts yet have different *orders of explanation* when it came to essence. As Fine puts it, the point is that, 'even when all questions of necessity have been resolved, questions of their source will remain ... [an essentialist question] should not be taken to be constituted, either in principle or in practice, by its claims of necessity' (Fine 1994a: 8).

Returning, then, to Socrates and singleton Socrates, the point about sources is this: not that Socrates's membership of the singleton 'is true in virtue of the identity of singleton Socrates, not of the identity of Socrates' (Fine 1994a: 9), but that the singleton membership is true because of the formal essence of singleton Socrates (it is a set with Socrates as its sole member) and *also* because of the virtual, but not formal, essence of Socrates himself (he is formally a rational animal, but virtually – in the special sense given above – an object). Fine does end up refining his position somewhat along the lines I have been suggesting, since he claims that the metaphysically necessary truths – by which he means what is necessarily true of anything – are 'the propositions which are true in virtue of the nature of all objects whatever' (Fine 1994a: 9). Hence he ends up asserting that *all* kinds of necessity – physical, logical, conceptual, and so on – can be taken as grounded in the essences of all the objects they are specifically about. Physical necessity is grounded in the nature of physical objects, and conceptual necessity is grounded in the nature of concepts. Metaphysical necessity, taken as what is necessarily true of all objects (e.g. that they are members of their singleton sets), will be grounded in the nature of objects *qua* objects. But as real essentialists we are far more interested in metaphysical necessity as applied to *things of specific kinds*. Metaphysics may be the science of being *qua* being, to use Aristotle's celebrated phrase, but although we begin with being we do not end with it: we want to know about the specific objects, the objects with specific natures, in the world around us.

Modalism cannot help us. It confuses the consequences of real possibility and real necessity with their constitution. Given the real modalities, we can use possible-worlds talk to illustrate them, and maybe even use possible-worlds thought experiments to uncover some of our intuitions about what modal realities there are. And perhaps we can even speak of real possible worlds as abstract structures within a formal theory (such as quantified modal logic) so as to test modal inferences. But in no way is real modality, and hence real essence, constituted by anything to do with possible worlds. Further, if we adhere only to modality without investigating its source in the essences of things, we will not carve reality at the joints; we will have no justification for any of the true classifications we make, whether in natural science or in everyday life. As James Ross puts it, 'there are no subjects of mere possibility. The possibility *of* contingent things is not prior to or explanatory of them, but consequent, a shadow projected by logic … from actual natures and dispositions' (Ross 1989: 264). To borrow a phrase from Edmund Husserl, we have to go 'back to the things themselves'.[18]

1.3 Reductionism: the illusory search for inner structure

The sorts of example that contemporary essentialists use when illustrating the theory of essence almost invariably involve chemical and atomic structure: 'Water = H_2O', 'Heat = molecular motion', 'Gold = the element with the atomic number 79' and so on. This is no accident, since reductionism is one of the hallmarks of contemporary essentialist thinking.

In the work of Kripke and Putnam, reference to 'internal structure' and cognate concepts abounds. In asserting that tigers are essentially non-reptiles, Kripke connects the 'internal structure' of tigers with their forming a species (1980: 120–1). His discussion of gold is in terms of 'atomic structure' (1980: 123–5), and that of water and heat in terms of molecular structure and molecular motion (1980: 128–9). His remarks on Putnam's example 'Cats are animals' again appeal to 'internal structure' (1980: 126). Putnam implicitly associates the essence of a lemon with its 'chromosomal structure' (1970: 141–2). Whilst he allows that some natural kinds may not possess a 'hidden structure', he claims that, 'if there is a hidden structure, then generally it determines what it is to be a member of the natural kind, not only in the actual world but in all possible worlds' (1975a: 241).

The focus on 'hidden' or 'internal' structure is not confined to contemporary – that is to say Kripke–Putnam-style – essentialists. It is also found in contemporary writers who are to be classified as real essentialists of a sort. The most prominent of these is Brian Ellis, whose important work on 'scientific essentialism' (see esp. Ellis 2001) concentrates almost exclusively on physics and chemistry, with only passing and doubt-filled reference to essentialism in biology and psychology (2001: 167–73); and although his discussion of economics and the social sciences in general is more extended (2001: 177–98), his main concern here is to deny, plausibly, that there are in these fields laws of nature to be discovered, at least in any form resembling the laws discovered in physics or chemistry. He asserts:

> Because of the messiness of biological kinds, and in order to develop a theory of natural kinds adequate for the purposes of ontology, I have broken with the tradition of biological examples, and taken the various kinds of fundamental particles, fields, atoms, and molecules as paradigms.
>
> (Ellis 2001: 170)

Moreover, his concentration on inner structure, in addition to his overall physicalist reductionism, leads him at one point to make the outrageous claim that, since 'they have diverse genetic makeups', human beings are 'not all members of the same strict natural kind' (Ellis 2001: 21).

Real essentialism needs, of course, to be concerned with internal structure. The epithet 'hidden' favoured by Putnam is merely a rhetorical gloss designed to provoke the thought that it is exclusively for scientists to discover the real essences of things concealed from everyday view. It is this, and the worldview that goes with it, which real essentialists resist. Scientists play an indispensable role in helping to explain the real essences of things – and for some kinds of entity, the ones *proper* to those fields of science requiring more or less elaborate technical devices of measurement and experiment, their role may be exclusive. But it is incorrect to hold that the job of the real essentialist just is the job of the scientist. It is also, and *primarily*, the job of the metaphysician informed by science, and additionally, for many kinds of entity, the job of everyone, expert or not.

Consider first, though, what it is that scientists have discovered – about water, for example. Although I have not surveyed all the textbooks, I doubt that you will find in any of them, as a record of a scientific discovery, the sentence 'Water = H_2O'. You may find the sentence 'Water is H_2O', but this does not mean that the 'is' used is the 'is' of identity. Rather, it will be the 'is' of constitution.[19] When Cavendish, Lavoisier, Gay-Lussac, Humboldt, Nicholson and others discovered the composition of water in the eighteenth and nineteenth centuries, they did not discover that water is identical to H_2O. What they found were processes that synthesized water from, and separated water into, its chemical constituents of hydrogen and oxygen, and that these constituents were bonded together in a certain arrangement or structure. But it does not follow from the fact that water has the constituents hydrogen and oxygen in a certain arrangement – even if it has them necessarily – that these just *are* the essence of water rather than, at most, *part* of the essence.

Put semantically, the point is that 'Water = H_2O' is either ill formed, necessarily false or just plain ambiguous. For what does 'H_2O' designate? Considered on its own, and let us suppose as read by a chemist, it might well be taken to stand simply for an abstract molecular formula expressed in the Hill system – but water is not identical to any abstract formula, whether expressed in the Hill system or any other. So suppose that what scientists discovered was that the following was true: 'Water is constituted by hydrogen and oxygen according to the molecular arrangement M', where 'M' is now conventionally expressed as 'H_2O'. No amount of Kripke– Putnam-style contemporary essentialist thinking can then demonstrate that this constitution is *necessary*: rigid designator theory no more allows us to move from 'Water is constituted by hydrogen and oxygen arranged according to M' to 'Water is necessarily constituted by hydrogen and oxygen according to M' than it allows us to move from 'Oil is always found near water' (let us suppose) to 'Oil is necessarily always found near water', even if 'oil' and 'water' are rigid designators.

Similarly, suppose what scientists discovered was that something like the following is true: 'Water is identical to the substance whose chemical constituents are arranged according to M'. Then they discovered an identity: but it no more follows that the referent of the right- and left-hand sides *necessarily* has its chemical constituents arranged according to M than that my discovery that Jones is the person who sits next to me on the bus every morning is also the discovery that he necessarily does so. So rigid designators have nothing to do with whether a discovery such as that of Cavendish, Lavoisier and others was of a whole essence, or part of an essence, or neither.

What they discovered was that water is constituted by hydrogen and oxygen in a certain arrangement. More precisely, they discovered that water is *a substance* with constituents of hydrogen and oxygen in a certain arrangement. That is to say, speaking accurately, they did not even discover that water is *the* substance with those constituents in that arrangement, since it took much further chemical analysis to learn that no other substance on earth had the *same* arrangement. Now we have such standard definitions as: 'Water is a binary compound that occurs at room temperature as a clear, colorless, odorless, tasteless liquid; freezes into ice below 0 degrees centigrade and boils above 100 degrees centigrade; widely used as a solvent';[20] 'Water is a substance composed of the chemical elements hydrogen and oxygen and existing in gaseous, liquid, and solid states';[21] and so on. That the definitions vary quite markedly or that they lack precision is not of importance. What matters is that, like all definitions, they propose a *genus* and a *specific difference* to explain what the definiendum is. The general form of definitions of water is: Water is a … (genus as indicated by the sum of the properties common to two or more species) with the following properties … (specific difference marking out water from everything else no matter how similar in other respects).

I will have a lot more to say about species and genus throughout the book, but this initial mention will help to illustrate how the real essentialist approaches essential definition. There is nothing in contemporary essentialism to license the view that essence is always given exclusively in terms of inner structure – that is a prior reductionist commitment, one that for the real essentialist is unjustified. As a 'scientific essentialist', Ellis too is committed to reductionism, though he is more explicit about this commitment. His reductionism, like most kinds, is physico-chemical, and it is based on an overall view that the objects of physics and chemistry are, as it were, theoretically more 'well behaved' than the macroscopic objects of everyday experience. But being theoretically well behaved is a notion that itself contains a metaphysical bias in favour of the quantitative over the qualitative, and this, too, real essentialism rejects.

There is no space here to canvass reductionism in its various forms and whether and to what extent it is true (I discuss it at more length in Chapter 7), though it is worth noting that even the most common putative examples of inter-theoretic reduction, such as that of classical thermodynamics to statistical molecular mechanics, are highly dubious. (In this case, one of the problems is that the same thermodynamic properties can be shared by quite distinct molecular systems.)[22] What is important for our purposes is that real essentialism, whilst incorporating into its definitions whatever correct science has to offer about the inner structures of things, takes all objects, from the very big to the very small, at face value. This means that the qualitative characteristics of things are held to be a real part of ontology, not mere epiphenomena of, or expressions of, or reducible to, the underlying quantitative characteristics of things given by a mathematical theory, no matter how predictively and explanatorily successful the mathematical theory may be.

Secondly, real essentialism does not privilege the microscopic over the macroscopic, unless the object of investigation is *specifically* the microscopic. Taking the macroscopic seriously is shown in the very form of the real essentialist definition, which gives both the genus and the specific difference, for example: 'Water is a colourless, odourless substance in liquid, solid or gaseous form that ... '; 'Gold is a soft, shiny, yellow, heavy, malleable, ductile metal that ... '; 'A fish is a cold-blooded, water-dwelling animal that ... '. Again, it is not important for present purposes whether the definition is exact. The point is that, unless we are speaking specifically about the microscopic, the macroscopic always figures in a real essentialist definition, either in the genus, or in the specific difference, or both.

I will have more to say in later chapters about the relations between the macroscopic and the microscopic, about inner structure and outward behaviour – in particular about what might be called the 'top-down' influence that the macroscopic exerts over the microscopic. But a key point to note at present is that real essentialism, more than any other ontological theory, stresses and seeks to explain the *unity* of objects. The central concept deployed to carry out this explanatory work is that of *form*. Form is decidedly not hidden or inner structure. It may *encompass* the inner structure of a thing if the thing possesses one, but the real essentialist neither insists that every genuine part of the furniture of the universe must have an inner structure nor reduces the essence of a thing to its inner structure if it has one. To take two extreme examples, at one end of the spectrum an artefact such as Michelangelo's *David* has no inner structure whatsoever – though it does have structure – but that does not prevent it from being a real entity, albeit artefactual.[23] At the other end, there might be fundamental physical particles that have no inner structure. (Maybe this is true of quarks, but the jury is still out since some physicists believe a sufficiently high-energy collision might reveal a quark substructure.) Again, there are non-artefactual objects that have no inner structure, only a structure that is wholly manifest – such as a naturally occurring pile of stones. Further, there may be immaterial objects that have an essence but no inner structure – for example immaterial spirits. In this latter case, the point here is not whether there *are* any, only that it would be a mere ontological prejudice to deny them a nature or essence simply *because* they had no inner structure.

Furthermore – and I am not claiming contemporary essentialists have adverted to such cases, though they are relevant to their overall worldview – there are abstract objects that have a structure that is not inner or hidden. Logical objects such as propositions and complex concepts are structural in nature but it is not even clear what it would mean to say their structure was internal: a conjunctive proposition, for example, has a structure given by its conjuncts and the operation on them, but the structure is manifest even though it can only be given by analysis. But having an analysis is not the same as having an inner structure. Complex propositions that do not wear their structure on their face, as it were, have a structure that can be revealed by analysis as well, but even though we might call the structure *implicit*, that is not to say it is 'inner'. An argument may have a more or less manifest structure, but to call it 'inner' even though it may require a lot of analysis to reveal it is at best a piece of ontological obfuscation. A mathematical object such as the number two, by contrast, does not seem to have any structure at all – it is not 'made up' of the number one taken twice over, even though its production by means of, say, the axioms of Peano arithmetic can be given in terms of the concepts 'one' and 'successor of'. Again, at least some phenomenal objects such as pains doubtfully have any structure at all, let alone an inner one, though they do have – *pace* physicalists – a wholly phenomenological essence that is manifest to the possessor.

Finally, perhaps there might actually – or at least conceivably – be objects with both an essence and an inner structure but where the latter is no part of the former. Consider a highly elastic substance with a certain number of constituents (let's make them metaphysical atoms to heighten the point), such that the substance can undergo highly radical and heterogeneous transformations that fail to preserve inner structure but do preserve the numerical identity of the constituents as well as the surface properties of the whole. At any time in its existence the object does have an inner structure, but no particular structure is essential to it. What is essential are the identity of the constituents and the surface properties. One might reply that it does have an essential inner structure, one given by some abstract mathematical formula stating the range of transformations it can undergo – and surely that range must be circumscribed to *some* extent. But if the transformations were sufficiently heterogeneous this would carry over to the formula, making it look decidedly ad hoc to call it a *structure* or even a structure-*type*. And mightn't the range be infinite yet not specifiable by a formula for an infinite series? Admittedly this is metaphysical speculation, but there is nothing obviously incoherent in the thought experiment.

It might be objected that if an object with an essence can be *synthesized* out of constituent elements, then those elements must make up the whole structure of the object. But it is not clear how this follows. By what metaphysical principle does it follow that when, say, Cavendish burned hydrogen in air and so produced water he thereby proved that water was *nothing more* than hydrogen and oxygen (in certain proportions and with a certain structure)? For what came into existence *at exactly the same time* as the hydrogen and oxygen combined in the requisite way was a whole ensemble of macroscopic properties, in short a *form* that gives water its essential unity as a certain kind of substance. This form, to be sure, has as one of its elements the existence of chemical constituents with a certain structure, but this does not show that *all there is* to water is the existence of those constituents with that structure. Nor does this reductionist thesis follow from the fact that there are no more inner chemical constituents to be discovered, only further properties of hydrogen, oxygen and their bonds. Nor does it follow from the facts – if they are facts – that there is a strict and precise correlation between all of water's microscopic properties and its macroscopic properties, and that the behaviour and effects of the latter can all and exclusively be traced back to the former. And if synthesis does not imply that all essence is inner in the inorganic case, how much more will this be so in the organic case, where it is highly doubtful whether all of the macroscopic properties of organisms can even be explained in terms of, or traced back to, physico-chemical constituents and their structural properties? (See Chapter 8.)

I do not pretend to have provided a wholesale refutation of reductionism. Rather, I have given a series of arguments as to why reductionism about essence, conceived particularly in terms of the concept of inner structure, is neither plausible nor derivable from contemporary essentialism, nor independent of prior physicalist commitments about the nature of reality. This should be enough at least to motivate the real essentialist outlook.

1.4 Why real essentialism?

Real essentialism starts with certain prior commitments, and it is right that these should be made clear from the outset. (I will have more to say about them in Chapters 2 and 3.) First, there is a real world, by which I mean a world that is wholly objective. It is common for realists to define objectivity in terms of mind-independence, but that can get the realist into somewhat unnecessary complications. (For an example, see Alston 1979.) Phenomenal objects such as pains, and mental objects such as particular thoughts and ideas, are mind-dependent in the sense that they depend on a mind for their existence. One could perhaps refine the notion of mind-independence, but the best way of speaking of realism from an essentialist perspective is to hold that something is real just in case the fact that it exists is not itself a matter of opinion or conjecture. I might not be able to have a pain without believing that I have it, but my having it is not itself a matter of opinion, mine or anyone else's (even though I might have the opinion that I am in pain without actually being in pain).[24] Of course there are many dimensions of contrast for the term 'real' – real v. fictional, real v. artefactual, real v. imaginary and the like – and the essentialist incorporates all of these distinctions into his ontology. But the overall position he holds is that there is a real world, and that the things in it are all real in the sense that they are *beings* of one kind or another and their being is not a matter of opinion or conjecture.

Secondly, the reference to being indicates that the real essentialist starts from the classic Aristotelian position that metaphysics is the study of *being qua being*: being in all its manifestations and varieties, classified according to a suite of concepts and categories that derive from the Aristotelian tradition. There are other kinds of essentialism, and we have already encountered 'scientific' essentialism. There is also Platonist essentialism, but I do not count this as real essentialism according to the sort of position I defend. Perhaps one can think of it as *hyper-real* essentialism (a nominalist might call it unreal!), but for all that it is inadequate and incorrect as a theory of reality. (More on this in Chapter 4.) Real essentialism takes nature seriously, and whilst it may countenance the existence of the immaterial – as I think it should – it does not reduce or refer nature as it is in concrete physical reality to a realm of the immaterial that is supposed to be its ultimate ontological ground.

Essences are real, they encompass all kinds of being and, thirdly, they are *knowable*. The essentialist is committed to the view that the human mind can come to know the essence of things. Knowledge of the truth just is the conformity of the mind to the way things are, and so knowledge of essence is the conformity of the mind to the natures of things. The knowledge is frequently only partial and incomplete, but it is no part of the real essentialist worldview that humans can always achieve complete, adequate knowledge of the essences of things. This not a counsel of despair but an encouragement to the increase and improvement of knowledge.

Fourthly, real essentialism holds that knowledge of essence is captured by means of *real definition*. As Fine puts it, '[j]ust as we may define a word, or say what it means, so we may define an object, or say what it is' (Fine 1994a: 2). The prejudice against real definition is a deeply held one, going back to the roots of empiricism. Yet it is hard to see why the concept is unacceptable. Indeed, since defining a word is best seen as giving the essence of a kind of object (the meaning), the opponent of real definition who at least concedes that we can define words has already conceded the principle that one can define objects of a certain kind; if that kind, why not others? (See further Fine 1994a: 13–14.) To define something just means, literally, to set forth its limits in such a way that one can distinguish it from all other things of a different kind. (To distinguish it from all other things of the same kind belongs to the theory of *individuation*, which I discuss in Chapter 5.4). Putting the point again in Aristotelian terminology (which will happen often throughout this book), to give the definition of something it to say *what it is*, to give the *ti esti* or *to ti ēn einai* of the object.[25] Put simply, the real essentialist position is that it is possible to say correctly what things are.

Fifthly, the real essentialist holds that the world is orderly and hence that things are *classifiable*, a point heavily emphasized, and rightly so, by Ellis. Describing the world accurately requires one to be able to classify the things within it into kinds of being. This does not depend on there being multiple examples of any particular kind, for even if each thing that existed were the only one of its kind it would still be classifiable as a member of some kind or other. (It is an a priori truth that for any object it is logically possible that there be another one of its kind according to *some* dimension of classification, since it is logically possible that there be another object similar to the first in some respect or other, given that universals are necessarily multiply instantiable. This applies to the form of the object considered as a whole as well. What is proper to the individual is what individuates it, and this, as we will see, belongs to the *material* side of the object, not the formal side.)[26] The real essentialist, however, is concerned primarily with classification not according to some real dimension or other, but according to what objects are in their entirety. This is given by the form of the object as a whole, and this too is multiply instantiable.[27]

It is remarkable that philosophers seem to have given up on taxonomy much sooner than scientists. In particular, biologists are notable for their continued reliance – fading in recent decades, admittedly – on the fundamentally Aristotelian system of Carl Linnaeus (1707–78) for their method of classifying living things. Yet philosophers, influenced by various forms of anti-essentialism, have on the whole taken a sceptical attitude to the idea that the universe is an orderly realm within which objects can be classified according to a system of categories, let alone one exhibiting the kind of hierarchical structure found in the Linnaean system. (Notable exceptions, though they do not talk too much about how the world actually *is*, include Woods (1967) and Thomason (1969), as well as Ellis (2001).) Real essentialism holds the existence of classification to entail the existence of a classificatory structure (of some sort or other), since the fact that essence is given by genus and specific difference already imports notions of inclusion and exclusion, the more general and the particular, and hence the possibility of hierarchy.

The short answer to the question 'Why real essentialism?' is that it is the metaphysical system that captures the reality of things. We have already seen that modalism does not deliver essentialism despite its promises. The reductionism found in scientific essentialism[28] is mistaken. But why not be a sceptic about essence altogether? Isn't the search for essence illusory? In this chapter I have already tried indirectly to chip away at anti-essentialism. In Chapter 2 I will look at some specific anti-essentialist arguments, in the course of which the positive aspects of the theory of real essences will begin to take on more definite lines.

2   Some varieties of anti-essentialism

2.1 Empiricist anti-essentialism

It is through examination of some of the anti-essentialist views that have dominated contemporary philosophy that we can begin to gain a grasp of what essentialism (that is, real essentialism) does and does not hold. We will see that anti-essentialism contains a number of misconceptions and outright errors that, when rectified, clear the ground for a view of essences as real and knowable.

Perhaps the most influential source of anti-essentialism can be found in empiricist thought.[1] There are various ways in which scepticism about the reality and/or knowability of essence appears in such thought: not all empiricists are nominalists, but the converse is almost certainly the case and nominalism, according to which all that exists are particulars, is incompatible with essentialism. Nominalism is consistent with belief in *individual* essences (haecceities), but real essentialism postulates essences as universals (quiddities), whether or not haecceities are also admitted (see Chapter 5.4). Again, instrumentalism is an outgrowth of empiricism, and instrumentalism is clearly anti-essentialist, since the search for essences is explicitly replaced by the employment of theories about reality as mere tools for the organization, explanation and prediction of observable phenomena.

Rather than canvassing all the main ways in which empiricism wrongly undermines essentialism, I want to focus on the broad theme of observability. Empiricists take essences to be paradigmatically unobservable, and hence as having no place in our scientific or non-scientific description of reality. The objection goes back at least to John Locke, for whom substance – as given by the most basic kind of real essence – is famously the 'something we know not what' support of the ideas we have of observable qualities (Locke 1975: II.23.2, p. 295). By the time of David Hume, essence receives barely a mention: it is not something of which we have an impression – hence we can have no idea of it.

Now, a relatively cheap essentialist response would be to make the anti-verificationist point that the unobservability of essence does not entail its unreality. As far as it goes, this is correct. Scientists routinely posit unobservables such as forces, fields and particles at the very small scale (where sometimes all we can observe are their effects). Both scientific and ordinary descriptions of reality involve postulating such things as powers or dispositions. The verificationist might produce more subtle arguments as to why at least some of these things do not exist, but the *mere* fact of their unobservability does not imply that they lack reality.

Verificationism aside, however, the more important essentialist response concerns what is meant by observability. The misconceptions here arguably go back also to Locke, since sometimes he equates real essence with substance, and this with a bare substratum or featureless support of observable qualities. On other occasions real essence is equated simply with the hidden, inner constitution of things – something 'unknown to us' rather than in principle unknowable (by observation). (Compare Locke 1975: 295ff. with 443ff. and 587ff.; and see the discussion in Mackie 1976: ch. 3.)

If the essentialist were to identify real essences with bare substrata, the empiricist complaint would have some bite. For how could a featureless support for the observable qualities of things have the explanatory role real essences are claimed to perform? The essence is the quiddity of a thing – its 'what-isness'. But a bare substratum, or bare particular as such entities are now usually called, cannot be the quiddity of anything since it *has* no quiddity, at least none that fits it into the taxonomy of observable entities characteristic of essentialism. Nothing that is essentially featureless can be at the same time, for instance, essentially a tiger or gold. The bare particularist can reply that its quiddity just is to be the bare support underlying substances of certain kinds. But then we run into a dilemma. If the bare particularist wants to define his entities in terms of the kinds for which they are the respective substrata, then he has to partition them according to those kinds: for kind F there will be F-type substrata, for kind G there will be G-type substrata, and so on. What, then, is the ontological ground of such a partition? It is not enough to say that each kind of substratum just is the support for the observable features of objects of each respective kind, for why could not the situation be reversed, with G-type substrata supporting Fs and F-type substrata supporting Gs? Is it just a contingent fact that this does not obtain? Presumably the bare particularist would hold that it is not, but then this commits him to the existence of some *intrinsic* features of the different kinds of substrata that guarantee their supporting all and only the kinds they in fact support. But then the substrata will not be essentially featureless, contradicting the initial assumption.

Could the tie between substrata and observable features be extrinsic only, so that the former would remain intrinsically featureless? It is hard to see how this could be so, given that the extrinsic connection between substratum and features would have to be essential in order for the necessary connection between them to be maintained, thus avoiding the possibility of a swap of the sort just mentioned. Yet it is difficult to see how there could be a necessary relation between substrata and features that was not at least in part grounded in some intrinsic feature of the former, just as is the case for all necessary relations. The substrata, then, would still have intrinsic features.

If, on the other hand, the bare substrata are essentially featureless, then what is to stop switches, not just between kinds but between particulars? Why couldn't the bare substratum of Fido, say, swap with that of Rover? Not only does this lead to intolerable scepticism about the identities of things[2] – since bare substrata are supposed to ground numerical identity – but it is metaphysically incoherent. For it allows, in the case of swaps across kinds and across particulars of the same kind respectively, that what kind a thing belongs to, and what numerical identity a thing has, is wholly independent of the way it behaves and the characteristics it possesses. It is not just that bare substrata are on this scenario theoretically redundant, but that the scenario renders kind identity and particular identity inexplicable. They do not become mere brute facts, but phenomena that are inherently separated from any physical (in the broad sense) or observable manifestation whatsoever. Yet *what* a thing is does determine *how* it is – in the traditional terminology, function follows essence.[3] Essence just is the principle from which flows the characteristic behaviour of a thing. And a thing's numerical identity as a particular member of a kind determines its particular behaviour: what makes Fido's particular behaviour Fido's and not Rover's is that Fido is an individual with its own identity, so to suppose that the identity of Fido may switch with that of Rover, with the attendant possibility of a radical discontinuity of characteristic behaviour, would be a metaphysical mystery. Fido might be tame, bark little, and have a small appetite. Should his bare substratum switch with that of Rover, who is fierce, barks a lot, and has a huge appetite, it would be one and the same dog *Fido* who exhibited an utterly inexplicable discontinuity of behaviour – one not traceable to anything observable even in principle. Needless to say, if there were substrata at all, then the discontinuity could be accounted for by attributing to them *features* by virtue of which the change of behaviour could be explained, contra the assumption that the substrata are bare.[4]

Rather than countenance bare substrata, the essentialist is committed to the existence of observable essences, and not because they are Lockean 'hidden structures' or 'inner constitutions' which simply await scientific discovery. Our observation of essence is like our observation of universals: indeed, since essences are themselves universals that give the definition or quiddity of a thing, observation of essence just is a species of observation of universals. But there is another sense in which observation of essences is the observation of particulars.

As to observation of universals, we observe, say, greenness, by observing green things. When a medical researcher wants to study cancer, he does so by studying particular instances – organisms with cancer, or particular samples of cancerous growth in vitro, and so on. If you want to study human nature, you have to look at individual human beings. Although all *immediate* sensory experience is of particulars, we have indirect or *mediate* sensory experience of universals *by means of* our observation of particulars. To say that this cannot be called observation because it is indirect is implausible. Every time a person looks at a reflection in a mirror, or an image on a television, or through a microscope, they see objects indirectly.

To this one might reply that the relation between universals and their instances, on the one hand, and that between objects and the physical instruments by which we see them indirectly, on the other, are quite different: the latter is causal, and so has no relevance to the former. But this disanalogy only serves to strengthen the essentialist's point, because the relation between universals and their instances is if anything *tighter* than that between objects and the instruments by which we can observe them. In the causal case, there can of course be situations involving illusion and deception, and so to explain how veridical indirect perception occurs we need to build in clauses concerning reliability and normal modes of perceptual operation. But the relation between universals and their instances is an *internal* one that excludes all possibility of illusion, deception or unreliability, on the assumption that one has perceived the instance veridically in the first place. If a green thing exists, then so must greenness; or, perhaps better, if a *mode* (or case) of greenness exists, i.e. a green trope, then so does greenness.[5] Hence one cannot *fail* to observe greenness when one perceives a green thing (or green mode/trope).[6] Thus the existence of an internal relation between a universal and its instances only strengthens the case for the observability – albeit indirect – of the former.

The indirect perception of essence mirrors the structure of our knowledge of essences as a case of our knowledge of universals generally. For when we come to know the essence of a thing – for example that a fish is a water-dwelling vertebrate with gills in the mature case[7] – we also do so indirectly by means of acquiring knowledge of particular examples. Not only does all knowledge begin with the senses, but all immediate sensory perception is of particulars. It is from the particulars that we advance, through a process of *abstraction*, to the knowledge of universals, of which we form abstract concepts. It is by the sensory presentation of repeated examples of a universal – the redness of this mailbox, of that fire engine, of that phone booth – that we are able, first to know that the objects concerned share a common characteristic and, second, to *reflect* on that common characteristic as predicable of many cases including ones yet unobserved or unknown. Our intellectual judgment to the effect that there is some universal shared, or capable of being shared, by more than one thing does not exclude our indirect perception of that universal but rather is elicited by it. The universal is not only an abstract object of rational apprehension, but something that manifests itself concretely in material reality.

As mentioned earlier, the observation of essence is also, in a sense, the observation of particulars. For we need to distinguish between *metaphysical* and *physical* essence. The metaphysical essence of a thing is its nature as represented in the metaphysical definition of it as falling under a certain genus and possessing a specific difference. So, to take the simple definition of man as a rational animal,[8] it tells us that the human being falls under the genus *animal* and possesses the specific difference of being *rational*. This essence, considered metaphysically, points us to the universals of *animality* and *rationality* as characterizing humans essentially (the complete essence being a complex universal composed of animality and rationality as parts). We can observe the essence of man by observing the universals indirectly, as instantiated in a given case. Or again, the definition of a fish as a water-dwelling vertebrate with gills in the mature case points us to the universals *water-dwelling*, *vertebrate* and *possessing gills in the mature case*, which we observe through observation of particular instances.

The physical essence of a thing, however, is its nature as concretely existing, containing real constituent principles or parts. In the case of humans, then, when we observe a particular human's rationality – rationality as exemplified in the mode of a particular human's existence – we observe a real, constituent part of the human; the same for his animality. Put more concretely, we can say that a human being is a composite of *mind* and *body*, the mind exemplifying rationality and the body exemplifying animality; and the human exemplifies both by virtue of his mind and body exemplifying each universal respectively. (Compare: Jack has a pain because his foot hurts; Jill is white because her skin is white.) Hence the physical essence of a person just is their particular mind and body, and we can observe it directly by observing these constituents.[9] Again, the physical essence of my pet guppy is its particular backbone, gills, and water-dwelling behaviour – when I observe these I observe its physical essence.

As long as we do not think of essences in terms of bare substrata, but as physically manifested constituents of a thing, we should not be troubled by empiricist scruples concerning unobservability. Even if we think of them as hidden internal structures (which, as I have suggested, is wrong at least as a general thesis), then so long as we do not make the unwarranted move of treating them as unobservable in principle the empiricist worry again has no bite. Real essences are amenable to observation both non-scientific and scientific, expert and non-expert. By combining these under the umbrella of metaphysical reflection, we have all we need to keep empiricist-style scepticism at bay.

2.2 Quinean animadversions

W.V. Quine, throughout his writings, expresses doubts about *de re* necessity in general and essentialism in particular. It might be thought that his doubts stem from his rejection of modal logic (at least in its quantified form), but it is more accurate to say that his rejection of modal logic stems from his overall rejection of necessity. Quine, in short, adopts a Humean view of necessity: there is no necessity at all in the real world. Hume, Quine says, 'was right ... in discrediting metaphysical necessity' (Quine 1990: 140).

Not only does the purported explanation of necessity in terms of possible worlds push the problem back a stage (with that we can agree), but so does the attempt to explain the necessity of the laws of nature: how can we distinguish them from what 'just so happens'? Talk of generality does not help, since most laws are general with respect to some subject matter but specific with respect to others.

Instead, says Quine, '*sub specie aeternitatis* there is no necessity and no contingency; all truth is on a par' (1990: 140). What distinguishes the laws from mere accidental regularities is 'how we arrive at them', in particular by induction and by the hypothetico-deductive method. Even when it comes to mathematical and logical truths, Quine famously accounts for the 'air of necessity' that surrounds them in terms of 'our prudence in not excessively rocking the boat' (1990: 140), invoking holism, maxims such as 'minimum mutilation', and overall scientific practice to try to gain for logic and mathematics all that we need from necessity without appealing to necessity itself.

One might wonder why Quine's *modus tollens* cannot become a *modus ponens* for the *de re* necessitarian. After all, faced with a choice between rejecting the proposition that the sum of seven and five is necessarily twelve and rejecting either another hypothesis to which we do not 'attach an air of necessity' or an empirical 'observation categorical', why would it not be a case of indisputable rationality to regard the arithmetical truth as *absolutely* non-negotiable and then to hunt for the error somewhere else? One common response of the modal sceptic is that our insistence on necessity has often led us astray in the past: witness non-Euclidean geometry, transfinite arithmetic, or the apparent transformation of one biological species into another. Maybe we will also be led astray if we insist on the necessity of the principle of bivalence, the logical impossibility of time travel or backwards causation, the necessity of the universe's having a cause, and so on. Hence it would be imprudent to persevere in claiming that any proposition, no matter how apparently obvious in its necessity or impossibility, should be immune from future revision.

There is no room to discuss all of the examples mentioned above (though on biological species see Chapter 9), but I want to emphasize the need to avoid confusing the questions of: whether a concept is senseless; whether it has sense but no application to anything; and, if it does have application, what it does or does not apply to. For the modal sceptic to cite examples such as those just mentioned is to fall into this confusion. To take non-Euclidean geometry as a case in point, what it teaches us is that some geometrical propositions are necessarily true in Euclidean space but not in non-Euclidean space. One can stipulate that 'triangle' means 'closed, three-sided, rectilinear figure in Euclidean space' and go on to say that this is what was always implicitly meant by the term before non-Euclidean geometry was discovered. After the discovery, the term became ambiguous (at least among mathematicians) as between this definition and the related one with 'non-Euclidean' substituted for 'Euclidean'; so that when we now talk about triangles we need to be explicit about what meaning we assign to the word or else assume that the context makes this clear.

On the other hand, one might say that 'triangle' is univocal, continuing, as it has always done, to mean 'closed, three-sided, rectilinear figure', following which one then stipulates whether one is talking about such figures as they appear in Euclidean or non-Euclidean space. (Further moves could be made in respect of 'rectilinear' as well.) Either way, it turns out that we now know that, although the internal angles of triangles in Euclidean space necessarily add up to 180°, this is not necessarily the case outside that geometry. We did not learn that necessity made no sense or had no application, only that we were mistaken about what things it applied to. As far as the ontology goes, there is no disagreement about interpretation. To put the matter in terms that will have become very familiar by the end of this book, when geometers discovered that Euclidean triangles were not merely a genus of triangle but also a species of triangle, they discovered that not all triangles had internal angles adding up to 180°.[10] (For what amounts to the same analysis of the situation, though framed purely in terms of meaning, see LaPorte 2004: 151–5.) In other cases, however, we might find that necessity does indeed apply despite the strictures of sceptics about the latest discovery or conceptual insight; this might be so, for instance, in the case of the principle of bivalence. What cases such as those above amount to, therefore, is not a call for the abandonment of necessity, but a call for clarity, rigour, and attention to detail in sorting out the necessary from the merely possible or contingent. If Quine's injunction is taken as one to prudence rather than outright scepticism, then, his remarks will have done philosophers a service.

Not so for some of his other arguments against necessity. Consider his famous argument concerning the cycling mathematician. Mathematicians, let us suppose, are necessarily rational but not necessarily two-legged. Cyclists, let us also suppose, are necessarily two-legged but not necessarily rational. So what do we say of Fred the cycling mathematician? Is he necessarily rational and not necessarily rational, necessarily two-legged and not necessarily two-legged? Quine concludes from this allegedly paradoxical situation that 'there is no semblance of sense in rating some of his attributes as necessary and some as contingent' (Quine 1960: 199).

The solution to the problem depends on whether the relevant propositions are given a *de re* or a *de dicto* reading. (See Marcus 1993: 227 for a brief mention.) If we take it to be true of mathematicians that they are necessarily rational, and of cyclists that they are not necessarily rational, Fred winds up having inconsistent properties. But if we take it to be necessarily true that if anyone is a mathematician he is rational, and not necessarily true that if anyone is a cyclist he is rational, Fred the mathematician turns out rational. And if we take it also to be necessarily true that anyone who is a cyclist is two-legged, and not necessarily true that anyone who is a mathematician is two-legged, Fred the cyclist turns out two-legged. So there is no paradox if he is rational and two-legged, as we would expect a cycling mathematician to be. The fact, moreover, that we do get a paradox if we ascribe *de re* necessary properties to cyclists *qua* cyclists, or mathematicians *qua* mathematicians, might lead the believer in *de re* necessity to suspect the very idea of attributing necessary characteristics to objects by virtue of their accidental features, which is what being a cyclist or a mathematician assuredly is.[11] And contra Alex Orenstein, who asserts that this resolution of Quine's paradox 'does not provide a positive case for essentialism'(Orenstein 2002: 159), it should in fact lead the sceptic in the direction of real essentialism, which tells us that the only way in which it can be true that Fred is necessarily rational is by virtue of his being a human, since all humans are, *de re*, necessarily rational beings. (Hence the misleading use of *rational* in Quine's paradox; *being good at arithmetic* would have been more accurate as far as being a mathematician is concerned.)

The believer in *de re* necessity might be led further by the thought that an appeal to relative essentialism will not do. Needless to say, Quine does not make it, but nor should anyone who actually wishes to uphold essentialism. On the relativist approach, Fred is necessarily rational *qua* mathematician but not *qua* cyclist, and so on. *De re* modal properties are thereby relativized to descriptions: nothing is necessarily *F* or not necessarily *F* absolutely, only relative to some description or perhaps context. Nonetheless the move will not work, since it merely invites the question 'What is Fred *qua* cycling mathematician?' To be told that this is an illegitimate description for relative essentialist purposes invites the charge of ad hockery, especially since the description is quite legitimate for all other purposes. How are we to sort the proper from the improper descriptions? Merely by whether they generate a modal paradox?

Another problem for the relative essentialist is that her position ends up looking either incoherent or in need of absolute essentialism as well. For how is she to respond to the question of what properties the number three has necessarily? For instance, suppose she asserts that three *qua* prime number is necessarily divisible only by itself and one; is three *qua* odd number necessarily so divisible? In fact it is divisible only by itself and one, but *qua* odd number all that is necessarily true of it is that it is not divisible by two. So does the relativist want to say that *qua* odd number it is not necessarily divisible only by itself and one? The question seems to lack sense precisely because, unlike being a cyclist or being a mathematician, being odd and being prime are themselves necessary properties of the number three. This being so, we want to say that three is necessarily divisible only by itself and one (and hence not by two) *however* we decide to pick it out – the description is irrelevant.

To force home the point, does the relativist want to say that, *qua* number, three is neither necessarily divisible by itself and one alone nor indivisible by two? Then *qua* number what is necessarily true of it? The answer, if we are to make sense of the question, has to be that, whatever other properties it has (such as primeness and oddness), it has those properties (such as divisibility by one, being abstract) that are the necessary properties of numbers. And this looks like the answer of the absolute essentialist, for whom objects have necessary properties however they are singled out and whatever the context, simply by virtue of what they are. The same goes for the question of what Fred is *qua* human being: he is, among other things, a living creature of necessity, however else we pick him out. For the relativist then to resort to isolating a class of properties $P_1...P_n$ for every kind of object F such that Fs have $P_1...P_n$ whatever the description of an F is simply to define the absolutely essential properties, not to do away with them.[12]

Finally, it is worth mentioning another of Quine's anti-essentialist doubts, this time the infamous example of the number of planets. (It was first raised in Quine 1943, but re-emerged in later work, including 1960: 196–7.) We know that

(1) 8 is necessarily greater than 7.

Let us also assume that

(2) The number of planets = 8.[13]

Leibniz's Law then seems to require us to infer that

(3) The number of planets is necessarily greater than 7,

which is false. What has gone wrong? Quine fingers *de re* necessity as the culprit.[14] The charge, however, is unwarranted, and as is well known there are various ways of answering it. On the standard Russellian analysis, 'the number of planets' is treated as a non-referring expression, and so (2) is analysed as

(2*) There is exactly one number of planets and it is identical to 8.

Substituting for '8' in (1) gives us the true *de re* proposition

(3*) There is exactly one number of planets and it is necessarily greater than 7[15]

as opposed to the false *de dicto* proposition

(3**) Necessarily, there is exactly one number of planets and it is greater than 7.

But one does *not* need to be committed to the Theory of Descriptions per se to see how to read (2) so as to generate a non-sequitur. For surely when we assert (2), what we are asserting is the existential claim

(2') There are eight planets.

This is the natural, unforced reading of the proposition. Now, from (1) and (2') one cannot derive (3) no matter whether (3) is read as a *de re* claim about the number of planets or as a *de dicto* proposition. One does not have to go further into a formal Russellian analysis in order to see the fallacy of the initial inference.[16]

Alternatively, one could claim that there is another, less natural but perfectly acceptable reading of (2) that takes 'the number of planets' to be a genuine referring expression. Using Kripke's terminology, we can read 'the number of planets' as referring rigidly to the number 8, thus preserving the form of (2) as a genuine identity statement, and mark this by use of the 'actually' operator. (2) then becomes

(2") The actual number of planets = 8.

From this it follows by Leibniz's Law, together with (1), that

(3") The actual number of planets is necessarily greater than 7,

which is a true *de re* statement. On either approach, then, one does not have to subscribe to Russell's theory, or indeed to the apparatus of quantificational analysis, to see what is wrong with Quine's use of (1)–(3) to cast doubt on *de re* modality, and thereby on essentialism.

2.3 Popper: avoiding 'what-is?' questions

Karl Popper is another critic of essentialism (Popper 1966: ch. 11; 1972: ch. 3; 1979: ch. 5). His attack occurs within the context of his fallibilism concerning scientific method, and though there is no space here to analyse his overall approach to science, still there are several themes in Popper's anti-essentialism that are worth extracting. They further illustrate some of the confusions and mistakes with which anti-essentialists can be charged.

The first is Popper's insistence on studiously avoiding what he calls 'what-is questions', that is, questions asking for the essence or 'true nature' of a thing. We should, he asserts, give up the view that 'in every single thing there is an essence, an inherent nature or principle (such as the spirit of wine in wine), which necessarily causes it to be what it is, and thus to act as it does. This animistic view explains nothing' (Popper 1979: 195). Now, let us leave aside the curious example of the spirit of wine, which is either a pejorative remark reminiscent of the nominalist and empiricist insult concerning 'occult qualities' supposedly posited by Aristotelians, or else perfectly correct – since wine is essentially alcoholic. And let us also put aside the sneering reference to animism, as though the essentialist is guilty by association with some mysterious pagan ritual or else foolishly – and falsely, needless to say – posits a soul in every object.

The nub of Popper's objection is that essentialism relies on what he calls an 'intellectual intuition' of essence and so is incapable of explaining anything (1966: 291–2). He summons to his cause Antisthenes,[17] who allegedly said, 'I can see a horse, Plato, but I cannot see its horseness'. Aristotle reports Antisthenes's criticism of essential definition (Ross 1928b: 1024b32) and Popper claims Aristotle was 'troubled by these difficulties'. If he was troubled, one wonders why in the passage cited by Popper he calls Antisthenes 'simple minded'[18] for thinking that there was only one way of describing an object. Popper's worry is that 'there is no way of distinguishing between a "true" and a "false" definition' (1966: 300). If, to go back to a familiar example, Fred says that a fish is a vertebrate with scales (D_1)[19] and George says it is a vertebrate with gills (D_2), then how can we say who is correct? The essentialist 'is reduced to complete helplessness' (1966: 292): Fred might insist that his intellectual intuition is the only true one, but then so might George and there would be deadlock. Or else Fred might concede that George's D_2 is as correct as his own D_1 but add that it is the definition of a different essence which George unfortunately denotes by the same name, 'fish'.

The essentialist replies that this is a caricature of his position. I will have more to say about knowability in Chapter 3, but the main point here is that the essentialist does not rely on intellectual intuition. If any definition were as good as another, it would, as Aristotle points out, be impossible to make a false statement. Similarly, if it were impossible to describe an object except by its true definition, one could never give a false description. But this is absurd, since we give false definitions all the time, and the history of science is littered with them. When we apply to one kind of thing a definition proper to another kind of thing – in Aristotle's example, the definition of a circle as applied to a triangle – we get a false definition. When Fred gives D_1, he gives a false definition since we know that some fish lack scales.[20] In general, defining an object by any of its accidents gives a false definition.[21] It is not intellectual intuition that discovers the true from the false definitions; rather, the process is a combination of the perceptual and the intellectual, whereby we perceive particulars and abstract their essence via a consideration of form (about which much more later). There is no special insight into essence generated by a dedicated faculty or perceptual organ, and no intuition is involved. What *are* involved, though, are the intellect – the rational faculties in general – and the organs of sense. Hence Popper's approving citation of Antisthenes's protest that he can see a horse but not horseness is beside the point. For Antisthenes raised this precisely against *Plato's* theory of essences, not Aristotle's, and in that respect it does have bite.

For an Aristotelian, however – which is what the real essentialist is – horseness is indeed observable, along the lines set out earlier. Again, there is no room to canvass Popper's fallibilism, but the essentialist will wonder whether Popper really thinks 'every definition must be considered as equally admissible' (Popper 1966: 292). Would he hold that a definition of electrons that excluded the possession of charge was as admissible as one that included it? That a definition of gold that included its being a metal was no better than one that left it out? Or that a definition of rivers that excluded their containing water did not fare any worse than one that mentioned it? In addition, Popper's critique suffers from an even more remarkable mis-interpretation of Aristotle, thus weakening his case further.[22]

Popper's second worry concerns the commitment of essentialism to 'ulti-mate explanation'. He denies '*the doctrine that science aims at ultimate explanation*; that is to say, an explanation which (essentially, or by its very nature) cannot be further explained, and which is in no need of any further explanation'. Essences, he says, may exist (though in the context of his overall attack I doubt he means this seriously), but they are 'obscurantist' and 'the belief in them does not help us in any way and indeed is likely to hamper us; so that there is no reason why the scientist should *assume* their existence' (Popper 1972: 105).

Popper's concern appears to be methodological. The search for ultimate explanation precludes the advancement of science by stifling questions that allow us 'to probe deeper and deeper into the structure of our world or, as we might say, into properties of the world that are more and more essential, or of greater and greater depth' (1979: 196). The phrase 'more and more essential' is a curious one, leading the reader to wonder what exactly Popper is concerned about. He cites only the case of Isaac Newton and gravity in support of his position (1972: 106–7), claiming that Newton's essentialism '*prevented fruitful questions from being raised*, such as, "What is the cause of gravity?"', or asking whether we could deduce Newton's theory from a more general, independently testable one. Newton famously said, with regard to the cause of gravity, '*Hypotheses non fingo*', 'I do not feign hypotheses' (see the General Scholium to the third edition of the *Principia*), and he wrestled with the nature and cause of gravity all his life. He refused to posit it as an inherent, essential property of matter since he found it absurd that an object could possess the intrinsic power to act at a distance. But he did think that his theory, though incomplete, did capture, mathematically, whatever the essential properties of matter were by which gravity could be effected.

The general lesson Popper seeks to draw from the case of Newton is that essentialism obstructs scientific progress. Now whatever might be said of Newton and gravity, it is difficult to see what justification there is for Pop-per's concern. Maybe he is right that Newton's essentialism was accepted until the late nineteenth century, whereafter wholly different conceptions of matter and motion came to be developed, leading in the end to General Relativity. Leaving aside, though, the point that General Relativity itself purports, for better or worse, to explain gravity in terms of the *essential* structure of the space–time manifold, why should we think that science was obstructed, or that it ever should be, by essentialist thinking? This would only be the case if it were part of essentialist doctrine that ultimate expla-nations are easy to come by, or that when we think we have an ultimate explanation most of the time we do have one. But essentialism is perfectly compatible with, and indeed requires, a level of modesty and humility in our investigative practices.

As is well known, for a long time whales were thought of as just another kind of fish. Observation seemed to suggest that water-dwelling animals with fins formed an essential (or, as is usually said now, natural)[23] kind. People were content with this classification for centuries. Was scientific progress thereby compromised, since people thought an ultimate classification had been reached and that all water-dwelling creatures with fins were united by a common essence? Perhaps there were sceptics who thought that no amount of observation would ever give us a reason to separate the whales from the sharks, but the fact is that we eventually did so, as a result of improved access to both and a better understanding of how whales and true fish differed in their anatomy and physiology. Now science would have been impeded had investigators insisted, *in the face of anatomical and physiological discovery*, that whales *had* to be classified essentially with fish *even though* they differed radically in their make-up. Maybe a few eccentrics so insisted. But if they did, they do not appear to have blocked the needed reclassification.

The example is almost folklorish, but is nevertheless typical of the progress of taxonomy in the biological sciences. And there is no reason to think the other sciences are any different. Georg Stahl's phlogiston theory, for example, was tenaciously held on to because for all its faults it had immense unifying and predictive power and seemed to explain such phenomena as the combustion of metals. Chemists thought they had alighted on an ultimate explanation, though it turned out to be false and was finally overthrown by Lavoisier. But there was no incompatibility between regarding phlogiston as ultimately explanatory while continuing to test the behaviour of metals in order to see whether the predictions of the theory were after all correct. In other words, one may think one has an ultimate explanation of a phenomenon without ceasing experimental endeavour. If the explanation is ultimate it has consequences, and the natural practice is to explore those consequences. If the consequences turn out not to obtain, then the scientist is bound to revisit the theory to see if it needs revising or rejecting. It would be a dereliction of scientific duty *not* to continue with experimentation after having found a putative ultimate explanation.

More generally, the effect of essentialism on scientific practice should be the exact *opposite* of what Popper claims it to be. Rather than hinder progress, it is a positive *stimulant* to progress. The search for ultimate explanations provides a conceptual terminus that focuses and unifies enquiry. As long as the scientist does not believe reality to be far less difficult to grasp and comprehend than it is – and it is no part of essentialism that reality is easy to fathom – the promise of an ultimate explanation is precisely what should goad him into ever more strenuous efforts to reach that goal. It is the search for how things *really* are, in their ultimate reality, that encourages the scientist not to rest content with whatever observable characteristics of things happen to cross his gaze. Appreciating that reality is complex and multifaceted, he should be reluctant to assume that this or that experiment, or one particular description of a thing's behaviour, has captured what really marks it off from everything else in the universe. There are many ways of describing things – most of them false. This thought alone should be enough to provoke the scientist into striving to get to the heart of the matter. And, contra Popper, it is essentialist thoughts that continue to permeate scientific practice, whatever philosophers may think about the effect of anti-essentialism on the scientific revolution of the eighteenth century.

Finally, there is also a point of principle behind Popper's unease concerning ultimate explanation. Although it is tied up with his overall falsificationism, we can extract the basic thought: it is that ultimate explanation by essences is incompatible with the goal of probing 'deeper and deeper into the structure of the world'. Since science is all about probing deeper and deeper, it should not rely on essentialism. For Popper, ever-deeper probing involves developing conjectures of higher and higher universality; leaving aside talk of conjectures, we can say that science is concerned with subsuming lower-level theories wherever possible by higher-level ones and hence increasing the generality of description and explanation of the phenomena.

The essentialist response is twofold. On the one hand, there is a sense in which ultimate explanation is not the same as explanation in terms of the highest possible level of generality. On the other, even if it were, explanation must come to an end and so a highest possible level of generality must exist. To take the first point, consider the explanation of why gold behaves as it does. It is a certain species of metal – a metal with certain physical characteristics. And let us suppose these are wholly explained by its particular internal physical structure. Now gold, being a metal, belongs to a genus, and that genus is itself a species of element, the elements being divided into the metals, non-metals and the metalloids, each group specified by its members' ionization and bonding properties. The behaviour of all three subspecies can then be explained, let us suppose, by a general chemical theory, and this might even be subsumed under a more general physical theory of electric charge, attraction of atoms, and so on. Maybe, for all anyone knows, this can all be explained in terms of quark behaviour. But the ultimate explanation, for the essentialist, of why gold behaves as it does is *not* that it falls under ever more *general* classifications and so is susceptible of explanation by theories at those higher levels, but that it falls under the *most specific* characterization possible for it. In other words, ultimate explanation is not explanation in terms of the most general, but precisely the opposite – explanation in terms of the most specific. The most specific characterization is what marks gold off from everything else in the universe and so explains the features that give it its particular identity in the scheme of reality.

It is logically possible for ultimate specificity to be reached *without* reaching an ultimate level of generality. The argument is as follows – I will frame it in 'hidden structure' terms that a contemporary essentialist might find congenial. Suppose there is some kind of thing K, and scientists discover at time t_1 that K is composed of particles of a certain kind P arranged in a particular structure S – call the particles so structured P_S. Now suppose that at t_2 they discover that P-type particles are always and everywhere composed of another kind of particle Q, and the Q-type particles in K have their own particular structure T – we call Q_T the Q-type particles that are T-structured in K. Suppose also that composition is transitive. (This is debatable, but it is a harmless assumption for the purposes of the argument.) The scientists know the laws governing P-type particles and the laws governing Q-type particles, and that the Q-laws are more general than, and subsume, the P-laws. Our scientists, then, being hidden structure essentialists, conclude they have found the essence of K – it is to be composed of Q_T. Their essentialist conclusion, however, relies on an implicit assumption that because the P-type particles are composed of Q-type particles, P_S constitutes a genus. That is to say, although P_S is wholly explained by the existence of Q_T in K, P_S *might* exist in and compose some wholly different kind of object L, and yet in L be explained by the existence of Q-type particles with a *different* structure altogether, say Q_V. Hence the essence of K could not be given by P_S, because P_S could be common to objects of different kinds – perhaps radically different – and so the essence of K would have to be given by the more specific Q_T with the more general laws of Q-type behaviour to explain why, in the T-structure, K-type objects behave as they do.

The implicit assumption, however, is not necessarily true. For all the scientists know, P_S might *not* form a genus, since it may be the case that being composed of P_S *entails* being composed of Q_T. In other words, it is logically possible that there may be no kind of thing L with P_S in the first place. That is to say, P_S might just be *as specific as it gets*, even though – and consistently with the fact that – P-type particles with structure S are in fact composed of Q-type particles with structure T, and there are Q-laws more general than P-laws, from which P-type behaviour can be deduced. Given this logical possibility, it follows that ultimate explanation and specificity of essence come apart: it is possible for scientists to reach a level of specificity that goes no further, even though they are still able to advance to a higher and more general level of description and explanation by means of physical law.

Although this argument is abstract, it seems to describe what typically is the case. So, for example, scientists have discovered that water has the H_2O structure. Are they justified in regarding this as the essence of water? (For the hidden structure essentialist it will be the whole essence, but for the real essentialist it is only part of the essence.) Not if being composed of H_2O forms a genus – because then it would not mark water off from every other kind of thing. But as far as anyone knows – and we have no reason even to suspect otherwise – being composed of H_2O does *not* form a genus. There is nothing in the world that is composed of H_2O and is *not* water. Hence water has nothing more specific about it – in real essentialist terms, no more specific difference – to mark it out from everything else. Being composed of H_2O is as specific as it gets. And yet it might be true, and many physicists would claim it is, that being composed of H_2O is wholly explicable in terms of a more general subatomic theory, perhaps a theory of quarks or some other fundamental particle. If true – if we can get even more general than H_2O to explain the behaviour of water – it does not follow that, to use Popper's inappropriate phrase, we have got 'more and more essential' in our explanation of water. We have got the essence of water once we have got its specific difference (for the contemporary essentialist, its hidden structure), and by moving to a more general theory to explain that specific difference we may have more success in unifying and simplifying our explanation of reality, but it does not follow that we will have overthrown the proposition that being composed of H_2O is of the essence of water, in favour of some other, 'deeper' essence.

There is no 'essence of the essence' of something – either you have its essence or you do not. But once you have its essence, that does not exhaust or preclude further investigation into the structure of that essence. And this helps to illustrate the difference between real essentialism and hidden structure essentialism: the real essentialist allows investigation into the structure of essence, but does not thereby end up claiming that what the discovered structure is a structure of was *not* the essence after all. The hidden structure essentialist, on the other hand, thinks that by delving into 'deeper and deeper' structures (to echo Popper) she is somehow getting closer and closer to the essence. From the real essentialist perspective, the irony is that the deeper and deeper she goes, the more and more likely it is that the essence she is searching for will vanish from sight altogether. No wonder that Locke thought real essences, understood as hidden structures, were 'something we know not what'.

Suppose, on the other hand, that this whole line of argument is wrong. Suppose that whenever the scientist ascends to a higher level of generality in his theories, then by that very fact he simultaneously descends to a greater level of specificity. Then what can the real essentialist say? All he can do is reply with the familiar refrain that explanation must come to an end somewhere. Note again that Popper's point about ascending levels of generality is detachable from his overall falsificationism. Falsificationism holds that no scientific theory can ever be conclusively confirmed; but the scientist can, if the position is correct, continue on a process of replacing one scientific theory with another, better-corroborated one, without moving to a higher level of generality: each new theory may be as specific as the one it replaces.

Rather, Popper's point about generality in the end comes down to a view of the categories of reality. If one can continue indefinitely subsuming theories by more general ones, then there is no ultimate level of generality. And if generality moves in tandem with specificity (by penetrating into deeper and deeper structures), then there really will be no essences. But if there is no most general *or* most specific level of description of reality, then it is hard to see how there can be any explanation of reality at all, of why things are as they are. This conclusion goes against the very 'Galilean philosophy of science' that Popper professes to uphold, whereby science aims at a 'true theory or description of the world (and especially of its regularities or "laws"), which shall also be an explanation of the observable facts' (Popper 1972: 100–3).

Yet without a most general or a most specific level of description, how can we ever have an explanation? And even if we have a partial explanation in terms of essences at the most specific level, doesn't a full explanation, one which unifies reality and shows how all the various kinds of things are related, require that there be a highest level of generality? The special sciences are always striving for this – witness the never-ending hope of physicists to arrive at a Grand Unified Theory of Everything that is so simple and elegant it can be written on the back of a postcard. Is the search itself irrational – even if it be doomed to failure? And is it irrational for the metaphysician to step in and assert that whatever the highest level of generality that may be reached within each of the special sciences, it is for metaphysics to provide the very highest level of description – that in terms of the fundamental categories of being such as substance and accident, essence and existence, form and matter, universal and particular?

Popper might reply that, for any level of categorization of reality, for all we know there might be one that is higher and so more general. The essentialist can reply from the opposite direction. Rather than consider our ascent towards higher categorization, we can begin with the concept of *being*, which in traditional metaphysics is called a *transcendental* concept.[24] By transcendental is meant that the concept applies to absolutely everything, and hence is supreme and exhaustive in what it embraces. Now being is not itself a genus (about which more in Chapter 5.3), but if the concept can be divided in such a way as not to leave a further classificatory gap in between it and the proposed further division we will have a categorization that cannot be subsumed under anything more general (i.e. apart from the transcendental concept of being itself). This will be what is traditionally called the *summum genus*, the highest genus under which everything either falls *or does not*; that is to say, the summum genus determines everything as belonging either to it or to its complement.

If we can come up with at least one summum genus we can counter the Popperian thought that there might be no highest level of generality. We can, because everything can be divided into things that either do or do not inhere in something else. Something that does not inhere in anything else is a *substance*, and something that does inhere in something else is an *accident*.[25] Everything falls into one or other of these categories (or is, on a certain construal of artefacts that I will give in Chapter 7.4, a kind of combination of both), and there is no way of subsuming them into a higher genus – at least none that anyone has ever been able to come up with. It is a matter of indifference whether we call substance a summum genus and classify everything as either belonging to it or not, or whether we call accidents the summum genus and classify everything as belonging to that genus or not. There are many more details that could be unpacked here, but some of these will have to wait until later. The point is that we are able to produce levels of generality beyond which we cannot go and which are sufficient to classify all of reality. There is thus no warrant for the Popperian tenet that the ascent to ever higher levels of generality is never-ending, and hence that there can be no ultimate explanation *for that reason*.[26]

2.4 Wittgenstein: the shadow of grammar

The Wittgensteinian attack on essentialism derives from his views about the multifaceted nature of language, which involves its not functioning as a calculus according to strict rules. This is most clearly and famously brought out in his doctrine of 'family resemblances' (Wittgenstein 1958: s.66ff.). More specifically, his view of essence is that it is, in the words of Peter Hacker, a 'shadow cast by grammar' upon reality (Hacker 1990: 438). As Wittgenstein himself explicitly says, '[e]*ssence* is expressed by grammar' (1958: s.371) and '[g]rammar tells us what kind of object anything is' (1958: s.373). It is remarks such as these that have led another commentator, Garth Hallett, to take Wittgenstein's philosophy of language as implying a full-fledged anti-essentialism in metaphysics (Hallett 1991).

Wittgenstein's views on language in general, and family resemblance in particular, contain far too much to be discussed here. I want instead to select several points that highlight the essentialist response to the Wittgensteinian critique. The first concerns family resemblance in general and Wittgenstein's famous example of the term 'game' in particular. For a start, it is at least arguable that his dismissal of the idea that games form a class defined by an essence was too quick. Jesper Juul, for one, has argued with some persuasiveness that games do indeed have an essence (Juul 2003), and that the essence is given by six features: (1) rules; (2) a variable, quantifiable outcome; (3) a value assigned to possible outcomes; (4) player effort; (5) attachment by the player to the outcome; (6) negotiable consequences. One interesting feature of Juul's definition is that he seeks to capture our intuitive understanding of what a game is, comparing it to a number of previous definitions found in the literature. This is important because the Wittgensteinian is right to warn essentialists to be on their guard against *re*definitions that masquerade as definitions. This is especially common in computer-related research, where terms (such as 'intelligence') are often appropriated for technical use and then redefined to meet prior assumptions (e.g. concerning whether a machine can pass the Turing Test) rather than defined in accordance with the phenomenon associated with the term outside the particular specialism into which it was imported.

Hence the 'variable, quantifiable outcome' in feature (2) does not require that a game have an outcome that is numerically measurable, only that it be clear, unambiguous, and such that, at the very least, one can in principle say that it has been achieved or not achieved (the quantification here can be thought of as binary – achieve (1) or not achieve (0)). Hence Wittgenstein's examples of patience and of a child throwing a ball against a wall, even if they do not involve winning and losing or competition, fall within Juul's definition. So does his other example of ring-a-ring-a-roses, where the outcome is precisely falling down on the word 'down!' So would rope-skipping as typically played by children, where a child either hands over to another the first time she misses the rope or does so after enough misses; in any case, simply staying clear of the rope is a variable, quantifiable outcome. A boxer's rope-skipping as part of his training is, on the other hand, not a game. Nor is finger-painting or (usually) playing with dolls – a child can play with dolls without playing a *game* with them.

Clause (6) is very important. As Juul puts it, '[t]he same game [set of rules] can be played with or without real-life consequences' (Juul 2003: 35): because of it, the definition includes sports as games, but not war or financial investment. I think Juul is right to include sports, even professional ones, since, as he says, if professional sport is counted as working rather than playing, a competition such as the London Marathon, containing both amateurs and professionals, would and would not be a game. It is better to say that all sport has negotiable real-life consequences, i.e. consequences outside the game itself. In the amateur case the consequences are negotiated *not* to extend outside the game, whereas in the professional case they are – they extend to career, financial status, celebrity status and so on.

The various moves of a game, according to Juul, should be predominantly harmless, even though they might be negotiated to involve some harm. This too seems plausible. The point about war's not being a game is that the harmful consequences are non-negotiable. Even though the parties can negotiate the terms of a peace settlement, the immediate consequences of engaging in warfare non-negotiably involve physical harm. If the parties decided to use toy guns and blanks they would no longer be engaging in war at all, but in something like war *games*. Hence unpleasant activities such as cock-fighting and bare-knuckle boxing are doubtfully called games, just as hunting is not a game. On the other hand, if the relevant consequences only extend to humans one might call cock-fighting a game since only the birds are harmed and the financial stakes themselves are negotiable – the spectators could just as well wager with fake money, though historically, and for obvious reasons, it was negotiated that the wagering should only be with real money.

Finally, many physical sports have injury as a real-life consequence extending beyond the game, but the best view here is that it has been negotiated (implicitly or explicitly) that injury be allowed. It is not, however, the *object* of the sport, whose players and organizers always seek to *minimize* injury; even defenders of boxing as it is now performed insist – whatever one may think of the acceptability of the risk – that the object of boxing is not to injure the opponent but to wear them down with superior skill.

There is a lot more that can be said about games, and I do not pretend that Juul's definition is necessarily immune to counterexamples. My point is simply that Wittgenstein's example is not as felicitous as it seems at first glance. Certainly, the essentialist should learn the precautionary lesson contained within his discussion, namely that a priorism about essence is untenable (where this is meant in a loose sense to involve mere reflection without inspection) – one has to 'look and see' (Wittgenstein 1958: s.66) whether one is confronted by something with an essence. But essentialists have never held otherwise. More importantly, essentialists must not be *hasty* in assigning essences: working out what the essence of an object is requires a complex mixture of technical and non-technical observation, classification, theory-building and rational reflection. Such is the harmless message that can be extracted from Wittgenstein's analysis of games.

A second point concerns his very choice of example. It is far easier for an anti-essentialist to make a specious point using an *artefactual* term such as 'game' than with a purely natural term. Suppose, then, that Wittgenstein had said something like this:[27] 'Do fish have an essence? Consider all the different kinds of fish there are. There are big fish, small fish; fish with scales, fish without scales; multicoloured fish, grey fish; fish that live in salt water, fish that live in fresh water – and fish that spend their time in both; fish with lungs, fish without lungs; fish with hard shells and fish without; fish that swim and fish that crawl along the ocean floor; fish that suckle their young, fish that don't. Is having a backbone essential to being a fish? Well, what about jellyfish? And what about breathing through gills? Well, lungfish have lungs as well as gills, and can breathe through both. And what about fish that breathe through holes in the top of their head? And what about flying fish – mightn't we just as well call them birds? I propose, then, that fish have no essence but form a *family*. There are crisscrossing features, but no one strand that goes through them all'. And so on.

The example might seem cheap and ludicrous, but it is neither. The point could just as easily – and perhaps even more strikingly – have been made using the example of subatomic particles, the kind of case on which scientific essentialists prefer to focus. More importantly, though, if Wittgenstein had been alive in, say, 1250 AD and used the above example, it might not have sounded so silly (though I grant this may be a slight on our forbears) – even to a medieval icthyologist. The 'grammar' of a term such as 'fish' might have told us something very different about the 'nature' of fish if the usage of several centuries ago had been considered. Yet clearly our knowledge of the world has progressed much since then, and we know far more about how to partition the water-dwelling animals into classes according to what they really are. The point is that by choosing the example of games Wittgenstein selected an *artefactual* term rather than a purely natural one.

An artefactual term is a term that denotes objects whose existence- and identity-conditions depend at least in part on human purposes. Games do not exist in nature – they are creatures of human purpose and activity, and share all of the flexibility and multiplicity to be found in human life. Hence it is only to be expected that we are not going to find it easy to see what is common to all games.

A contrary thought suggests itself, however. It is that when it comes to inspecting the terms of our language to see which do and which do not denote things that have an essence, the following is more likely: that the terms for things *without* essences will denote things existing in nature rather than those of our own making. Why? For the simple reason that humans often have *better* access to their own goals or purposes than they do to nature itself. So when it comes, for instance, to a term such as 'work of art' and a term such as 'matter', it is in some ways easier to specify the essence of the former than of the latter. (The fact that people differ strongly over what the essence of a work of art *is* does not mean that works of art do not have an essence. But there is no space for a digression on this topic.)[28] Clearly, the ease of finding an essence depends on the kind of thing one is examining, and in general artefacts bring with them all the difficulties associated with identifying human purposes. But for the essentialist this is only a counsel to deeper investigation.

The broad point about Wittgenstein's anti-essentialism concerns the relationship between language and metaphysics. To think that grammar can tell us what an object is (apart from a grammatical object)[29] is, to adapt a favourite simile of Popper's when talking about linguistic philosophy generally, like thinking that our spectacles determine what it is that we see through them. Rather, it is the *world* that determines what we see through our spectacles, and our spectacles are tools to help us focus more clearly on the objective reality that we see using them.[30] There is, of course, a conventional aspect to language. To return to the (probably exaggerated) story of medieval fish observation, once our fanciful medieval ichthyologist came to realize that there was something about whales, or crustaceans, or jellyfish, that put them objectively into a different category from the water-dwelling vertebrates with gills, he was perfectly free to stipulate that the term 'fish' would henceforth be used for, say, whales and things sufficiently like them in respect of their form, and that the term 'whale' would be used for what we now call fish. Needless to say, had this happened it would not have been the case that fish were whales, only that the terms used to designate both would have been the opposite of what they actually are. So much is familiar from the Twin Earth debate. What are not conventional are the specific differences between fish, cetaceans, and crustaceans that require us to use our grammar in some way to mark those distinctions for the purpose of having an accurate description of reality.

Presumably, the reason the term 'fish' was retained for the vertebrates with gills is that something like Putnam's story about stereotypes was true in this case:[31] the term 'fish' was, from the beginning of its entry into the language, used to designate a particular kind of thing precisely by virtue of certain observable characteristics. It was never up for grabs, as it were, that 'fish' should at least denote all of *those* things given that it denoted any of them at all. What was up for grabs, and has been throughout the history of ichthyology, is what the extension of the term 'fish' is. Note, however, that the first matter 'up for grabs' was one of linguistic convention – whether the word 'fish' would be used for things with certain observable features. What was up for grabs later on, though – at least epistemically speaking – was not a matter of convention but of determination by the world. Icthyologists had to discover whether whales were in fact sufficiently like stereotypical fish in terms of their form to continue to be denotable by the same term. Once it was learned that they were not, it was no longer a matter of choice as to whether they still should be called 'fish', as long as the ichthyologist (and the rest of us who depended upon his classifications) cared about whether he was describing the world accurately by partitioning it into distinct classes just in case a partition was available and known.

The semantic story, however, is not the essentialist's central concern, since essence is no more a matter of modal semantics than of Wittgensteinian grammar. That this is so is betrayed even by some Wittgensteinians themselves in the way they approach metaphysical questions. For example, when Peter Hacker discusses whether any sense is to be made of the idea that a person is essentially an immaterial soul as opposed to a living human animal,[32] he denies the former on grounds that look explicitly ontological rather than grammatical – the apparent absence of identity conditions for immaterial substances, their lack of behaviour (the assumption being that only material substances can behave), and the usual problems of causal interaction with bodies (Hacker 2007: ch. 10). These are not questions that can be settled by examining whether conventions exist, or could ever be given, for the sensible use and application of terms such as 'substance', 'identity', and 'cause' to immaterial substances. They are, on the contrary, questions that can only be settled by rational metaphysical reflection. Rather than the cloud of metaphysics being condensed into a drop of grammar (Wittgenstein 1958: 222),[33] the truth is the reverse: the more the Wittgensteinian engages in metaphysics, the more the drop of grammar is dissolved by ontology.

The final, and perhaps most damaging, point is that the Wittgensteinian approach to metaphysics in general and essentialism in particular falsifies the way language itself behaves. The Wittgensteinian approach, supplemented as it sometimes is by Rylean considerations concerning category errors (an example being Bennett and Hacker 2003), takes natural language to be a set of rules and practices that is 'in order as it is' (Wittgenstein 1958: s.98). When the metaphysician tries to analyse the nature of reality it is not long before he takes language beyond the bounds within which it has sense, and gives expressions strange new meanings that inevitably get him into knots. Yet the truth is quite different – for *there is no such thing as ordinary language in the first place.* By this I do not mean that there is no such thing as *natural* language, as opposed to artificial language or formal language. Natural language exists, but not in the state that Wittgensteinians mean when they speak of 'ordinary language'. By ordinary language they mean natural language as it is used in a kind of ideal, or pristine, pre-metaphysical state. If such a thing existed, then one could track how 'language goes on holiday' (Wittgenstein 1958: s.38) and so how language users engage in metaphysical discourse that itself leads, almost inevitably, to conceptual confusion. When they did this they would, as it were, be falling from linguistic grace by traversing the bounds of sense as laid down by 'ordinary', i.e. pre-metaphysical, usage. It is language of this kind – free of metaphysics – whose existence is illusory.

Natural language is permeated and saturated by metaphysics, and has been so ever since philosophy began with the pre-Socratics. Every time any speaker makes a claim about the nature of reality she is implicitly, often explicitly, invoking metaphysical categories and precepts, whether they concern substance, quality, identity, cause, being, essence, mode, and so on. Hence there simply is no vantage point from which the Wittgensteinian can cast his eye over the ordinary functioning of language in order to see how a speaker – whether philosopher or layman, scientist or causal observer – gets his understanding into knots when he stretches everyday use beyond the bounds of sense. It is not that there is no vantage point because there is a problem in the very idea of using language to analyse language, or grammar to analyse grammatical error. The problem is in thinking there is a vantage point from which one can espy language in its 'ordinary', pre-metaphysical state. There is no such vantage point because there is no such language to be observed in the first place. Yet the existence of such a vantage point is a necessary condition of the entire Wittgensteinian enterprise.

The inevitable consequence, then, is that either the Wittgensteinian, when looking at problems concerning essence or any other metaphysical topic, ends up being forced to do metaphysics in the non-linguistic way by engaging with the metaphysical concepts and principles that underlie all of language; or he gets himself into knots by floundering about in the net of a mythical ordinary usage that is wholly detached from extra-linguistic reality. The essentialist is in no doubt which course he should take.

3 The reality and knowability of essence

3.1 Why essences are real

It is a metaphysical truth that the world contains both unity and plurality. There is a multiplicity of things and they all have features in common. In one sense, everything in the world is united to everything else, at least by sharing in being – everything is a being of some kind or other, whether concrete, abstract, actual, possible, mental, physical, natural, artefactual and so on. The phenomenon of multiplicity is explicated by the principles of individuation. The phenomenon of unity is explicated by the principles of essence.

There are two aspects to unity. First, there is the unity of multiple entities that fall under kinds. At one level, Fido and Rover possess a unity of a different sort to that possessed by Fred and Wilma, and vice versa. At other levels, they have the same sort of unity. Why? There are two general lines of response. One is to attribute unity to something in human practice, convention, or stipulation, for whatever purpose. Another is to attribute unity to reality: 'There is unity' is true because the world contains it, not because we impose it. The first response is usually called subjectivist, or relativist, or conventionalist. It sees unity as some sort of artefact of human classificatory practices. There is much that can be said against it. In a recent discussion, Crawford Elder argues that conventionalism about essences is self-defeating. For we are the source of our conventions, and if conventionalism were true in general it would have to be true about us. But then our conventions would have to be logically prior to us; but, on the contrary, we are logically prior to our conventions. Hence conventionalism about us could not be true. (See Elder 2004: ch. 1.) The implication is that if conventionalism is not true in respect of us, why should it be true in respect of anything else? (There is a conventional aspect to the essences of artefacts, but that is not the same as saying that conventionalism about artefacts is true.)

A similar sort of argument could be levelled against evolutionary theories of our classificatory practices, themselves stemming in large part from empiricist and Quinean scepticism about 'natural kinds'. (See Quine 1969.) If, as Quine claims, our 'sense of comparative similarity ... is presumably an evolutionary product of natural selection' (Quine 1969: 171), the problem is that our existence as beings capable of classification according to principles of comparative similarity is presupposed by our implementation of those principles. Hence the principles cannot be applied to ourselves since we have to exist before we can apply them. But if they do apply to ourselves, then they have been implemented without any creature to implement them (unless they have been applied to us by alien beings, which in turn have been classified as a natural kind by some further beings, and so on in a vicious regress). Note that the point is not temporal but logical: even if our emergence as a natural kind were contemporaneous with our formation and application of principles of classification, our status as a natural kind could not, *logically*, be constituted by the application of those principles to ourselves. This is because our applying them presupposes that we have an independent existence as a real, natural kind – independent, that is, of the implementation of the principles. But if we exist as a real natural kind independently of the application by us of principles of classification, why not others? What is special about us in *this* regard?

So one aspect of the reality of essence is that it explains the objective unity among multiplicity we find in the world. On the other hand, various opposing theories, of one or other nominalist flavour, that seek either to deny unity in multiplicity or to account for it in other ways, are inadequate to the task. There is no space to discuss nominalism here in any detail, but I want to focus on what can be labelled 'bundle' theories and their relation to what I will call *the unity problem*. Their inspiration comes in large part from David Hume and his bundle theory of the self (Hume 1978: I.iv.6), about which he concluded: 'All my hopes vanish, when I come to explain the principles, that unite our successive perceptions in our thought or consciousness. I cannot discover any theory, which gives me satisfaction on this head' (Hume 1978: 635–6). Trope theory is the most common form of bundle theory currently proposed: concrete particulars are bundles of compresent, or co-occurring, tropes or modes, i.e. property instances, and universals are classes of resembling tropes. Such theories (e.g. Stout 1921; Williams 1953; Campbell 1990; Bacon 1995; Simons 1994, 1999) have all sorts of problems with them (see, e.g., Daly 1994; Lowe 1999a: 205–9; Mertz 1996: 156–62), but what concerns the essentialist is how they can account for the second aspect of unity, namely unity *within* a concrete particular. The unity problem is broadly this: how can metaphysics account for the existence of objects that display a unified, characteristic repertoire of behaviour, operations, and functions indicative of a single, integral entity?

One aspect of this general question, for example, is the problem of identity through change. The problem of change, in other words, is a particular manifestation of the broader phenomenon: there are things in the world that display a characteristic unity and integrity. One way some of them do so is by persisting through change, whereby they act as supports (but *not* as bare particulars) of qualities that can be true of them at one moment and not at another. But there are other aspects to unity. Substances, such as humans, trees, lumps of gold, gases, and electrons, all possess a range of properties that bear causal, explanatory, and constitutive relations to each other. Gold's malleability and high lustre are no coincidence, even though there are substances (such as lead) that have one property but lack the other: it is by virtue of gold's free electron structure that it both is malleable and reflects more light than some other metals. It is no coincidence that trees have trunks and leaves, even though some plants have the latter but not the former: again, it is part of the overall structure of trees that these are their primary constituents. Again, it is no mere accident that mice have hearts and lungs, since that is part of their structure as a land-dwelling vertebrate. And it is no coincidence that human beings have a capacity for humour and a capacity for speech: these are properties stemming from human rational nature.

It is no way around the unity problem to argue that the search for a principle of unity, such as Hume vainly (in his view) looked for in the case of persons, is confused and misguided because for any bundle of particular properties of an object *F*, it is simply tautological to say that they belong to *F* (Hacker 2007: ch. 10). It is analytically true that my thoughts are *mine* and not yours, and hence to say that my thoughts might not have belonged to me is a logical mistake.[1] But the problem should not be expressed in those terms. Rather, the question can be phrased as follows: how is it that although I have certain thoughts, I might not have had any of them but might instead have had other thoughts? (A simple distinction of scope is enough to bring the problem back into focus.) Hume's problem, given his theory, was a genuine one. I as a person am able to have thoughts. But there is no particular thought that I necessarily have. If I am just a bundle or aggregate of thoughts, I therefore have no unity. But surely I *am* a unified entity, capable of supporting some qualities but not others. I can think, but I cannot be in two places at once. Some properties I *must* have – I cannot rid myself of my rationality, though I might act irrationally.[2]

There is no escaping the unity problem even if one subscribes to an 'amorphous lump' theory of reality (as Michael Dummett (1981: 577) appears to). For even if, on such a picture, there were no multiplicity in unity – only a Parmenidean 'block' – still the question would arise as to what gave the amorphous lump its unity; by virtue of *what* would it be one rather than many? (I will return to this issue in the discussion of prime matter, in Chapter 4.3.) And no matter how Humean one tries to get – denying necessary connexions in nature, asserting the possible combination of anything with anything – one will still run up against the problem of unity for whatever ultimate constituents one posits as the building blocks of reality. In short, there is no escape from the unity problem in some shape or other. But the real essentialist takes at face value the real existence of the entities given to us in everyday perception and in scientific observation (with all the necessary caveats about error, illusion, and false theory). These all have an integral, unified mode of operation that calls out for an explanation.

Nevertheless, the appeal to explanation must be made with caution. First, the claim that essence explains unity should not be taken as a kind of inference to the best explanation. Essence is not a scientific or even a philosophical posit that is subject to revision or elimination in the light of a better explanation of the unity and integrity of real existents. There is nothing probable about the existence of real essences. They are – so the real essentialist claims – as certain as existence itself. There must be an essence for everything that exists: it must be possible to say *what* it is, what it could *not* be, and *why* it is as it is.

Secondly, although it is important and informative to include as part of essentialist theory an account of the explanatory relations between the characteristics of things, essence is not reducible to those relations. I will say more in Chapter 7 about the relation between essence and property, but the basic point for present purposes is that we need to distinguish between the two. It is correct that some features of things explain other features of things and that we should expect there to be relations of explanatory basicness; moreover that some features of things, where 'feature' is taken very broadly, are not explained by any other feature of the object in question. Yet this is all compatible with the existence of features that are essential to a thing – what are called *properties* in the strict sense[3] – but that it would be misleading to describe as *part* of the thing's essence. For example, that humans are capable of humour is an essential feature, or property, of human beings. (It is *not* falsified by the existence of people without a sense of humour!) But it is not accurate to call such a capacity *part* of the essence of the human being, since essences, contrary to contemporary essentialism (and even real essentialists seem to fall into the mistake more often than they should), are not mere bundles of essential features. Having a capacity for humour is essential to Fred, but his *essence* is to be a rational animal and it is *this* that explains why he has the capacity for humour. So essence does indeed play a crucial – the crucial – explanatory role in accounting for the features of things. Fundamentally, however, the role of essence is not explanatory but *constitutive*.[4]

3.2 The 'problem' of the universal accidental

Locke was correct to criticize a priorism in the theory of essence, at least as far as knowledge of actual essences is concerned, and as far as those essences do not belong to objects that are themselves the matter of a priori enquiry (such as mathematics). Whatever the undoubted deficiencies of late Scholasticism, infected as it was by nominalism, it is inaccurate to suppose, to use Mackie's words, that the Scholastic method as such was guilty of using 'processes of ratiocination and verbal disputation' to arrive at a knowledge of essence (Mackie 1976: 86; on medieval science generally, see Grant 1974). Real essentialism has always regarded knowledge of essence in its actuality as an a posteriori matter, supplemented by a priori metaphysical reflection concerning such things as classification, structure, explanation, causation, unity, specificity and generality, and so on.

If the essences of material objects are knowable through everyday and scientific observation, though, shouldn't this mean that there is at least one *empirical test* for essence? Yet it is not clear that this follows, and here there is a good analogy with another metaphysical phenomenon, namely dia-chronic identity. Both everyday and scientific observation allow us to track the identity of things through time – we do it on a regular basis. But it would be wrong to think that there is an empirical test for diachronic identity, in anything like the sense that there is a test, say, for whether something is an acid, or whether exposure to a certain chemical causes dis-ease. When it comes to diachronic identity, we observe the similarities between things, their characteristic behaviour, their properties, and on the basis of such observations we form judgments – more often correct than not – that certain things are diachronically identical. But there is no general *test* for the accuracy of such judgments. To be sure, in individual cases there are often certain crucial observations we make that enable us to reach as close to certainty as we can that a at t_1 is identical with b at t_2. But this is compatible with there being no test as such for identity – no test that will yield certainty, or anything close to it, in all cases. The same goes for essence. We make observations concerning the behaviour and features of things, and on this basis, often supplemented in the scientific case by plenty of theory, we make judgments about what the essence of something is. Often we reach as close to certainty as we can get as fallible enquirers; other times our judgments are and may remain highly provisional and subject to revi-sion in the light of new information. There is no magic test, no piece of metaphysical litmus paper, that we can apply so as to know in all common cases – let alone uncommon ones – what the essence of something is.

We can begin to see why this is so by considering what Stephen Mumford calls the problem of the 'universal accidental' (Mumford 2004: 116–18). According to Mumford, the essentialist has no way of distinguishing between essential properties and accidental properties that are universally possessed by the members of the kind K for which the question of its essential properties arises. By universal he says he means 'at all times', but presumably he means 'at all places' as well. Given K and a set of properties $F_1, F_2, F_3 \ldots F_n$ that belong to all members of K, 'we have no way of knowing that ... there doesn't lurk a universal but accidental property' (2004: 116). Since 'there must be more to being an essential property than simply being a property possessed by every kind member', we should expect the essentialist to say what it is. But 'essentialists have failed to show what this extra something must be. They have failed to show how we ascend from being a property universally possessed, by all kind members, to the status of being an essential property' (2004: 117). The essentialist cannot simply help herself to the claim that the essential properties are the ones that are possessed always and everywhere *and* in every possible world in which

K-members exist, since that would be 'to assume the very essentialism that the universal accidental problem has cast into doubt' (2004: 117). Even in what he calls the 'infimic case where there is exact similarity of all kind members', as in the case of electrons, the essence/accident distinction is a distinction without a difference. The essentialist would assert that any particle lacking a negative unit charge was by that very fact not an electron, but it does not follow that having negative unit charge is essential – it is universally possessed by electrons, and that is the most the essentialist can say (2004: 117–18).

The supposed problem of the universal accidental looks worrying, yet it is anything but this. The first thing to note is that, as with virtually all philosophers who discuss essentialism in contemporary debate, Mumford speaks interchangeably of essences and essential properties, as though an essence just is an essential property or bundle thereof. But this, as I have argued, is already a mistake. Having a capacity for humour is an essential property – a *proprium*, to use the traditional terminology – of human beings, and in this sense we can say it flows *from the essence* of human beings to have a capacity for humour. But the *essence* of being human is to be a *rational animal*, and humans have a capacity for humour *only because* they are rational animals. Being rational animals *explains* why they have a capacity for humour, because rationality implies the capacity to think in an abstract way about things, to form concepts and combinations of concepts. And it is at least plausible that, when combined with animality, rationality implies the possibility of forming combinations of concepts that show various kinds of dissonance with everyday experience, that highlight the surprising and the absurd in the world around us or in possible situations, and so on. Having an ability such as this metaphysically guarantees the ability to find things comical or amusing. Hence the capacity for humour is a characteristic feature of human beings and stems from what it *is* to be human. It is for this reason that we judge, correctly, that all humans have a capacity for humour, that no human, no matter how dull witted or serious minded, lacks that capacity, and that no human *could* lack it. Hence it is an essential property, whereas, say, being six feet tall is not. Thinking in this way, the essentialist can easily make the 'ascent' from the universal to the essential.

Secondly, Mumford slides misleadingly between metaphysics and epistemology. Of course the essentialist cannot without circularity prescribe as a *test* for whether a universal characteristic was essential that it be one possessed by all members of *K* in every possible world. But no essentialist has ever done so. What they routinely do is *define* as essential any characteristic that has this modal property, and as we saw in Chapter 2 this sort of approach to essence is inadequate. But there is nothing wrong with any essentialist's saying to a sceptic, when faced with universal characteristic *U*: 'If you're worried about whether *U* is essential to kind *K* or whether it is a mere universal accidental, then although neither of us may be able to tell, I can assure you that if *U is* essential it will be true of all members of *K* in every possible world in which they exist'. In other words, for a given universal characteristic *U* it may be the case that *for all anyone knows* it is merely accidental, but there will be an objective answer one way or the other.

Thirdly, the real essentialist, whilst acknowledging the possibility just mentioned, will count it as exceptional. Universal characteristics – those found in kinds of thing everywhere and at all times – are nearly always essential, and so there is nothing wrong, methodologically, in regarding them as essential in the absence of further argument or demonstration to the contrary (since what is universal at t_1 may not be so at t_2). The sceptical doubt will hardly be such as to impede the progress of science, let alone the judgments of everyday observation.

Finally – and most importantly – when it comes to the true *essence* of a thing, not just its essential properties, the essentialist *is* able to make the ascent from mere universality without holding either that there is any empirical test for essence or that certainty in essentialist judgments can be reached on all occasions. To continue with the case of human beings, suppose I am walking through a field and come across a creature that has a vaguely human shape, is supported by two planks of wood, and has a torso consisting of a sack stuffed with straw, from which protrude two more bits of wood. On top is something that looks a little like a human face, only it too is wood, with pebbles for eyes, a twig for a nose, and two more twigs protruding from either side. Is it a human being? Of course not, I realize – it's a scarecrow. How do I know? Well, because human beings are essentially animals and this thing is not even alive. But how do I know humans are essentially animals?

For the real essentialist, there is nothing intrinsically impossible about the sort of reasoning that goes into establishing such a proposition, whatever the epistemological difficulties when it comes to particular kinds of thing. We all know what counts as a paradigmatic human being, or a stereotypical human, to use Putnam's terminology. Human beings have natures, as I have already argued in respect of things in general. When a thing displays a range of characteristic operations and behaviour, a characteristic set of functions, and we are able to observe a range of similarities and differences between it and other things, and thereby to classify it, no matter how approximately, within a taxonomic scheme that ascends in increasing generality and descends in increasing specificity – then we are justified in ascribing to it an essence or nature, even if we don't know what that essence or nature is; or, though we do know part of the essence, yet we do not know the *complete* essence.

We are then able to use our reason and our common experience to ask ourselves various questions, of which the most important is: if I took away this or that quality of the thing in question, would its nature remain the same? Would it continue to display the characteristic properties, functions, operations and behaviour that it does when it possesses the quality that I remove in thought? If so, the quality is no part of the essence. If, on the other hand, removal of the quality would cause a general disturbance or radical change in the thing's operations, functions, and so on – then the quality would be part of the essence. (Or it might be a property that flows from and is explained by the essence rather than part of the essence itself – but more about this in Chapter 7 and elsewhere.)

And it is quite obvious that a human being relies for its characteristic operation on being an animal – it has an animal nature, even though that is not its *complete* nature. This is how I know that the most cunningly decorated scarecrow could never be a human. It is how I know that being an animal is not merely universal in humans, but essential as well. It is important to emphasize that asking this sort of question does not involve peering through Kaplan's 'Jules Verne-o-scope' (Kaplan 1979) at possible worlds, or positing Lewis-style real possible worlds (Lewis 1986), or stipulating possible worlds with certain things in them (Kripke 1980: 44). As Mumford rightly points out in respect of Ellis's scientific essentialism, 'all possibility [is] immanent and all essences [are] this-worldly' (Mumford 2004: 117). Hence when we pose the fundamental essentialist questions as stated above, we think about the object as it is in *this* world and ask how it would behave in *this* world were such and such a feature removed from it. And if we can answer the question in respect of a simple case such as the animality of the human being, the point is established in principle and there is no reason in principle why we cannot answer it in respect of human rationality, or the possession by fish of gills, or the negative unit charge of an electron.

In this latter case, it should be remarked, Mumford mistakenly characterizes *infimic* species as those whose members are exactly similar (Mumford 2004: 117). This is incorrect: Ellis gets it right when he says that the infimic species (more accurately, *infima* species) have no subspecies and hence are such that their members are 'essentially identical' (Ellis 2001: 3). Being essentially identical and exactly similar are not the same. Ellis, however, goes on to make the mistake of claiming that infima species 'are the simplest kinds of substances' (Ellis 2001: 70). This too is wrong. They are exactly the species that have no subspecies, the most specific of all species. Human beings form an infima species as there are no species of human beings (contra Ellis 2001: 21, as noted in Chapter 1). Electrons, as far as anyone knows, are an infima species, though they themselves are a species of lepton. (Some suggest muons are a species of electron due to their similar interactions.)

For simplicity, let us assume electrons have a single intrinsic property of negative unit electric charge. (Whether its mass is a property distinct from its charge, whether its radius is another separate property, and so on, can be left to one side.) According to Mumford, the essence/accident distinction is 'inapplicable' in cases of exact similarity of kind members. Yet it is not clear why we should say this. If a particle lacks the negative unit charge, it will behave very differently from one that has it. The electromagnetic interactions will be very different, it will figure differently in the composition of atoms and molecules, and so on. It is a matter for physicists to determine what these differences are, how great they are, and how the electron should be classified. But what physics tells us is that a difference in polarity of electric charge would radically alter the characteristic behaviour and function of the thing we know as the electron. This is enough for us to judge, with confidence (if not with certainty), that an electron's charge is part of its essence. It does not exclude the fact that physicists could have used the word 'electron' for a different kind of object and called electrons something else. What it excludes is that *this* kind of thing – the electron – could lack a negative unit charge. Mumford's universal accidental is, I conclude, a pseudo-problem.

3.3 An empirical test for essence?

The second issue I want to look at is whether my claim that there is no empirical test for essence is mistaken. Maybe there *is* such a test, and the real essentialist Crawford Elder has provided it. Elder notes an important fact about essences: 'any essential nature includes some properties such that, were they to be absent in a roughly similar essential nature, certain other properties in the original nature would have to be absent as well' (Elder 2004: 35). Essential properties occur in tightly connected clusters: take away a human's capacity for humour and you take away their capacity for rational thought, for language, and so on – in short, you take away their humanity and what you are thinking of will not be a human at all. Moreover, properties can be classified according to sets of contraries – red/yellow/green, square/circular/triangular, having charge +1/having charge −1/having charge $^2/_3$, and so on. These thoughts lead Elder to propose what he calls an empirical test for essentialness, the 'test of flanking uniformities': 'To gain evidence that f characterizes Ks not just uniformly but essentially, see whether, among the members of (what seem to be) natural kinds roughly similar to Ks, differing from Ks by possessing some one property or another contrary to f, there are uniformly found *other* properties contrasting with *other* properties uniformly possessed by Ks' (Elder 2004: 37). Elder believes this is a test we actually use 'without quite realizing it' (Elder 2004: 23).

An initial worry about the test of flanking uniformities is what is meant by 'roughly similar'. Suppose Max is a field essentialist from Mars, having travelled to Earth on a voyage of discovery to find the essential natures of things. He walks into room A full of male humans all of whom have short hair and brown eyes. He walks into an adjoining room B full of female humans all of whom have long hair and blue eyes.[5] Max thinks, plausibly, that the things in room A form a kind, the things in B form a kind, and the kinds are roughly similar. He notes that the things in B differ from those in A by possessing a contrasting property,[6] namely eye colour. Lo and behold, he also observes that the things in B uniformly possess other properties contrasting with other properties uniformly possessed by the things in

A – concerning length of hair and maybe a range of further properties as well. Using Elder's test of flanking uniformities, Max concludes that having brown eyes is essential to the things in A. In other words, he will have concluded falsely, not only that male humans essentially have brown eyes, but that human beings essentially have brown eyes. He may not express the conclusion to himself in those terms, but Max's field essentialism will have gone seriously awry.

Another worry is that Elder's test requires that the field essentialist observe not merely that certain contrasting properties are absent when others are, but that they *must* be: '*f*'s absence, in an essential nature roughly similar to that of *K*s, must go together with the absence there of some other property (say, *g*) likewise present in the nature of *K*s' (Elder 2004: 36). This might be thought to solve the above problem – the absence of brown eyes does not guarantee the absence of short hair. But this won't help Max because he will have no idea whether there is such a guarantee. If he did know that such a guarantee was lacking he would *already* be on the way to knowing the essence of human beings and so he would not need Elder's test in the first place! Hence any suggestion that metaphysical entailments between essential properties could be usable by the field essentialist as part of his test would make the test circular or redundant.

Elder says that his test provides 'evidence' of essentialness, rather than that it is guaranteed to reveal the essence of anything; but it is doubtful to what extent it even provides evidence, at least credible evidence, in many cases. Suppose our field essentialist Max has moved on from the humans in rooms A and B, and now stalks his way into rooms C and D. In C he finds humans of varying appearance, but all sharing the characteristic of being six feet tall. They are all, needless to say, lacking in a covering of fur. In D he finds a roomful of chimpanzees, all of which are three feet tall and very hairy. Max thinks that the chimps and the humans are *roughly* similar, which is fair enough since he may not have seen much else on Earth to compare them with – and anyway they *are* roughly similar. He notes the following: the chimps differ from the humans by possessing a feature – being three feet tall – contrary to that of being six feet tall which is possessed by the humans. Further, uniformly found are other features – in particular being hairy – contrasting with other features uniformly possessed by the humans, in particular lacking a generous covering of hair. Applying Elder's test, he concludes that being six feet tall is an essential property of human beings. Clearly the test has again led him badly astray. (This is so even though, as Elder requires for his test of flanking uniformities (2004: 28), the pairs of features involved in these cases are ones that contrast as a matter of degree. He thinks contrast by degrees is necessary to make sense of 'proper rivalry' between properties. But this too is a doubtful aspect of the test, as plenty of contrasting essential properties[7] – such as being a man and being a mouse (or being a non-man) – do not contrast by degrees. Including them as material for the test of flanking uniformities, however, even more clearly will presuppose a grasp of essence before the test can be applied.)

Yet in this second case it is no accident that chimps are both hairy and short, and that humans are hairless and relatively taller. In both cases the phenotype, at least when it comes to basic body plan, is fixed by the genotype. Max, were he armed with a good quantity of biological knowledge, could refine his interpretation of what he observed (e.g. in terms of ranges of heights rather than determinate heights) and so arrive at a better understanding of why it is that chimps differ from humans in so many ways. But applying the test of flanking uniformities will not help – and will lead him into serious error – absent what would have to amount to an overall grasp of essence in general and its biological aspects in particular. He would have to have so much knowledge that he would not need to apply the test at all, though he could continue to examine ways in which properties belonging to objects with different natures contrast, which properties occur in which clusters, and so on. All of this would be part of his overall repertoire for arriving at a judgment of essence. But to suppose that there is an empirical test for essence is mistaken.

3.4 Coming to know essence

It might be thought that there is some sort of circularity lurking within the epistemology of essence that I have outlined. I have said that everything has an essence. This implies that all we need to do in order to know whether we are confronted with an essence (though we might not know what that essence *is*) is to identify something. But then how do we identify a thing without first knowing that it has an essence? Aren't we caught in a circle?

The charge is specious. This can be seen most strikingly in the case of mathematics, where things have essences and we know they do. The first person to identify the essence of a circle presumably had identified circles before he did so, and was able to distinguish them from squares and triangles. This is of course more striking in the case of complex geometrical shapes, where identifying them prior to identifying their essence is quite plausible. Once the point is established in such cases, it is made *in principle* for the knowability of essence.

The sceptic might reply that there are important differences between mathematical and material objects, and she would be right to do so. None of the differences, however, supports the sceptic's case. The most significant disanalogy seems to be that mathematical objects are typically identified by part of their essence, and then the rest of their essence is analysed and explicated. In the standard case, when a mathematician identifies a kind of geometrical figure, or a function, or an arithmetical operation, he thereby identifies something that belongs to its essence – having three sides, being discontinuous, being transitive, and so on. Often, however, when material objects are identified this is done by fixing on some accidental quality – being of a certain size, or colour, or shape, none of which might be essential to what is identified.

Note first, however, that, if genuine, the disanalogy only involves standard cases of identification at most. For some mathematical objects might be, and presumably have been, identified by wholly accidental qualities that the object might lack without ceasing to be what it is essentially. No one knows who identified the first triangles, but it is not wholly implausible that this person came across, or perhaps imagined or constructed, triangles that were iso-sceles, right-angled, or scalene before realizing (and eventually demonstrat-ing) that none of these qualities was essential to triangles *qua* triangles (even if they are essential to the three *species* of triangles, which is another matter). It is not important whether this is how anyone actually came to know about triangles; that it *could* have happened that way is all that matters.

Secondly, if the disanalogy is genuine there is a good reason for it – namely that mathematical objects have far more essential properties than they do accidental ones. More precisely, they have far more that is true of them either as part of their essence or as flowing from their essence than they do qualities that are wholly extraneous to their essence and so con-tingent on the kind of object under consideration. It might be accidental to circles as a species that they have any particular radius, and accidental to a particular circle that it has a given colour or that it is shaded, and so on. But when anyone identifies a circle, they are far more likely to do so via one of its essential properties, such as shape or having a radius equidistant from all points on the circumference. The reverse might seem to be true for material objects such as trees and tables, which tend to be picked out very often by wholly accidental characteristics. Now, if this is so, it is no aid to the sceptic's case. All it shows is that since mathematicals have more essen-tial than non-essential features, they are more likely to be identified by the former than is the case for material objects. It does not show we cannot *know* the essences of material objects – only that we have to work harder.

Thirdly, all the hedging and qualification above are because it is not clear that there is a disanalogy at all. For we do not merely identify material objects by their accidents, even if they have far more of them than mathe-maticals do. In the standard case we identify things also as living or non-living, animal or plant, rational or non-rational, body or non-body, sub-stance or non-substance, spatial or temporal or both – and so on. Unless a person is a metaphysician he will not know the exact definition of sub-stance, or of rationality, for instance. Unless he has some biological knowl-edge he will not have much technical grasp of the distinction between life and non-life. But, as has already been stressed, it is no part of essentialism that a person who knows the essence of something must know *all* of its essence or know its essence in precise detail. If I identify a human as an animal and a scarecrow as inanimate, I have identified *part* of the essence of each. It is at least arguable that in *most* cases of material object identifica-tion, just as in mathematical, we identify objects by parts of their essence, even if in the material case we also rely heavily on accidental characteristics. If, then, there is no disanalogy, the case against the sceptic is even stronger. We can know the essences of mathematicals. We identify them most often by their essential features. Since identifying them involves coming to know their essences, there is no circularity, contrary to the initial worry. The process is not crucially different for material objects, even though we rely more heavily on accidents when identifying them. Hence there is no circularity here either.

In general, it is true to say that we mostly identify and come to know the essences of material objects *indirectly* via their properties and accidents, whereas this is not the case for mathematical objects. Indirect knowledge, however, is still knowledge, just as indirect observation is still observation, as was pointed out in Chapter 2. The medieval Scholastics used to say that the human mind hunts after the essences of things,[8] by which they meant that we do not have an intellectual intuition of essence or a faculty other than the general rational one for finding out what things are. Objects present themselves to our understanding with varying degrees of immediacy, mathematicals doing so more immediately and directly than material things. In most cases, however, when an object presents itself for inspection, as it were – even in the case of simple geometrical figures – we have to delve into its nature by finding out how it behaves, operates, functions, changes (if at all), what powers it has, what similarities or dissimilarities it bears to other things, and so on. By all of these means we are able to identify things and suppose them to fall under some genus or other, with some specific difference or other, yet without knowing what these might be (except perhaps at a very abstract level: for example, the thing concerned is physical, or mental, a quality, or a substance with some sort of independent existence, extended or unextended, and so on). All we need to do is to grasp the fact that there is some portion of reality before us, some kind of being or other. We never apprehend *being in general*, or being as such, even though this is the formal object of all metaphysical study. All we ever apprehend is being in its various manifestations, and since we do this we are already in a position to affirm that things have essences, that everything is something or other. It is enough for us to get started on the hunt for essence.

The hunt would not be possible for a field essentialist who happened upon a Shoemaker-style frozen universe (Shoemaker 1969). Suppose Max, our field essentialist from Mars, flew his craft over a wholly frozen Earth, meaning that no events at all were occurring.[9] It would be impossible for him to form any conception of whether there was a distinction between the essential and the accidental on frozen Earth, let alone which characteristics of things fell into which categories. Perhaps, being a good metaphysician and so an opponent of bare particularism, he might work out a priori that not every feature could be accidental; but it is doubtful that he could exclude the possibility that every feature was essential to the thing that had it. And even if he could, he could not know *which* features were essential and which accidental. Max would not even be in a position to formulate thought experiments about the things on frozen Earth. He could not, for instance, work out whether a human being with a green coat on could exist without it. (Needless to say, he would not identify such an entity *as* a human being wearing a green coat.) For all Max knew, the green coat might be an essential body part. Note that this reinforces the point that counterfactual reasoning depends essentially on knowledge of actual objects and how they behave. Since such knowledge would be unavailable to Max, he could not carry out his field essentialist project on frozen Earth and would be advised to move on to a more flexible planet (or else wait for a thaw).

3.5 'Paradigms', 'stereotypes', and classification

As is well known, Putnam's theory of the meaning of natural kind words relies on the notion of what he calls a 'stereotype': a stereotype is a 'conventional idea' associated with a natural kind term (Putnam 1975a: 250). This idea involves a number of features by which speakers pick out a typical or paradigmatic member of the natural kind in question; hence the stereotype functions like Kripke's reference-fixing descriptions (Kripke 1980: 135–6). A stereotypical feature of a kind K might not be possessed by all members of K, not even by all normal members of K (Putnam 1975a: 250). All that appears necessary on Putnam's account (and, as far as one can tell, on Kripke's) is that most normal K-members have most of the features associated with the stereotype. What 'most' means is obviously vague, but it seems to mean that the possession of such features is sufficient to enable a competent speaker to know the meaning of the natural kind term in question by means of acquaintance with at least one of those normal members. Or he may grasp the term by means of knowledge that someone else in the linguistic community, often an expert, is so acquainted. And part of his grasp involves understanding that to be a referent of the term is to bear an equivalence relation – the 'same kind' relation (Putnam 1975a: 232) – to stereotypical members of the kind.

The notion of a stereotype has come in for plenty of criticism (see, e.g., Zemach 1976; Mellor 1977; for a defence of Putnam, see Sterelny 1983), much of it pertaining to its semantic role (Mellor 1977: 74); but these are not the concern of the real essentialist, for whom semantics does not tell us anything about essence. Hence, when I said in Chapter 2 that something like Putnam's story about stereotypes explained how a term like 'fish' was ultimately restricted in such a way as to exclude whales from coming within its extension, I was simply using the most plausible part of Putnam's semantic theory to illustrate how essentialists understand classification. Whatever the merits of his semantic theory, the idea of a stereotypical or paradigmatic member of a species[10] is crucial to understanding essence. And in this context there is a criticism of Putnam that is metaphysical in nature and does shed light on how essences should be understood.

The criticism, by Mellor, is that even accepting the notion of a stereotype (what he calls an 'archetype'), '[n]o reason is given why particular properties must be common to all things in all possible worlds that are of the same kind as the archetypes' (Mellor 1977: 74). Suppose we have a stereotypical or paradigmatic sample of some kind K – call it S_1. Suppose also that S_1 and all other such samples in the actual world have a certain set of characteristics $C_{1...n}$ by virtue of which they are (according to experts, perhaps) members of K. Now unless the essentialist begs the question by presupposing that all members of K must have *exactly* $C_{1...n}$, then we can suppose: a world w_1 in which K-members have most of $C_{1...n}$; a world w_2 in which the K-members have most of the C_i possessed by the K-members in w_1; a world w_3 in which the K-members have most of the C_i possessed by the K-members in w_2; and so on until we reach a world in which the K-members have very few of the C_i possessed by the stereotypical K-members in the actual world. Again, we can suppose: a world w_1 in which the K-members share most of the features of the stereotypes in the actual world; a world w_2 in which the K-members share most of the features of the stereotypes in the actual world; but that the K-members in w_1 and the K-members in w_2 do not share with each other most of the *same* stereotypical features as those had by the K-members in the actual world. Thus a relation such as *x has most of y's S_1-features*, where an S_1-feature is a stereotypical one, i.e. one possessed by the stereotype S_1, cannot ground the *same kind* relation, since the former is not an equivalence relation. Yet it needs to be for Putnam's account to work.[11]

Now it may be that this sort of objection does succeed against Putnam, inasmuch as he, like other contemporary essentialists, tends to think of essences as bundles of properties (typically micro-structural) not all of which need be shared by all objects having the essence – not even by all the normal members of the kind. But it does not work against real essentialism, for which the same-kind relation most definitely is an equivalence relation. For the relation is not specified in terms of bundles of properties at all, but in terms of species and genera. For two things to be of the same kind is for them to be either generically identical or specifically identical. The relation of being specifically identical is certainly an equivalence relation. In particular, it is transitive: to deny this would be to allow that a thing could fall under two species, which is impossible. Species logically exclude each other: gold is not water, men are not mice, trees are not mountains, and vice versa. So much should commend itself to reason. But mightn't a Mellor-style objection arise again in respect of genera? After all, most things fall under more than one genus: animal and body, rodent and mammal, water-dweller and whale, and so on.

So we might imagine the following situation: object a falls under the same genus G_1 as b; b falls under the same genus G_2 as c; but a and c do not fall under the same genus. Similarly, a might fall under the same genus G_1 as b; a might also fall under the same genus G_2 as c; but b and c do not fall under the same genus. Hence being generically identical is not transitive. However, the objection fails. The reason is that the conclusion in each case is false: in the first case a and c will indeed fall under the same genus, and the same is true for b and c in the second. But which genus will they fall under? The answer is: the higher of the two genera G_1 and G_2. In other words, G_1 and G_2 will have to be logically dependent inasmuch as G_2 falls under G_1 or G_1 falls under G_2 (and if they fall under each other they are the same genus and so trivially all of a, b and c are generically identical).

Take, for example, the most extreme sort of case: if we can see the explanation hold there, it must by implication hold for less extreme cases. Suppose a is a tiger, b is a human, and c is a box. a is generically identical with b because they are both animals. b is generically identical with c since both are material substances. (It is irrelevant whether b is *wholly* a material substance, since we are only talking about *generic* identity.) But then a will be generically identical with c since both too are material substances. Again, a is generically identical with b (both animals), a is generically identical with c (both material substances), and so b is generically identical with c (both material substances). As long as there is a logical dependence between the genera, there is guaranteed to be generic identity between all the objects considered, because what enables generic identity between one pair will also enable, by virtue of entailing higher genera, generic identity between another pair (where the pairs share a member) on the assumption that they are generically identical at all.

But what if there is no logical dependence between the genera? Again, take an extreme case, one familiar to traditional metaphysicians. It might be supposed that tigers are generically identical with humans (both animals) and humans are generically identical with angels (both rational), but angels are not generically identical with tigers.[12] Hence generic identity is not transitive after all. This objection fails because *animal* and *rational* are not both genera. It is true that they are logically independent, in that 'x is an animal' does not entail 'x is rational' and vice versa. But if they were both genera it would be possible for one thing to fall under logically independent genera. Yet this cannot be, since it would entail that the thing in question fell under two distinct species (since the genus is part of the species),[13] which we noted earlier was impossible. For the real essentialist, the species gives the *nature* of the thing – its characteristic mode of operation, which includes various properties the thing *must* have if it is to fall under that species. But if something fell under two species it would have two distinct characteristic modes of behaviour and so possess distinct and *incompatible* properties; for if all the properties were compatible there would not be distinct natures after all and hence there would only be one species. More precisely, for any two species some properties of each are either contrary or contradictory. Contrary properties would be, for example, being able easily to dissolve and resisting dissolution, or attracting a certain particle and repelling it. Contradictory properties would be, say, being able easily to dissolve and *not* being able easily to dissolve, or attracting a certain particle and *not* attracting it. In either case, if there were no such pairs of properties entailed by putatively distinct species there would not be two species after all, since there would be nothing to mark one species off from the other. Hence nothing can be both gold and water, or an electron and a proton, or a tiger and a monkey.

Mightn't we suppose a case in which one of the putatively distinct species was such that either F-ing or not F-ing, for some property F, simply didn't apply to things falling under it, so one could have compatibility in this way? In other words, mightn't there be an x such that it fell under species S_1, by virtue of which it F-ed, as well as under species S_2, by virtue of which it neither F-ed nor failed to F, and so there was no incompatibility between S_1 and S_2? But this sort of case would be even more remarkable for the essential incompatibility between the species, since it would have to be one in which one of the species was *so* distinct from the other that things falling under it were of a wholly different category from things falling under the other. So, for instance, no one would think that anything could be both a mammal and a number, even though mammals lactate and numbers neither lactate nor fail to lactate. Lactating is not a property that it makes any *sense* to apply to numbers because numbers are a wholly different sort of thing from mammals. Hence there will be radical incompatibility between mammals and numbers, involving obvious ranges of properties. Thus the further one tries to go in securing compatibility between some properties of distinct species, the more different the species one has to choose, and so the more other kinds of radical incompatibility manifest themselves.

So if, to return to the case of tigers, humans, and angels, *animal* and *rational* are not both genera, what are they? The standard classification holds that *animal* is a genus and *rational* is a specific difference rather than a genus. But shouldn't there be an ineliminably relative character to classification? Couldn't we, without inaccuracy, take *rational* to be the genus, under which would fall both *angel* and *human*, so that the specific difference of humans would then be *animal*? I will return to this question in Chapter 5.2, since it raises the further issue of whether there is one correct scheme of classification for every essential kind (for every species, to use the traditional terminology). The main point as far as the present problem goes is that *animal* and *rational* cannot both be genera for the reasons given above, and so we cannot use them, or similar cases, to produce a counterexample to the transitivity of generic identity.

All of this anticipates somewhat the later discussion of taxonomy in Chapter 5, but the moral is that knowledge of essence requires us to engage in processes of classification according to genera and species. Reference to relations such as sameness of kind and sameness of structure, or to how stereotypical members of some species behave, are mere aspects of an overall approach that presupposes a metaphysical (as opposed to natural-scientific) grasp of how objects are grouped together or marked off from one another by appeal to fundamental ontological categories. Natural science may tell us the essences of certain kinds of thing, at least in part, but it is neither the source of essence per se nor the source of our knowledge of it. For this we have to go deeper: rather than resting content with a superficial explanation of essence in terms of 'hidden' or 'internal' structure, we have to delve into the structure of essence itself.

4 The structure of essence

4.1 Hylemorphism: act and potency

The world of concrete material bodies is the place to start when analysing the structure of essence. The fundamental thesis of real essentialism is as follows: *every finite material body has a twofold composition, being a compound of act and potency.* Since there are no actual infinites in the material universe (Smith and Craig 1993: 9–24 and *passim*), in fact every material body is finite, but this needs to be mentioned explicitly. To be finite is to be limited in various ways, in particular spatio-temporally, in terms of the characteristics a thing has, and in terms of the characteristics it is *capable* of having. Every material body is such that it is limited in these three ways. Essentialism focuses on the second and third. For any material body, there are some things it just is and some things it is not, and there are some things it cannot do and some ways it cannot be, but also things it can do and ways it can be. Further, reality is in a constant state of flux – it is dynamic rather than static. Things go out of existence and others come into being, and existing things lose characteristics and take on new ones. Reality is, as it were, constantly in a state of being carved up in new and different ways: bits of reality are constantly changing through the agency of other bits of reality. All of these phenomena call out for an explanation, yet essentialism in its contemporary and scientific varieties has little to say about them.

The only possible explanation for the fact that reality is able to take on new kinds of existence, whether substantial or accidental, is that there is some principle of potentiality inherent in reality. The existence of such a principle was denied by Parmenides and the Eleatics,[1] who rejected the reality of both change and multiplicity. They contended that: (1) nothing actual can come from what is already actual, since the former would have to exist already, actuality being wholly static and incapable of generating anything; (2) nothing actual can come from what is non-actual, since what is non-actual is not real, and hence is nothing; and nothing can come from nothing.[2] There are philosophers, usually four-dimensionalists of one stripe or another, who deny the phenomenon of 'temporal becoming', as real change is sometimes called, and who at least implicitly accept the sceptical

Eleatic consequences; but this is to deny a fundamental metaphysical datum that is obvious to the senses – what might be called a non-negotiable aspect of our picture of reality. (For more on change and four-dimensionalism, see Oderberg 2004b.)

The problem disappears, however, once we admit the principle of potency into our ontology. Actuality does not come from actuality alone, nor does it come from nothing: it requires actual agents and causes but is educed from the *potentiality* in reality to take on new existences. There are a number of truths about potency which need to be made explicit so we can see how it functions as one of the two fundamental divisions of reality. First, the sort of potency I am referring to is *purely passive*. When water dissolves salt, it does so via an *active* potency, a power *to act*, namely the power to break the sodium–chloride bond due to the polarity in the water molecules. Active potency, then, requires actual properties of things in order to operate. It is therefore characterized in part in terms of determinate features of reality. Purely passive potency, however, is not so determined. It is wholly *indifferent* to how it is acted upon. What this means in practice, as it were, is that as far as reality is concerned *anything can be anywhere – except* where there is already in place a restriction on what can come into existence due to the prior existence of some reality. As far as the nature of reality goes, a tiger could appear anywhere in the universe, *except* for where it is prevented from doing so by some actuality already in place. It cannot come into existence right where a tiger already exists, for instance, and it might be nomologically impossible for it to appear somewhere, say next to the sun, but this too will be due to prior actuality. Nevertheless, pure potentiality in itself is completely indifferent to how it is activated.

Secondly, pure potency cannot actualize itself: nothing can bring itself into existence, but whatever does come into existence requires some actual agency to effect this, at least in part. Hence, if there were only pure passive potentiality in the universe, nothing could come into existence, which is false to the facts.

Thirdly, pure passive potency (I will call it simply potency for now, and make distinctions where necessary) is not temporally prior to actuality. It is not as though, when something comes into existence, there is some potency at t_1 which is acted upon by something at t_2 with the result that the entity comes into existence. Hence one should not think of the coming into existence of something, say water from hydrogen and oxygen, as being like the coming into existence of a statue by the shaping of a lump of clay. In the latter case, the clay is temporally prior to the statue; in the former, although the hydrogen and oxygen atoms are temporally prior to the water, the pure potency necessary for the water to emerge from the hydrogen-oxygen bonds is not temporally prior to the water. It is, we might say, *constitutively* prior and logically prior, but it does not exist in its own right prior to the water's coming to existence. When hydrogen combustion in the presence of oxygen produces water, what emerges is a wholly new substance: two elements are synthesized into a new compound. Pure potency *must* be involved in this substantial change, on the assumption that the change really is substantial. (I will give the argument for this in section 4.3.)

A standard reply here is the atomist one, to the effect that there is no substantial change, only the constant arrangement and rearrangement of indestructible particles. Apart from the huge burden of proof the atomist has to discharge, of showing how all of the multiplicity and diversity in the universe are a product of mere recombination (needless to say, no one has ever shown it), the problem is that there is substantial transformation *all the way down*, as far as anyone knows. According to current physical theory, even quarks can be substantially transformed into other quarks: for example, a quark triplet of [bottom, top, top] can, by virtue of the strong nuclear force, be changed into a triplet of [down, top, top]; indeed the bottom quark could also have been changed into a strange or charmed quark. This is held to be consistent with the conservation laws, and according to quantum theory quark transformation must eventually occur. Hence, even if the atomist could, *per impossibile*, demonstrate that all apparent substantial change at the macro level was an illusion generated by the recombination of elementary particles, he would still have to account for substantial transformation among the particles – and pure potency would still be needed.

The second fundamental aspect of reality along with potency is *actuality*. We know this from the mere fact that reality is *not* in a state of total indifference or indeterminacy. It is not an 'amorphous lump', an undifferentiated whole, but it presents itself to us pre-packaged, so to speak, or parcelled up into bits and pieces. These parcels or divisions of reality are actual, consisting of objects and their characteristics (and of course relations). The world is not populated by *potential* trees, but *actual* trees; not by potential electrons, but actual electrons. If the whole universe, implausibly, were just the excitation of a quantum field, the excitation would be actual, not potential; and virtual particles are not a kind of potential particle, but either an actual but essentially unobservable particle (perhaps necessary for Hawking radiation, if it exists) or a mere mathematical abstraction.

Actuality is made up of *perfections* – objects and qualities that give reality a definite shape. To say that actuality involves perfections is not to say that reality or the things in it are perfect in the familiar sense of all-powerful or lacking in nothing – the qualities attributed to a divine being when we speak of it as perfect. What it means is that potency is *completed* by actuality such as to constitute reality as it is, and that each thing that exists has its own characteristics that give it a definite place in reality as something with distinctive properties and accidents enabling it to be marked off from everything that is different from it either individually or essentially.

Now within the material universe, just as there is no pure potency without actuality, so there is no actuality without pure potency. Just as reality is not an amorphous lump, so it is not a homogeneous whole consisting of only one kind of actuality either. Hence there is a *reciprocal relation* between actuality and potentiality. On the one hand, actuality limits potentiality by carving it up into discrete and qualitatively distinct elements: undifferentiated reality is differentiated by actuality. On the other hand, potentiality limits actuality by restricting it within boundaries so that we can truly say that different actualities are present in different regions of reality: unlimited actuality is limited by potentiality. This is why not everything is green, or wise, or negatively charged; why not everything is a tree, or a philosopher, or an electron. For that matter, it is why the universe is not just one big electron. It is also the reason why the universe could not possibly be just a bundle of universals, for if it were what would stop those universals being present anywhere and everywhere? But they are not: there is not in the universe mere wisdom, but the wisdom of Socrates, the wisdom of Plato, and so on. Hence there are modes (tropes, if you like) as well as universals: you will find the wisdom of Socrates, but you won't find the wisdom of Nero. Nor can you find the wisdom of the tree in my back garden, because trees are categorially incapable of either having or lacking wisdom. But this categorial incapacity is itself evidence of the existence of radical potentiality in the universe: the potentiality of the tree, in conjunction with its actual features, metaphysically excludes wisdom. That is to say, as far as the tree goes, potentiality has already limited actuality in such a way that the tree is simply not constituted either to have or to lack wisdom.

This twofold division of reality into the actual and the potential is the necessary beginning for an understanding of essence. It is the origin of the Aristotelian theory of *hylemorphism*,[3] which real essentialism employs to explain what essence is and how it operates. Essence reveals itself in things. But all things (remember, I am here talking only about material objects) are a mixture of actuality and potentiality. Since things are constituted by their essences, those essences themselves must in some way be mixtures of actuality and potentiality. Hylemorphism says that they are – their actuality is *form* and their potentiality is *matter*.

4.2 Substantial form

Here is a standard definition of form: it is the 'intrinsic incomplete constituent principle in a substance which actualizes the potencies of matter and together with the matter composes a definite material substance or natural body' (Wuellner 1956: 48). In fact this is a definition of *substantial* form rather than form in general, since form in general is no more than the principle of specificity of any thing, that by which it is what it is. The generality of such a definition, however, since it covers accidents as well as substance, and also non-substances, means that it is clearer to approach an understanding of form in general via the form of substance in particular, since substance involves the paradigm of form according to which other kinds of form are correlatively understood.

I will say more about substance later, but for the moment we need only note that typical substances are animals, plants, human beings, lumps of matter such as gold, wood, rock, as well as atomic and subatomic particles, molecules, drops of water, clouds of gas, and so on. Now substantial form is *intrinsic* since it is a constituent solely of the substance. It is a *constituent* because it is a real part or element of it, though not on the same level as a substance's natural parts such as the branch of a tree or the leg of a dog. Rather, substantial form (or 'form' for short) is a radical or fundamental part of the substance in the sense of constituting it as the kind of substance it is. It is a *principle* in the sense of being that from which the identity of the substance is derived – that *by virtue of which* the substance is what it is. It is *incomplete* in the sense that it does not and cannot, contra Platonism, exist apart from instantiation by a particular individual. In the specific case of material substances, i.e. substances that have a material element even though they may not be wholly material, this means the form cannot exist without correlative *matter* to individuate it.[4] And form *actualizes the potencies of matter* in the sense of being the principle that unites with matter to produce a finite individual with limited powers and an existence circumscribed by space and time. Together with matter, it composes the distinct individual substance. Hence all substances in the material world are true *compounds* of matter and form.

Now it is an understatement to remark that the concept of substantial form has taken a hammering in the last four hundred years, this being probably the single greatest philosophical reason why real essentialism went into almost terminal decline. Descartes scorned the notion.[5] Locke claimed to have 'no idea at all' of substantial form, a term he described as having been introduced by 'mistaken pretenders to a knowledge that they had not' (Locke 1975: II.31.6, p. 380; III.8.2, p. 475). And Hume, altogether a nonbeliever in substance, descried substantial form as 'incomprehensible', a 'fiction', one of the 'spectres in the dark' conjured by the 'ancient philosophers', from which delusions 'modern philosophy' promised to free the mind (Hume 1978: I.iv.3, p. 222; I.iv.4, p. 226).

These condemnations are without foundation, whatever the explicable deficiencies in the empiricists' learning concerning the doctrine of substantial form,[6] whatever the state of science at the time, and whatever the faulty teachings of late Scholasticism that gave rise to so much misunderstanding. There is no explanation for the unity of any material substance without the postulation of substantial form. Most contemporary metaphysicians confronted with the unity problem would either feign ignorance of just what the problem was or attempt to explain it in terms of some sort of arrangement of, or relation between, micro-particles at some level. (I use 'some sort of' and 'some' advisedly.) Crawford Elder has provided a strong argument against the very idea that arrangements of micro-particles can take the place of real substances. Suppose a reductionist wanted to claim that all that being some kind of substance *S* amounted to was the *S*-wise arrangement of some micro-particles (let her pick her favourite kind of particle). Then either the reductionist *must* quantify over *S*s in the analysis so as to get the right bundle of particles – which would be circular – or there is no way for her to specify what that bundle might be. She needs to identify a relation that binds *all and only* the particles that belong to *S*, i.e. that excludes any other particles not belonging to *S* – yet no such relation is forthcoming (Elder 2004: 50–8).[7] He concludes that 'there is no causal relation that, as a general matter, joins individual microparticles within a given familiar object to all and only the others that are within it' (Elder 2004: 59).

There is, however, a different though related problem for reductionism, also focusing on the very idea of specifying a reductive relation among micro-particles. Elder presupposes that there might be a relevant relation that at least relates all of the micro-particles within *S*, even if no such relation relates only those particles. But why should we even suppose that this is the case? There is no way, for instance, of describing gold by means of a single relation between gold atoms: they possess a cubic crystal structure *all* of which has to be described in order to specify the particular arrangement of gold atoms that makes for something to be gold. And if we descend to the level of protons, neutrons, and electrons, let alone anything more fundamental, the task of giving a single relation becomes even more difficult. If you want to mark gold off from everything else in the universe you have to define a structure, not a relation. There will be no relation that all gold atoms in any sample of gold bear to each other, though they will all be parts of a certain structure.

The distinction is important because reference to structure is *holistic* in a way that relations are not. If being gold were simply a matter of finding some relation *R* such that a certain minimum of micro-particles all bore *R* to one another, the reductionist could list all those particular relations and claim, with some plausibility, that gold could be defined just by giving the list. There would be no room for form – there would only be a collection of relations. To insist that there was something more to being gold than being a concretely instantiated list of relations really would be 'occult', to use Hume's pejorative terminology. But such a list cannot even be given for something so simple as a straight line, let alone gold, or water, or elm trees, or tigers.

To return to the circularity problem, Joshua Hoffman and Gary Rosenkrantz have ingeniously proposed necessary and sufficient conditions for the unity of both inorganic mereological compounds and living things (Hoffman and Rosenkrantz 1999). Their proposals are instructive for a couple of reasons. First, by 'mereological compound' they explicitly exclude things such as houses, trees, and mountains (1999: 78–9). What they mean is a 'compound piece of matter' that has its parts essentially. Now, leaving aside the doubtful claim that such objects belong to 'commonsense ontology' (which they assert), if they cannot give a successful principle of unity for such objects there is little hope they could ever do so for genuinely commonsense elements of ontology such as houses, trees, and mountains. There is no room here to go into the technical details, but the result of their proposal is that a nut tightened firmly onto a bolt counts as a compound piece of matter just as much as a wooden cylinder, which is highly implausible. So does a flimsy cotton thread glued to a heavy object, but not if it is weakly attached by a small lump of putty (see further Hoffman and Rosenkrantz 1999: 84–5).[8]

Secondly, when it comes to giving conditions for the unity of living things, their proposal involves the notion of *functional* unity, which is in turn analysed via the idea of the functional subordination of the parts of a living thing to a master part that regulates the life processes of the whole (Hoffman and Rosenkrantz 1999: 87–101). Such a proposal is patently circular if intended as a definition, since the concept of functional subordination presupposes a prior grasp of the unity of the whole. Now Hoffman and Rosenkrantz *acknowledge* this. They explicitly assert that they are not aiming to provide a definition, explanation, or analysis of unity, whether of living or non-living things (1999: 87): they are only offering necessary and sufficient conditions. But this is an acceptance of the fact that no *explanation* of unity in terms of relations between parts is possible. Hence their proposals are instructive for what they implicitly demonstrate *cannot* be done. The project of giving necessary and sufficient conditions for unity does not succeed. To make it succeed, one would have to introduce reference to the workings of the whole of which the parts are members. But then there is no hope of a *definition* or explanation of unity in terms of parts only.

The upshot of this discussion is that form is required to explain unity and form is an irreducibly *holistic* concept. The explanation is not circular because form itself can be defined – as on p. 65 – independently of unity, as the real constituent principle by virtue of which a thing is determined to be of a specific kind. We might need to appeal to unified behaviour in order to understand what the form is in a given case, but this is no more than another way of putting the point, which I emphasize throughout this book, that essence is known indirectly via a thing's properties. Epistemically, we need to observe unity in order to know form – but form is the *principle* of unity, not unity itself.

We can better understand the holistic nature of substantial form via a defence of the unicity of form, a thesis hotly contested among medieval philosophers.[9] Unicity of form means that for any substance there is one and only one substantial form which it possesses. This is because a substance is one kind of thing, and substantial form determines the kind of thing it is. Hence when a substance comes into being it does so by virtue of acquiring a single substantial form, and when it loses that form it ceases to exist altogether as that kind of thing, even if something else is left over which is not that kind of thing. So when a lump of clay is smashed to pieces it ceases to exist altogether even though other, numerically distinct lumps of clay may come into existence by virtue of the persistence of clay material which is not itself a lump of any kind but rather the referent of the mass term 'clay'.

Suppose, on the contrary, that the lump of clay possessed two substantial forms, that of *lump* and that of *clay*. Then we would have to say that if the lump form were removed, say by smashing, the clay form would remain and the lump of clay, not having been completely destroyed, would continue to exist. But how could it exist? One might think it existed as the clay itself. But this is absurd: in what sense would the *lump of clay* have persisted – as clay? But a lump of clay is not mere clay. Or suppose it existed as in some respect 'partially identical' to the clay. Yet this is unintelligible, whatever the proponents of 'degrees of identity' or peddlers of the idea of 'survival' (a kind of persistence short of full identity) may think. Further, it would then seem impossible even to *destroy* a lump of clay without removing the clay form as well, which would require disintegrating it into its atomic or subatomic parts – but surely destroying a lump of clay can't be *that* difficult.

Whatever one might say about the substantiality (indeed the reality) of such objects as lumps of clay – and some recent writers have cast doubt on it[10] – the unicity doctrine is even more apparent in the case of objects over whose substantiality there is no dispute, such as living things. Let us go back to Fido. If substantial forms were multiple in Fido, the multiplicity theorist would have to say either that one substance, Fido, instantiated two substantial forms, or that there were actually two substances where it looked as if there was only one. Take the first alternative. Suppose we say that Fido, being both a living thing and a dog, falls under the two substantial kinds *living creature* and *dog*. These being distinct forms, why could they not come apart, with Fido instantiating one but not the other? One scenario is that Fido goes the way of all doggy flesh, leaving behind a canine corpse. It might be said, pointing at the corpse, 'There is Fido', meaning that Fido is still a dog, albeit a dead one. But a dead dog is not a kind of dog any more than the proverbial rubber duck is a kind of duck, or, to change the analogy, than a dead parrot is anything other than an ex-parrot. A substantial form supplies the proper functions and operations of its instances. Since no such functions and operations take place in a dead dog[11] – indeed the processes undergone by and taking place in a corpse are in general the very *reverse* of those undergone by and taking place in a functioning dog – clearly a dead dog does not fall under the substantial kind *dog*.

Another scenario is that Fido acquires the powers of Proteus and morphs into various other kinds of substance whilst retaining the form of *living creature*. Does this indicate that Fido would have ceased to fall under the substantial form *dog* whilst continuing to instantiate the separate form *living creature*? No, because in the case of Protean change the transient forms are not substantial but accidental: they do not determine the kind of thing Protean Fido is in his *essence* or *nature*, but reflect merely the diversity of forms which that essence or nature allows him to take on. Observing Protean Fido in his canine form, we do not behold a substance that is essentially a dog and a Protean living thing, but an essentially Protean living thing that has taken on the form of a dog. Therefore neither of the scenarios just described gives us a way of positing distinct substantial forms possessed by a single substance.

Might there, taking the other alternative, be two substances where there only appeared to be one? We can easily dispense with this thought in respect of Protean Fido, because we cannot plausibly say, observing the living creature in its canine form, that here there are *two* things, viz. a dog *and* a Protean organism: rather, there is one thing, a Protean organism appearing *as* a dog. For the organism, the sortal 'dog' is as much a phase sortal[12] as the sortal 'teenager' is for a thirteen-year-old person, in which latter case there do not exist two things, a human being *and* a teenager. More plausibly, however, it might be argued in the case of normal Fido that there are two substantial forms, viz. those of *dog* and of *body*, and that either there are two substances, for example a certain body constituting a dog, or one substance instantiating the forms of both body and dog. The basic confusion at the root of both proposals is that they misunderstand the concept of substantial form. Substantial forms do not make up a hierarchy within a substance: the canine form is not an add-on to the inferior corporeal form, for example. For how would one specify exactly what kind of body the canine form was superadded to?

We can eliminate the idea that the canine form is the form of a certain kind of corpse. It is tempting to think that a living dog just is a dead dog plus something extra, and one might imagine dead Fido's being miraculously brought back to life and call that the re-addition of canine form to canine matter. But dead flesh is not a formally impoverished kind of living flesh: in dead flesh, from the moment death occurs, not only is the substantial organic canine form absent but it is replaced by the very form of a dead thing, in which new functions of decay and disintegration immediately begin to occur.[13] The reanimation of dead Fido by means of the re-addition of the organic canine form would involve not the superaddition of something to a corpse, but the actual *reversal* of disintegrative processes already commenced. In other words, Fido's form *qua* living dog is the form of living flesh, i.e. the living flesh has a formal cause in Fido's substantial form; there simply is no metaphysical space for another kind of flesh to which the organic canine form is added to produce a living, breathing dog.

Another way of putting the point is to say that substantial form *permeates* the entirety of the substance that possesses it, not merely horizontally in its parts – there is as much dogginess in Fido's nose and tail as in Fido as a whole[14] – but also *vertically*, down to the very chemical elements that constitute Fido's living flesh. To use the traditional Scholastic terminology, the chemical elements exist *virtually* in Fido, not as compounds in their own right but as elements fully harnessed to the operations of the organism in which they exist, via the compounds they constitute and the further compounds the latter constitute, through levels of compounds – DNA, the proteins coded for by that DNA, the organelles that make up the cells, the organs made up of the cells, and so on.[15]

Supposing there to be elementary particles (a proposal I deny),[16] and supposing these to be quarks, it does not follow from the fact that every material substance is *made* of quarks that every substantial form is the *form* of a bundle of quarks, because in the existing substance the quarks *have* no substantial identity of their own, their behaviour having been fully yoked to the function and operations of the substance in which they exist. The substantial forms of the particles exist *virtually* in the substances they constitute. In other words, the quark is ontologically dependent on the whole of which it is a part, but its causal powers persist, albeit in a way radically limited by the whole.[17] The substantial form is what determines the permissible and impermissible behaviour of the quarks in the body, which is why some chemical reactions typically occur, others rarely, and others not at all. Nor is there any particular bundle of quarks of which the form could even be the form, given the familiar fact that every body loses and gains quarks all the time. Again, it is the form that determines the when, how, and how much of the loss and gain may occur, with external circumstances merely operating upon predetermined possibilities.[18]

4.3 Prime matter

Just as actuality is to be understood as *form*, so potentiality is to be understood as *matter*. However, just as the core of the analysis of essence requires the notion of substantial form, so it also requires a notion of matter which is as conceptually beyond sensible matter as form is beyond *shape* (which is often used heuristically to help the grasp of form).

According to the hylemorphic theory, the unique substantial form of any material substance must be united to something to produce that substance, since in itself it is only an actualizing principle. What does it actualize? It does not actualize anything whose actuality already presupposes the existence of the substantial form. Here it is useful to distinguish between two senses of 'of' in the expression '*x* is the form of *y*'. In one sense, the substituend for '*y*' is simply that whose identity depends on the substituend for '*x*', as when we say that a father is the father of his son ('he is his father's son'). In the other, the substituend for '*y*' is the object whose identity does not so depend, the object with its own real existence apart from that to which it is functionally related, as when we say that a father is the father of a person. In the first sense, then, we can say with Aristotle, when speaking about life, that the soul, understood as the organic principle, is the first actuality of a natural body with organs.[19] In other words, the soul is the form of an organism, that which makes the organism an organism; we could also say that the soul is the form of a body that has *these* kinds of property. In terms of the real unity relation, however, the soul is the form of something else, something not itself shot through by the very soul to which it is united – and this is what the hylemorphist calls *primordial matter*, or prime matter.

Hence we can truly say that a statue is made of bronze matter, a tiger is made of living flesh, a lump of gold is made of matter with a certain structure, and so on. But none of these are *prime* matter; rather, they are all what might be called sensible, or secondary, or proximate matter, since they are all already informed by the substantial form of the essential kind to which they belong. Prime matter *underlies* all of these kinds of matter. It is a pure passive potentiality, without any form whatsoever, nor subject to any privation (i.e. it does not lack some form that it *needs*, in the way that a blind person is deprived of sight), but it is wholly *receptive* of any form whatsoever. It is the completely undifferentiated basic material of the physical universe. It is not *something*, in the sense of something or other, but it is not nothing either. It is the closest there is in the universe to nothingness without being nothingness, since it has no features of its own but for the potential to receive substantial forms. (This potential includes that for spatiotemporal extension, as will be explained when I come on to the question of individuation in Chapter 5.4.) It is changeless, but is the *support* of all substantial change, and as such is subject to numerical identity, so that prime matter is conserved throughout substantial change.

This looks, to use a somewhat non-technical term, like spooky metaphysics. Certainly the concept of prime matter went the same way as that of substantial form during the early modern period. But there is nothing spooky about it, though the hylemorphist readily admits that prime matter, like essence, is something we can only know indirectly, not something with which we can ever be directly acquainted. Yet there has to be something to which form unites, and primordial matter is the only thing that can fill that role. For there is no other acceptable way of accounting for substantial change, the ceasing to exist of one substance and its replacement by another. I have already mentioned that quarks cannot do the job since they too are capable of substantial transformation. But substantial change occurs at higher levels as well, as when wood is burned to ash, food is digested, hydrogen and oxygen are synthesized into water, an animal dies, one element radioactively decays into another or is turned into another by bombardment with high-speed particles, a piece of paper is ripped to shreds, and so on.

Now *something* has to remain the same throughout substantial change. We can see that in the case of accidental change – qualitative, quantitative, and local – the support is precisely the bearer of the accidents: when a red wall is painted green, it is the wall that supports the change. The same goes for micro-level change, for instance the ionisation of an atom, where it is the atom that undergoes accidental change. The same applies to local change, where the support is the thing that moves;[20] and, again, this applies as much at the micro level as at the macro level: the emission of an alpha particle[21] from an atom of uranium 238 involves the movement of the particle. But what about the case of substantial change, such as the hammering of a wall into a pile of rubble or the transformation of an atom of uranium 238 into thorium 234 as a result of alpha decay? Here it is not so obvious that there is a substantial support, but it is also by no means clear that the notion of support can be done away with in this type of change.

The point can be brought out by means of a general argument. There are three alternative ways of explaining substantial change. First, one might do away with talk of supports altogether. When the wall is hammered into rubble, what changes? The wall pure and simple, it might be said. But to say that the wall itself changes is ambiguous as between substantial and accidental change; the wall also changes when it receives a coat of green paint over its red surface. So how, then, can we distinguish between the two kinds of change? One might say that when the wall is hammered into rubble it *turns into* something else; but that will not do, since the red wall turns into a green wall when it is painted; and a child turns into an adult but there is only one human being. Alternative locutions will inherit the ambiguity of the verb 'change', so we will need a new locution to mark the distinction; or else we will have to deny the distinction altogether.

Denying the distinction is problematic, for what does it mean? Are we to say that all substantial change is really accidental, or that all accidental change is really substantial, or that there is simply unqualified change? The first two options deny the existence of evident facts: some things just do survive change and others do not. Hence it is incumbent on the opponent to come up with a theory of unqualified change that does not distinguish between survival and non-survival, or at least assimilates every change to one or the other in a principled and plausible way. Perhaps certain kinds of process philosophy take this approach, but they are of doubtful coherence if they invoke the concept of a process whilst refusing to answer questions such as: What is it that undergoes the process? Does anything survive a process? As usually understood, process philosophy denies fixed realities in nature and so might be thought of as advocating only substantial change; but the process philosopher does not want to invoke the concept of substance, even substance that is short lived, since substances are fixed realities. Yet it cannot be only accidental change that the process philosopher believes in, since accidental change entails the existence of a fixed subject of change. The concept of a process is subject to just the same sorts of concern as that of change itself insofar as gain or loss of existence is in view.

On the other hand, marking the distinction between substantial and accidental change with a new locution does not explain the phenomenon; it merely names it. So the denier of a support for substantial change has to find an alternative metaphysical account of what is going on when one substance turns into a numerically distinct substance. And the only way, it seems, is to speak of *creation and annihilation*: when the wall is hammered into a pile of rubble, the wall is annihilated and replaced by a newly created pile of rubble. The problem with this account, however, is that in nature there is *no* pure creation and annihilation. The sorts of phenomena we speak of when we speak of creation and annihilation are ones in which prior material is turned into something else (where we do not assume by 'turned into' that the prior material survives the change). Hence the creation of a human being by reproduction is properly called *procreation* rather than creation pure and simple, since the previously existing gametes are the material out of which the child is formed.

Similarly, when the wall is reduced to rubble it is the previously existing matter which is turned into rubble. Creation and annihilation, strictly speaking, are out of nothing and into nothing, respectively. In physics it is a fundamental truth that energy can neither be created nor destroyed (the first law of thermodynamics), and this simply reflects the metaphysical truth that since all changes in nature require natural causes, and since those causes are finite, and since finite causes cannot create something out of nothing or turn something into nothing, a natural substantial change is not a series of creations and annihilations. Positively speaking, a substantial change is an actualization of the potentiality which some substance has with respect to some new substance: walls can be turned into rubble but not into fish. It is the potentiality which stretches across the change, becoming actualized by it, and so there cannot have been pure annihilation and creation when one substance is turned into another.

The first way of explaining substantial change, which involves doing away with all talk of supports, is therefore ruled out. The second way appeals to an apparently obvious fact: that when the wall is turned into rubble it is the matter of the wall – conceived as secondary or proximate matter – which survives the change and acts as support. So why can't we simply posit this kind of matter as the support of substantial change? The reason is that the support used to explain substantial change cannot be something whose existence during the change is not guaranteed. When the wall is hammered into rubble some matter survives in the rubble but other matter is dispersed to the winds. The matter of the wall undergoes all sorts of atomic and molecular changes as a result of the hammering: if the wall is pulverised, are we to say that the heap of fine powder before us is the same matter as that of the wall? Even if it is, the fact is that substantial change can occur without the preservation of sensible matter: the matter can undergo radical molecular change, as when flesh is burned to ashes.

Could it be the quarks that persist – at least enough of them to support the change from, say, wall to fine powder? But since quarks themselves can substantially change, they cannot do the job: there is no metaphysical guarantee of substantially changeless quarks throughout the substantial transformation, and so we would be back with the impossible scenario of creation and annihilation. Moreover, for reasons already alluded to, the very fact of substantial transformation means that all matter is totally converted from one substance to the next whatever the details of molecular, atomic or subatomic transformation. For instance, suppose we had samples of hydrogen and oxygen which we synthesized through combustion into a sample of water, with no loss of matter (admittedly an ideal rather than a real situation, but this is irrelevant). What reason is there for thinking that the hydrogen and oxygen atoms, or quarks for that matter, are *actually* present in the water, as they were in the original samples of hydrogen and oxygen? Well, if the water contained actual hydrogen, we should be able to burn it – but in fact the opposite is the case. If the water contained actual oxygen, it should boil at −183°C – but in fact it boils at +100°C (at ground level).[22]

Of course the response is that the oxygen and hydrogen are bonded in water and so cannot do what they do in the absence of such a bond. But that is precisely the point. The combustibility of hydrogen and the specific boiling point of oxygen are *properties* of those elements in the technical essentialist sense – they are accidents that necessarily flow from their very essence. Since the properties are absent in water, we can infer back to the *absence* of the essences from which they necessarily flow. Therefore neither hydrogen nor oxygen is actually present in water. Rather, they are *virtually* present in the water in the sense that some (but not all) of the powers of hydrogen and oxygen are present in the water (though all properties requiring the elements to be actually present will be gone), and these elements can be *recovered* from the water by electrolysis – not in the way that biscuits are recovered from a jar, but in the way that the ingredients of a mixture can (sometimes) be reconstituted.[23] Electron configurations are restored to what remains of the elements (in particular the nuclei), and in all other necessary ways the hydrogen and oxygen atoms are reconstituted by electrolysis, with their properties intact.

If this analysis is correct, then it seems to be even more strikingly so for quarks, which do not – at least on current physical theory – exist in a free state. If this is true, there is no way of recovering them from the hadrons to which they belong and their existence is always virtual: they are always and everywhere circumscribed by the larger particles to which they belong, and so on up the hierarchy of forms so that they are always circumscribed by the unique substantial form to which they belong. (Note that I am *not* saying there is a hierarchy of substantial forms in every substance. Rather, there is a hierarchy of substantial forms among the world of substances, and for each substance there is a single form it has. The quarks in that substance are circumscribed by the one and only form for that substance.) Just as Fido's animality is only separable in *thought*, but not in reality, from his being a dog, so his quark-composition, if he be composed of quarks, is not separable in reality from his essence. How the quarks in Fido behave is wholly determined by his substantial form, and hence different from how the quarks in me behave, whatever the constancy of some quark properties that all material objects share by virtue of being material. But if free quarks are recoverable, then their position is no different to that of hydrogen and oxygen: when they compose a new substance they lose their own substantial existence and contribute only virtually to the operations of the substance they compose. Hence my earlier talk concerning substantial transformation of quarks needs to be taken cautiously. We do not know nearly enough about their substantiality or otherwise; but this only goes to strengthen the case for prime matter against the idea that quarks provide the support for substantial change that such change requires.

The third way of explaining substantial change appeals to prime matter. Is there much more that can be said about it beyond the sketch already given? By its very nature, not much – at least without going into areas that cannot be explored here. A few things should be noted, however. First, there is nothing wrong with speaking of the *nature* of prime matter as pure passive potency, as long as we take 'nature' loosely and not as meaning essence in the strict sense. Strictly, prime matter has no essence. Loosely, it has the nature of being pure potentiality unmixed with any determining form, substantial or accidental.

Secondly, prime matter is not to be confused with the 'world-stuff' proposed, for example, by Sidelle (1989) (briefly discussed in O'Leary-Hawthorne and Cortens (1995: 144–5) and criticized in Elder (2004: ch. 1)). For, to the extent that one can make out what 'world-stuff' is supposed to be, it seems to be capable of arrangement and to appear to us in certain ways. Prime matter does neither – it has no appearance and does not of itself come in arrangements. It is, as we shall see when we discuss individuation, radically disposed to dimensionality, but this is manifested wholly through the forms that prime matter takes on.

Thirdly, might prime matter be energy? It is an intriguing question that I cannot pursue here. One problem is that the hylemorphist has a better grasp of what prime matter is than the physicist has of what energy is, and since metaphysics has to be informed by science there will be severe limits to what the former can say about the possible identification of prime matter with energy. If there are substantial energy transformations (e.g. heat to sound, chemical to light) by which a wholly new kind of thing comes into existence, there will have to be prime matter distinct from energy as a support (as noted in Johansson 1989: 38–9). But if such transformations are but phases of an underlying pure energy that has no determinate form in itself, then *perhaps* one might venture the thought that they are one and the same. For present purposes, I will tread no farther down this obstacle-laden ontological path.

4.4 Substance

The category of substance is one of the fundamental categories of being, indispensable to a correct inventory of everything that exists (or could exist). Its demise as such within ontology was wholly due to mistaken notions, mainly from the empiricists, by which it was conceived either as an unknowable, featureless substratum or bearer of sensible qualities, or as dispensable in favour of some or other bundle theory.

Trope theory is by far the most popular anti-substance theory among contemporary metaphysicians, with some claiming, somewhat incongruously, that '[t]he ordinary everyday notion of a continuant individual substance is in its own humble terms all right as it is', but that substances are analysable as bundles of tropes (Simons 1999: 29). Whatever our ordinary, everyday notion of substance is, and whatever its inaccuracies, it is decidedly *not* of a thing that is so analysable, even if ordinary people have no pre-theoretic conception of tropes in the first place (though they experience them all the time). More importantly, all trope theories, of whatever ingenuity and complexity, fail because they cannot get around the ontological dependence of tropes on the substances in which they inhere. The redness of a particular apple is a *feature of the apple* and requires the apple in order to exist, but this is not explicable on trope theory.

First, might the trope theorist plausibly say that being a feature of something *x* just is to be a member of the trope bundle that constitutes *x*? No, because being a feature of something and being a member of something are not the same relation. Socrates is a member of the sets containing him but he is not a *feature* of those sets. The membership of the apple's redness in the trope bundle putatively constituting the apple does not make that redness a feature of the apple, something that is true of the apple or characterizes it.

Secondly, why couldn't the apple's redness *leave* the trope bundle and migrate to another apple or some other kind of object altogether? In fact the apple's redness could not possibly do so: not only does its existence entail the existence of the apple, but it entails that it be a mode (to revert for a moment to the preferred terminology) *of* the apple, i.e. a modification of it. What is it about a trope bundle that makes this true? It couldn't be that the trope bundle necessarily contains the apple's redness as a member, because then the apple would necessarily have this particular redness, which is false. Yet it is hard to know what else the trope theorist can say. Even if he can establish that the existence of the apple's redness entails the existence of the trope bundle supposedly constituting the apple, it does not follow that the existence of the particular redness has to be a feature of the particular apple by bearing some sort of relation to the trope bundle.

Thirdly, not only are tropes ontologically dependent upon the substances that possess them[24] in the sense of entailing the existence of their possessors and characterizing them, but they also depend for their *identity* on their possessors. Which particular wisdom a wisdom trope is depends on which thing possesses it. Hence the wisdom of Socrates is distinct from the wisdom of Plato precisely by virtue of one's belonging to Socrates and the other's belonging to Plato. Now, as Lowe points out (Lowe 1999a: 206), the trope theorist is committed to holding that the identity of a given trope depends on the bundle to which it belongs; but the identity of the bundle itself depends on the identity of the tropes belonging to it. Hence the identity conditions of tropes will be circular and so not well defined. This might be thought an unfair objection for a hylemorphist to make to a trope theorist,[25] since the same charge might be thrown back at the former. After all, doesn't the identity of a substance depend on its substantial form, and doesn't the identity of substantial form depend on that of the substance to which it belongs?

For reasons I will go into in Chapter 5, this is a mistake. The identity of substances is primitive in the sense of being unanalysable. A substance is *individuated* by its matter. *Which* substance it is (i.e. of what kind) is given by its form, but its identity conditions are not given by those of its form. Nor does its form have identity conditions – to speak of the same substantial form in a substance just is to speak of the identity of the substance. By coming to know the form of a substance one comes to know the identity of the substance. The substance has an identity – it is one or another kind of thing – and its identity is traceable through time. But it has no *conditions* of identity, nothing else that has to be true in order for it to have the identity it has or to be reidentifiable. This is less mysterious than it sounds and will be explored in Chapter 5.5. The point for now is that a similar thought cannot be applied to trope theory. Which trope a trope is *must* depend on something outside the trope, because tropes are dependent beings. And trope bundles must have their identity fixed by their members: their identity is no more primitive than that of sets, whose identity is given by their members, even if trope bundles are not sets themselves. Nor does it matter whether the identity of the bundle is given by all or only some of its members. Since the identity of every member must be fixed by the bundle it belongs to, there will be a vicious circle of identity conditions whichever favoured tropes are selected as those that fix the identity of the bundle.

A substance is in some sense an ontologically *independent* entity. It has existence in itself and by virtue of itself as an ultimate distinct subject of being. This definition encompasses several notions. Substance has existence in itself in the sense that it is not *in* anything else, not a modification of, a part of, an aspect of, some other thing. It exists by virtue of itself since its continued existence does not require it to be a product or projection of something else. As a distinct and ultimate subject of being, it is the bearer of qualities but nothing bears it or is a subject of it. All of these marks of substance come down to the fact that substance has a complete essence consisting of matter united to form such that no reference to any other object is required to constitute it as the thing it is.

Perhaps the best way of capturing these ideas in a definition is the proposal of Lowe that substances are identity-independent in the following sense (Lowe 1999a: ch. 6; 2005):[26]

x is a substance = $_{df}$ x is a particular and there is no particular y such that y is not identical with x and x depends for its identity upon y, where

> x depends for its identity upon $y =$ df there is a function f such that it is part of the essence of x that x is $f(y)$.

So, for instance, singleton Socrates depends for its identity on Socrates but not vice versa, since it is part of the essence of the singleton that it is the unit set of Socrates. It will be recalled, though, that in Chapter 1 I said that it was a *virtual* part of Socrates's essence that he be a member of the singleton containing him, by which I meant that a virtual part of what it is to be Socrates is to be something or other, and what it is to be something or other is, formally, to be a unit of being in a class apart. Singleton membership is a way of understanding this individuality. Now that idea depended on the claim that Socrates's being human logically presupposed his being some individual or other. Hence it is a virtual part of his essence to be an individual. But why not say that, because it is part of his formal essence – the explicit definition of him as a human being – to be rational, it is formally part of his essence to belong to the class of rational things? Isn't it part of the very essence of rational things to form a set (united by a certain characteristic)? But unless we want to reduce predication to set membership (itself undesirable and implausible), we have to distinguish ontologically between Socrates's being rational and his belonging to the set of rational things. So why isn't the latter *also* a part of his essence, thus falsifying Lowe's definition?

The reason this does not follow is at the same time the reason why Lowe's formula is not really a *definition* at all, even though it may be extensionally adequate. (Recall what was said in section 4.2 about Hoffman and Rosenkrantz's distinction between necessary and sufficient conditions on the one hand and illuminating analyses on the other.) By employing the notion of essence in the putative definiens, Lowe *presupposes* a grasp of substance rather than defines it, since essence (in the primary sense in which we are now discussing it) is an abstraction from substance. Or, to put it the other way around, substance just is the concretization of essence. A substance has an essence by virtue of being a compound of prime matter united to substantial form. The coming together of these two fundamental realities constitutes the substance as a new, complete reality in its own right. Unless we already comprehend this, we cannot comprehend why non-substances are non-substances. But once we do grasp the true analysis of substance as compound of matter and form, we can see immediately why Socrates's identity is independent of his singleton membership but not the reverse. His identity is given wholly by his being a compound of matter and form. Although it may be part of what he is as an individual to be a member of a singleton set, it is *not* part of what he is *as a human being*, and hence not part of what he is as rational. What he is as rational is given wholly by the definition of rationality, in other words by the explanation of what it is to be rational.

Similarly, events are non-substances, and are rightly excluded by Lowe's formula, because an event is a change, or a collection or series of changes, in a substance or substances, but a substance is not a change in anything. Hence we cannot begin to understand why an event is a non-substance without already understanding what a substance is. A substance is a compound of matter and form; an event is no such thing. Again, a mode is not a substance, but a modification *of* a substance. A universal is not a substance but that which is shared by substances (or indeed by other things). A substance is not common to, or shared by, anything. (True, Aristotle calls substantial kinds, i.e. genera and species, 'secondary' substances (Ross 1928b: 2b ff.), but by this he means that genera and species are derived entities, abstractions from the individual or *primary* substances, i.e. substances strictly so called, for which they give the essence. What *animal* is derives from what animals *are*, what *gold* is derives from what gold things *are*, and so on.) Parts of substances are not substances, although we might call them *incomplete* substances, since their identity derives from the substances they are parts of, not the reverse. Being a dog entails having canine parts; we can even say that canine parts are essential to dogs, and that being a dog entails having parts that are organized in such and such a way. Why not then falsify Lowe's formula by reading '$f(y)$' as 'possessor of canine parts'? Lowe would no doubt object that the definition would then be circular, since grasping what it is to be a canine part presupposes grasping what it is to be a dog in the first place. But I have argued that his proposal is not really a definition anyway, and in any case why not read the function variable as 'possessor of parts organized in the following way ... ', where the dots are replaced by a non-canine-presupposing account of the organization of (what are in fact) dog parts? Isn't this how a biologist would define a dog?

The objection has force, and arguably militates against the extensional adequacy of Lowe's proposal. In any case, the hylemorphist will say that what makes a dog a substance but its parts not (except in an attenuated sense) is that the essence of canine parts is to contribute to the functioning of a dog, but a dog does not, of its essence, contribute to the functioning of anything. In fact it is, I contend, of the essence of many things, organic and inorganic, that various substances contribute to their functioning; but it is not of the essence *of the substances* that they contribute to the functioning of anything. In fact, the things of which it is their essence that certain substances contribute to their functioning are not substances themselves, but events and processes. (See further Oderberg forthcoming a.)

A leg is not a leg once amputated any more than a corpse is a human being. The essence of a leg is to contribute to the functioning of its animal possessor. Once amputated it is still a lump of flesh, but lumps of flesh are not parts of animals. When a chunk is removed from a lump of gold it is no longer a part of the prior lump – it is a *new* lump of gold. Lumps of gold do not have lumps as parts, though they do have chunks. A relation is not a substance because its identity derives from its relata, either the particular ones in the case of a particularized relation (Romeo's love for Juliet) or the potential relata (as in the relation of loving). Propagated objects such as beams of light are not substances because what it is to be a beam of light is (partly) to emanate from some source or other, and substances – except according to neo-Platonists, among whom hylemorphists are not numbered – are not emanations of, or propagated by, anything. (God conserves substances in existence, but His conservation of them is not analogous to the propagation of light by a source – except according to neo-Platonists. For more on progagated objects, see Oderberg 1996.) Privations are not substances since privation involves a *lack* of form, not a presence of form. Are space and time substances? I do not propose to canvass this thorny issue here, but the hylemorphist knows how to go about answering the question: it depends on how space and time (or space–time, for that matter) are defined, on what they *are*. If the best way of understanding them requires thinking of them as prime matter–substantial form compounds, they will be substances. And we can get a better grip on whether this *is* the best way of thinking of them by seeing whether they are in any way identity-dependent on, or modifications of, or parts of, or propagated by what we know to be substances, or whether instead they have a complete reality of their own that is not *communicated* (to use a traditional term) to something else, i.e. that is not essentially shared or united with something else.

So there are a number of ways of understanding substance, all converging on its definition as a compound of prime matter and substantial form. We can analyse substance into its constituents, but we should not expect to be able to define those constituents in terms that do not refer, explicitly or implicitly, back to substance itself. And this just shows that substance is a fundamental category of being – analysable into parts that do not ever or anywhere exist separately from it, but not analysable into anything that can truly be understood apart from it. The situation might be unusual to contemporary metaphysical eyes, but then so is much else that commends itself both to common sense and the wisdom of the ages.

4.5 The immanence of essence

I end this chapter with some remarks on Platonism about essences. Real essentialism, understood as having hylemorphism at its core, is fundamentally anti-Platonist. This means not only that there are no uninstantiated essences, but that the essences of things must be *in* the things that have them. Note that this is *not* the same as the claim that essences can never exist apart from matter, for there might be entities that are essentially immaterial – God, disembodied minds – or that, whilst essentially embodied, are also capable of existing apart from matter. (I will argue in Chapter 10 that human beings satisfy the second possibility, though the relation between the human person and his body will need to be spelled out carefully.) Even in such cases, the essences of these beings will be instantiated, whereas Platonists allow essences that are wholly unin-stantiated. Note further that anti-Platonism about essence involves more than the claim that there are no uninstantiated essences, since one could be a Platonist and still coherently hold (though no one does, for good reason!) that there must be concrete instances of Platonic essences, even though the essences are in no way in their possessors. The kernel of the anti-Platonist case is that essences are *immanent* – they are in some sense in their pos-sessors. It then follows that they must be instantiated.

The arguments against Platonic essentialism, including the one I want to focus on, overlap those against Platonism about universals generally, which is only to be expected since essences are a kind of universal. I will not rehearse those specific arguments here. (For a standard critique, see Arm-strong 1978a; and see also Lowe 1999b.) Not all critics of Platonism about universals, however, accept that they are immanent in the sense defended by the real essentialist. Lowe, for instances, takes immanence to be no more than that there are no uninstantiated universals (Lowe 2006: 98–100) and can make no sense of any stronger thesis. I contend that the real essentialist must adhere to a stronger thesis – that essences are in their possessors.

The word 'in' is notoriously ambiguous. In what sense are essences in their possessors? The short answer is that they are in their possessors in the very way in which form is in matter. Once there is a union of matter and form there is an individual, and the essence is in the individual immediately and with no further ontological step to be taken. Hence the way in which essence is in substance is distinct from any sort of physical containment, since the relation between form and matter is one of *union*, not contain-ment. But it is also distinct from particular spatio-temporal location, if this is understood as the location of a particular. Hence when Lowe asserts with justified incredulity that if the universal of redness coincides spatially with one rose, and also does so with another, the roses must be wholly spatially coincident (Lowe 2005: 99), he wrongly takes the relation between a uni-versal and a particular – and by implication that between an essence and a substance – to be one of spatial coincidence. Essences do not coincide with their possessors – they *constitute* their possessors. Substantial forms do not coincide with prime matter – they *determine* it. Hence essences, and the substantial forms that are their primary constituents, do not have a spatial location akin to that of particulars. A given essence is located wherever its possessors are, and has no location – and does not exist – if it has no pos-sessor. To this extent it is, to use David Lewis's terminology, 'wholly present' (1986: 202–5) wherever and whenever it is instantiated; but he then wrongly goes on to construe universals as non-spatio-temporal parts of their instances (1986: 205). They are not parts of anything *except* in the sense that sub-stantial form is one of the two constituent parts of substance – which I do not suppose Lewis had in mind. Nor do they lack a kind of spatio-temporal existence – not the kind that particulars have, to be sure, but the kind proper to themselves.

What kind of spatio-temporal existence? It is an existence that requires them to operate only in and through their instances. This is because universals in general, and essences in particular, do not exist *as* universal in mind-independent reality – they only exist as multiplied in particulars. But if they don't exist as universal in reality, surely universals only exist in the mind? Again this is not true either. If it were, there would be no real similarity between anything, by which I mean that things would not literally possess other things that were strictly identical with each other. (I follow Armstrong's terminology (1989a).) Needless to say, the nominalist will not baulk at this consequence, and I shall not pursue nominalism here. The point is that if there *is* real similarity between things, this must be founded on the strict sameness of other things. Hence universals cannot exist wholly in the mind – they must exist in reality as well. But they do not exist *as universal* in reality, only as multiplied into particulars.

How can this make sense? Consider what all squares have in common: there is something they literally share, namely squareness. But one might complain, 'We never encounter squareness, only square things.' To which the immanent realist replies that we *do* encounter squareness all the time – *in* the square things. 'But I mean we never encounter squareness *in the abstract*.' To which the reply is that this is correct: we do never encounter squareness in the abstract, because squareness in the abstract is not something we ever *could* encounter – what would such an encounter be like? Rather, we do not encounter squareness in the abstract because squareness is something that *we* abstract – *from the square things*. In short, nothing abstract exists without abstraction. And abstraction is an *intellectual* process by which we recognize what is literally shared by a multiplicity of particular things.

The only reason why we might find all of this mysterious is that we have been thrown off track by a wholly misconceived view of the abstract–concrete distinction. This distinction, as it exists in contemporary metaphysics, seeks to divide reality into abstract and concrete entities. Generally, the former are non-spatio-temporal and the latter spatio-temporal, though we can query whether modes or tropes are spatio-temporal even though they are called by trope theorists 'abstract particulars'. For if they are not spatio-temporal, in what way do they enter into spatio-temporal causal relations? How could the particular lustre of a gold nugget catch the attention of a prospector if the particular lustre were not in space and time? But if tropes are in space and time, in what sense are they abstract? Surely they are as concrete as the individuals that possess them? If we maintain the contemporary abstract–concrete division of reality, this looks like a dilemma. If we abandon the distinction, the problem disappears. For modes exist only concretely in mind-independently reality, but abstractly in the mind. There is no abstractness without abstraction, and so the only way a mode could exist abstractly is if someone thinks of it without thinking of the individual that possesses it. That modes are *capable* of being thought of in this way is a fact about them as well as about us, and this is sufficient as a real foundation of their abstractness.

The same goes for universals. The real foundation of their abstractness is that we are capable of abstracting from the particulars in which they inhere and thinking of them – forming concepts of them – apart from thinking of those particulars, even though universals cannot exist in reality separately from the particulars that instantiate them. Since essences are a kind of universal, the same is true of them. No one ever encounters humanity in the abstract, though we encounter humanity all the time by observing the particular human beings who instantiate it. To this extent and this extent alone does humanity exist in particular humans – really but not abstractly. This conception makes a nonsense of the contemporary abstract–concrete distinction. Everything in the spatio-temporal world is spatio-temporal. Nothing that exists in the spatio-temporal world exists as anything but particular. But what exist in the spatio-temporal world are more than particulars. There are universals, but these exist only as particularized – except in the mind, where they exist as universal and hence as abstract.[27] Thus the simple question of whether an object is abstract or concrete becomes an oversimplification requiring a more complicated answer than simply attaching the label 'concrete' or 'abstract' to the object in question.

That, in a nutshell, is the theory of immanent realism about essence. And the main argument as to why essences must be immanent is simple enough. It is that Platonism does away with material substance altogether; but since there are material substances, Platonism must be false. Hence the essence of a substance cannot consist in the substance's instantiating, or copying, or mirroring some non-spatio-temporal Platonic Idea. Moreover, it cannot consist in the substance's instantiating, mirroring, or copying anything other than the form that is a real constituent of the substance itself – where it is only instantiation that obtains, not mirroring or copying. For the substance to instantiate the form that makes it what it is does not render the substance ontologically dependent in the senses discussed earlier. The substantial form determines the identity of the substance, so of course the substance is ontologically dependent on it in a trivial sense – how could it be otherwise? But for the substance to be what it is only on condition that it instantiate something – such as a Platonic Idea – that is *not* a real constituent of the substance is to make it ontologically dependent in a strong and objectionable sense. It is to regard the substance as a non-substance – incomplete in itself and requiring something else to give it its identity. Needless to say, the neo-Platonists thought just that about substances: they were all, on their conception, emanations of Platonic Ideas, or of the Form of the Good, or of the Divine Intellect. But while the hylemorphist can accept that God exercises a conserving and sustaining power over created substances, he cannot accept that substances are not complete in themselves, not determined to be what they are by their form united to matter.

Again, this is in accord with common sense. Whatever it is that makes Socrates what he is, it must be something true intrinsically about *him* – about the way *he* is constituted – not about the way he is related to something else. (The bearing of this upon the proper conception of artefacts, as well as on the theory of historical essences, will be considered in Chapters 7 and 9.) We intuitively think of the humanity of a person as *in* the person, not in a Platonic Idea, or in the mind of an artificer. Even if Socrates was created by God, and even if in creating him God executed a blueprint in His own divine mind, this only gives us the efficient and exemplary causes of Socrates's existence. It gives us the exemplary cause, since Socrates would have been created according to a plan, just as an architecturally designed house has the blueprint as its exemplary cause, the model on which it was built.[28] It gives us also the efficient cause, since Socrates will have been created by divine action. But the *formal* cause of Socrates – what makes him what he is – will be the very form that God brought together with matter to create the individual Socratic substance (if I may speak that way for a moment). And if Socrates is born naturally, his efficient cause is his parents. But his formal cause is something in him.

The problem with Platonism is not just that it runs into Third Man and other regress arguments (as it does), or that it runs into problems with causation (as it does), but that it does away with material substance altogether and so collapses the proper division of reality into things that are complete in themselves and things that are in some way 'of' another (as exemplified by the sorts of entity mentioned earlier). Indeed it is hard to see how the Platonist could resist treating substances as no more than another kind of accident, a characteristic of the Ideas that give them life: for since everything a substance is and does involves its instantiating some universal or other, how can everything it is and does involve anything more than its copying an Idea? What independent reality does it have?

Platonists have historically drawn, and continue to draw, elaborate pictures of what the world would be like if everything instantiated some Platonic Idea or other. The more elaborate the picture, the more divorced it is from both common understanding and the evidence of the senses. The hylemorphist can happily leave Platonists to their devices and concentrate instead on the sublunary world of real substances with real essences. Having said that, however, lest the Platonist think I have given him short shrift I will return to Platonism in Chapter 6, where further considerations reinforce the truth of immanent realism.

5   Essence and identity

5.1 Real definition and the true law of identity

From the trivially necessary property of self-identity, i.e. the relation every-thing bears exclusively to itself,[1] we can recover an important and non-tri-vial truth – the *law of identity*. It can be expressed in several ways, one of which is 'Everything is something or other'. In other words, everything is a this-such. Put another way: everything has an identity. As Joseph Butler put it, '[e]verything is what it is, and not another thing' (Butler 1914: 23). In terms of essentialism, it is stated as 'Everything has its own essence or nature'.

Butler's refrain was famously taken up by Kripke (1980: 94), though the latter's concern was with the possibility of ever giving non-circular analyses of philosophical concepts. This is not the concern of the law of identity, which is a fundamental truth about essences. It is far more than the ema-ciated contemporary version of the 'law of identity', namely that everything is self-identical, or even that everything is necessarily self-identical. To see that the true law of identity, or law of essence as it might be called, is in fact informative, it helps to consider what it is denying. Return to the 'amor-phous lump' theory of reality, according to which there are objects (better, one big object) that do *not* have an identity as something or other, which do not fall under some sortal or into some kind. ('Amorphous' might just as easily have been replaced by 'formless', since the first is simply the Greek rendition of the second.) Now if the amorphous lump view is true, the law of identity is false, and vice versa. According to the law of identity, every-thing *has* one. Moreover, everything just *is* its own nature. (This is the most plausible way of reading Lowe (2005) when he identifies Socrates with his humanity, claiming that the distinction between them is a mere distinction of reason, not a real one.)[2]

Reality is not formless. But why should we believe this? The simplest reason – apart from the considerations already given in previous chapters – is an inductive argument to the effect that no such formless reality has ever been discovered. No matter how deep we penetrate, no matter what material objects we discover, we always find them falling into some kind or other.

Note that the kind need not be natural – it may be artefactual, or logical, or conceptual. (One might argue that disjunctive kinds such as *grue*, though not natural, are nevertheless logical.) Even the subatomic and quantum levels of reality (as far as any of the discoveries we have made are concerned) are full of form, whether it be kinds of particle, or of field, or of energy, force, dimension, and so on. We simply never encounter amorphous reality.

Now someone of a Kantian bent would no doubt say that this is not surprising since we cannot but impose on 'things in themselves' the classificatory schemata with which we are endowed, and that hence the inductive argument has no strength at all. Perhaps there are formless things in themselves and we can (necessarily) never know about them. Unfortunately, however, it would take a separate discussion to refute the Kantian view, so the question has to be left in suspension here.[3] But it can also be conveniently short-circuited by replying that even if there were unknowable noumena the law of identity would still apply at the empirical level (as Kant himself does not appear to have doubted), and so the Kantian can read what is being claimed here as applying with equal force to that level alone.

As I have already argued, however, a priori considerations also support the law of identity, since it is the foundation of all demonstration, scientific and non-scientific. In seeking to show, for instance, that copper conducts electricity, or to explain *why* it does so, we proceed by means of the proposition that copper is a metal. In order to predict or explain why whales give live birth, we use the truth that whales are mammals. If I want to know why paper burns, I need to know what paper is. The examples are simple but the principle is not. Knowledge of the material world proceeds by way of definition, and the law of identity can also be formulated as 'Everything is definable'. Thus stated, 'definable' should not be read epistemically since it is no part of the law that we human beings are able to define everything we come across. Not only are there almost certainly things for which we cannot give a complete definition (perhaps *matter* itself, or *time*), but it may be that there are things for which we cannot even give a partial one (maybe *energy*?). Further, the law as stated is consistent with the thesis that there are material *primitives*, namely objects for which no definition is possible since they are unanalysable (perhaps *identity* is an example, as I will argue in section 5.5 for the diachronic case). Such objects would be trivially definable in terms of themselves.

How, it might be objected, do we get from the proposition that everything is a this-such to the claim that everything has an essence? Mightn't it be the case that everything has an identity even though nothing has any of its properties essentially? But suppose there were an object that had all of its properties accidentally: it is *F* but it could have been *G*, it is *H* but it could have been *J*, and so on. Then we can take the disjunction of all the properties it could have had (including those it actually has), and *this* will be its essence. In other words, there may be some objects with ineliminably disjunctive essences,[4] but the disjunction will be necessarily true of the object all the same, and so pure contingency of qualities is impossible. Having said that, one must never be too willing to accept that an essence is disjunctive, since the natural question should always be 'By virtue of *what* must the object be either *F* or *G* or ...?' Furthermore, nothing follows about whether the disjunction can be infinite. For material objects, which are finite, one would expect disjunctive essences to be always themselves finite.

There are a number of criteria that correct definitions should meet, though we should not expect the criteria to be listed with the pseudo-precision of mathematical formulae, unless we are dealing with mathematical objects. As Aristotle emphasizes time and again, we can only be as precise as the subject matter allows, and when it comes, for instance, to natural bodies, let alone artefacts and other more exotic kinds of thing, we can only expect the precision that such objects allow. We want our definitions to be (1) clear, (2) extensionally adequate, (3) positive where possible, and (4) stated in terms different from the definiendum. Clarity usually requires that the definition be (i) brief, (ii) not metaphorical, and (iii) such as not to define the obscure in terms of the more obscure. Needless to say, (i)–(iii) admit only of approximate application. Brevity is needed for communication. It does not exclude the possibility that a definition be complex, or that when unpacked it will be extremely long. But ordinarily we should want a definition to sum up the complexity, length, or technicality in a simple proposition. 'Man is a rational animal' does this in an exemplary way, as does 'A fish is a water-dwelling vertebrate with gills in the mature form'. A definition that simply lists all the known characteristics of a thing does not.

Our definitions must be stated in terms of genera and species. Take gold:

(G₁) Gold is a shiny yellow substance with (whose atomic constituents have) atomic number 79.

This definition might be extensionally adequate, but it is incorrect since the first part expresses a collection of accidents, not a genus. But why don't shiny yellow substances form a genus? After all, we could classify the world using such a set of accidents. And Eli Hirsch has raised worries about why we (or some alien linguistic community) mightn't choose to carve the world up in exotic ways, using a term such as 'gricular' (anything gricular is defined as green or circular) (Hirsch 1988, 1993). It should be noted that Hirsch is more concerned about languages than how the world itself is carved up (Elder 2005), and that disjunctive predicates are tangential to the present point. But the general worry remains – what constitutes a genus?

The answer is that the genus of something is part of its *form*, not its *accidents* or even its *properties* (i.e. the proper or necessary accidents). Yes, we can classify the world, in part, according to the shiny yellow substances, but being a shiny yellow substance is not part of the form of anything – it is to have two accidents and to be a kind of thing that *has* form (i.e. a substance). If you asked a metallurgist, or some other materials scientist, why he didn't use *shiny yellow substance* as part of his scheme of classification, he would tell you it was because the shiny yellow substances were not all metals, or were too heterogeneous, not scientifically interesting, and so on. All of this is true, and implies that one will not be able to make many interesting predictions about how something will behave on knowing only that it is a shiny yellow substance. It also implies that being a shiny yellow substance is not going to explain very much about the known behaviour of things either. The fundamental metaphysical reason for this is that shininess and yellowness are accidents, not genera or parts of genera: the genus of a thing is part of its *form*, so when we hunt for the genus we are looking for a (partly) *constitutive* rather than a *characterizing* principle.

Although being a material substance is partly constitutive, we cannot define gold this way:

(G$_2$) Gold is a material substance with atomic number 79.

This is because *material substance* is not the lowest genus into which gold falls, and so, although extensionally adequate, it is still incorrect. For it fails to capture with enough specificity what gold is. Generically, it is not a *mere* material substance, and hence we need to find the lowest genus into which it falls, that is, the *proximate* genus with respect to gold as a species. *Material substance* is its remote genus and science tells us we can get more determinate. So why not:

(G$_3$) Gold is a substance that is malleable, ductile, melts at 1064.43°C, has a cubic crystal structure, and possesses atomic number 79.

The problem here is that, again, whilst extensionally adequate, and whilst involving necessary truths about gold, these truths refer to *properties* of gold, not constitutive principles. The malleability, ductility, and melting point of gold are properties fixed by more fundamental facts about gold, in particular its atomic structure. Gorman (2005) usefully puts this point in terms of explanation: the question 'Why is gold malleable?' is answered by pointing to more fundamental features of gold, in particular its atomic structure. Conversely, its atomic structure is not explained by its malleability. To the objection that explanation is not an extensional relation, the essentialist can reply that we do not have to speak in terms of explanation but can appeal to extensional relations like determination, and even supervenience, though this latter does not really capture what the essentialist wants to say. The point is that, from what science tells us, the atomic structure of gold determines it to be malleable. It is something about what gold *is* that determines how it *behaves*.

This points to one of the problems with Twin Earth thought experiments, for we have no reason to think it even *metaphysically possible* that there be, say, a substance with *all* of the properties of water yet that is composed of

XYZ rather than H_2O. As far as we know, having the properties of water is wholly explained by the molecular structure of water.[5] By 'wholly explained' here, I mean that the entire collection of properties possessed by water is understood by science as caused by the constitution of water and realized (to echo John Searle's (1991) way of speaking) only in that constitution. I would go further and venture that every specific property of water is realized only in water's specific constitution. To clarify, it is true that some of the individual properties of water can be realized in substances constituted otherwise: after all, liquidity is realized in many different substances. But when I refer to specific properties, I refer not to liquidity pure and simple, but what we might call – perhaps infelicitously but not circularly – the *water-like* liquidity of water. We could say the same for its water-like boiling point, for instance – not merely the temperature at which it boils, but the manner in which it boils, which is different from substance to substance (the average number of bubbles formed, their frequency, and so on). Perhaps this makes property individuation too fine-grained a matter, or maybe there are straight counterexamples. Still, that the entire collection of water-like properties is realized only in water seems to be what science holds; and the Twin Earth scenario is about the whole collection.

If this is true, then not only does having the H_2O structure metaphysically guarantee having the properties of water, but having the properties of water guarantees having the H_2O structure, and so Twin Earth is metaphysically impossible. One might call this a two-way supervenience between the properties of water and the H_2O structure – no difference in one without a difference in the other. But for the essentialist the matter is more subtle than that. The *explanatory* or *determinative* relation goes only one way – from H_2O to the properties of water, not the converse. The kind of relation that goes from water's properties to the H_2O structure, on the other hand, is something different: ' ... is realized only in ... ' captures fairly accurately what the essentialist wants to say, but the important point is that, whilst the relation is also an entailment (as in the case of the relation from H_2O to water's properties), it is not a causal or explanatory one.

To return to gold, then, our genus needs to be something constitutive of gold, and what scientists tell us is that being a *metal* is constitutive, and metaphysical reflection confirms that for something to cease to be a metal is for it to undergo substantial change. This looks like a good candidate for a genus. But is it the proximate genus of gold? It depends on whether the metals can be further divided into subspecies in ways that exhibit common properties and behaviour indicative of a distinctive kind of substance. I express this with deliberate imprecision, since it is not clear how far metaphysics can go in answering such a specific question: it is principally one for the metallurgists and materials scientists themselves. But the metaphysical point is untouched whether the metals are further classified or not. If *metal* is gold's proximate genus, we have all we need. If it is only a remote genus, requiring a further classification – say into the ferromagnetic and non-ferromagnetic metals, or the d-block (transition) metals and the rest – then one of these (non-ferromagnetic or d-block, both of which gold falls under) will be gold's proximate genus.

Why not both? Because if the ferromagnetic/non-ferromagnetic and d-block/non-d-block partitions were both into genera, and gold belonged to both yet one was not contained in the other, it would have to be two distinct substances, which nothing can be. If we have a case of apparently competing genera, then it must be the case that one is really contained within the other. (Fred can only be both an animal and an organism because the genus *animal* is contained within the genus *organism*.) The genera are real, the competition apparent. By contrast, if the competition is real – the object or species really does fall into two categories that are not related by containment – then one or both will not be real genera. This is the case with gold, which falls into both the d-block category in the periodic table and the non-ferromagnetic category. Yet *d-block* and *non-ferromagnetic* are overlapping but not co-extensive categories.[6] They cannot both be genera, even though they are both types of metal and gold falls under them. On examination, we can see that whilst being a d-block metal is a plausible candidate for a subgenus/subspecies of metal, being non-ferromagnetic is not. A metal is classified as d-block due to its electron configuration. It is classified as non-ferromagnetic due to its not having a certain kind of magnetism. The former is a good candidate for a constitutive principle of the metals that fall under it, whereas the second is a category of *accident*, not a constitutive category.

So the first possibility is that two apparently competing genera are not really in competition. The second is that two apparently competing genera are not really both genera. Note that if *neither* of the apparently competing genera is really a genus the object will fall under a different genus altogether, no matter how much it may *appear* that it falls under both. To take a fanciful example, if Fred looks like he falls under *human* at midday and under *wolf* at midnight, he really will not fall under either – he will be a *werewolf*, and hence fall under a distinct genus of which human-like and wolf-like appearance are both phases.

Whatever the empirical technicalities, then, for present purposes we can rest content with the following:

(G$_4$) Gold is a metal with atomic number 79

as giving the correct definition of gold. (More precisely, we should say that gold is a metal whose atomic constituents have atomic number 79; but the shorter version in (G$_4$) will suffice.) For as well as assuming that *metal* is the proximate genus, we can be fairly sure that *having atomic number 79* gives the specific difference, marking out gold from everything else in the universe, no matter how similar. If having atomic number 79 turns out to be identical with some more fundamental state, say a particular quark configuration, we could name the more fundamental configuration as the specific difference, but would not have to as having atomic number 79 would still be as specific as one could get in respect of gold. If having atomic number 79 turned out to be realizable by distinct fundamental configurations, we would be obliged to revise (G_4) and name as difference the configuration possessed by gold.

Could gold exist without having atomic number 79? No amount of mere Twin Earth speculation can answer the question any more than for water. We need to look at how gold or water are *actually* constituted and what properties they actually have. As far as we know, even if the details have not all been discovered, having atomic number 79 and being composed of H_2O metaphysically determine, and thereby explain, at least some, and perhaps all, of the specific properties of gold and water, respectively. Not all of the properties, it must be reiterated, since others – those that flow from being a metal and being a liquid, for example – are determined, and thereby explained, by more generic atomic features of gold and water. Given that gold and water are generically a metal and a liquid, that is just what we would expect. Now this does not answer all of the questions that could be raised about the relationship between a compound material stuff such as gold or water and its underlying structure. We will look at some of these when the discussion turns to properties in Chapter 7.

5.2 The Porphyrian Tree

The basic idea behind the Porphyrian Tree, as it has come to be called, goes back at least to Plato, was highly developed in Aristotle, refined in Porphyry (*c.*234–305 AD) and handed down through medieval philosophy to the modern period, where it survived in Aristotelian logic (all logic prior to Frege) and still survives in contemporary taxonomy, particularly biological, via the work of Linnaeus.[7] The subject of taxonomy is a huge and fascinating one, but there is no room to go into any detail. All I will do is briefly sketch how Porphyrian taxonomic principles are used by real essentialism to partition the world.

Bear in mind that what taxonomy aims at is *real* classification. Hence Robert Pasnau is incorrect, or at least misleading, when he states that the species–genus framework of the Porphyrian Tree 'need not correspond to any real differences within things' (Pasnau, forthcoming).[8] It aims precisely at the real classification of things based on their essences. Since everything has one and only one essence, there can only be one correct scheme of classification for each thing. It may look as though there can be competing schemes, but this is because certain rules will not have been adhered to. (The details will have to be supplied on another occasion.) For instance, the omission of intermediate (or, as they are traditionally called, subalternate) species will produce a structure that looks different from a more complete one that includes them. Again, if the taxonomist ignores levels of generality between species she will produce a structure that is extensionally correct but classifies things in the wrong order. Further, if she ignores the precise sifting or filtering process involved in constructing a Porphyrian Tree she will produce a non-exhaustive classification, whereas correct taxonomy aims at completeness.

There is much that needs to be said, and cannot be here, about whether there is only one correct way to classify every species. But let's go back to the question left hanging in Chapter 3.5. Could it be that we can alternatively choose *animal* as the genus to which *human* belongs, with *rational* as the specific difference, or the converse? I think we do not have liberty here, but that one choice – the former – is more correct than the other. The reason is to do with hierarchy. Humans belong to a hierarchy of living things – from the merely vegetative, which we call plants, through the sentient, which we call animals (pure and simple), to the rational, which is the humans. Now in case the reader should think this a highly simplistic categorization that ignores the subtleties of evolutionary biology, I discuss and defend it at length in Chapter 8. I note here simply that one does not need to know much about biology to see that living things do come in grades – that sentience *adds* to mere vegetative nature, and that being rational is, ontologically, something over and above mere sentience, in terms of the powers conferred on the living thing. (For more on the entailment relations between powers and a general notion of superiority of powers, see Chapter 10.5.) Because rationality is best seen as a power that adds to mere vegetative and sentient nature, to classify a human as a rational animal is to recognize this ontological truth: a human being is a kind of animal, possessing both vegetative and sentient powers, as do all animals, but with the addition of rationality that puts humans on a higher level in the ontological hierarchy. This does *not* mean that humans have more than one nature, viz. a vegetative nature, a sentient one, and a rational one. There is one and only one nature for each entity (see Chapter 4.2). What it means is that the single, unified nature of the human being is structured in such a way that the genus *animal* is combined with the specific difference *rational*.

Consider a different case. Recall the definition of fish as a water-dwelling vertebrate with gills in the mature case. Here the genus is *water-dwelling vertebrate* and the specific difference is *[possessing] gills in the mature case*. Why couldn't the definition reverse the genus and specific difference? Here the answer has nothing obviously to do with hierarchy, but is connected to the idea that gills are a modification of a more general aquatic vertebrate body plan. Hence there is more than one way in which the order of categorization of genus and specific difference can be justified. Two matters should, however, be noted – one irrelevant and the other of possible but doubtful relevance. The irrelevant point is the order of evolutionary development. Suppose, as the evolutionary story goes, humans evolved from more primitive animals and that fish evolved from more primitive vertebrates without gills. (I say more about evolution in Chapters 8, 9 and 10.

Note also that 'more primitive than' means no more than 'earlier in the evolutionary tree', though the use of 'primitive' by biologists still usually connotes, in the traditional metaphysical sense bequeathed by Linnaean taxonomy, hierarchy and levels of perfection.) Still, the justification for categorizing the genera and differentia in each case has nothing to do with the thought that the specific difference appeared later in evolution than the genus, i.e. that vertebrates without gills appeared before ones with gills and that non-rational animals appeared before rational ones. Even if the order of development turns out to have been the reverse, the reasons for categorization would be the same, namely having a power, in the case of humans, that went beyond the merely animal, and having a variation, in the case of fish, on a more general aquatic vertebrate body plan. Neither chronological order nor the order of efficient causation of one species by another is to be confused with the levels of generality and specificity inherent in a species. This confusion is, as I argue in Chapter 9, at the heart of the cladistic approach to species classification.

The other point, which I consider doubtfully but possibly relevant, concerns numbers. Why can't the essentialist just say that having gills is specific to fish, and being an aquatic vertebrate generic, because there are more species of aquatic vertebrates than there are possessors of gills? (I do not know whether this is true, but suppose it is.) And isn't *animal* the genus for humans, and *rational* the specific difference, because there are more animals than there are rational beings? Doesn't the identification of genus and specific difference, then, depend on which of the two is more common? Now this might be relevant. It might be that, although the nature of a thing is a wholly non-relative matter, the carving of that nature into genus and specific difference is at least relative to which is more common. If so, it would not make essences in any way subjective; nor would it make them contingent. It would mean simply that the way in which we separated out the genus and specific difference within the essence depended on other facts not dependent on the target kind's intrinsic constitution.

Nevertheless, I do not see any good reason for taking this approach, since we have adequate resources for justifying the choice of genus and specific difference without it. Even if the universe contained far more kinds of rational beings than it did animals, we should still treat *animal* as the genus of *human* because we can see that rationality adds to the purely sentient and vegetative nature of a thing. What about a world containing only many different kinds of disembodied rational minds and no animal apart from humans? Granted it would be harder in such a case to conceive of the way in which being rational was more specific than being merely animal, but conceivability is not always a good guide to possibility and the fact is that there could, even in such a world, have been non-rational animals. Similarly, even if there were far more kinds of possessors of gills than aquatic vertebrates, having gills is still a more specific modification of a more general aquatic vertebrate body plan. How an animal's body is structured overall is, in other words, more generic than how it carries out a specific function such as respiration. It is for reasons such as these, then, that I conclude that generality and specificity are not to be interpreted statistically, and that they are non-relative matters.

To return from this slight digression, then, the easiest way to construct a classificatory tree is to work from the bottom up, thinking first of the species one wants to classify, and tracking backwards through higher and more general classifications until one reaches the highest generality, or the *summum genus* within the classification. At every stage, the aim is to filter out the classes of objects that do not share the species of the target class, working at a higher level of generality at each stage. Any complete classification is going to be detailed and complex, so we can only work here with simple examples designed to illustrate the basic method. So, for instance, the structure in Figure 5.1 gives the classification of fish.

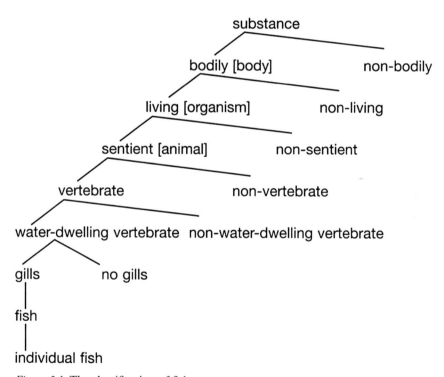

Figure 5.1 The classification of fish

Note: The terms in square brackets are simply the nominalization of the adjectival, positive species term on the same level conjoined with its immediately higher genus: bodily + substance = body, living + body = organism, etc. Sometimes the noun is already expressed by the species term, e.g. vertebrate, and sometimes there is no term ready to hand, in which case we can just nominalize and neologise at the same time. Henceforth I will omit terms in square brackets unless clarity requires it.

Since modern taxonomy is only roughly in accord with Porphyrian principles, the current state of things makes it very difficult just to read off a
metaphysical classification from the scientific classifications currently available.
Figure 5.2 gives a metaphysical classification of gold. This classification
makes use of scientific (chemical, metallurgical, etc.) divisions, but would
not be found as presented here in any scientific textbook, since for one
thing scientists do not use disjoint classification. Instead they simply
place kinds under other kinds without aiming at exhaustiveness and
without filtering out everything not belonging to a kind so as to concentrate
on the particular kind being classified.[9] Secondly, the Porphyrian Tree
makes use of metaphysical as well as natural scientific categories. The classification is metaphysical: it is designed to display what a thing *is* in its
essence. But metaphysics must be informed by science; hence scientific

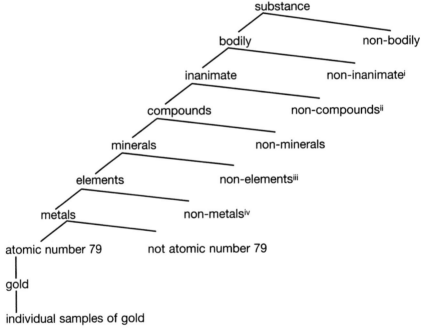

Figure 5.2 A metaphysical classification of gold.

Notes:
[i] The Porphyrian Tree essentially involves partition into disjoint classes – for some
class F, the Fs and the things that are not F. It also requires, where possible, a
positive classification for the entity being classified. It is difficult to see how one
could give a wholly positive classification of the non-living, since the very concept
is parasitic on the concept of the living; hence the best we can do for the non-living
is to classify it as such – as inanimate. But to register the fact that we are focusing
on positive features of the non-living, we mark its complement by a negative classification – hence the awkward-sounding 'non-inanimate'. Of course, looking at it

categories will always be involved in classifying anything which is, at least in part, the proper object of study of one of the sciences.

By employing metaphysical categories as well (such as *substance* and *body*), the Tree shows that nothing is *only* a proper object of scientific study in the narrow empirical sense. The lower down the Tree one progresses, the more the categories take on an empirical character, as one would expect. Hence it is wrong to separate metaphysical trees from empirical ones as Lowe does (1999a: 184), the former called by him 'categorial hierarchies' and the latter 'taxonomic structures'. Reality is a unity, and whatever falls under an empirical classification by that fact falls under some metaphysical classification: hence there must be a single tree for any species of thing that is an object of natural science, one that represents both its empirical and its metaphysical status. Lowe is right that categories such as *dog* or *tiger* are not metaphysical: still, all animals fall generically into the same metaphysical

purely logically, 'non-inanimate' is still a positive classification, being a double negative. But conceptually, and metaphysically, we should think of it as negative – all those entities that are not in the category for which we are making further partitions, irrespective of what the members of the complement may have in common. That is, we abstract away from their commonality and focus instead on the commonality between the non-living things.

ii A note about the compound/non-compound distinction: I leave it open for present purposes whether there are any material metaphysical simples, though I doubt it (see further Chapter 10.5). One might countenance the possibility of objects that are physically indivisible even though metaphysically complex – perhaps certain 'fundamental' particles fall under this category. If this were true, the particles would have parts, but the laws of physics would prevent their being separated. Since I take the laws of nature to be metaphysically necessary (see Chapter 6.4), however, this is not a distinction I can admit. If the object is physically indivisible, it will be metaphysically indivisible – indivisible in no possible world in which the object exists. Yet that this could be true and the object genuinely have parts is highly doubtful, at least given the plausible view that any object with parts seems to have an innate tendency to disintegration under certain conditions. Does an atom of gold fall under *compound* or *non-compound*? Since we know atoms not to be physically simple, it should fall under the former. But we may also wish to distinguish between homeomerous and non-homeomerous substances, i.e. ones that have parts essentially the same as the wholes and ones that do not. Gold can be divided into gold parts, but a gold atom cannot. Hence we may wish to include this partition under *compound*; gold would be a homeomerous compound, whereas a gold atom, like other atoms, would be a non-homeomerous compound.

iii Among the non-elemental minerals are such things as phosphates, sulphides, oxides, and sulphates.

iv Among the non-metallic elements are such things as antimony, bismuth, graphite, and sulphur, as well as natural alloys, phosphides, and silicides. Some are classified as semi-metals, others as definite non-metals, but for our purposes all of these come under non-metal, that is to say anything which is not a metal, including semi-metals.

category of *substance*, and the species of animal are in that sense all on a par. Moreover, among the animals there are, for instance, the sentient and the merely vegetative; and of course also the rational. (For more on this see Chapters 8, 9 and 10.) These too are categories of animal, but they are not the sole province of zoological or biological study: the metaphysician too must take a direct interest in categories such as *sentient animal* and *rational animal*.

Thus it is the unity of reality, as shown by the blending of the metaphysical and the empirical in categories of object, that demands the unification of taxonomic structures. Moreover, I would go further and claim that it is for the metaphysician to determine the extent of a category's empirical content (again, informed as much as possible by the relevant scientific discipline). It is also for the metaphysician to oversee the final structure of the Tree. Empirical classification only gets us so far, sometimes gets it wrong, is not as organized as one might hope, and must be governed by metaphysical oversight if it is to make a proper contribution to the essentialist enterprise and to the pursuit of knowledge in general.

The Porphyrian Tree forms an upper semi-lattice, as attributed by Thomason (1969) to all taxonomic systems (without reference to the Tree). Hence any two kinds K_1 and K_2 have a least upper bound (LUB), that is, a lowest higher kind that contains them both; if they are on the same path, the LUB will be one of K_1 or K_2; if they are on different paths, it will be a third kind K_3. Further, for any K_1 and K_2, if they have a greatest lower bound (GLB; a highest lower kind), it will be either K_1 or K_2; hence there can be no cross-classification, i.e. no third kind K_3 which is the GLB of K_1 and K_2. (Ellis wrongly attributes the disjointness feature to the system's being an upper semi-lattice (Ellis 2001: 56); in fact this is an *additional* property not generally held by semi-lattices. Universal cross-classification would produce a lower semi-lattice, which if added to an upper semi-lattice would yield a complete lattice.) Moreover, the Porphyrian Tree essentially contains both a *summum genus*, a genus above which there is no other, and an *infima species*, a species lower than which there is no other: these correspond to the universal and empty elements in Thomason (1969).[10] The reason why there must be a summum genus and an infima species within a tree is that otherwise there could be no definition at all. If an entity could fall, in principle, under ever higher genera, or be a member of a species that contained ever lower species, it would be impossible to give its definition. In the former case, the proximate genus would be undefinable since there would be no final answer to the question 'What is it?' Whatever answer one gave to the question of the proximate genus, it would be incomplete. One could say, for instance, 'This thing is an animal', but what is an animal? One could say, 'A sentient organism', but then what is an organism? One could say, 'A living body', but then what is a body? If we could not stop at a supremum, in this case *substance*, we would have only the appearance of a proximate genus, not the reality. Similarly, if species could forever be broken up into smaller species, we could never reach a specific difference. For every time we thought we had reached it, it would turn out that what we had reached was either an accident, and so no part of the definition, or else just another part of the genus of the object being classified, with the differentia yet to be found.

The illustration and explanation of the Porphyrian method of classification could easily occupy a book in itself. I will have more to say about it in the course of this one, but for now let us look at one more example, the classic tree of man (see Figure 5.3). There are a number of things to be said about this tree. First, it does not look remotely like the sort of classification of humans given by contemporary biologists. There is no single agreed scheme among them, but they all look very different from that given in Figure 5.3. (See further Bilsborough 1992: 18–21.) A typical, albeit abbreviated, example is given in Figure 5.4.[11] From *Hominoidea* to *Homo*, a fuller tree looks like that in Figure 5.5. Secondly, the Porphyrian division does not look especially scientific in itself, whatever its differences from current classifications. Thirdly, it might be thought to get the definition of human beings wrong. Finally, as a general parting shot, opponents of such a tree, and of the Porphyrian method in general, would regard it as hopelessly out of date and reminiscent of the worst armchair biology.

I will say more about species generally, and human nature in particular, in Chapters 9 and 10. For the moment, the following points should be made. First, a principal reason why the contemporary classification, along with many other taxonomic schemes in biology, looks a lot unlike the Porphyrian

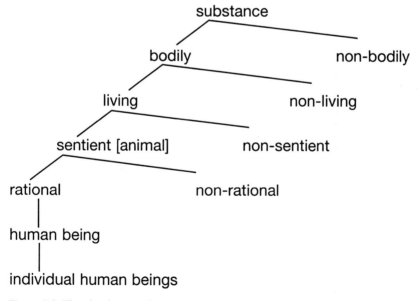

Figure 5.3 The classic tree of man.

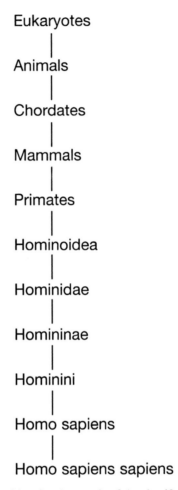

Eukaryotes

|

Animals

|

Chordates

|

Mammals

|

Primates

|

Hominoidea

|

Hominidae

|

Homininae

|

Hominini

|

Homo sapiens

|

Homo sapiens sapiens

Figure 5.4 A typical but abbreviated example of the classification of humans given by contemporary biologists. [11]

Note: Hominoidea include 'lesser' apes such as gibbons and 'great' apes such as chimpanzees, gorillas, orangutans, 'human-like' ancestors of modern humans, and modern humans. (By presenting this taxonomy I should not be taken to endorse it, especially as regards humans and 'human-like' species.) The line of descent then separates these out until *homo sapiens sapiens* is reached, i.e. modern man.

scheme is that since the advent of evolutionary theory it has been the increasingly explicit purpose of taxonomists to make classifications that reflect lines of evolutionary descent. As Joseph LaPorte succinctly puts it (2004: 20), 'in biological classification, the first aim is to reflect history' (LaPorte 2004: 20). He goes on to cite David Hull to the effect that the main aim of taxonomy since Darwin has been to mirror evolutionary descent in hierarchical classifications using the basic Linnaean categories (such

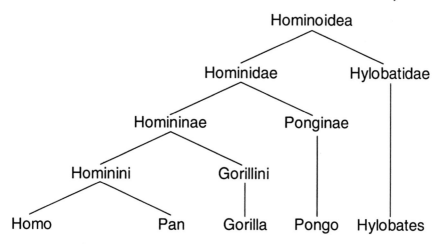

Figure 5.5 A fuller classification of humans, from *Hominoidea* to *Homo*

Note: I have reconstructed this tree from the classification by Andrews cited in Bilsborough (1992): 20. However, in light of the common view that *pan* (chimpanzees) are the closest relatives of *homo*, I have grouped the former with the latter rather than under *gorillini*. This should not be taken to be an endorsement of such classification, only a representation of current thinking among biologists.

as kingdom, class, order, genus, species, now supplemented by many other ranks such as domain, phylum, family, and super- or sub-ranks of these).

It is central to real essentialism that historical origin and essence are separate notions. This is explained by means of the fourfold distinction of causes. We have already noted that essence has a material cause, in the sense that all material substances are compounds of form and matter. For substances that have a natural goal or purpose (paradigmatically, living things), there is also a final cause – that to which substances with teleology naturally tend. Substances have in addition, and as I have already explained at length, a formal cause – the substantial form that makes them what they are. But they also have an efficient cause – that by which they come into existence.

Now one of the main problems in identifying essence with historical descent is that it confuses the efficient and formal causes both of a substance and of the species to which it belongs. It does not follow from the fact that a substance or species has a certain historical origin that its *essence* is to have that origin, even if it has its origin necessarily. In the case of a particular substance – say, a lump of gold – if the Kripkean thesis of necessity of origin were true (about which more in Chapter 7), and if it were necessarily true of the lump of gold that it could not have been originally composed of different atoms, it would not follow that its essence was to have come into existence by the composition of those atoms. Its essence would still be that of being a metal with atomic number 79. The lump's line of descent – the historical process that actually led to its being formed, which for all we know might be traceable back to the earliest moments of the universe – does not tell us what gold *is*. So why should we expect it to be different for species as such, including biological ones?

Hence if we accept the evolutionary story according to which human descent historically followed something approximating the line given above, we have no reason to think that this will tell us what humans are. The Porphyrian Tree, by contrast, must not be read as an account of historical origins – whatever the entity classified. It is a *synchronic* structure designed to partition the target species (the one being classified) in such a way as to distinguish it from everything else in the universe. That is the main reason why it looks so different from a taxonomic structure informed by facts of descent or historical origin.[12]

Secondly, the Porphyrian Tree is scientific in the broadest sense: it aims to display our knowledge of what a thing is according to strict principles of classification. But it is also not a pure product of empirical or natural science. Rather, it is a metaphysical structure informed by natural science. The higher one ascends in the structure, the more metaphysical the categories involved – such as substance, body, material, immaterial, compound, simple, quality, quantity, and so on depending on what one is classifying. The lower one goes, the more empirical are the categories – such as mammal, vertebrate, water-dweller, metal, and the like. Categories around the middle of a given structure are likely to be a mix of the metaphysical and the empirical. I will show in Chapter 8 that categories such as *living* and *animal* are like this.

Real essentialism is committed to the position that natural science does not tell us everything there is to know about what there is and what things are like. It also holds that metaphysics is superior to natural science in that, by providing the fundamental principles for reasoning about things, it governs natural science by drawing the boundaries beyond which the latter must not stray. Nelson Goodman espoused a weaker form of this idea when he famously said that 'the practical scientist does the business; but the philosopher keeps the books' (quoted with approval by Wiggins 1980: 119). The only business the natural scientist legitimately engages in is empirical observation and/or the construction of theories to unify, explain, predict and control natural phenomena using the tools that are specific to his trade. The 'bookkeeping' function of the philosopher in general, and the metaphysician in particular, goes beyond the maintenance of logical consistency and conceptual clarity (the sorts of activity Goodman had in mind) and extends into ensuring that the natural scientist abides by the non-negotiable principles of ontology, some of which I have already discussed and more of which will follow. Hence the essentialist makes no apology for employing a taxonomic structure that, although informed by the best observations, discoveries, and conjectures natural science has to offer, is ineliminably metaphysical in nature.

Finally, maybe the tree of man given above is just wrong? The objection is that if there were an example of, say, Locke's famous 'rational parrot' (Locke 1975: II.27.8, pp. 333–4), then there would be a rational animal that was not human, so this cannot be the definition of human beings. This raises some important issues I will broach here and expand in Chapter 10. First, there is the question of why *animal* should be the proximate genus of *human*. Why not *mammal*, or *primate*, or one of the genera in the modern line of descent presented above?

On the negative side, in case the essentialist should think that we need to go lower than *animal* so as to ward off the possibility of rational parrots, going lower will not help. Leaving aside rational parrots, which are, I would contend, metaphysically impossible given everything we know about *parrots*, there is the apparent metaphysical possibility of a rational animal that isn't human. Suppose there were, unknown to us, on some distant planet a species of creature – call its members *ranimals* – that satisfied the criteria for rationality and animality. Maybe it evolved according to the laws of evolution on that planet; maybe God spontaneously created this race of rational animal without telling us. Why couldn't ranimals be a new kind of mammal as well (let alone a bird or a reptile, for that matter)? Or a new kind of primate? Returning to planet Earth, suppose – as some conjecture[13] – Neanderthals were not of our species, incapable of breeding with us; and that their body plan and behaviour were such that we would not think of them as recognizably human. But suppose they were rational. Again, no matter how similar they were to us, they would not be us any more than ranimals would be us; hence going even lower down the genera will not help.

Modern taxonomy has us now as *homo sapiens sapiens*, to distinguish us precisely from what are thought of as archaic *homo sapiens* (*rhodesiensis*, *idaltu*, and even *neanderthalis*), distinguished from us at least by skull shape and capacity (and probably by much else, though we have little hard evidence to go on). If they were rational, and if they were significantly different from us bodily, then not even *rational primate* or *rational homo* would give the definition of human beings on the assumption that *rational animal* did not. In other words, if we allow the definition of human beings to be refuted by the possibility of rational animals with a distinct bodily constitution, then descending the hierarchy to find a more determinate genus will be of no assistance.

On the positive side, I contend that we get into problems with possible counterexamples to the definition of humans as rational animals only if we think of *animal* as a purely biological category. Instead we need to think of it as partly biological and partly *metaphysical*. Animals are distinguished by a certain range of properties that are accessible not just to biologists, even though biologists can assist in providing the *detail* of what processes support or characterize animals and in filtering out those entities that do not undergo the relevant processes, have the requisite characteristics, and so on. But animality is primarily a metaphysical concept since it marks out beings with certain kinds of power and capacity (sensory awareness no matter how primitive; appetition – the power to act on sensory knowledge in the pursuit of what is good for the entity and avoidance of what is bad; locomotion; and more). I will say more about this in Chapter 8, but the point is that if we treat *animal* as a partly metaphysical category we can still regard it as the proximate genus of *human being*. Metaphysically, a human is a sentient organism, an animal, even if humans belong to more determinate, purely biological categories such as *mammal*. Since, in searching for essence, we are after a metaphysical definition, not a biological one (whatever the biological aspects), we need not – and cannot – go further down the hierarchy, since lower genera are purely biological.

Now Elizabeth Anscombe briefly addresses the question of the rational parrot, and she contends that the definition of man as a rational animal 'suffices if, so far as we know, there *are* no animals except men that satisfy it' (Anscombe 2005: 28). Unlike mathematical or logical definitions, where merely imagining a thing that satisfied the definiens but not the defini-niendum would suffice to refute the definition, a definition of a plant, animal, or chemical substance is not, she says, refuted by the mere possibi-lity of such a thing. She says one would have to 'believe' in rational parrots and so on. Belief has nothing to do with it, though: instead she must mean that such animals would have to exist. Anscombe's approach must be resis-ted by the essentialist, because if it is followed there will be no definition of human beings at all. Now, she could say that even if my hypothetical rani-mals were possible, the proposition that man is a rational animal would still be necessarily true. This is correct, but only insofar as *rational animal* would then become the *genus* of *human being*, so man would still necessarily be a rational animal, but only generically.

What, then, would be the specific difference? Man is necessarily whatever he is essentially, but if he has no specific difference there will be *nothing* that he necessarily is as a matter of his essence. For all we know, ranimals might be lurking in some as yet unexplored remote rainforest (as was once sup-posed of orangutans). Anscombe cannot reply that this is a mere epistemic possibility and so irrelevant, since she denies that *metaphysical* possibility is relevant to the definition of man as well. But I contend that, since ranimals are metaphysically possible, on her understanding of the issue man will necessarily still be a rational animal, only rationality will be part of the genus. If she insists it is the specific difference, then it will only be con-tingently so. But man is necessarily what he is *both* generically *and* specifi-cally, and if the specific difference of rationality is contingent, where is the necessary difference? We have already seen that going lower down the hier-archy will not help, since there might be rational primates, rational apes, rational *homo*, even rational *homo sapiens*, all no less rational or animal than rational animals of any other kind.

The better answer, I claim, is that any truly rational animal, *if* such were metaphysically possible, would still be human. Hence, even if it did not have the body plan or physical constitution were are familiar with, still, if it were genuinely an animal and genuinely rational it would in fact be one of us; which would only go to show that having what is now thought of as the specifically human body plan or genotype, and so on, were not essential to humans after all, but only contingent accidents much like race, hair colour, or skin colour. This conclusion is less bizarre than it sounds. It will seem strange only if we are convinced that being human is merely a biological category, or a genetic one, or even a matter of belonging to a certain line of descent. (Not even line of descent would help Anscombe, since it is metaphysically possible for there to be ranimals with the same line of descent as us.)

I claim that it is none of these. Being human, just like being an animal, is primarily a metaphysical category with biological content that gives us the ways in which humanity physically manifests itself. (There will be a biology of ranimals too, if they exist.) If we remove the fixation on biology (supplemented by chemistry and other natural sciences) as the source of all knowledge of what it is to be human, we remove the supposed self-evidence of the idea that rational animals without what we think of as the specifically human body plan or genotype would not be human. Further, if we place the appropriate emphasis on *rationality* we will have more reason to see ranimals as human. If they really were rational – if they had the full panoply of characteristics that make for rationality in us, including, crucially, the capacity for abstract thought and the communication of it – then I do not think we would have nearly as much trouble in recognizing them as one of us as one might think. Anything less than full rationality and they would not be rational, so they would lack the specific difference of humans. (Such might be true of the pre-human hominids.) Anything less than full animality and they would not fall under our genus. (Such would be true of rational robots or computers, if such were possible – though I deny it. It would also be true of disembodied spirits such as angels and God.) I conclude that we do not have a good reason for abandoning the definition of man as a rational animal, but we do have good reasons for maintaining it.

5.3 The Analogy of Being

It is tempting for the real essentialist to think that we can construct a Tree of Everything. We begin with *being*, it might be supposed, as the highest genus of all, and then we break it up into the kinds of being, descending to ever greater specificity, until we reach the individual beings. There are various reasons why even the most ardent essentialist should resist this thought. For instance, certain categories cut across other categories, making anything like a perspicuous tree impossible. Privations are not real beings but what are called *beings of reason* or *logical beings*, that is to say neither forms, nor matter, nor compounds of matter and form, nor in any way a determination of some potentiality. A hole in the ground is not a presence but an absence. Nor is it a mere modification of something positive, namely its physical container. It is a kind of being, but one that is in some sense logically constructed out of real beings that are positive determinations of potentiality. This does not mean you cannot fall into a hole, or that when you do you are only falling into a logical construction! What it means is that the very act of falling into a hole has to be analysed in terms of positive being in order to understand what it really involves. You can describe the shape and structure of the hole in positive terms and analyse the process of falling as a complex relation between your body and those positive modifications of the ground.[14]

The category of *privation*, however, cuts across many other categories, including most if not all of the categories of accident. It would have to be on the putative Tree of Everything, but it would lack perspicuity to give it a separate listing altogether, as Hoffman and Rosenkrantz (1994: 18–21) do, or to add it as a rider to every other category for which privation is possible. Neither approach shows clearly the relation between privations and other kinds of being. The same goes for negations, relations, and possibilia considered *as logical beings*. Yet to divide the Tree of Everything into the real beings and logical beings again obscures the phenomena by treating the logical beings as though they bore no relation to the real beings from which they are constructed in the mind. The same again applies to contingent being and necessary being, or complete and incomplete being (e.g. substance and part), which cut across the other divisions. For reasons of both practice and principle, the Tree of Everything is not something for which the essentialist should strive. At most he should aim at constructing Trees of Things, with the objective that everything there is appear on at least one tree. This is, I believe, achievable.

What I want to concentrate on, though, is the main reason of principle for opposing a Tree of Everything, namely that *being* is not a genus. This takes us to the famous Scholastic doctrine of the Analogy of Being. (For a useful commentary on Aquinas's explanation of the analogy, see Bobik 1965: 106–18.) In brief, the argument is as follows. Being cannot be a specific difference of any thing, nor a property, nor an accident. If it were a specific difference it would differentiate things of different kinds. But being does the very opposite: it *unites* things of different kinds, all of which are beings, whether real, logical, actual, potential, necessary, possible, substantial, accidental, and so on. So being cannot be a specific difference, or indeed a differentiator of any sort. Nor is it a property of anything, since properties are what follow from a thing's nature, i.e. because of its nature. But being doesn't *follow* from the nature of anything, it is *part* of the nature of everything: not a part distinct from matter or form, but of the nature of matter and form themselves, since they are beings. (Since being is not a property, neither is existence, which is actual being. It is consistent to hold (1) that I do not have the property of existing, since existence is not a property of anything (not even concepts, contra Frege), and (2) that it is true of *me* that I exist, since I consist of the actualization of matter by a substantial form; and that is what it is for me to exist.) Nor is being an accident of anything, as though it were present in a thing but could be absent. Every being is necessarily a being.

What's left? Well, maybe being is a *species*, i.e. a combination of genus and specific difference. Yet if it were a species it would be contained in a higher genus – but there is no concept more general than being. Moreover, if being were a species, then it would give the essence of everything that fell under it, i.e. all beings would be essentially beings. But then all beings would have the same essence, which is obviously false. The only other possibility, as far as being as a category is concerned, is that it is a *genus*. That is to say, being is the summum genus under which all other things fall in the Tree of Everything.

There are, however, serious difficulties with the idea that being is a genus. First is how we are then to break up being in order to form the first divisions in the tree. The standard, and most plausible, first division is into substance and accident – everything is either one or the other. If this is right we need to find the specific differences of being that constitute substance as substance and accident as accident. What could these be? The obvious answer is that substantiality itself and accidence itself are the differentiae of being. But substantiality and accidence are themselves beings – universals instantiated by all substances and all accidents, respectively – and so we would have being differentiated by being. Yet this cannot work, because the specific difference of something has to be wholly *extrinsic* to what it differentiates. So, for example, the specific difference of gold is to have atomic number 79. This difference is wholly extrinsic to gold's genus *metal*, since being a metal is no part of what it is to have atomic number 79. Having atomic number 79 may *entail* being a metal, but the difference itself is in no way explained or understood in terms of being a metal: it is explained and understood solely in terms of an atom's having 79 protons in its nucleus.

By contrast, being a substance does not merely entail having being, but it is part of what it *is* to be a substance that substances are beings. Therefore substantiality is not wholly extrinsic to being, and if it were a differentia of being this would mean that being was differentiated partly by itself. Yet nothing can differentiate itself in whole or in part, on pain of the relevant definition's being circular. So what could differentiate being? The only thing, as it were, that is wholly extrinsic to being is – nothing. Yet it is impossible for nothing to be a differentia: differentiae are always something or other, some element of reality that determines the specific identity of a thing. This is one reason why being cannot be a genus.

The second concerns whether 'being' is univocal, equivocal, or analogous. If it were univocal it would be like terms such as 'human', 'dolphin', 'water', 'oak tree', and so on. All of the things that respectively fall under these terms do so in the same way, for the same reason – they share the essence expressed by each term. Being does not work this way. When we abstract *humanity* from individual humans, or *oak tree* from individual oaks, we abstract away the accidents and are left with the essence. We cannot do this with being, since it is heterogeneous: there is substantial being, accidental being, complete being, incomplete being, necessary being, contingent being, possible being, absolute being, relative being, intrinsic being, extrinsic being, and so on. These features of being are not accidents from which we can abstract to form a clear, complete, and homogeneous concept of being.

For each and every kind of being, the way in which being manifests itself is essential to that kind (contingent beings are essentially contingent, accidental beings are essentially accidental, and so on). To try to abstract away from these essential features in order to arrive at a concept of being *as such* is a metaphysical and conceptual mistake, since it is to abstract from what is essential to the kinds of being.

It might be objected that we do not abstract only from accidents, because we also abstract from specific differences: we can abstract from *rationality* and consider man only as *animal*, investigating what humans have in common with other animals that are not rational. But, as I argued earlier, the kinds of being are not specific differences. When I try to abstract from, say, substantiality, I abstract from the entire essence of the thing that is a substance, *its being included*. What I am left with is not being as such, but nothing. Hence 'being' is not a univocal term.

Nor, however, is it equivocal. If it were an equivocal term, like 'bank', 'letter' or 'table', I could disambiguate it and so form wholly distinct concepts of wholly distinct kinds of thing, as we do with other equivocal terms. But the kinds of being are not wholly distinct: they do have something in common, namely that they are all *beings* of one kind or another. Were we to think of being as equivocal, we would lose the unity of things, the oneness in the many, just as we lose the diversity in oneness if we treat being as univocal. We must, then, treat being as neither univocal nor equivocal, but as *analogous*. 'Being' is an analogous term, i.e. it is applied analogously to the things that fall under it, just as we can apply the term 'angry' to people and skies, or 'healthy' to animals and diets. We can, if we like, say that being *acts* like a genus. 'Being' expresses the essence of all beings, but incompletely. It does not differentiate between beings. But it is not a true genus. It does not single out some things from others by what the former have in common with each other but not with the latter. *Everything* is a being of some kind or other. Contra Hoffman and Rosenkrantz (1994: 18) and Lowe (2006: 39), then, it does not belong on any ontological tree. Being is like a genus but not truly a genus. It is a genus by analogy, and, as it is traditionally called, a *transcendental* concept.[15]

5.4 Individuation

When it comes to the problem of individuation, real essentialism holds most generally that individuation depends on the kind of thing we are concerned with. So, for example: accidents are individuated by the substances in which they inhere; propagated objects such as beams of light are individuated by their sources of propagation; and privations such as shadows and holes are individuated by the real objects that give rise to them – in the former case the relevant source of occlusion, in the latter the relevantly shaped source of enclosure. I will say more about various non-substantial entities in Chapter 7, including artefacts, which I take to be ontologically dependent entities of a certain sort. Here I want to outline the essentialist theory of individuation of material substances, since these are the paradigm, both ontologically and epistemologically, for our understanding of individuation in general. (Further details can be found in Oderberg 2002a.)

Since every substance is a compound of matter and form, the hylemorphist unsurprisingly looks for the principle of individuation in one of these metaphysical constituents. Although hylemorphists differ, by far the dominant theory is that *matter* has to be this principle. The fundamental thought is that form is universal, giving ('communicating', to use the traditional jargon) to each thing that shares it, for some particular essence, the identity by virtue of which it can be truly said to be *united* to everything else that has the essence – its *co-essentials*, as we might put it. Since the reality of substance is a phenomenon of unity in diversity, and since form is the principle of unity, the other major constituent of substance, namely matter, must be the principle of diversity. In other words, matter must in some way give each substance its individuality within a kind. This way of thinking, the hylemorphist contends, is but a refinement of commonsensical thinking about the relationship between unity and plurality in the material world.

The thought that matter is the principle of individuation, however, has to be made more precise. We can do this by showing why certain other options, and certain interpretations of the fundamental thought, have to be ruled out. To begin with, although prime matter is one of the basic constituents of material substances, it is – perhaps surprisingly, one might think, given hylemorphism – *not* the principle of individuation. The reasons are: (1) it is common, i.e. multiply instantiable (wherever there is actuation by a substantial form), and it is a hallmark of individuality, including that of material substances, that it is, to use the traditional term, incommunicable.[16] We can say (following Lowe 1989: 38): x is an individual if and only if x is an instance of something y (other than itself) and x itself has no instances other than itself.[17] (2) Prime matter is indivisible, being mere potentiality, so it cannot serve as the basis of the division of a species or nature into individuals. We cannot say, 'Here is some prime matter, and there is some more', but we can say, 'Here is Socrates, and there is Callias', or in other words 'Here is prime matter informed by the nature of Socrates, and there is prime matter informed by the nature of Callias'. (We can call these 'Socrateity' and 'Calliaeity', but must not confuse them with haecceities or individual essences as postulated by Duns Scotus; these I reject as at least unwarranted. Socrateity just is general human nature as particularized in Socrates. The particularizing is done by matter, not by 'thisness'.)[18]

Secondly, the principle of individuation cannot be matter as possessing such-and-such determinate quantity, i.e. size, shape, volume, location ('quantity' should be taken broadly to include location, since it is really *dimensionality* which we should understand by quantity in this context). This is because determinate quantity is accidental, but accidents presuppose the existence (and hence individuation) of the individual substance in which they inhere, so the individuation of substance by accident would be circular. (I give only qualified endorsement to this standard objection, for reasons to be suggested shortly.)

Thirdly, the principle of individuation cannot be matter as disposed for the possession of such-and-such determinate quantity. Now, although such a disposition may not be accidental but essential to a thing's nature, it will not do. (1) Few if any substances have matter disposed to a determinate quantity (though many micro-particles do, and perhaps some micro-organisms), only to a *range* of quantities. (2) A disposition to quantity *follows* from the possession by matter of substantial form: it is *because* Socrates is human that he is disposed (speaking now of ranges) to a height greater than six inches; Socrates would not be so disposed if he were an ant. Hence, as will be explained, even if matter with a disposition to quantity were the principle of individuation, form would have to play a role in individuation by giving otherwise indifferent prime matter whatever it is that enables matter to individuate.

Fourthly, the substantial form, though it is in a sense the primary factor in individuation, is not the principle of individuation itself. It is the primary factor in individuation because of the sortal-dependency of identity.[19] This means that information by a specific form is what lays the ground, as it were, for numerical identity and diversity. Since the individual substance is brought into being by the union of prime matter and substantial form, it is not surprising that substantial form plays a role, and indeed a far more complicated one than is often thought. As for the basic point being made here, we can quote Aristotle in support:

> We assert, then, that substance is one of the categories of being; and that this substance is partly what is called matter, which by itself is not this individual; and partly form and specific difference, by which a thing is at once denominated individual; and, lastly, the composite of both.
> (Aristotle, *De Anima* II.i, 412a6–10) [20]

And commenting with approval on this passage, Aquinas says:

> Form is that by which a particular thing actually exists.[21]
> (Aquinas 1994: s.215, p. 73)

Since the question 'Is *a* the same as *b*?', in order to be answerable, must be expandable in terms of some kind *F* – 'Is the *a* the same *F* [dog, man, lump of wood] as *b*?' – we know that specific information makes individuation possible in the first place, and is in that sense primary, even if not the principle of individuation itself. Two reasons suffice to show that form cannot be the principle of individuation itself. (1) Form is common, whereas individuality is not (i.e. it is incommunicable to many, as noted earlier). (2) Matter is an essential part of the material substance, which is a composite of matter and form; but individuality must take account of the individual's essential parts; so form alone cannot confer individuality.

Fifthly, the existence of the material substance cannot be the principle of individuation. For we can conceive of individuals which do not exist, such as fictional objects, the hundredth president of the USA, and so on. One might object to this by saying that fictional objects, for example, have existence within their domain of quantification (Hamlet exists *in* the play, but not *in real life*). The reply is that we should not confuse existence as a presupposition of an object's behaviour or actions, or more broadly of its role within a certain frame of discourse, with real existence as the actualization of some form. We cannot conceive of Hamlet's being indecisive without conceiving of him as existing within the play; and we cannot conceive of the hundredth president of the USA's making an inarticulate speech without conceiving of him as existing. But we can, otherwise, conceive of a wholly non-existent individual, say a big brown bear, or a man who wins the presidency, without embedding the conception within any identifiable frame of discourse, and so without presupposing the thing's existence. Such a thing is still conceived of as an individual – as a particularized essence – and it contracts its species just as a species contracts its genus whether or not the species has any actual members. (Think of the genus *polygon*; now think of the species *chiliagon*; now think of some chiliagon.) Similarly, a sculptor's ideal prototype of a Greek muse already has individuality before he brings it into existence. Hence individuality must be contained in the essence of a thing, not in its existence.

So what *is* the principle of individuation? There are three elements to this, but only one which we should in general speak of as *the* principle of individuation. First, every material substance is the principle of its individuation by its own proper entity.[22] It is the very union of prime matter to substantial form that constitutes the individual substance, as surely as the coming together of cogs and wheels (or chips and plastic) constitutes an individual watch. Individuality follows necessarily from substantial being, and if this is how we should take the Quinean slogan 'no entity without identity', that slogan expresses an important truth.

Secondly, to add to what was said above concerning the primacy of form, we must say that form holds a higher place than matter in the identity of the complete composite substance. Matter as such is inchoative, and *of itself* no more inchoative of this rather than that substance; whereas form perfects and determines the substance, turning what is wholly indifferent into something determined and singular.[23] It is a lack of regard for this point that seems to be at the root of worries had by some philosophers about whether the matter that individuates is 'thick' or 'thin', an issue I will attempt to resolve in the ensuing discussion.

Thirdly, it is matter which is the principle of individuation, in this sense: it is the *chief intrinsic principle* by which the entire substantial composite is individuated.[24] It is matter which divides common form, i.e. which turns the communicable into the incommunicable, and which in union with form results in that which is 'indistinct in itself and distinct from others'.[25] The three claims are, then, to be reconciled in this way: it is the initial or logically prior influence of common form on otherwise indifferent matter which gives to matter the character by which it individuates the substance which, as a whole composite, is constituted as an individual entity. So when we say that the substance is the principle of its individuation by its own entity, we pay regard to the fact that every material substance, being a this-such, is therefore individual; but we do not exclude the further fact that every material substance has a component, namely its matter, by virtue of which it is a this-such. Individuals can self-individuate without that self-individuation being primitive or incapable of further analysis, just as pianists can by definition play the piano without their pianism being incapable of further analysis.

But what kind of matter is it that is the chief intrinsic principle of individuation? The traditional formula adopted by medieval philosophers following Aquinas, which I call PDM, is that the principle of individuation is 'designated matter' (*materia signata*), more exactly matter possessing *quantity*, even more precisely matter possessing *indeterminate* quantity.[26] The quantity is generally recognized as having to be indeterminate because of the simple fact that substances vary in their material quantity over time without losing their individuality. (I say individuality rather than identity – although it is also true that they can vary in material quantity without losing their identity – because of a crucial difference between individuality and identity which will be mentioned later.)

Again, omitting details, I suggest we can elaborate PDM by adopting a proposal made but rejected by Kit Fine (1994b: 32 ff.) in his work on Aristotle's theory of individuation. It is well known that Aristotle did not go so far as to formulate the idea of *designated* matter, but only of matter as such as individuating substance. This leaves it open whether he meant thin (prime) matter or thick (proximate) matter, and if the latter in what *way*, or by means of what *characteristics*, it individuated. Fine, critical of Aristotle in this regard, is impressed by the puzzle of Socrates and Callias: 'Suppose that Socrates has at one time the same matter as Callias has at another time. Then their matter is the same; their form is the same; and since each of them is a compound of matter and form, they themselves are the same' (Fine 1994b: 14).

Now, although Fine canvasses various options for dealing with the puzzle, and appears to dispose of them all, he has not, in my view, successfully disposed of the solution he calls *Relative Composition*, whereby the time at which a substance is enmattered can individuate it. 'Can', because one need not always appeal to the temporal dimension: if Socrates and Callias are in different places, then this property of their respective matters individuates them; if they are different sizes, then that also individuates them. But suppose, as Fine encourages us to do, that Callias undergoes an imaginary process whereby he slowly sheds his matter while eating Socrates for breakfast. He takes on the matter of Socrates at exactly the same rate as he loses his own, and ends up consisting of all of Socrates's matter, as well as being exactly the same size as Socrates once was, and placing himself in exactly the same portion of space as Socrates once occupied.

If this is all imagined, then what prevents Socrates from ever having been identical to Callias is that they never shared the same matter *at the same time*. Elsewhere (Oderberg 1996) I have argued that two substances of the same kind cannot be in the same place at the same time;[27] and the reason is precisely that it would be impossible in principle to say, on such a hypothesis, which matter belonged to which substance, and they would then not be individuated. Form is 'parcelled out' by matter in space and time, so if matter is shared (and by shared is of course meant *wholly* shared – substances can overlap) it makes no sense to speak of distinct parcels, i.e. individuals. Socrates and Callias might share their matter, and they might even do so in the same place; but it will not be at the same time. Note that the reverse is not a possibility: they cannot share their matter at the same time but in different places; rather, they simply cannot share their matter at the same time. This follows from the asymmetry between time and space, but does not in the least make a difference to my claim that Relative Composition solves Fine's puzzle of Socrates and Callias.

Fine's objection to Relative Composition is that it makes the unifying role of form mysterious: 'It cannot be that time is one of the elements that is unified . . . . Nor can it be that unification is relative to a time; for how can a time, as such, affect the manner whereby the form makes some given matter into one thing rather than another?' (Fine 1994b: 34). Fine is correct on both counts. In particular, time does not affect the way form unifies. Rather, the way form unifies affects the temporal characteristics of a substance. As has already been suggested, it is through the exigency of form that matter receives the disposition to indeterminate quantity, where it can now be stated that we should understand indeterminate quantity as *whatever range of definite quantities, prescribed by the form itself, a substance happens to have*. Form unifies; matter receives; part of what it receives is a propensity to have the range of dimensions prescribed by the form, whether it be the range of dimensions appropriate to human beings, or snails, or lumps of marble.

Further, contra Fine, there is nothing unduly 'selective' about Relative Composition: it is not as though the temporal index of a compound gives a certain portion of matter a privileged position as, say, the matter of Socrates. Why is Socrates made of this stuff rather than that? Because he is. That his stuff exists at one time rather than another is simply a by-product of the fact that he exists at all, and there is no objection I can see to regarding a thing's by-products as the way in which that thing is individuated, as long as the by-products flow *essentially* from the nature of the thing (i.e. as properties), as indeterminate temporal dimensions certainly do.

There simply can be no substantial union of matter and form without matter in dimension.

Another case Fine proposes is that of an amoeba A_1 that divides and whose descendants then fuse to form a distinct amoeba A_2 with the same matter and form as A_1. Now it might be tempting to say that this is a case of intermittent existence, so that $A_1 = A_2$ but the amoeba did not exist during the interval in which the two fission products existed. Whether or not this is correct (and it would be a logically adequate response to Fine), it is worth noting that Aquinas, for one, does not appear to countenance the possibility of intermittent existence in the course of nature. (See Hughes 1997: 98–9.)[28] We can again, however, appeal to Relative Composition and say that what numerically distinguishes A_1 from A_2 is that they do not have the same matter at the same time.

In addition, Fine suggests the possibility of a Ship of Theseus scenario for amoebae: A_1 with matter M splits into a large and a small amoeba, surviving (let us suppose, plausibly) as the large one. It then fuses with a small amoeba, surviving as the fusion; and so on until the resulting amoeba A_2 possesses none of the original matter M, having shed a number of small amoebae which then fuse into an amoeba A_3 with all and only the matter M. Is $A_1 = A_2$ or is $A_1 = A_3$? Common matter and form suggest the latter, but a certain continuity of history suggests the former. As with the original Ship of Theseus puzzle, my response is that the original amoeba (or ship) goes out of existence at some time (though exactly when is another, and difficult, question) and that the descendants A_2 and A_3 are both numerically distinct from it. What about the fact that A_1 and A_3 share the same matter and form? Again, they do not do so at the same time.

But now we run up against an important problem for Relative Composition, which Fine recognizes. For does not Socrates himself have the same matter at different times? So how can the relativization of matter to time of existence be the principle of individuation? And again, can he not have different matter at different times (by variation)? So how can matter designated (inter alia) by temporal dimension be the principle of individuation? It is at this point that we must return to the distinction between identity and individuality which I mentioned on p. 112. Recall that matter possessing determinate quantity could not be the principle of individuation because it would entail the loss of a thing's individuality were it to vary in the determinate dimensions of its matter, as virtually every substance does. It can be replied[29] that the objection confuses individuality with diachronic identity: a principle of diachronic identity different from the principle of individuation can ensure identity over time through change of dimensions.

This point is correct, though it must be qualified by saying that it does not follow that the principle of individuation should indeed be determinately quantified matter after all. For the indeterminacy of dimensions, under the exigency of form, applies both modally, i.e. across possible worlds, and temporally. The point is that if Socrates, for instance, can be six feet tall in the actual world and six feet two inches in some possible world, what individuates him in an arbitrary world, i.e. what individuates him pure and simple, is whatever dimensions his matter happens to have in a given world, i.e. his matter under *indeterminate* dimensions. Since, as has been argued, it is temporal dimensionality which matters chiefly in individuation, given the shareability of spatial dimensions, what individuates Socrates (in any world) is whatever temporal index his matter happens to have (in that world).

Continuing with this point, the indeterminacy of dimensions also applies temporally, as I have said. Within a given world, substances change their dimensions, their size, shape, and so on, and also the time at which their matter exists. Further, they can even (at least conceivably) change their entire matter without ceasing to exist. At any given time, every substance has some matter, and that matter is simultaneously unshareable in its entirety with any other substance (or so I have claimed). So why be concerned about variation? Surely it must have something to do with the fact that the principle of individuation should not just capture what obtains at a slice or slices of the history of the universe, but also what happens during an *interval* or intervals in the history of the universe. To be sure, a candidate principle of individuation is a non-starter if it cannot, at any given moment in the history of the universe, capture what it is, metaphysically, that distinguishes every substance existing at that moment from every other one existing at that moment; or what distinguishes what exists at one moment from what exists at some other moment.

But one would have thought that another requirement was for it to be able to capture what it is, *during a given interval*, that distinguishes every substance persisting during that interval from every other substance persisting during that interval; and what distinguishes that which exists during one interval from that which exists at some other interval. Now, during an interval, a substance simply may not *have* determinate dimensions. So if we want to be able to say what it is that numerically distinguished, say, Churchill during the period 1940–5 from Stalin during the period 1947–50, or what distinguished Churchill from Roosevelt during the interval in which their lives overlapped, we cannot appeal to determinate dimensions but rather must speak of *ranges* of determinate dimensions; and this, both the modal and temporal variability of dimensions, is what we should mean by *indeterminate* dimensions.

Naturally, when the moments or intervals being compared are the same we cannot appeal to distinct temporal dimensions, but will have to appeal to spatial ones: Churchill and Roosevelt (rather, their matters) occupied distinct spatial ranges during the time their lives overlapped. Further, since a substance can change its matter over time, we cannot speak of a *single* parcel of matter designated by indeterminate dimensions as the principle of individuation. Fine proposes as another possible response to his puzzles the idea of Plural Composition, and I think that we can adapt this to the question of individuation by saying that individuation is sometimes grounded in the several matters which a substance possesses over time; but since dimensionality is crucial those matters must be indexed just as a single parcel of matter is indexed according to Relative Composition. And what we end up with, as Fine notes, is *Plural Relative Composition*, where (to adapt his proposal again) we take individuation throughout an interval as grounded in the series of temporally indexed matters which a substance possesses during that interval – its several matters, in order of appearance, during that interval. So, what distinguished Churchill during the period 1940–5 from Stalin during the period 1947–50 was their possession of distinct matters during distinct intervals.

In fact, the approach in terms of Plural Relative Composition is almost certainly too strict because it is clear that, whatever the changes of non-proximate matter in, say, a living body over time, the body itself remains numerically the same, and what individuates a human, for instance, is his proximate matter, which is his body; mutatis mutandis for other organisms and possibly even some inanimate objects to the extent that they are not mere lumps of matter. In this case we can leave Plural Relative Composition to one side as a useful adjunct elaboration of our general principle of individuation, and speak solely of Relative Composition, where the temporal relativization is either to a moment or an interval, as the case may be.

Despite all that has just been said, however, we are still no closer to being able to employ the PDM to specify what it is that grounds the identity of a given substance *over time*. The principle of individuation must state by virtue of what a substance at a time or over time is distinguished from every other substance at every other time or over every other time. The glaring exception to this, however, seems to be the substance itself. Can we say, in terms of the PDM, what it is that ensures that Churchill at a given moment in 1947, or over a given interval during 1947, is *not* distinguished numerically from Churchill at a given moment, or over a given interval, in 1960? It seems we cannot. All of the dimensions are different. By the principle of individuation, then, they should be two distinct people; but they are not.

Hence it is at least prima facie correct to distinguish the principle of individuation from the principle of diachronic identity, whatever it may be. The principle of individuation only applies on the assumption that we have a separate principle of diachronic identity, one which secures the persistence of a substance such as Churchill from one moment to the next. Assuming this, we can say that it is substance S's matter, under indeterminate dimensions, which individuates it. For any *given* moments t_1 and t_2, we must appeal to the principle of diachronic identity, rather than individuation, in order to state whereby S at t_1 is the same as S at t_2. In other words, once given our individuals at a time (through actuation by substantial form) and over time (through a form-invoking principle which secures persistence), we can state how the principle of individuation applies for both synchronic and diachronic individuation. Variation does indeed require that the dimensionality of individuating matter be indeterminate (though of course determinate at any specific moment), but this does not imply that matter designated by indeterminate dimensions is just what secures substantial identity through variation in the first place.

5.5 Identity over time

To say, however, that there is a principle of diachronic identity is *not* to say that identity over time has an informative analysis in terms that do not presuppose the very concept itself. I end this chapter by saying a little about this idea, leaving further questions concerning diachronic identity for another occasion.

I have argued elsewhere (Oderberg 1993) that there is no non-identity-presupposing analysis of diachronic identity in general.[30] The most popular current proposal for analysing identity over time is the four-dimensionalist account, according to which every persisting object is taken to be a four-dimensional 'space–time worm'. (Defenders include Heller (1990) and Lewis (1986); Sider (2001) offers a different kind of four-dimensional analysis; see also references in Oderberg (1993).) Inspired (if not necessarily justified) by contemporary relativistic physics and the supposed amalgamation of the three spatial dimensions and that of time into a 'four-dimensional manifold', this theory has it that persisting objects are really complexes of temporal parts, more or less momentary 'slices' or 'stages' of matter across space–time. What we think of as three-dimensional objects persisting through time are, on this view, four-dimensional objects 'smeared out' across the space–time manifold. Yet four-dimensionalism, in whatever version, suffers from many flaws.[31] For one thing, it denies the self-evident fact of real change. Connected to this is the fact that there is a perfectly adequate semantic solution to the so-called 'problem of temporary intrinsics' that does not require singular terms denoting temporal parts.[32] But perhaps the fundamental weakness is that there is no way of analysing the supposed temporal parts of persistents that does not either presuppose the very phenomenon of identity which is supposed to be analysed or else reduce to absurdity by invoking literally instantaneous object-stages that cannot give rise to any temporally extended object.

The correct position, I contend, is that identity over time is primitive. Yet there is a right way and a wrong way of interpreting this. The right way is to take the phenomenon of identity per se to be primitive. In other words, there is no way of defining identity across time in other terms: it is a basic, unanalysable phenomenon. The wrong way is to take it as meaning that the identity of material substances themselves is primitive: in other words, it would be incorrect to claim that when it comes to identity *nothing further can be said* about why it is that an object of a certain kind, existing at a given time, is numerically identical to an object of a certain kind identified at a later time; or why an object at one time is identical to *this* object rather than *that* object at a later time. It would, to elaborate a little, be wrong to claim that when it comes to *kinds of thing* the criterion of identity for a given kind is primitive, that nothing further can be said about why, say, objects of kind K continue to exist in certain conditions but cease to exist in others – other than that's just how things are for Ks. But even if a sympathizer with nominalism were to say that there *are* no real kinds of object, that every object is purely an individual, it would still be wrong to assert that nothing further can be said about why individuals persist in these circumstances rather than those.

The reason the wrong way is wrong is that it simply ignores self-evident truths of identity. We can explain why it is, for instance, that Bessie the cow seen at t_1 is not identical to Rover the dog observed at t_2, and why Rover at t_2 is not the same as Fido at t_3 – also why, say, a Lego house at t_3 is distinct from the pile of Lego bricks at t_4 that constituted it at t_3. In all such cases we do not rest content with saying that Bessie is Bessie and Rover is Rover, that Fido and Rover are just not the same, and that a Lego house is something different from its Lego bricks. Even if the criteria of identity invoked are quite simple, they are informative: a cow and a dog are different kinds of animal; this cow and this dog have different properties; the two dogs are of different breeds, or else differ otherwise in their accidental characteristics; a pile of Lego bricks does not make a house; and so on. The notion of primitive substance identity does not explain what we *do* when we account for the identity of substances.

Clearly what we do is more than simply make assertions about what is identical with what. And what emerges is that the criteria we invoke all, whether directly or indirectly, refer back to the forms of things, and, *pace* the nominalist, to those forms considered as universal entities instantiated in particular cases. The identity of the substance is primitive in this sense – that it cannot be decomposed into elements that do not themselves presuppose either the identity which is the subject of analysis in the first place or the identity of other things on which the identity in question is dependent. So the identity of Rover, for instance, is *evidenced* by those features we typically point to as features of Rover – Rover's bark, Rover's bite, Rover's characteristic way of chasing postmen. But it would be patently circular to claim that Rover's identity *consisted* in these things; or, in the case of an inanimate natural formation such as a river, the identity is evidenced by typical features of that thing – its characteristic shape or flow. Aggregates such as a pile of bricks have an identity wholly dependent on the identity of their constituents, which need not commit us to mereological essentialism – the idea that even the slightest addition to or replacement of parts destroys a thing – even though it is notoriously difficult to say just how many bricks need to stay the same for the pile to be the same pile. We refer to evidence, and evidence is all we have to go on. Even the much-vaunted phenomenon of spatio-temporal continuity only gives us evidence rather than an analysis.[33]

The sorts of feature to which we point, however, when we try – impossibly – to analyse identity (as distinct from the actual practice of reidentification, which we do successfully all the time) are notable for having this in common: they are all features referable back to, and deriving from, the form of the object in question. In general, what matters are the congeries of powers, operations, activities, organization, structure, and function of the object, whether it be something as bare as shape in the case of the diachronic identity of a circle drawn on a piece of paper, or something as complex as character in the case of the identity of a relatively higher animal such as a dog. Hence it is Rover's special way of barking at dinner time which is of more relevance than his colour – after all, he could have been swapped for a twin from the litter – and more his mournful mien when refused a walk in the park than his enthusiasm for chasing postmen. There seems to be a hierarchy of attributes to which we attach relative importance in grasping a thing's identity. Better, perhaps, is to think of it as a series of concentric circles, moving from the periphery, where certain attributes – perhaps (but not necessarily) colour, shape, posture, having been at a certain place at a certain time – have a fairly transitory importance, towards the centre, where, in the case of, say, a higher animal, features such as manner of behaviour and characteristic function assume dominance. The closer we get to the centre, the nearer we approach the *essence* of the thing.

Why can we not simply refer identity criteria back to spatio-temporal characteristics? Apart from the impossibility of an analysis in terms of spatio-temporal continuity, and apart also from the well-known Max Black-style counterexamples to the Identity of Indiscernibles (Black 1952), the possibility of exact spatio-temporal coincidence of objects precludes any analysis in terms solely of such characteristics. I have argued elsewhere (Oderberg 1996) that coincidence is impossible for substances of the same kind because of the problems of individuation, but that for non-substances (at least of certain kinds) it is possible since individuation is effected by appeal to the identity of the coincident objects' ontological sources, since non-substances are ontologically dependent entities. For instance, coinciding objects such as two shadows or two beams of light, one on top of the other, are individuated by their sources (the distinct occluding objects and the distinct light sources, respectively).

Again, for substances of different kinds, if coincidence is possible it will be referred back to distinct identity criteria for those substances, and this may include modal features, i.e. features concerning how things *might* have been with respect to one or both objects (these being genuine features of objects as much as their non-modal features such as shape or size). For instance, a statue is distinct from the lump of marble constituting it because of the different identity criteria for statues and lumps of marble; one *could* have existed without the other, say if the lump had been rearranged into a differently shaped object.[34] In all cases where coincidence is possible, reference to distinct identity criteria entails reference to the distinct forms possessed by the entities in question, substances or not. (In the case of non-substances of the same kind, such as property instances or such entities as shadows and beams of light, reference is to the identity criteria for the substances on which they are ontologically dependent.)

The moral of the story is that form is the root cause of identity: another way of putting it is that identity has a *formal cause*. Since, however, substances are individuals and form is not of itself individual, we have to posit a *material* cause of identity as well: in other words, the identity of a substance is given by the form as instantiated in matter. That the matter is not the root cause of identity is shown by the fact that many, if not most, macroscopic objects can and often do change all their matter without ceasing to persist.[35] No substance can change its form – i.e. its *substantial* form – and continue to exist. Another way of expressing the proposition that identity has a formal cause is to say that form is the *bearer* of identity. For a substance to persist is for it to possess *this* substantial form: not merely *a* substantial form, but a form instantiated by *this* matter – where *this* matter is not identified by there necessarily being a single parcel of atoms or other stuff, since, as noted, this may itself change over time. The matter is simply the matter of the persisting substance. Only if this were offered as an analysis of identity would there be a problem of circularity.

Rather, what I am offering is an analysis of the *causes* of identity, and seen as such there is no circularity: a substance persists because it consists of a form instantiated in matter, the form being the actualizing principle by virtue of which the substance is what it is, and the matter being the limiting principle of that form by virtue of which the substance is individual.

6 Essence and existence

6.1 The real distinction in contingent beings

Not all distinctions between things are real. Some are what we might call 'notional', 'conceptual', or 'logical'. As noted in Chapter 5, there is no real distinction between Socrates and his humanity, or indeed between anything and its essence (as individualized, of course), for according to the Law of Identity everything just *is* its own essence, whatever it is. To take another example, it is commonly argued by mind–brain identity theorists that there is no real distinction between mind and brain, only a conceptual one deriving from the different ways – third-personal and first-personal – in which the mind/brain presents itself to observation or reflection. (Which of these aspects is more fundamental is another matter: for materialists it is brain, for idealists mind, and for neutral monists neither.)

There was a long debate throughout the Middle Ages as to whether the distinction between essence and existence was real or merely notional – a 'distinction of reason', as the latter might also be called. A respectable line of philosophers defended the view that it was notional, though the dominant position was that the distinction was a real one.[1] Here I will briefly defend the real distinction and show that the debate is not sterile but has important implications in ontology and epistemology.

First, though, what needs to be clarified is that the thesis of the real distinction between essence and existence is not that between existence and *metaphysical* essence, but that between existence and *physical* essence, i.e. not essence considered in the abstract, but essence as it is in the concretely existing being. The nature of humans or of dinosaurs in the abstract cannot be identified with their existence, nor can their existence be any *part* of their abstract essence, since existence is precisely what *actualizes* an essence: it is no part of the essence of any kind of thing that it exist. Rational animals do not essentially exist; nor does anything with atomic number 79. Note, however, that this does not commit the essentialist to Platonism. The essentialist is an *immanent* realist – there are no uninstantiated essences. But the distinction between essence and existence can be drawn without invoking Platonic essences, since we must not confuse real distinction with ontological *separability.* The possibility of an instantiated essence is expressed by the following proposition:

(1) Possibly there is a form *F* which is instantiated,

from which it does not follow that

(2) There is a form *F* which is possibly instantiated.

Hence the essentialist *qua* immanent realist can countenance the possible instantiation of a form – including a form that has no actual instances, such as *element with atomic number 1000* – without countenancing the prior existence of an uninstantiated form. To suppose otherwise is to make a simple confusion of scope. No essence can *exist* apart from its actual instances, but that is not the same as saying that its existence just consists in the existence of its actual instances.

But what about the idea of identity, or at least overlap, between the actual, particular essence of something and its existence? Isn't it true that Socrates's existence is identical with, or at least a part of, his particular humanity, just as much as it is true that Socrates's particular humanity is identical with Socrates? If so, it would imply that Socrates was identical with his existence or that his existence was part of him – and isn't this right, namely that Socrates and Socrates's existence are one and the same or at least overlap? After all, it might be argued, particular existence is true of the particular that exists, yet it is not a *characteristic* of anything existent. But then it should be thought of as identical with the particular that exists in the same way that *being Socrates* is true of Socrates without being a characteristic of Socrates – it just means that Socrates is Socrates. Or, at least, if Socrates's existence is neither a characteristic of him nor identical with him it should be regarded – the only remaining option – as in some sense part of him.

Defenders of the real distinction between actual essence and actual existence – which is where the historic controversy obtains – have various arguments for it. They all take their inspiration from Aristotle's remark that '*what* a man is and *that* he is are different'. (See the *Posterior Analytics* in Ross 1928a: 92b10.[2]) Taking substances again as our paradigm, the basic idea is that Socrates's actual existence and his particular essence, though ontologically inseparable, are really distinct, every bit as much as a particular triangle's sides and its angles. For his existence forms no part at all of the concept of his essence. I can think of Socrates in terms of his essence – as a human being – without thinking of him as existing. But before the same criticism is raised as was levelled by Arnauld at Descartes's argument for dualism,[3] the point is not merely that I can think of Socrates without thinking of him as existing, but that I can grasp the *entire essence* of Socrates, *qua* human being, without either explicitly *or implicitly* thinking of him as existing. Suppose I am a sceptic as to whether Socrates ever did exist – maybe he is an invention of later historiography, for all I know. I can still think of him as essentially a human being and not remotely entertain his having existed.

I can, of course, think of Socrates without explicitly conceiving of him as an animal, or even as rational, or as belonging to a higher genus such as *material substance*. This doesn't imply that it is no part of his essence to be any of those things, only that I can grasp his essence without grasping his complete essence, and without analysing it into its constituents. This is most clearly the case with things whose complete essence I do not know, such as relatively unfamiliar objects from the natural sciences; and for many people it will apply even to familiar things such as water or uranium. Given that we do not, and maybe cannot, know the complete essences of many things, it would be too stringent to require that grasp of essence require grasp of everything in the essence. But we cannot grasp essence if we exclude, either explicitly or implicitly, any of its constituents. At most our grasp will be incorrect, at worst non-existent. I cannot grasp the essence of whales correctly if I think of them as fish, and not at all if I think of them as land-dwelling creatures. The question we must ask is: if I exclude a certain element from the essence of a thing, do I thereby misconceive it? In the case of existence in respect of contingent things, the answer is surely that I do not misconceive any such thing if I exclude existence from it. Hence existence cannot be of the essence of contingent things.

One objection to the real distinction is that it seems to imply the truth of the Ontological Argument. For if essence and existence are really different in contingent things, they must be the same in necessary beings, and since the paradigmatic necessary being is God, whose essence is His existence,[4] we can know that God exists merely by knowing His essence. In fact it might be thought that Aquinas himself refutes his own position by rejecting the Ontological Argument (Aquinas 1920a: I.2.1, p.19ff.). The inconsistency is only apparent, however, because when I grasp (incompletely, to be sure) the essence of God as inclusive of existence, all I grasp is that *if* God exists He exists necessarily – but I can still without contradiction deny that He exists in the first place.[5] I can, in other words, have the concept of a certain thing as necessarily existing without being committed to its actually existing.[6] (Compare: I might have the concept of necessarily existing metaphysical simples, and therefore be able to define them, without being logically compelled to accept their existence. For that I will need a separate argument.)

Another objection might seem to follow from the standard modalist criterion of essential properties (Chapter 1, p.10), namely that x has F essentially if and only if, necessarily, x has F if x exists. But necessarily, if x exists then x exists, so x exists essentially. Hence there must be no real distinction between x's essence and x's existence, for any x. This is less a reason to believe there is no real distinction between essence and existence than to abandon the criterion. For it forces us to accept that Socrates, say, does not necessarily exist although he essentially exists, which is absurd. (See further Fine 1994a: 6ff.).[7]

To elaborate the point made earlier, it might be objected that to treat essence and existence as really distinct is by that act to treat existence as some sort of characteristic of contingent things – a kind of metaphysical 'add-on' to essence. The opposing view takes existence to overlap or be identical with essence, a position that might be thought more plausible. But the objection only serves to reveal the paucity of vocabulary (and of conceptual resources) in contemporary metaphysics. Existence is indeed something that is true of existing things. It is arguably incapable of being defined, not because, like *being*, it is too general and so analogous, but because it is a simple notion not susceptible of analysis into constituents (this applies as well to the concept of identity).[8] But we can still describe things that we cannot define. To exist is to be not in mere potentiality only, but to be in actuality. Hence existence is the actualization of something – more precisely, the actualization of an essence. A substance comes into existence when form is united to matter, resulting in a compound of both with its own real essence. An accident comes into existence when a substance is modified by it, i.e. when the accidental form actually comes to inhere in it. All existence, even the existence of privations, ontologically dependent entities, fictional entities, and so on, requires that something be actualized.

Does this make existence a characteristic of anything? It is not a property, since properties flow from the essence of a thing and, given what I have already said, existence does not flow from the essence of anything, whether contingent or necessary. (Even with a being whose essence is not distinct from its existence, the latter does not flow from the essence but is a part of it.) Neither is existence an accident, since accidents inhere in and modify already-existing substances. A substance can lose an accident and continue to exist; it cannot lose existence and continue to exist. Hence to that extent we can agree with the broadly Kantian critique of the Ontological Argument, to the effect that existence 'is not a real predicate' (Kant 1933: A598/B626, p. 504).[9]

This should not, though, lead us to the still-dominant Fregean view that existence is a second-level property of concepts. Existence is something true *of things that exist*, not of our concepts of them. It is as patently true *of mammals* that they exist, and *of Fido* that he exists, as it is true of them that they have fur or breathe oxygen. Hence we should also reject the view recently defended by Fred Sommers that existence is a characteristic of the world (Sommers 2005: 211–14; for details, see Sommers 1997). For Sommers, to say that elks exist is to say that the world is elk-ish – that the domain of reality contains elks.[10] But the existence of elks is a fact *about elks*, and this is logically prior to its being a fact about the world, if there be such a fact as well. Existence, though neither a property nor an accident, is true of existing things and a fact about them. Just as form actualizes potentiality to produce a substance, so existence can be thought of as actualizing form itself. Form actualizes matter; existence actualizes form. These are not really separable, since when the former happens the latter by that very fact obtains, and vice versa. But they should be thought of as really distinct acts, and existence should be described (not defined) as, using the medieval jargon, the *last* actuality of a substance. (For non-substances, existence is had derivatively from the actualization of the forms of the substances on which the non-substances are ontologically dependent.) Hence existence is not a part of essence, nor identical with essence, nor a characteristic of existing things. Yet it is still true of them. This explanation brings into focus the way in which contemporary ontology has lost the conceptual resources to explicate fundamental features of reality.

I said that the real distinction between essence and existence has important philosophical consequences, so I will briefly mention two. First, in epistemology, if we collapse essence as a metaphysical constituent of being into the existence of the concretely existing thing, we exclude the possibility of intellectual judgment altogether. All knowledge begins with our acquaintance with concrete particulars, but if we are to ascend from mere knowledge of things as *this thing* or *that thing*, we have to form judgments based on the abstraction of the universal from the particular. This we do by means of our knowledge of form, beginning with substantial form, hence with essence. But if essence just is existence, or even has existence as a part, we cannot so abstract and so cannot have knowledge (beyond that of bare demonstrative knowledge, which is arguably not even a kind of knowledge at all, but mere acquaintance). We are forced either into a radical and barely coherent empiricism or else into some kind of idealism that denies all epistemic access to mind-independent reality.

Secondly, by grasping the real distinction we make room for the very idea of contingency, for in contingent beings no essence *must* be actualized. But at the same time we make room for the idea of a being whose essence *is* its existence, in the sense that there is no mixture of potency in it. Theists identify this being as God, and it is traditionally held that God is *pure actuality*, i.e. a being that has no potentiality in its constitution, this absence being the root cause of its unlimited and infinite nature. Only atheists who hold the very concept of God to be incoherent will fail to find anything of philosophical importance in this idea. If the concept of God is coherent, it needs explication. Listing the properties of God is the usual way, but we should expect that for God, as for any other being, properties flow from nature, so we need an explanation of God's properties (His omniscience, omnipotence, eternity, etc.) in terms of more fundamental truths about the divine nature. The real distinction between essence and existence in contingent beings, and their identity in necessary beings, provides the framework for such an explication.

6.2 Everything is contingent ... almost

I have spoken of the idea that existence is the actualization of essence. Sometimes it is said that existence takes an essence from the realm of the merely possible to that of the actual. Many readers will, despite the arguments against Platonism in Chapter 4, suspect a lurking Platonism in this way of thinking. Surely the essentialist is after all committed to essences subsisting (though not existing) in a realm of potentiality, only to be actuated by existence (via the causes of existence) and hence realized in the world?

The idea of a 'realm of potentiality' is, for the immanentist, only a metaphor. Potentiality is, to be sure, not metaphorical, but wholly real. It does not follow, however, that essences have their own mode of being in an immaterial realm, waiting to be united with real potentiality so as to form the actual substance. Actuation of matter by form is caused wholly within this world[11] by the efficient causes that bring substances into being. This does not mean, however, that possible essences (e.g. of some non-existing but possible chemical element) have no reality whatsoever. Given the real potentiality of matter to receive form, resulting in a determinate something-or-other, the possible essence itself has a certain reality. But the reality is not Platonic.

I have already claimed that possibilities are grounded in the natures of things. Even logical possibilities can be seen as grounded in the natures of logical objects. Fine has suggested that the logical necessities can be taken to be 'propositions which are true by virtue of the nature of all logical concepts' (Fine 1994a: 9–10). If true, we can correlatively understand logical possibility in the same way. There is no space to examine this proposal, but I do want to clarify and supplement the general idea of modality as grounded in reality. As far as existence is concerned, its possibility is ultimately grounded in pure potentiality, in the sense that possible existence requires the potentiality for the actualization of form in matter. Matter – that is, prime matter – is wholly indifferent to the reception of this or that form. Relative to pure potentiality, we can endorse the idea that anything can exist anywhere, anytime. Put more graphically, and omitting for the moment questions of creation, we can say that the development of the material universe might be metaphysically constrained – not just nomologically constrained – by how things were at the origin of the universe. For instance, given that the laws of nature came into existence at the origin,[12] there is not merely a nomic constraint on how things are or can be (e.g. that objects with mass be attracted by the law of universal gravitation), but a metaphysical one. Given that the universe contains colour, it is metaphysically impossible that an object be wholly of two distinct colours, and the like. This notwithstanding, it was a matter of indifference what *kind* of universe came into existence.[13] It could have been a universe of free quarks, of uncombined electrons, or a universe containing one single atom. The prime matter informed by whatever form or forms the universe happens to contain is wholly indifferent, and does not therefore determine what exists.

Nevertheless, given that the universe contains what it does, and is the way it is, metaphysical possibility is further constrained by the existing forms. So, given that a certain object is green all over, metaphysically it cannot be at the same time red all over. Given that a certain hunk of matter is gold, metaphysically it cannot at the same time be silver. If it is possible for a given element to transmute into another, say through radioactive decay, this possibility is determined not just by prime matter but by the existing forms: if an atom is of a form that allows decay into another element, this is a metaphysical possibility (as well as a nomological one). But a thing may be of a form such that it is metaphysically impossible for it to transmute into another kind of thing: to take a glaring case, it is metaphysically impossible for an electron to transmute into an elephant. Thus, given the way the world actually is, metaphysical modality is grounded not just in matter but in the existing forms: both substantial change and accidental change will depend for their possibility in a particular case on which forms already exist and the kind of generation and corruption to which they are or are not liable.

It is readily seen how this proposal differs from standard accounts of modality. It is not combinatorial (see Armstrong 1989b), since what can exist,[14] while constrained by what already exists, is no mere combination of what already exists. Hence there is room for so-called 'alien' essences, wholly new kinds of thing that are not mere recombinations of existing kinds of thing, something the combinatorialist has to accommodate at the cost of watering down his theory (Armstrong 1997: 166–7). Nor is there room for concrete possibilia of the kind espoused by David Lewis (1986). Indeed, Lewis-style modal realism eliminates all real possibility since on his account everything is actual relative to its own world. To call that which is non-actual relative to our own world 'possible' is not to countenance real modality but to get rid of it altogether, and it is this that is, it seems, at the heart of the 'changing the subject' objection levelled by Kripke (1980: 44–6) at Lewis. How can possibility in *this* world be explained in terms of what is *actual* at *another* world?

Similarly, the idea of real modality is incompatible with accounts that treat modality as a kind of fiction (Rosen 1990) or as a kind of abstract object such as a set of propositions (Plantinga 1970). Though modality is explained in terms of matter and form, it is in the end unanalysable. Like identity, it can be described as a phenomenon, explained in terms of the structure of essence, and our knowledge of it can be explained in terms of our knowledge of essence. But it cannot be reduced to non-modal terms, since matter just is potentiality, and form constrains potentiality without eliminating it. Hence every substance has some potential for something, and all non-substances have potential derived from the substances on whose existence they depend.

What is left unanswered by this conception of modality, though, is how we should understand the possibility of whatever first came into existence at the origin of the universe. Since there was no prime matter before that – it came into existence along with the forms that informed it at the beginning – and since there are no Platonic Forms, how do we account for the fact that the world contained just what it did contain at its origin? We could leave it as a brute fact that the world is thus-and-so, and since whatever is actual is possible, it was thereby possible; but it is not clear we can rest content there.

Another kind of universe *could* have existed – so why doesn't it? Here, I submit, we need to refer this primal possibility, as we might call it, to something outside the universe. Theists can say that we must refer the primal possibility to ideas in the divine mind. If so – and it is indeed plausible, in my view – something like the Leibnizian view is correct, that possibility has at least its *root* cause in the divine intellect, since whatever is or has been possible throughout the history of the universe depends on what possibility was realized at its origin. (See Leibniz 1998: 99–100 (correspondence with Arnauld), 273–4 (*Mondaology*).)

Returning now to the real distinction between essence and existence, we must note one of its most important consequences – that the only necessary existents are those beings whose essence is (or includes) their existence. Contingent beings are contingent precisely because it is no part of their essence to exist. Hence it is possible that no contingent being exists, since again the possibility of non-existence is just what it is to be contingent. So might there have been *nothing at all*? Intuitions differ here: you might think it perfectly coherent to suppose that nothing existed whatsoever, and you would be committed to this if you thought that there might have been no material universe (including space and time) and that no necessary being existed.

But what about supposed necessary existents such as numbers and logically necessary truths? If there are such things, then it is not possible after all that there is nothing whatsoever. Yet there are good reasons for denying that numbers (let's confine ourselves to the natural numbers), and by extension all of the logico-mathematical operations on which the necessary truths depend, could exist without anything else. The main reason is that such things are *abstractions* from other things that are not themselves abstractions from anything, i.e. abstractions from particulars. There is a temptation to regard numbers as particulars, and since they are not spatio-temporal or in any way physical they would have to be abstract particulars. But, as Paul Benacerraf showed, there is more than one kind of abstract particular that numbers could be, and since there is no good reason to choose one over the other, numbers should not be identified with any of them (Benacerraf 1965). The better approach is to regard numbers as universals rather than particulars: they are abstract objects in the same way that other universals are abstract, in being abstracted from particulars. Jonathan Lowe has made a strong case for regarding numbers as *kinds* rather than *properties* (Lowe 1999a: 223–7; 2006: 81–3). More precisely, he treats numbers as kinds of set (not as *a* kind of set), i.e. kinds that have as their instances, for each number *n*, the *n*-membered sets. One advantage over treating them as *sets* of sets (à la Russell), apart from sets' being particulars, is that sets cannot change their members; hence, since numbers have identity across possible worlds, as sets they have to have the same members. But which and how many contingent things there are vary from world to world, so numbers could not be sets of sets of contingent things.

So one would have to identify numbers with sets of sets of necessary things, usually the null set and sets constructed from it. And this leaves it a mystery how numbers are actually *taught*, given that we learn about numbers long before we can form a conception of the null set (even if, *perhaps*, we can form the conception of a set of things quite early in life).

Kinds, however, can vary in their membership, so regarding numbers as kinds allays any concern about a kind's retaining its identity across possible worlds despite change of membership. In response to worries about how numbers can be taught if sets are abstract, Lowe does not offer one solution, but makes several proposals (Lowe 1999a: 226), including the one of regarding numbers not as kinds of set but as kinds of plurality: the number 2 might be the kind with pairs as instances rather than two-membered sets, these being distinct. I cannot pursue this here, but instead remark that this loosening of the account of what are the instances of numbers as kinds suggests that he is perhaps too hasty in rejecting the idea that numbers are properties. All he says is that if numbers are properties rather than kinds they must have modes as instances, 'but this seems to make little sense' (Lowe 2006: 82). Yet why can't we regard the instances of numbers as particularized properties identical to the particular *n*-tuplenesses (to coin an unfortunate barbarism) of the *n*-tuples that possess them? On this account, the number 2 would be the property having particular *dualities* as instances (where 'duality' is construed adjectivally, not as just a synonym for 'pairs'), the number 3 would have *trialities* as instances, 4 would have *quadralities*, and so on. One reason for taking this route is that properties, as I have explained, flow from the essences of things, and having duality clearly flows from the essence of a pair. This may not be a reason in itself to prefer the account of numbers as properties over that of numbers as kinds, but it is a reason nonetheless.

If numbers are abstractions, then, they must be abstractions from something. Moreover, they cannot be mere abstractions from themselves, since their individuation conditions would be circular. (For a related point, see Lowe 1999a: 227.) We can count, say, the set or plurality containing only 1, 2, 3 and 4 as instantiating the number 4 itself (mutatis mutandis for the numbers-as-properties view), but only because we already have an independent understanding of number as instantiated by sets or pluralities that do not contain only numbers. But if numbers must be abstractions from something other than themselves, there must *be* something other than numbers in any world in which there are numbers. Yet nothing contingent might have existed. And without having space for the details, I contend that all logical and mathematical objects (operations, propositions, functions, etc.) must be treated in a way similar to numbers. But we cannot simply regard numbers in a world without contingent objects as abstractions from other, non-numerical abstractions, since these too are abstractions from things other than themselves and cannot be abstractions from numbers on pain of either circularity or incoherence.

We are faced, it seems, with the position that either there might be nothing at all – nothing contingent and nothing necessary[15] – or, if there are necessary things such as numbers (and other logical or mathematical objects), there must be things *other* than numbers from which numbers are abstracted. But since no contingent thing might exist, there must be something else. As Lowe puts it in a parenthetical remark, 'we see that, of logical necessity, the natural numbers exist provided anything at all exists' (1999a: 226). But he adds that what else exists is 'perhaps' a concrete object 'such as myself, whose existence is ensured by the Cartesian *cogito*' (1999a: 226). Yet this will not do, since I might not have existed (whatever we think of the *cogito*). We need something else, something necessary and particular that is (by that very fact) not a number or any other logical or mathematical object.

The only plausible candidate for such a being, as far as I can see – one whose essence is its existence – is God. Hence either there might be nothing whatsoever or if the numbers must exist, then so must God. And if God exists, the numbers exist and will be abstractions from Him (provided that He is of a kind, say *divine being*, even if the kind necessarily has only one member).[16] Hence anyone committed to the necessary existence of numbers, or other logical or mathematical objects, must countenance the existence of God, moreover the necessary biconditional that God exists if and only if the numbers exist. Whether there might, on the other hand, be nothing whatsoever – no God and no numbers – must be left to another occasion. Suffice it to say for now that either everything is contingent or if something is not contingent, then God exists.

6.3 Powers

Whether or not there is a being whose essence is its existence, as long as we admit the coherence of such an idea we have a way of understanding the powers of contingent beings, in particular the inhabitants of our spatio-temporal universe. A being whose essence is its existence suffers from no limitation whatsoever, because its existence is not explained in terms of the actualization of any potentiality. A material substance, on the other hand, is precisely a combination of actuality and potentiality. Its coming into existence involves the taking on by prime matter, which is pure poten-tiality, wholly indifferent to what it might become, of a limiting or deter-mining principle – a substantial form – that, to speak metaphorically for a moment, 'pins down' the prime matter and thereby gives it a determinate identity as something or other. To use the Aristotelian/Scholastic terminol-ogy, form combines with prime matter to produce a *quiddity*, a this-such. Hence, when we speak of such things as divine omnipotence and other properties involving divine power, we must not think of the divine being as having power in the same way in which contingent beings have power. There is an analogy between them, however, deriving from the role of actuality and understood in terms of the distinction between *active* and *passive* power, a distinction playing little part in contemporary discussions of powers and 'dispositions'.

The basic idea is that the passive quality of a thing's powers derives from its prime matter, and the active quality from its form. This is because passivity is a kind of receptivity – a capacity to receive and undergo change, to be subject to causes and ultimately to be destroyed. Activity, on the other hand, as the term connotes, is a capacity to do – to produce or effect change, to cause and ultimately to destroy. Hence the more a given capacity of a thing is passive and receptive, the more it partakes of prime matter, which is pure receptivity. The more it is active and effective, the more it partakes of actuality, i.e. of form. On the assumption (which I will not defend here) that beings can be arranged in a hierarchy from the least active/most receptive to the most active/least receptive, whereas we find pure potentiality – prime matter – at one end of the spectrum we find pure actuality at the other end. Pure actuality is wholly unmixed with any receptivity or potentiality, so cannot receive or undergo any change. But it can still *cause* change in other things, and *act* in various ways towards other things. Such a thing still has power, and we can call that power a kind of potentiality, i.e. active, but we must not take such power to derive in any way from the receptivity of matter; rather, it derives wholly from form unrestricted and unlimited in any way. This is how traditional metaphysics conceives of divine power.[17]

The contemporary debate about dispositions and powers has so far shown little interest in the distinction between active and passive power, and hence it is no surprise that hylemorphism has played no role in the debate. We can better put the point the other way around, by noting that the absence of hylemorphic considerations has made for a lack of necessary distinction between powers, and more generally a lack of concern for the very concept of power (though that is slowly changing, as evidenced by the increasing popularity of talk of powers and potencies rather than dispositions). I contend that a proper understanding of form and matter, and hence of essence, will enable us to understand powers. As I outline the idea in this section, I will show how some of the issues that have been the subject of recent debate can be resolved.

Since every substance is a compound of matter and form, hence of potentiality and actuality, we should not be surprised that it is difficult, if not impossible, to separate its features (its accidents and properties) into those that are purely actual and those that are purely potential (where by 'potential feature' I do not mean a characteristic the substance could but does not possess, rather something it does possess but in a way involving potentiality rather than actuality). This mixed composition of substance is what is at the heart of the debate over whether a viable distinction can be drawn between the 'dispositional' and the 'categorical'. In fact, neither term is a happy one. 'Categorical' could mean 'real', 'actual', 'unconditional', 'episodic', 'occurrent', all of which are distinct aspects of phenomena. (On this point, see also Mumford 1996: 86–7; 1998: 20–2.) And 'disposition' does not capture what it is metaphysicians worry about when analysing properties such as solvency, solubility, fragility, and so on – the paradigms of 'dispositions' in the literature. For 'disposition', as well as sometimes connoting potentiality, also connotes actuality – as in, for instance, the disposition of a thing's parts, where this means 'arrangement'. It can also connote such qualities as mood, tendency, and inclination – all of which may involve a certain degree or kind of potentiality, but none of which is always and unqualifiedly a power.

We get closer to the distinction we need to make when speaking of potentiality versus occurrence. Lowe (2006: ch. 8) eschews the dispositional/categorical distinction in favour of the dispositional/occurrent distinction, where dispositional predication is grounded in the characterization of a substantial kind by a property, and occurrent predication is grounded in the characterization of an individual substance by a property instance (a mode) that itself instantiates a property. Hence 'Salt is water-soluble' is a dispositional predication and 'This salt is dissolving in water' is occurrent; the same goes for 'Rubber stretches' and 'This rubber is stretching'. Whilst suggestive, this proposal will not do. First, since it assimilates all powers[18] to what is true of *kinds* (in particular substantial kinds), it makes no room for *accidental* powers, i.e. powers possessed by individuals of a kind, where the kind is not characterized by the power in question. Suppose Fred is one of the few people (maybe the only one) capable of genuinely hypnotizing others. He has a hypnotic power, but 'Humans can hypnotize other humans' is false – it does *not* characterize humankind. There are rare people, known as '*idiots savants*', who, whilst having an abnormally low IQ, have extraordinary intellectual powers in particular areas, such as arithmetical calculation, that transcend anything that characterizes the human species. Hence an individual human may have such a power yet it not be true of the species that having such a power characterizes it. The moral is that not all powers characterize kinds or, more precisely, essences. Some do – such as the power of speech[19] – but others do not. This is why we need a theory of essence to help us distinguish between the powers that do and do not belong to the essence of a thing.[20]

Secondly, Socrates possesses rationality – this rationality is particular, and true of him. Where does it fit into Lowe's four-category ontology? Lowe bifurcates universals into the substantial (kinds) and the non-substantial (which he calls 'properties'), adding individual substances and modes to his fundamental categorization of what there is. Now rationality does not seem to be a substantial universal, i.e. a kind, in his sense. *Human* is indeed a substantial kind, but *rational* is not, since the instances of rationality will be modes (particular rationalities) rather than substances. It is not certain that Lowe would say this, but one reason for thinking he would is that he understands kinds as characterized not just by properties but by laws, and there is no guarantee that rational substances would all be subject to the same laws – they might form too heterogeneous a kind. Or some rational substances (such as God) might not be subject to any laws. Although there are hints (Lowe 2006: 127) that *water-soluble* is a substantial kind, since water-soluble things are governed by the laws of water-solubility, I am not sure Lowe should countenance this since one might as well say the same for *green* or *having mass*, since green things and things with mass are governed by the laws of colour and of mass (inertial and gravitational), respectively, however heterogeneous a kind each might otherwise constitute. Rightly, he takes *green* to have as instances modes not substances, but then the same should be said of water-solubility, which will be a property rather than a kind.

To go back to rationality, then, why not say the same as well? On this interpretation, rationality would be a property rather than a kind and Socrates would be characterized by his particular rationality, which instantiated the non-substantial universal of rationality. If so, however, on Lowe's theory this would make 'Socrates is rational' an *occurrent* rather than a dispositional predication, which is false. Rationality is manifested by various occurrences (speech, thought, art, and so on) but is itself a power, not an occurrence. Moreover, it is a power true of the *kinds* whose members have it; more precisely, it is what its possessors have by virtue of their essence, whether or not all its possessors have the same essence.

The problem with the four-category ontology, then, whatever its important insights (of which there are many) – a fortiori with even sparser ontologies – is that it does not make enough of the distinctions necessary for a correct classification and characterization of reality. The exhaustive division of universals into kinds and properties collapses the distinction between accidents and *propria*, i.e. properties in the strict sense. Hence it cannot distinguish between accidental powers and powers proper to a kind. It also collapses the distinction between genus, species, and specific difference (*differentia*) into the overly general category of 'kind'. This means that a specific difference such as rationality either gets mischaracterized as a property or else is treated as a kind whose instances are substances, with the result that there is no way of determining why *rational* should be a kind term and *green* not, given that both characterize the things that have them – both are 'ways things are' (Lowe 2006: 92–3). Moreover, if substantial universals are only the *species* (e.g. *human*), then there is no room at all on Lowe's 'ontological square' for either genera (such as *animal*) or specific differences (such as *rational*). The point is not that Lowe would *want* to call 'green' a kind term, or even that he would want to call 'rational' a property term. It is, rather, that the four-category ontology does not allow us to say what needs to be said: that *human* is a species; *rational* a difference; *is able to hypnotize people* an accidental power; *is able to use language* a proper power; and so on.

I submit that the term 'occurrent' is as useless as the term 'categorical' to mark a distinction from 'potency' and 'power', except insofar as it might be used as a synonym for 'actual'. But 'actual' is incapable of definition, like the other basic ontological categories. It can be described as a definite or determinate way of being, as a *perfection* of a thing, where 'perfection' is used in the traditional sense. This is contrasted with 'potential', but we must be careful to avoid confusion. Powers are determinate and definite, in the sense that their possessors really have them, they are real states or ways of being. But they are indefinite and indeterminate in the sense captured by the common idea of manifestation: a power is manifested in its operation, by which I mean that the result of its operation is some definite or determinate actuality, such as a state of dissolution (in the case of solubility), of break-age (in the case of fragility), of speech or other symbolic representation (in the case of linguistic capacity) and so on. But it now becomes clear that we really cannot understand actuality independently of potentiality, and vice versa. Neither is strictly definable, but each must be understood partly in terms of the other. This can be seen clearly in the problem of the relation between powers and subjunctive conditionals.

Those who deny the existence of real powers in the world have usually taken the Humean empiricist approach, seeking to analyse powers in terms of subjunctive conditionals expressing what would happen to a thing, or what it would do, were it to be exposed to a certain stimulus. (See examples from Locke, Hume, and Ryle cited in Mumford 1998: 38–9 and Molnar 2003: 99.) C.B. Martin, however, has refuted the very idea of analysing powers in terms of subjunctive conditionals, and even of providing either necessary or sufficient conditions for the possession of a power in terms of the truth of a subjunctive conditional (Martin 1994).

The powers (or dispositions, to use the more common terminology, which, as noted on p. 132, is imprecise) he focuses on have come to be known as 'finkish'. This is because Martin describes a situation in which an object x can have a power P at a given time even though the conditional is false at that time since the situation is rigged by a device such that, whenever x is exposed to the relevant stimulus S, x loses P and so is unable to manifest the relevant response R. (The relevant stimulus and response are the ones named in the conditional proposed as the analysis of the possession by x of P). Conversely there could be, as Martin explains, a situation in which the conditional is true at a given time yet x lacks P at that time because the situation is rigged such that, whenever x is exposed to S, x gains P and so is able to manifest response R. The device he imagines is an 'electro-fink' that interferes with a live wire in such a way that the wire is rendered dead whenever exposed to a conductor, and conversely interferes with a dead wire to render it live whenever exposed to a conductor. In the former case, the wire indeed has a power (of losing current through a conductor) at a certain time even though it is not true at that time that were it exposed to the con-ductor it would lose any current, since it would be rendered dead by the electro-fink. And conversely for the latter case. This sort of example breaks the logical connection between powers and the propositions describing their conditional manifestation.

There are other sorts of case, such as 'masking' dispositions (Molnar 2003: 92–3) which a thing may possess and which prevent another of that thing's powers from ever manifesting itself. Molnar cites an example from Greek mythology: Tantalus, son of Zeus, was punished for abusing his privilege of sharing food with the gods by being immersed in water – every time he tried to drink, it drained away; and every time he reached for fruit, the wind blew the branches beyond his reach.[21] In fact the case looks more like finking than masking, but we can imagine that the gods endowed Tantalus with intrinsic powers: his body was such that it forced water and fruit away from him whenever he tried to consume them. Yet Tantalus had the power of eating and drinking. And there are universal antidotes: there could exist a lethal snake in a situation where, any time it bites anyone, they are rescued by an antidote. The snake would have the power to kill, but this would be frustrated on all occasions and the conditional 'If x were bitten by S, x would die' would be always false. (For more on antidotes, see Bird 1998.) Modalizing the conditional by saying, for instance, 'It is possible that were x exposed to S it would manifest R' weakens the putative analysis intolerably: all sorts of cases can be conceived in which an object *might* behave in a certain way given a certain stimulus, without *actually* possessing the power – in particular, if it were *endowed* with the power, assuming the power to be non-essential, as many powers are (see p. 132).

All of these sorts of case – and one can easily imagine others – militate either against the entailment, by truths concerning the possession of powers, of subjunctive conditionals concerning stimulus and response/manifestation, or else the reverse, or both. This has led some, notably Martin and Molnar, comprehensively to reject any conditional analysis of powers (see Molnar 2003: 83–94 for a good overview). Yet, as others have said (e.g. Mumford 1998: 81–91), we should at least expect power possession to entail the truth of certain kinds of conditional, even if we reject a reductive analysis. But attempts to forge a connection that looks informative have not been promising. Mumford (1996) proposed an entailment by any truth concerning power possession of a conditional specifying response in the absence of conditions preventing manifestation of the power. He later rejected this as vacuous (Mumford 1998: 86–91), replacing it with an 'ideal conditions' approach. According to this, if an object x has power P, then, were conditions to be ideal, if x were subjected to stimulus S it would manifest response R. Yet what 'ideal conditions' are remains elusive. Mumford distinguishes between 'ideal' and 'ordinary', as he must, since some powers are such that they manifest themselves in unusual or extreme conditions. But he ties 'ideal' to 'conditions that can vaguely be understood as "normal"' (Mumford 1998: 89). And he adds that which conditions are ideal is relative to the context of the power ascription, yet no explanation is forthcoming of how we determine either context or relativity to context. The proposal looks, then, either intolerably vague or merely a reformulation of the ceteris paribus-style analysis Mumford rejected.

The force of the Martin–Molnar rejection of entailment between power possession and subjunctive conditionals has not yet been successfully deflected – at least as long as we expect our conditionals to be free both of terms that explicitly or implicitly refer to potentialities and of terms whose grasp requires a prior understanding of potentialities. In other words, the Humean/empiricist project of even *partially* explaining (via one-way entailment), let alone analysing, powers in terms solely of actualities is doomed. Yet it is also false that conditionals that explicitly exclude preventing mechanisms such as finks (which destroy the power), antidotes (which prevent the power from having an effect), masks (which prevent the power from even being exercised) and the like are *not* entailed by truths of power possession. Of course they are so entailed, and this is precisely how we explicate powers to others and come to know of them ourselves. There is nothing vacuous in this as long as we have to hand a metaphysical analysis of potentiality in general via the hylemorphic theory. Hylemorphism tells us that there is no matter without form, since everything has a quiddity – is something or other. Matter, on the other hand, as pure potentiality, is nothing in particular (though it is not nothing, as I explained in Chapter 4). Hence there is no potentiality without actuality: this is a fundamental, necessary truth of ontology not subject to finkish refutation. Hence Molnar misses the point, and misinterprets Aquinas on the way, when he insists that powers are 'actual properties' rather than 'unrealized possibilities' (Molnar 2003: 126), as though this were the correct contrast to make. Powers are not actualities, nor are they mere possibilities (and hence logical beings) – they are *real potentialities*.[22] And since there is no potency without act, so also there is not – at least in the material world – form without matter (on which more in Chapter 10), since form requires individuation by matter in order for there to be any particulars at all.

Given these truths, we know that matter and form – potentiality and actuality – form a correlative pair, always found together and each inexplicable without reference to the other. Neither can be defined, since they are too general and instead constitute the basis for all definition. But they can be explained and described, as I have done at length already. Hence it should be no surprise that particular powers and actualities can only be explicated in terms that presuppose the general notions of act and potency. Terms such as 'stimulus', 'manifestation', and 'response' refer to actualities that can only be grasped via a grasp of potency: they are what bring potency to actuality, or else what follow from the actualization of potency. And we cannot do away with them.

So, for example, imagine a naturally occurring system S in an environment rigged by God so that whenever S is subjected to force F in any possible world, S produces effect E and a distant bell rings, i.e. a bell causally isolated from S. There is an entailment between 'S is subjected to F' and 'A distant bell rings', but the ringing of the bell is no manifestation of S's power to produce E in the presence of F. We must include the concept of manifestation in any explication of powers. Note, though, that we do not need to include the concept of stimulus, at least not in any sense reflecting an efficient causal process. I have the power spontaneously to conjure up images in my mind, but need no stimulus to do so. (One may have to appeal here to final causes, but these are not the sorts of stimulus dispositionalists typically have in mind.) It may be, in fact, that our knowledge of power in the material world derives from first-personal knowledge of our own powers, as might be suggested in respect of causation generally. If so, the concept of stimulus has in such a context only limited relevance.

There is, then, an entailment between truths about the possession of powers and conditionals concerning manifestation, but these conditionals are inevitably power-invoking in their formulation. So when Mumford asserts that conditionals invoking the absence of preventing factors reduce to conditionals of the form 'If *F*, then *G*, unless not-*G*' (Mumford 1998: 87), he makes the mistake of expecting the conditionals to be potency free. There is, however, all the world of difference between 'If this wire were exposed to a conductor it would lose current unless prevented from doing so' and 'If this wire were exposed to a conductor it would lose current unless it did not lose current', which is indeed vacuous. The former contains a term, 'prevent', which can only be explained in other terms that invoke potency, since prevention essentially involves interference with a thing's doing what it is capable of doing. (You cannot *prevent* a rock from eating.) Nevertheless, the former conditional is entailed by the proposition that a given wire is live, and it is *informative* about a particular power even though it invokes the general concept of potentiality. (Compare: I can informatively explain the structure of a triangle's lines in terms of its angles, even though I cannot explain what angles are without invoking the general concept of a line.)

One does not need to understand hylemorphism as a metaphysical theory in order to have a grasp of potentiality sufficient for understanding what stimuli, responses, and manifestations are, and how they apply to particular powers. But the theory is available as the metaphysical underpinning of any analysis of powers. Moreover, it is hard to see how Molnar, for one, can avoid commitment to it. For one of the marks of powers on which he places great emphasis is what he calls 'physical intentionality', the 'directedness' of powers towards their manifestations (Molnar 2003: ch. 3). There is no room to explore the details, but his general idea is important and supports the case for reviving the notion of what I call inorganic teleology (Oderberg forthcoming a), which fell by the wayside under the anti-Aristotelian assaults of empiricism and materialism and has not yet recovered. The point here is that if, as Molnar suggests, one of the hallmarks of powers is that they are in some sense directed at their manifestations, it must be true that possession of a given power entails that the possessor will manifest it under an appropriate sti- mulus (in the case of wholly material substances) and in the absence of preventing conditions. Having the power essentially involves being in a state of *readiness* to manifest it, by taking on or producing actuality in the right conditions.

Hylemorphism also resolves the problem of the so-called 'dispositional–categorical' distinction. This is the worry about how to distinguish 'dispositional' from 'categorical' properties (with 'property' used here in the loose, contemporary sense), supplemented by the question of whether 'dispositional' properties have 'categorical' grounds. As I have indicated, the very terminology needs to be replaced by the 'act-potency' terminology of hylemorphism. Since there is no potency without act and (in the material world) no act without potency, we can never encounter a portion of reality in which potency is evacuated and only actuality remains, and vice versa. Hence we will never encounter powers without actualities, or actualities without powers.

But this does not mean they cannot be distinguished. Some accidents, such as spatio-temporal, geometrical, and quantitative ones, do not *manifest* themselves under a certain stimulus. It is no part of the explication of an object's actual circularity, say, that if appropriately stimulated it will take on a circular shape, since it already *has* that shape. This is so even if the object does have the power to take on other shapes when, say, subjected to certain forces. (Lowe mentions this (2006: 124–5), but note that his use of 'dispositional' and 'occurrent' in this context belies his own account of dispositional predication in terms of substantial kinds characterized by properties. A rubber eraser, to use his example, may be dispositionally square though, under distorting forces, occurrently trapezoid, even though this belongs to no substantial kind characterized by the property of squareness. But see also the discussion of accidental powers on p. 132.)

I would extend this notion to many properties that others would treat as dispositional, such as colour. Hence, *pace* Lowe (2006: 124), a red object in a dark room is *not* occurrently black. Its redness is not reducible to its power to look red in appropriate light; hence what it possesses in a dark room is not the power to *be* red, but the distinct power to *look* red. So there is an adequate notion of actuality applicable to various kinds of accident, namely the ones that require no stimulus to manifest themselves. We can broaden it to include the kind of case mentioned above, of the spontaneous exercise of a personal power, by speaking not of manifestation but of going through a process. I may need no stimulus to conjure up images in my mind, but this sort of behaviour is still the exercise of a power since I need to go through a process in order to manifest it – I have to *do* something. Red objects, square objects, and six-foot-long objects, by contrast, do not need to *do* anything in order to manifest these qualities, even though *we* may have to do something in order to notice them.

There is, then, an important insight as well as a confusion in this striking passage from Martin:

> Pure categoricity of a property or state is as much of a myth and philosophical artifice as is pure dispositionality. Any intrinsic property is

Janus-faced, a two-sided coin, and only at the limit of an unrealizable abstraction can one think of these as separate properties in themselves. No intrinsic properties, right down to the ultimate properties of elementary particles or the ultimate properties of spatio-temporal regions of fields, are – in Aquinas's terms – 'in pure act' or purely categorical. They are not, and indeed cannot be, manifesting all of which they are capable.

(Martin 1993: 184)

The first thing to note is Martin's explicit identification of being categorical with being in act, i.e. being an actuality. He is no hylemorphist, yet pays some obeisance to the traditional distinction at its heart. Secondly, he is insistent that you will never find potentiality without actuality or vice versa: it is both all the way down (and, I add, everywhere and at all times, and in all possible worlds where material substance exists). Thirdly, by denying the existence of pure actuality in the material universe, he states an important truth. Pure actuality would have to be immaterial.

The rest, however, is confused.[23] Lowe rightly objects to Martin's view according to which there is a dispositional and a categorical – better, a potential and an actual – *aspect* to each property (better, accident or quality), finding it a difficult view to make sense of (2006: 133). If second-order properties are not at issue (see Heil 2003: 119), then it is hard to see what could be meant, since actuality and potentiality are distinct and *incompatible*. By 'incompatible' I do not mean that a thing cannot contain both, since that is just what hylemorphism endorses. Rather, insofar as something is in act, it is *not* in potency, and insofar as it is in potency, it is *not* in act. So how could any property have an actual and a potential aspect, if this means that it is really both in act and in potency, or that its actuality is identical with its potentiality, there being only a logical or notional distinction between these aspects? Moreover, talk of aspects might suggest talk of perspectives, and there is no perspectival note in either act or potency: something either is or is not in act or in potency. The same sorts of criticism apply mutatis mutandis to Mumford's 'property monism', according to which 'the dispositional and the categorical are correctly understood just as two modes of presentation of the same instantiated properties' (Mumford 1998: 190). Such a position explicitly denies, as Mumford does, that the act/potency distinction marks an ontologically real division. We are then left with something we know not what kind of properties and are unable to explain what *in reality* accounts for the actualities and potentialities we find. Moreover, it gives all properties a 'manifestation aspect' even where it is wholly inappropriate, as in the case of shapes, structures, and spatio-temporal characteristics – whatever causal roles they may *also* be associated with.

The search for a 'categorical' grounding for all powers, then, is misplaced. If Ellis is right (Ellis 2001; also Ellis and Lierse 1994), then some powers – those of at least some of the subatomic particles – are ungrounded. More than that, however, *all* powers are ungrounded in the sense that they are not actualities or in any way (*pace* Mumford's functionalism about dispositions) instantiated by actualities, since actuality *excludes* potentiality in the way I have explained. But they are inseparable as well, and this is the important insight in the passage from Martin just quoted. Wherever we find potentiality we will find actuality, since form is what delimits pure potency and gives it a specific nature. This explains how pure potentiality – pure, undifferentiated power to receive this or that existence via the actualization of this or that form – is restricted and delimited so as to produce specific powers, whether it be the active powers of an animal to digest food or of water to dissolve salt, or the passive powers of a glass vase to break on being dropped or of a piece of metal to expand on being heated. In other words, actualities give rise to powers – indeed they entail the existence of powers. They do not 'ground' them in the sense of instantiating or realizing them; rather, they shape and determine them. The powers a thing has will, therefore, be wholly determined by its essence.

Unfortunately, though, talk of essence (despite the work of Ellis) is still in short supply among dispositionalists. Yet without essence we cannot explain *why* a thing has the powers it does. Essentialism tells us that a thing has the powers it does because of the kind of thing it is. Its essence bestows on it a range of powers, none of which is ever exhaustively manifested (as Martin 1993 rightly insists); otherwise, the object would lose all potentiality and be in a state of pure actuality, which is impossible. Passive powers, or powers to be affected by the actions of other objects, partake more of the material component of essence than the formal component, even though form still determines such powers. Take a hunk of homogeneous, highly plastic and flexible gunk (not exactly a scientific example, but it suffices to make the point). The piece of gunk, let us suppose, cannot *do* anything: it cannot dissolve or destroy other compounds; it cannot effect accidental changes in anything *except* through the actions of other things: I can throw the gunk at a window and break it, but that is *me* doing the work. The gunk has a range of passive powers, however: it can be bent, distorted, deformed, broken up and scattered to the winds, and so on. These passive powers derive from the material component of the gunk, albeit as shaped by its form. What this means is that the gunk's essence as a hunk of relatively undifferentiated, pliable *matter* makes it susceptible to being acted on, as matter, in a range of ways. Still, not *anything* can be done to the gunk: it cannot be turned into a proton or a monkey; it cannot, let us suppose, be stretched to a length greater than ten metres or compressed into a ball with radius less than a centimetre. Hence its range of passive powers is shaped and determined by its form, but the form *works* on matter, thus giving the gunk its particular passive characteristics as matter.

On the other hand, the power of an animal to digest food, as with other active powers, partakes more of the formal component of its essence than the material component. Unpacking this idea, there are two elements. First, like any passive power, the active power to digest food necessarily involves matter and its receptivity to change. In particular, when the animal digests, it too is changed by the food: its stomach expands, enzymes are stimulated into activity, and so on. These are all parts of the activity of digestion. But the special component that distinguishes the activity *as activity* from the mere passivity possessed by the hunk of gunk is due to form, not to matter. This is because matter is receptive, and digestion is not mere reception but action on other things, in which those other things (particles of food) are destroyed and assimilated into the body of the animal. Such action cannot derive wholly from a principle of passivity, and so it must derive from actuality, i.e. from form.

It will be objected that this distinction between powers is a misconceived legacy of empiricism,[24] that we now know matter to be not wholly inert or passive but also dynamic and active, and hence that the distinction marks a division in powers that does not reflect how nature works. Martin (1993: 182), for one, can make no sense of this way of talking. Yet if we take activity and passivity to be but two sides of the same ontological coin, as it were – that there is no real distinction between them – then the question arises: why *can't* the hunk of gunk act? Why can't it change anything or destroy anything of its own accord? The reply will be 'It's just not like that' or, more precisely, 'It's just not structured that way'. But this merely makes the point for the hylemorphist. If matter were always and everywhere both active and passive, if it were such that of its nature it had these two 'aspects', then we should expect matter always and everywhere to be both acting and reacting. Yet it is not. (Even if there is action by the particles within the hunk of gunk, the hunk itself is not active.)

Moreover, even if matter were like that we should expect any hunk of matter to be able to do what any other hunk of matter can – but this is not the case. To say 'This hunk of matter is not structured like that one' is just to concede that matter requires more than mere existence to be able to act: it needs to be formed, or actualized, in certain ways in order for it to have the range of powers it does, whether active or passive. To speak of 'structure' is not very helpful either, in fact, since this looks either like a placeholder for something we know not what about matter's arrangement or like a weak substitute for *form* or *actuality* as the ontological principle explanatory of the active powers of material substances. A structure, in the pure sense, can be described purely mathematically and geometrically. Yet how can this give rise to any action? Even an account of how salt dissolves in water involves more than a description of mere structure, but of the actions of charged particles in breaking molecular bonds. Hence talk of 'structure', if it is to have any explanatory force in respect of active powers, must include reference to the form and actuality of matter – the essences involved, with all of the activity they make possible. There is no escaping the distinction between form and matter, or – what comes down to the same distinction at a more general level – between actuality and potentiality.

I have said that all powers, not just the powers of fundamental particles, are ungrounded in anything actual, but are shaped and determined by actuality. This does not mean that powers mightn't be grounded in other powers, in the sense that one power might be but an instantiation of another power and wholly explained by it. (By contrast, actuality does not instantiate, or wholly explain, potentiality.) For example, the power of speech is grounded in the power of abstract symbolic representation. The power of digestion is grounded in the power that animals have of sustaining their own existence by their own teleological behaviour. The power of salt to be dissolved by water is grounded in the power of its individual molecules to have their bonds broken by water molecules. (In all these cases there will or may be further powers involved, some more basic, but the details need not concern us here.) Why not say, then, that we can do away with talk of essence and replace it with talk of powers pure and simple? Why not say that some powers are derived, others are basic, and what makes a member of some substantial kind *K* just that sort of thing is that it has a congeries of powers arranged in some sort of hierarchy from the basic to the non-basic?

Some philosophers do talk like that (e.g. Bennett and Hacker 2003). They think that we can get by with talk of powers without having to ground them ultimately in essence. Or, if they are partial to essences, they would reduce them (without eliminating them) to collections of powers. (Let us loosely call these positions reductionist.) Yet this takes us back to the unity problem, outlined in Chapter 3. If to be a *K* just is to have a collection of powers, then what unites the powers? To say that they are all just essential to *K*s is a mere linguistic variant of 'They are all of the essence of *K*s', and the concession to essence is made. Yet the reductionist does not want to say that a *K* could *lose* any of the powers; but if there is no essence, why couldn't any of the powers be lost without the *K*'s ceasing to exist? What holds them together? Even if they are each individually essential, why should we expect there to be any entailments *between* any of the powers?

Yet we see such entailments everywhere. For instance, being able to eat[25] entails being able to digest,[26] and vice versa. Now suppose the reductionist comes across a *K* that can both eat and digest. Since she denies that *K*s have an essence, or holds that if they do it is just a collection of powers, and she correctly takes the power to eat and the power to digest as individually essential to *K*s, then how does she explain the entailment between these powers? From '*K*s essentially can eat' and '*K*s essentially can digest' it does not follow that if anything essentially can eat it essentially can digest.[27] What does follow, of course, is that if anything is a *K*, then if it essentially can eat it essentially can digest. But the reductionist wants to explain being a *K* just as having a collection of powers, including being able to eat and to digest. So she will have to explain the entailment between these powers as follows: if anything essentially can eat and essentially can digest, then if it essentially can eat it essentially can digest. This is a logically necessary truth.[28] But it does nothing to illuminate the connection between the powers. By eschewing reference to *K*s in a way *independent* of reference to their powers, the reductionist loses the ability to explain what unites the powers.

Why not postulate an entailment loop between the powers? To take a simple case, why not say that *K*s have powers P_1, P_2, and P_3, that having P_1 entails having P_2, having P_2 entails having P_3, and having P_3 entails having P_1? There is no need for a unitary essence or form, just a circular relationship between the powers. This seems every bit as problematic as causal loops. Each power ends up being explained by itself, which is no explanation at all in the case of contingent existents, and here we have a case of the contingent obtaining of an entailment loop. Its circularity means that the existence of each power is 'explained' by its existence, and hence that the whole contingent loop is 'explained' by its existence, which is nonsensical and no explanation at all.

So why not take the entailment, say between being able to eat and being able to digest, to be a brute fact? First, it looks like the sort of relation that calls out for an explanation – why *is* it that things that can eat can also digest, and vice versa? Secondly, there *are* explanations of such relations between powers, in this case *because a thing that can eat and can digest must be an animal*. Now there may be no explanation as to why anything in particular is an animal (Why is Fido an animal? Well, he just is!), though there must be an explanation as to why animals exist at all. But being an animal explains why it is that if some things can eat they must be able to digest. (Thought experiment: could God produce or evolution throw up a kind of creature that can eat but has no capacity for digestion? Well, if it can eat it must need to sustain its existence, and digestion helps it to do that. I am not talking about a hypothetical *mutation*, but a design feature, if you will, of the organism. Yet there's no *evolutionary* explanation of why such a creature should exist, and fathoming a divine purpose for such a creation is not easy. In any case, even if such a creature were metaphysically possible, my claim would be the more limited one that there is an essentialist explanation of why *some* creatures, namely the animals, are such that their being able to eat entails their being able to digest, and vice versa.)

I conclude that only the essentialist – i.e. the believer in unitary essences explained in terms of substantial forms – can explain the necessary relationships between certain kinds of power, namely the ones possessed essentially. The unitary essence explains the powers: the powers *flow* from it, to repeat the metaphor. Hylemorphism explains what needs explaining.

6.4 Laws of nature

I end this chapter with a consideration of some of the issues concerning laws of nature, in particular how real essentialism accounts for them. I want to look at two broad questions: (1) whether any of the laws of nature are metaphysically necessary; (2) whether all are. The idea that the laws of nature are metaphysically necessary, contrary to the common view (e.g.

Armstrong 1983; Carroll 1994), is defended by 'dispositional essentialists' such as Ellis (2001) and Ellis and Lierse (1994). According to dispositional essentialism, the dispositional properties of fundamental particles (and fields) are essential to them, and the natural processes involving such particles are essentially manifestations of those properties. These processes are embodied in laws governing the way the particles behave. Since the dispositional properties are essential, in their absence there would not *be* the particles that possessed them, hence there could be no situation in which the particles existed but they did not manifest, or at least tend to manifest, the behaviour to which their dispositions give rise. The laws embodying the processes involving those dispositions are, therefore, metaphysically necessary.[29]

The scientific essentialism of Ellis, however, is at least implicitly reductionist, as I noted in Chapter 1. He doubts that there are many, if any, essentialist explanations in biology or psychology, for instance; or at least nothing that is not ultimately an explanation involving the essentialism in physics and chemistry. Real essentialism rejects this reductionism, and I will have more to say about it, at least in respect of biology and psychology, in Chapters 8, 9, and 10. Nevertheless, a proper understanding of essentialism shows that a necessitarian position on the laws of nature is correct, and to this extent Ellis is on the right track. Still, various objections have been levelled at the idea that even some laws could be necessary,[30] and I want to address several of them.

The a priori argument *for* necessitarianism, shorn of scientific essentialist accretions, runs as follows. Laws of nature are truths about how objects must behave. How objects must behave depends wholly on how objects must be. Hence the laws depend wholly on how objects must be. Hence they obtain in every world in which the objects they are about exist. In other words, every world in which certain objects exist will be a world in which those objects must behave in a certain way. Therefore every such world will be one in which the truths about how those objects must behave – i.e. the laws – obtain. There is no world, then, in which the objects exist and the laws about them do not obtain. So the necessity of those laws is metaphysical, since it is a necessity derived from the essences of the objects.

The short way of making the necessitarian point is to assert that *the laws of nature are the laws of natures*. For natures just are abstract essences in concrete operation. Nature is the collection of all the natures of things. So to say the laws are *of nature* is to say that they are *of the natures* of things. The first point to make in clarification is that it is an a posteriori matter *what* the laws of nature are, since it is a matter for investigation what the properties of objects are, i.e. how they must behave. This is so whether the laws are derived from observations of regularities (such as the laws of heredity) or whether they are postulates (such as the constancy of the speed of light irrespective of the motion of the source),[31] or whether they look like stipulations (which is arguably the case for Newton's second law, as it stipulates a measurable quantity, called force, as the product of two other quantities, mass and acceleration). In each case, the method for arriving at the law is somewhat different, as is its role in the relevant theory, but it is still an a posteriori matter whether the law holds. In the case of a postulate, its truth will be assumed, but empirical investigation can refute it. In the case of a stipulation, such as Newton's second law, empirical investigation could reveal that there is no constant correlation between a stipulated quantity and the quantities on which it is allegedly dependent, in which case it would turn out to be wrong to have postulated a single quantity that varies in a predictable way. Needless to say, this applies to the empirical sciences, but for a priori sciences (logic, mathematics, geometry) the investigations involved are not empirical; still, one produces proofs or refutations to show whether a law in these sciences holds, or else takes them to be self-evident. But one must not confuse the method of arriving at a law with the reason the law holds, since even in the a priori sciences the laws hold because of the natures of the objects being investigated.

Secondly, and related to the first point, sceptics about the role of essence in explaining laws sometimes express a worry about circularity, at both the ontological and epistemological levels (see, e.g., Drewery 2005). The ontological worry is that although laws are, for the essentialist, supposed to hold by virtue of the properties of things, it looks also like the properties hold by virtue of the laws that are true of them. For instance, can there be a conception of the essence of an electron independent of the laws that determine what electrons do, including how they interact with other particles (Drewery 2005: 387)? The epistemological worry is that, although the essentialist claims we know laws via essences, maybe we can only know essences via laws, and so we are caught in a circle.

These dual concerns can be allayed together. Since the laws just are truths about the properties of things (and the essences from which the properties emanate), there is no circularity but identity. That is, the laws have no content over and above that involving objects, their essences, the properties that emanate from them, and the relations between these. That reference is often made to other objects apart from the one whose properties are being investigated simply shows that if we want to know the properties of one thing we often have to find out the properties of other things: if we want to know what powers of interaction electrons have, we need to know what other objects there are and how electrons interact with them. And this means we might first have to know *other* laws; but these laws too will be truths about the properties of other things.

To take the standard example, if we want to know whether it is a law that salt dissolves in water, we need to know both about salt and about water: but this does not show that there is no conception of the essence of salt independent of the essence of water. All it shows is that the passive power of salt to be dissolved by water can operate only if water has certain properties. Moreover, even if water lacked those properties, salt would still retain the internal chemical bonds that gave it the power to be dissolved by any substance that possessed the active powers we mistakenly thought water had. Furthermore, if (let us suppose, without assuming it possible) we had a case where two kinds of object were such that we could only know about the essence of each via knowledge of the essence of the other, then although we would have no independent conception of the essence of either, we could conclude that what we were investigating was a *system*, and the independent essence was the essence of that system, of which the wholly relational essences of the objects were but elements.

Thirdly, and related to the second, there is the worry that scientific essentialists tend to treat the intrinsic properties of fundamental particles[32] as all dispositional (Ellis 2001: 135), in which case what is left of the notion of intrinsic essence? Isn't the use of the term 'intrinsic' for such properties merely honorific? (See Drewery 2005: 387.) What this shows is that scientific essentialists are wrong to suggest that the essence of anything, fundamental particles included, is purely dispositional, even if some of a thing's properties are ungrounded potentialities, and even if the essence itself involves some ungrounded potentiality. As I have argued, there is no pure potentiality, i.e. potentiality existing in the absence of actuality to shape and determine it. The same applies to particles such as electrons. In fact it is arguable whether, say, the mass or charge of an electron is purely dispositional, given that they are precise, measurable quantities, whatever the electron's potential behaviour in relation to other particles, given its mass and charge. The existence of actual quantity excludes pure dispositionality. The electron is a measurable entity with spatio-temporal location; it is not a mere bundle of powers. Electrons have angular momentum, orbit, and are countable. They are discrete packets of energy obeying the laws of quantum mechanics. All of this shows that electrons are material substances with form – not mere potentialities, but a mix of actuality and potentiality. Hence they are no exception to the hylemorphic account of essence. Even if it turned out that what we thought were discrete, measurable quantities were nothing but perturbations of fields or some such, then electrons might not exist as described; instead they would be accidents or properties of some other entity, such as a field. And this entity would be a mixture of actuality and potentiality.

Fourthly, there is a worry, expressed in various places, that, for all we know, the fundamental 'constants' of nature may not be constant at all but variable, in which case any law that depended on a variable quantity, where the existence of the objects it was about was not dependent on that quantity, might fail to hold in a world in which such objects still existed (Lowe 2006: 151–2; Drewery 2005: 389). Water might not boil at 373 Kelvin if this law depended on a quantity, independent of the existence of water, that could vary from world to world. The same goes for the dissolution of salt in water. Isn't this a reason to think that the laws of nature might come apart from the natures of the things they are about?

The essentialist has two related responses available: both involve the thought that if such a scenario were possible we would know that 'Salt dissolves in water' was not a law after all, rather than a law that held in some worlds but not others. Both responses are stronger than Bird's (2001, 2002). According to him, physics and chemistry strongly suggest that if Coulomb's constant[33] were other than it is, not only would dissolution of salt in water not occur but salt would not exist either. Hence the law that salt dissolves in water would not fail to hold. But, as he concedes, we need to know more about physico-chemical laws (more particularly, about quantum mechanics) to know whether this would in fact be the case. Yet Bird is happy with this position, as it shows that whether a law is necessary is an a posteriori matter. He concedes that some laws may be contingent. I submit that the essentialist needs a stronger response, rather than to proceed on a case-by-case basis and so allow that contingency of law may hold where, say, the existence of an object covered by a law stating its behaviour is not dependent on the law itself.

As I said, both responses available to the essentialist involve treating 'Salt dissolves water' as not being a law at all, on the scenario envisaged. First, we can say that *if* salt and water can exist in a world where the former does not dissolve in the latter because of a variation of Coulomb's constant, this shows that the complete statement of the relevant law (as with many laws) requires attention to background conditions. In the case of salt and water, one condition would be that Coulomb's constant has the value it does. The truth would be not that salt dissolves water absolutely, but that salt dissolves in water only in conditions $C_1 \ldots C_n$. If one of the conditions fails, salt does not dissolve. Hence in a world where Coulomb's constant has a different value, the law that salt dissolves water in conditions $C_1 \ldots C_n$ still holds. This in itself does not require treating the law as a ceteris paribus law, since ceteris paribus clauses apply to cases of interference, non-normal cases, and the like (Bird says a little about this (2001: 273)). It may be that these considerations require adding a ceteris paribus clause as well, but that is another matter. The point here is that putative laws of the form 'Ks do F to Js', and similar propositions stating interactions between kinds of object, are rarely if ever true laws.

The second response is more subtle, and relies on immanentism. Physical constants are not free-floating quantities; they are properties of something or other. In the case of Coulomb's constant, it is a property of electrostatic fields, contributing to the precise proportion by which the electrostatic force between charged particles varies.[34] If we look at constants this way, as abstractions from concrete particulars, we can regard 'Salt dissolves in water' as not being a true law, since the true law governing their interaction is a greater-than-two-place relation. It is at least a three-place relation, which we could formulate along the lines of 'Salt dissolves in water relative to k', where k is Coulomb's constant. To be more precise, we should say something like 'Salt dissolves in water according to E', where E is an equation instantiating Coulomb's Law and containing, as well as k, ranges for the charge variables and a range for the distance separating the charges. Spelling out the details might produce a very long equation, or in some cases we might not even know how to spell it out. The point remains, however, that *this* would be the true law governing the interaction of salt with water, not the simplistic 'Salt dissolves in water'. In a world where k did not obtain there would be no such law – it is *not* that it would be false. This would merely be an instance of the necessitarian position that the laws governing objects hold in all worlds in which those objects exist.

According to the first response I gave, in a world where the actual-world constant varied, the law would still hold, since the failure of background conditions would be irrelevant. According to the second response, just given, there would be no such law at all, since one of the kinds of thing necessary for its obtaining – e.g. an electrostatic field yielding Coulomb's constant – would be absent. This would be no different in principle to the water–salt law's not obtaining in a world without salt or water. In order to say which response is preferable, we need to know more about what the constants of nature are, of what exactly they are true, and how they might be regarded as differing from mere background conditions. We cannot canvass that here. Both responses, nevertheless, are superior to Bird's response, which, whilst in some ways congenial to essentialism, holds too many hostages to empirical fortune and so eschews the general a priori argument I gave at the beginning to the effect that the laws of nature are the laws of natures.

Although what I have said so far is concerned mainly with the very idea that any laws of nature might be metaphysically necessary, it inevitably implies that *all* the laws of nature are metaphysically necessary. This does not exclude the possibility of miracles. It is commonly thought that a miracle, if such were possible, would involve a *breach* of one or more laws of nature, thus reinforcing the idea that the laws are not metaphysically necessary. In other words, a miracle is usually thought to show that a law of nature might fail to hold. This, however, is the wrong way of conceiving of miracles. A miracle would not be a breach in the laws of the nature, but a *suspension* of the laws. We can see a rough analogy with the case of human positive law. For some reason or other, the state might decline to uphold or enforce a certain law, say one requiring payment of a particular tax. It might do this either by not bothering to pursue or investigate breaches of the law, or by constantly declining to punish anyone apprehended breaking it. The law remains on the books, but fails to hold and breaches are allowed. By contrast, the state may revoke a law temporarily, removing it from the statute book. During this period, no one who omits to pay the relevant tax (better, what *was* a tax when the law was on the books) breaches any law, and there is no relevant law that fails to hold.

Miracles are like the second sort of case. During the time a miracle occurs (assuming miracles can occur and a particular case is indeed miraculous), the laws of nature that would otherwise be violated were they operative are suspended – they are *not* operative. But if they are not operative, why wouldn't miraculous events occur throughout space and time at the same time a particular miracle was occurring? In an extreme case that might be so: God could, if He wanted, suspend all laws throughout space and time, and miracles would be pervasive. But in the typical case – let us suppose a dead person's coming back to life, or water being changed to wine – what happens is that the relevant laws are suspended *only in the spatio-temporal region of the miracle.* I contend that it is a mere terminological matter whether one goes on to say that in all the regions outside the miracle the laws continue to be in force, or else that the very universality of law implies that what are in force outside the miracle are no longer to be regarded as laws, but as something like pro tanto natural injunctions, or specific ordinances of nature, or something similar, which regain the force of law once the miracle has ended.

But if the state can choose to fail to enforce a law or else to revoke it altogether, why doesn't God have the choice? Since the laws of nature are the laws of natures, for God to interfere with an operative law would by that very fact involve God's preventing natures from operating according to what they are, which is not a mere semantic impossibility but a fundamental metaphysical one. God is bound by the natures He creates as much as by the laws of logic, which, as I have claimed, are but a species of essentialist necessity. He could, of course, annihilate the natures he has created and replace them with new ones that operated according to different laws: He could, perhaps,[35] replace all current organisms with new kinds of organism that could rise from the dead according to a law of reverse entropy that replaced the current thermodynamical law. That is not, however, the same as preserving the natures that do exist but frustrating their operation according to the current laws. For the current laws simply describe how the natures that do exist *must* operate. Why couldn't God, say, prevent salt from dissolving in water by a momentary interference, without annihilating the natures of salt and water? But then He would have to change the nature of something else – space, time, the atmosphere, or something else involved in normal dissolution – and to change the nature of a thing is to annihilate it altogether, whether or not it be replaced by some other kind of thing with a different nature. I conclude that the possibility of miracles does not refute necessitarianism about the laws of nature.

Another objection comes from Katzav (2004). He focuses on the fact that there are global physical laws or principles governing the operation of all physical systems and their constituents. In particular, the Principle of Least Action (PLA), formulated by Pierre-Louis Moreau de Maupertuis in the eighteenth century,[36] states that all physical objects move along a path that minimizes action. One statement of the principle has it that '[i]f we examine the laws which prevail in the physical world, we find that whenever there is more than one conceivable method of operation, nature follows the one in which the product of the time multiplied by the energy is the least possible amount' (Fee 1941: 497). And again, Maupertuis himself expresses his idea that 'nature is thrifty' by saying that 'in all the changes which occur in the universe ... that which is called the quantity "action" is always the least possible amount' (quoted in Fee 1941: 503). An example of the general principle is Fermat's Principle, or the Principle of Least Time, according to which light travels between two points along the path of shortest time. Classical mechanics can be reformulated using the equations deriving from the work of Lagrange,[37] where the trajectory of an object minimizes action as expressed in the Lagrangian (the difference between kinetic and potential energy). The PLA is also used in quantum mechanics, relativistic physics, field theory, and it seems that all the laws of motion can be derived from it.

Katzav uses the PLA to argue against dispositional essentialism. If, as dispositional essentialists hold, the dispositions and other intrinsic properties of objects suffice to determine how they will behave, it contradicts the PLA. For the PLA implies that the way an object behaves is not determined by its intrinsic properties. The PLA itself, as a wholly general principle, fixes an object's dispositions and behaviour in conjunction with whatever intrinsic properties the object possesses. Its behaviour cannot be read off from its intrinsic properties alone, including its dispositions, or from its intrinsic properties coupled with those of any objects with which it can interact.

Ellis replies that the PLA should be understood as being 'of the essence of the global kind in the category of objects or substances', which kind he takes to be *physical system* (Ellis 2005: 91). Hence, if we attend properly to the hierarchies of kinds that are part of essentialism, we need not regard the PLA (more precisely, whatever it is that makes it true) as ontologically more basic than, or other than, just another essence – only a highly general one. Since Ellis regards the world as 'one of a kind' (Ellis 2001: 249–53), it is clear why he responds in this way. Some worlds have as part of their essence that they are governed by the PLA (and perhaps other highly general laws – see Ellis and Lierse 1994: 43); others do not.

Whilst not wanting wholly to dismiss this response, I think another is available, at least given our limited knowledge of the ontological ground of the PLA. For a start, Ellis is wrong to place *physical system* as the global natural kind in the category of substance. The global kind – the *summum genus* – is just *substance*. Systems are collections of substances and their modifications, including their relational accidents. If *physical system* were the summum genus, then individual substances would be species of system, and this is just wrong, whatever the reality of systems within and involving those individuals. Now there may, as suggested on p. 146, be systems whose elements must be understood at least partly in relational terms. Perhaps the universe is like that. Maybe, whatever its conceivability, it is metaphysically impossible for there to be a universe containing just one thing, say a metaphysical simple. (On the very possibility of metaphysical simples that are by nature material, see Chapter 10.5.) Maybe space and time (or space–time) are necessary as well, and these must be understood substantively rather than as modifications of that single simple. Or maybe they must be understood relationally, so if it is impossible for the putative simple to exist without space and time, at least one other thing must exist. If the single simple in an otherwise empty universe were impossible, then the application of the PLA in any universe would require the existence of a system, and we could say that what made the PLA true was the essence of the system.

On the other hand, were the singleton simple possible (maybe it does not even have to be a simple), and space and time reducible to mere modifications of it, would it be clear that the PLA did not apply to it? I do not think so. Why could such an object not be subject to the PLA? Suppose it had been created by God, and was endlessly changing according to the divine blueprint for it. Might it not also be the case that its series of changes, and so the action integral describing them, followed a minimum of action relative to all its other possible trajectories through space and time?

The point of this admittedly highly speculative supposition is that we cannot rule out the possibility that what makes the PLA true is no more than the intrinsic powers of material substances. Katzav would have us believe that we can fix the intrinsic characteristics of objects and still not be able in principle to work out their actions since we need the PLA to do so as well. But if the PLA is made true by a highly general power – one shared without exception by all material objects – then fixing the intrinsic characteristics of objects requires *also* fixing their general intrinsic disposition to act according to a minimum. If the PLA is true, then we can regard it as made true by a high-level disposition which, taken in conjunction with all of the other intrinsic properties of objects, enables us to derive their action integral, hence their equations of motion. It is an overly narrow understanding of what dispositions or powers are that prevents Katzav from leaving this option open.[38]

7 Aspects of essence

7.1 Kinds of accident

In this chapter I want to look briefly at some aspects of real essentialism. Although a detailed exploration of these topics is not possible here, an outline of some of the issues concerning each one will help to shed light on how the overall essentialist position should be understood.

The first concerns accidents. Contemporary metaphysics lumps all accidents together and gives them the name 'properties' but, as we have seen, essentialism distinguishes between non-essential and essential accidents, the latter being *propria* or properties in the strict sense (the qualifier 'essential' being somewhat misleading, as I will explain). They are a kind of accident, and what is true of accidents in general is true of them, but I will say more about what is particular to properties in section 7.2.

Like everything else, accidents have an essence – they are a this-such, a something-or-other. Hence they can be categorized and placed in hierarchies, with something like a species/genus structure, but this will not look exactly like the Porphyrian Tree as applied to substances. The reason is that substances can be fully defined in terms that do not presuppose a prior grasp of the essence being defined, whereas this is not the case with many (perhaps all) accidents. Yet this should not surprise us, once we reflect on the way substance and accident are apprehended. The apprehension of a substance involves finding the specific difference that marks it out from the various genera to which it belongs. This typically involves specifying one or more properties of the object, sufficient to enable us to place it in an appropriate category. (The same goes for the genus.) For, as I have argued (and will argue further in section 7.3), essences are known to us via properties, hence via certain kinds of accident.

Since, however, accidents have essences as well, if we could define an accident using the genus/species method we would have to specify further, second-order accidents to enable us to categorise our target first-order accident. But these second-order accidents would have to be definable via third-order accidents, and so on. Yet this process must come to an end, otherwise nothing would be definable – no substance and no accident –

since definition is precisely the *limitation* of an object in the sense of that which gives it its boundaries and marks it off from everything else. Infinite definition is no definition at all, not even, I contend, of an infinite being: even that should be capable of definition in terms of finite elements, though the definition may not be complete, as most definitions are not given our finite capacity to grasp the essence of anything.

At some point in the process of definition, we must come to an end, accidents being no exception. This means something must always remain undefined, perhaps because the indefinable is essentially phenomenal and so only graspable by acquaintance rather than strict definition, or perhaps because the indefinable is some simple phenomenon not specifiable in other terms. Where we end depends upon what we are defining, but I would argue, for instance, that an accident such as colour, and any specific colour, is indefinable in the first sense. We might draw a tree for, say, red, as in Figure 7.1. Although such a tree goes some way to defining red, it would be clearly wrong to say that red had *phenomenal* as its genus and *colour* as its difference, since the other colours fall under this as well. And it would be incorrect to take *colour* as the genus and *red* as the difference since *red* is what we are trying to define. Red is clearly a kind of colour – but what kind? Many philosophers will opt for placing under *colour* a wavelength division, in particular *has wavelength 630–760 nanometres* and *has wavelength other than 630–760 nanometres*, and then place *red* under the former. I think this should be resisted, not because of worries about vagueness or about extensional adequacy, but because, even if adequate, and even if precise, the putative definition would not get close to capturing the essence of red, which is phenomenal. Redness just has a certain look, a certain appearance to a certain kind of perceiver,[1] and when we grasp that – by acquaintance – we

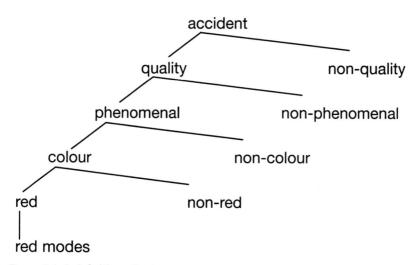

Figure 7.1 A definition of red

grasp what it is about redness that marks it off from other qualities in general and other colours in particular. It seems that Jackson-style arguments (Jackson 1982, 1996) and the sorts of consideration presented by Hacker (1987) reinforce this view. The same can be applied to phenomenal qualities such as pain and heat.

But even if this view of phenomenal qualities were wrong, and they could all be defined correctly in non-phenomenal terms, indefinability would still remain when it came to at least some of the accidents used to define the putative phenomenal qualities. Accidents involving dimensionality, such as length, shape, size, duration, will be either indefinable or definable in terms of accidents that are themselves indefinable, as will at least some accidents of fundamental particles, such as mass, charge, spin, energy state, and so on. I make no claims about particular accidents, only the general claim that we should not expect all accidents to be definable, and hence not expect to be able to fit accidents into the general Porphyrian structure, except in an attenuated way such as that exemplified above. We can, however, categorize accidents, and Aristotle did about as good a job as anyone has ever done, dividing the accidents up into nine categories: (1) quality; (2) quantity; (3) relation; (4) place; (5) time; (6) posture (arrangement and disposition of parts); (7) habit (arrangement and disposition of external adjuncts such as dress, cover, decoration); (8) action (doing); (9) passion (undergoing).[2] (See further Ross 1928a.) His tenth category of being is, of course, substance.

Accidents are actualities, but they are not pure act, not even mathematical properties (see Chapter 6, note 23). They are all mixed actualities, i.e. combinations of actuality and potentiality, even though it is also correct to speak of all accidents as forms themselves – as 'accidental forms', in contradistinction to substantial forms. The explanation of this apparently inconsistent way of speaking is that every accident is a determinate actuality, not a pure potentiality. Even powers themselves, as argued in Chapter 6, are not pure potentialities, and this even though they may be irreducible and so not wholly explained by (or 'grounded in') some one or more actualities (or 'categorical' qualities).[3] All powers are given their determinate being by the actualities that shape them, even though there remains an irreducible potentiality in their nature. The power of water to dissolve salt is not wholly explained without reference to potentiality, including the active power of the water molecules to attract sodium and chlorine ions from the salt molecules, and the passive power of these ions to be attracted. But what makes such a power a *solvent* power rather than some other power is the actualities of the molecules, such as polarity, charge, molecular structure, and so on.[4]

Thus even irreducible powers are shaped by actuality, i.e. given their determinate nature by actuality, and so we can correctly speak of them as actualities, as determinate ways of being, and hence as forms – but in a *secondary* sense. As observed in Chapter 6, powers are not actualities in the sense of being wholly determinate, like shape, size, structure, and the like. They manifest themselves in a range of ways. So they are not strict actualities: to describe them as such would implicitly be to eliminate the actuality/potentiality distinction. But powers are not wholly indifferent either: each has a *range* of manifestations associated with it; each is a determinate way of being shaped by strict actuality.[5]

Accidents that are not powers, such as shape, size, structure, and colour (so I contend), are also of course actualities, and so forms in the strict sense, though it is plausible that they all have powers associated with them (more accurately, true of them) such as the power of shapes to exclude other shapes, of sizes to resist certain forces, of colours to induce certain perceptual experiences, and so on.[6] So the fact that powers are shaped by actualities, and that actualities are often, perhaps always, attended by various powers, evidences a mixture of act and potency in all accidents, whether they are strictly denominated powers (such as solvency) or actualities (such as shape).

The other way in which accidents partake of both potency and act is via their natural *inexistence*, i.e. their inherence by nature in the substances that possess them. Since the substances are compounds of act and potency, they are limited, finite beings, and this finiteness is, as it were, inherited by their accidents. Only certain kinds of thing can be coloured, only certain substances are capable of reproduction, and so on. The old Scholastic maxim that a thing behaves as it is (*agere sequitur esse*) sums up this idea: finite beings have a finite range of behaviour, and the latter is determined by the essence of the former. Given the ontological tie between substance and accident, then, one might ask, thinking of *Alice in Wonderland*, could there be a grin without a cat? In other words, could accidents exist without a substance? The most famous context for such a question is the Catholic doctrine of transubstantiation, according to which the unconsecrated bread and wine are converted, by the action of the priest pronouncing the words of consecration, into the Body and Blood of Christ. The accidents of the bread and wine remain, but the substance has changed: where there was truly bread, there is now only truly Christ (present in His substance, but not with His material accidents, such as height and bodily qualities, as when He was on earth in first-century Palestine).

Brian Ellis regards this doctrine as 'madness' and 'bizarre' for a scientific essentialist: 'Same observable properties, different substances. Fine, if you think that what a thing is is logically independent of what it does. But madness if you think otherwise' (Ellis 2001: 246). Hence 'it is metaphysically impossible for flesh and blood, constituted as they are, to behave as the doctrine of transubstantiation requires' (Ellis 2001: 247). Yet this logical independence – hence metaphysical independence – not only does not contradict real essentialism, but is required by it. For, as I have argued, there is a *real distinction* between a substance and its accidents, including its properties. A substance is *not* a bundle of accidents, or identical with any particular privileged accident. Similarly, no accident is identical with any substance – they are really and metaphysically distinct. So it must be possible for them to come apart – *not* according to the order of nature, however.

Natures are essences in operation. By its nature, a substance must have accidents, and accidents require a substance in which to inhere. Not even God could change this, given what substance and accident are. But were He to *suspend* the operation of nature by miraculous intervention, He could prevent a substance from having any of its accidents, and accidents from having a substance in which to inhere. What He could not change, short of annihilating a substance or an accident, is the very essence of these beings – that a substance has a quiddity by which it is constituted according to genus and species, and that accidents are those forms that require a substance in which they *naturally* inhere. Transubstantiation violates neither of these metaphysical truths. The accidents of bread and wine are still genuine accidents; they still have a natural requirement for inherence; that is, in the course of nature they exist by being possessed by a substance fitted for them. By their essence, accidents are distinct from substances and have their own reality. But a suspension of the laws of nature (and so of the laws of natures) allows them to exist without their natural correlate, viz. an appropriate substance.

Note, first, that since everything requires a principle of individuation, what God could *not* do, in my view, is create accidents that never were and never will be possessed by any substance, because accidents are individuated precisely by the substances that have them. Hence the individuality of the accidents of bread and wine during and after transubstantiation is secured cross-temporally by the substance of the bread and wine that used to exist and in which they used to inhere. (I will say more about cross-temporal individuation in Chapter 10.) Secondly, the real essentialist view of the matter does not involve bare particularism. Bare particularists hold that particulars have nothing intrinsic that constitutes them as belonging to one kind or another. By contrast, were a miracle to deprive a substance of its natural accidents, the substance would still have an intrinsic essence – it would still belong intrinsically, by virtue of its constitution, to one kind or another. So, too, during and after transubstantiation, Christ remains God and is distinguished from all His creatures by His very essence. No bare particularist would allow that. I conclude that although God could not create a grin that never belonged and never will belong to any cat, still, by direct intervention in nature and suspension of its operation, He could deprive a grin of its cat. Prejudice against the very possibility of a miracle aside, scientific essentialists such as Ellis have to demonstrate exactly what ontological principle is violated by such a thought.[7]

7.2 The nature of properties

Once we are clear on the real distinction between substance and accident, we can see that the real distinction between essence and property follows immediately. For a substance is constituted by its essence, and properties are a species of accident. No property of a thing is part of a thing's essence, though properties flow from the essence. The idea that properties flow from real essences might seem stranger than it is. Locke himself uses the term 'flow' (Locke 1975: III.vi.19, p. 449), though he was merely expressing the common Aristotelian/Scholastic thinking that had been handed down to him (albeit in an impure state). Leaving aside the question of miraculous intervention, and so using essence and nature interchangeably, we can say that properties flow from a thing's essence in the sense that what it is metaphysically guarantees what it does. It is because humans have the rational nature they do that they can engage in certain kinds of thought, and because diamonds have the nature they do that they have such a high hardness index, and so on.

It might be thought, however, that the distinction between essence and property is arbitrary. Humans are rational, yet surely rationality is a property or cluster of properties; and tigers are mammals, so to be a mammal must be to have a certain property or cluster of properties. This way of looking at essence, effectively collapsing the distinction between it and property, is ubiquitous among contemporary essentialists, scientific essentialists being no exception, yet it must be resisted. The reasons are by now familiar. Without such a distinction, we have no explanation for the unity of an object or for the support of its properties, for it becomes just a bundle of properties, with all of the problems attendant on bundle theories. Even real essentialists are sometimes prone to collapsing the essence/property distinction. Hence, although Gorman (2005) is correct to hold that accidents are explained by essences (and not the reverse), he speaks of essences as 'characteristics' of things that possess them. What marks these characteristics as essential, and so to be distinguished from accidents (including properties), he argues, is that essential characteristics are not explained by any other characteristics of their possessors. And this leads him to claim that if the possession by a hydrogen atom of one proton were explicable in terms of a 'deeper fact' involving, say, quark structure, then having one proton would not be essential to it, whereas the quark structure would be 'a candidate for essentiality' (Gorman 2005: 284–5). Since, however, we do not know that such an explanation holds, we can rest pro tanto with the possession of a single proton as a 'fundamental, unexplained fact' about hydrogen, and hence as an essential characteristic.

This way of thinking, I contend,[8] falls into the confusion, discussed in Chapter 2.3, between specificity and generality, thus reinforcing the more general mistake of hidden structure essentialism. We know that having a single proton marks hydrogen out from everything else in the universe. (Well, we could be wrong, but there is no evidence we are.) Hence *having a single proton* is most plausibly regarded as the specific difference of hydrogen. I say 'most plausibly', because the very nature of properties is such that they too necessarily characterize a species, and are typically possessed by every member, marking it out from every other species – yet a property is not a specific difference.[9] Properties flow from and are explained by essences, not the reverse. Hence specificity gives us the strongest independent evidence we can have for a differentia, but we still need to engage in investigation of explanatory relations before we can have the greatest evidence we can have, taken as a whole, that a candidate constitutive principle really is such, and not a mere property flowing from such a principle. In the case of hydrogen, we can be all but certain that having a single proton is part of the essence of this element, i.e. a constitutive principle.

Yet we must qualify the position further, lest it be thought that my appeal to explanation is by that very fact an appeal to reduction. For even if it turned out, say, that the atomic number of hydrogen were explained by quark structure S, it would not follow that this single-proton quark structure was part of the real essence of hydrogen. This is so whether or not the constitution relation between having a single proton and having quark structure S was just identity. Of course, if it were identity, then we would not have advanced to a 'deeper' essence of hydrogen: all we would have done is clarified just what the essential principle *having a single proton* consisted in.[10] If it were not identity (and I hold that there is a genuine distinction between constitution and identity) it still would not follow that finding the constitution of protons by quarks meant moving from an apparent essence to a real essence.

This is because there is a difference between what is *constitutive* of a thing and what *constitutes* it. Once we have located an object's genus and specific difference, we have its essence – that which is constitutive of it. If we then find out that the object is *constituted* by something else, say by fundamental particles, what we discover is not its 'deeper' essence but its *material* cause. Now the root material cause of all substances is prime matter, but since there is no matter without form, when we discover a thing's constituents, whether fundamental or not, we discover *proximate* matter, i.e. its proximate material cause, and this comes to us already packaged by form, as it were. That is to say, the constituents and their structure are already informed by the substantial form of the object whose constituents they are. In the case of hydrogen, its putative single-proton quark structure S is not a free-floating structure that happens to constitute a single proton, but a structure that is itself informed by the substantial form that is *constitutive* of hydrogen. Similarly, a human being is constituted in part by cells, but those cells are already informed by the body that is partly *constitutive* of the human being. The only sense in which having a body explains what it is to be human is the constitutive one. And if S constituted hydrogen's single proton the only sense in which it would explain what it is to be hydrogen would be in terms of the constitutive way in which having a single proton explained the specific difference of hydrogen. Hydrogen's properties, i.e. its behaviour, operations, states, and so on, would be explained, at least in part, by its single-proton structure.

Were you to ask, 'But why does this particular proton in this particular atom have quark structure S?', to be told 'Because that is a hydrogen atom' would be to give you an informative answer, hence an explanation. If quarks are fundamental, there would be no further explanation. If they were not, then the situation would be that there was a lower-level structure S_l that constituted S, and that the former was a constitutive part of the proton's quark structure. But this fact would get you no nearer to a 'hidden essence' of either the proton or the hydrogen atom of which the proton is a part. In short, a lower level of constitutive explanation does not by that very fact get you closer to the essence of a thing, which is why hidden structure essentialism is confused.

What this shows is that the question as to the essence of hydrogen is a different one from the question as to the essence of a proton. It may be that the essence of a proton is partly given by a certain quark structure – [up, up, down] – just as the essence of hydrogen is partly given by having a single proton. But it does not follow, without prior reductionist assumptions, that the essence of hydrogen is partly given by a certain quark structure. All that follows is precisely that the essence of hydrogen is partly given by having a particle *whose own essence* is partly given by having a certain quark structure. Similarly, it is part of the essence of human beings to have rationality. And it is part of the essence of rationality to manifest itself, let us suppose, by a certain range of powers exercised by the object that has rationality. But it is not part of the essence of *human beings* to manifest a certain range of powers, for these are *properties* of humans flowing from their specific difference of rationality, not part of the human *essence*.

Even a real essentialist such as Gorman, on the most natural reading of his (2005), is led astray by contemporary essentialist thinking when he treats essences as characteristics. If having a single proton were a characteristic of hydrogen, it would naturally call out for an explanation – 'Why is hydrogen so characterized?' When the real essentialist replies, 'Because that's just what it is to be hydrogen', adding the rider, 'No matter how much deeper you go into hydrogen's inner structure', an essentialist such as Gorman, influenced by the reductionism at the heart of contemporary essentialism, wonders why the deeper structure does not get you closer to the essence of hydrogen. If having a single proton were just another characteristic of hydrogen, the concern that we had not yet got to hydrogen's essence might be warranted. This way of thinking, derived in a virtually straight line from Locke's 'something-we-know-not-what' approach to essence, implies that scientists, or anyone else for that matter, might *never* get to the essence of anything. Even if there were an a priori argument that there had to be genuinely fundamental particles, i.e. ones not composed of any others, all that could show us at most is that everything must *have* an essence, but not that we have ever grasped it, since we might not have alighted yet on the fundamental particles (as we may not have in respect of quarks). It also implies that when scientists first discovered hydrogen's single-proton structure, and satisfied themselves that no other element shared this atomic number, they had not in fact made a genuine advance in getting at the essence of hydrogen, even though they had found the specific difference and already knew the genus.

There is nothing wrong with using the term 'characteristic' in a loose sense when speaking of a substance's constitutive principles, but the metaphysical truth that must be borne in mind is that the difference of a thing is neither an accident in general, nor a property in particular. In traditional Aristotelian terminology, it is a *predicable*, that which is capable of being *truly predicated* of a substance. Genus and species are also predicables, but they too are neither accidents nor properties. Whereas genus, species, and difference are *constitutive* predicables, accidents and properties are *characterizing* predicables. The distinction is, in effect, marked by Lowe (2006), with his division of universals into substantial kinds and attributes, and by Aristotle, with his denomination of substantial kinds as 'secondary substances' in the *Categories* (Ross 1928a: 2a12).

Hence, for instance, since *mammal* is a genus, being a mammal is *not* a property of any mammals. This will sound strange to contemporary essentialist ears, but less so once the distinction between essence and property is grasped. To be sure, there are mammalian properties – having fur, lactating, and so on – but being a mammal and having mammalian properties are not the same thing. A mammal has mammalian properties *because* it is a mammal; these properties point to its essence. But isn't it a mammal because it has these properties? Isn't the real essentialist order of explanation upside down? To reverse the order of explanation, however, is ultimately to do away with essence, not to explain it. More accurately, it does away with real essence and replaces it with a surrogate bundle theory of essence as a collection of properties. And the problems with such a conception resurface. What holds the properties together? What supports them? What *has* them? Why – if modalism is to be avoided (recall the discussion in Chapter 1) – are some of the properties essential and others merely necessary? There is, though, a reading of 'It is a mammal because it has these properties' which is perfectly consistent with real essentialism, but it interprets 'because' epistemically, not metaphysically. The statement is elliptical for 'We know it is a mammal because we know it has these properties'. Or, for the naturalists who first categorized the mammals, it means something like the following: 'We have observed these properties occurring regularly among certain animals. They all point to these animals' forming a distinctive class, one marked out from other animals. Let us call these animals the mammals.' This is precisely how early naturalists would have understood their observation-based taxonomy.

A final reason for maintaining the essence/property distinction is to avoid a certain kind of taxonomic error. The attribution of properties to kinds is always made with implicit reference to normal members of the kind in question. When we say that mammals have the property of lactating, the implicit qualification is that normal mammals are like this. We would not take the existence of a mutant female mammal born without nipples or milk-secreting glands to refute the attribution. We can use a ceteris paribus clause to mark such a qualification, but such use presupposes a grasp of what it is to be a normal member of a species. This might look as though it leads the essentialist into circularity: to know what a normal member is, you have to know what properties the species has; but to know what properties the species has, you have to identify the normal members. The circularity is only apparent.

To take a toy example, when naturalists identified swans as a kind they fixed on certain accidents that seemed to be properties, in particular swans' distinctive shape and overall body plan. They made a defeasible judgment that swans formed a distinctive kind. They knew that whiteness was too common among animals to be the main feature to fix upon when classifying swans. But they observed it to be ubiquitous among the swans they encountered, and made another defeasible judgment that whiteness too was a property of swans. They were proved wrong by the observation of black swans, and revised their judgment about the properties of swans, relegating whiteness to a mere accident. Moreover, the development of biology allowed naturalists to judge confidently that being black (or white, for that matter) was not a genetic mutation in the swan population, like albinism found in the occasional crow. The moral of this simple story (which, in its outlines, is true) is that taxonomists work in a piecemeal fashion, making defeasible judgments along the way via the holding of certain putative properties as fixed for the purpose of determining essence. They then make a defeasible judgment about essence, and further investigate other putative properties of the kind they think they have identified. They could be proved wrong at any step of the way. Swan specialists might have discovered that the supposedly distinctive physiology of their target kind was not distinctive after all, so that swans formed neither a species nor even a genus.[11] Or they might have discovered that black swans were after all a genuine mutation, and so maintained that whiteness was a property. When naturalists looked to classify monotremes (the echidnas and platypuses), they were able to judge with certainty that being an egg layer was not a mutation but just a part of the monotremes' physiology. They observed enough similarity between known mammals and the monotremes to enable them to judge defeasibly that monotremes were a species of mammal. So they revised their defeasible judgment that bearing live young was a property of mammals.

There is nothing especially mysterious about this process. What it does reveal, though, is that essentialists have sufficient conceptual machinery not to be inevitably led astray in their attempt to locate the properties associated with essences. Just as we have enough understanding of what it is to be a crow to see that albinism does not refute the truth that crows have the property of being black, so we can also see that an anencephalic or severely brain-damaged child, say, is still a human being – a rational animal – even though it lacks some of the properties associated with the human essence. We have, on the one hand, enough knowledge of what damage and deformity are in human beings and, on the other hand, enough knowledge of human anatomy and physiology, to know that although a severely brain-damaged child does not have the *use* of reason, still it has rationality precisely because it is human. To put the point in hylemorphic terms, possession of the actuating principle by which a being is human (mutatis mutandis for other kinds of substance) does not entail that every potentiality associated with this principle must itself either be, or be capable of, actuation. (Consider people who are drunk, drugged, asleep, very young, very old, etc.) Nor does it entail that there is a standard of 'perfect instantiation' – a standard distinct from, and beyond, *normal, typical* or *paradigmatic* instantiation – whereby anything failing to meet the standard of perfection associated with a substantial form thereby fails to have the form. If instead rationality, which is the specific difference of the human species, were a mere property or cluster of properties, then we could no longer even say what the human species was, or whether the brain-damaged child was a member of a *new* species or of no species at all. But we do know what humans are, and that such a child does not belong to a new species. The anti-essentialist might demur to both propositions, but then anti-essentialism is an overall metaphysical position full of holes (see Chapter 2 for some of them). The implications for ethics are manifest.

7.3 Knowledge of essence via properties

Properties point us to the essences of things. As things are, so do they behave. Since properties are kinds of accident, and all our knowledge of things begins with empirical knowledge of accidents, our knowledge of properties is similarly a matter of observation. But to know properties *as* properties we have to make an intellectual judgment that is metaphysical in nature; it is not an empirical observation that some accident *is* a property of something. Similarly, it is a metaphysical judgment that certain properties indicate that an object has a certain essence, i.e. that it has a substantial form that puts it into one category rather than another. Hence even the most empirically minded of taxonomists, whether biologist, chemist, physicist or, for that matter, psychologist, anthropologist, or sociologist, practise metaphysics when they assign an essence to the proper object of their study and categorize the object as being of some kind.

We should not, however, expect properties always to drop out of reckoning once we have judged them to indicate a given essence. Often the properties must do duty, or stand proxy, for the as-yet-unknown essence. So, for instance, before the chemical composition of water was discovered, chemists had to do the best they could, taxonomically, given their limited knowledge. They knew water had certain properties (solvency in respect of certain other compounds, the power to enter into certain mixtures, various boiling points, and so on), and they used these to fix the essence of water as belonging to a certain genus (a liquid, or more precisely a substance capable of existing in solid, liquid, and gaseous states) and possessing a specific difference (the liquid which behaves in such-and-such ways distinctive as a whole from all other liquids). But the properties used to fix the difference did duty for that difference until it was discovered to be the H_2O composition and structure.

Another way in which properties stand proxy for essences is when there is no name for a part of the essence. For example, mammals are known to be a species of vertebrate, but there is no name for the difference other than something like 'mammalian' or 'mammal' itself. Typically, mammals are defined as vertebrates characterized by certain properties such as the presence of mammary glands in the female, bearing of fur or hair, and so on. These properties point to a certain substantial form, namely the mammalian form. There is nothing incorrect about calling the difference *mammalian*, but it is more informative to be explicit about some or all of the properties that point to that form. The same goes for, say, *organism* defined as *living body*. The difference is *living*, but one might as well have said *organic*. It is more informative to be explicit about some or all of the properties indicative of being living, such as reproduction, nutrition, and the like. There is no reason why we should *have* a readily available, informative name for an essence or part thereof; indeed we should expect otherwise precisely because it is properties that take us to the essence, and because judgments of essence are often provisional. We fix on certain supposed properties, and if they turn out to be mere accidents we try to find the real properties. Were we to go too readily to the naming of an essence we might be too hasty to fix a name to a thing and so entrench it in scientific or ordinary thinking, making dislodgement by further investigation all the more difficult. Such was arguably the case with the use of the name 'phlogiston' for a putative substance that could not be detected and yet explained quite well many of the phenomena associated with combustion (see Ball 1999: 125ff.). The caricature of hasty naming is, of course, the infamous *virtus dormitiva* of Molière's *Le Malade Imaginaire*. Yet if the doctor in Molière's play had not been trying vacuously to explain why opium is a narcotic in terms of its having a narcotic power, but rather had been engaging in taxonomy, his remark would have been perfectly acceptable. Opium even now is classified generically as a narcotic analgesic, though these terms denote properties of the compound that indicate a certain essence, given explicitly in terms of chemical structure.[12]

The process of coming to know essence via properties is not a matter of language, even though decisions have to be made about how language must be used given a particular discovery. This important fact is missed by LaPorte (2004: ch. 4) in his otherwise illuminating discussion of cases such as jade and water. As LaPorte shows, contra hidden structure essentialism, there is more to essence than chemical or other micro-level structure. The Chinese worked and prized jade for thousands of years, and this jade has the chemical structure $Ca_2(Mg,Fe)_5Si_8O_{22}(OH)_2$. It was probably in the eighteenth century that another compound, with the structure $NaAl(SiO_3)_2$, made its way into China from Burma, and was found so similar to Chinese jade that the Chinese eventually accepted as genuine jade both the original Chinese jade (nephrite) and the 'new' jade (called jadeite in 1863 by Alexis Damour, the French scientist, to distinguish the chemical compositions of the two compounds). Discovered difference in chemical structure in this case did *not* lead to the conclusion that jadeite was not really jade.

Now Putnam's account of jade is far too brief to allow us to be sure of what moral he was trying to draw (Putnam 1975a: 241), but his thought – as applied to water – was that the subsequent discovery of XYZ on Twin Earth would not lead to Earth speakers calling it water, whereas if it had been plentiful on Earth for a long time, we would, on discovering its composition, have called it the XYZ kind of water. Why the assignment of essence, at least for naturally occurring substances, should depend on where they are or how long we have been familiar with them is quite mysterious. LaPorte's point, though, is that Putnam is wrong on the facts anyway. Jadeite was not known to the Chinese for thousands of years, yet when it was discovered – a case relevantly the same as Twin Earth – they did eventually come to regard it as a kind of jade. (Putnam says that 'two quite different microstructures produce the same unique textural qualities' (Putnam 1975a: 241), but this too is wrong. Jadeite is harder than nephrite, they can differ slightly in their colouring and jadeite is usually more translucent – not to mention their different specific gravities and other dissimilarities.) So although Putnam, for reasons that are somewhat odd, treats inner structure as decisive of essence in some cases but not in others, when he does regard it as decisive real historical examples show that macroscopic properties play as much of a role in determining essence as inner structure.

Yet, for LaPorte, cases such as jade point to the conclusion that 'there is no clear answer as to what we should say: Such a split [between macroscopic properties and underlying structure] exposes vagueness' (LaPorte 2004: 93). We could, he says 'go either way' (LaPorte 2004: 100). The same goes for cases such as those of ruby and topaz. When scientists discovered that the compound Al_2O_3 (corundum) comes in different colours, the term 'ruby', which was applied to the red varieties, continued to be reserved by speakers for these and not extended to, say, the blue varieties. On the other hand, when it was discovered that the compound $Al_2SiO_4(F,OH)_2$ comes in blue as well as yellow (among other colours), speakers *extended* 'topaz' from the yellow varieties to include the other colours as well. These actions by speakers were, says LaPorte, *decisions* and not *discoveries*. The decisions are about how, if at all, to refine existing terms (LaPorte 2004: 102).

LaPorte is right that micro-structure is not all there is to essence (though he speaks vaguely of natural kinds rather than essences). He is also right that the discovery of essences sometimes necessitates decisions about how to use language. But he is wrong that this is all there is to the explanation of cases such as those typified by jade, ruby, topaz, and also water (LaPorte 2004: 103–10). English speakers, once apprised of jadeite and nephrite, with their different chemical composition but very similar macroscopic properties, could have decided to reserve 'jade' for nephrite only (the same for the Chinese term 'yü', which now in fact covers both compounds). They could have used 'jadeite' for jadeite. They might also have chosen not to use any term to refer both to nephrite and to jadeite. But if they had not then introduced a term to refer to both, their use of language would *not* have captured all there was to the reality of these minerals. For jadeite and nephrite *are* sufficiently similar to form a distinct class of substance, despite their chemical differences. And that is why mineralogists *have* ultimately decided to extend 'jade' to both. If they hadn't, and if they had wanted to state a truth about the essences of jadeite and nephrite, they would have been obliged to introduce a *new* term to denote the genus to which both jade, as used by them, and jadeite belonged as species. Which terms we use is a matter of convention. That we use terms to denote essences is not.

Similarly, 'topaz' could have been reserved, by stipulation, only for the yellow varieties of that compound. And 'ruby' could, by stipulation, have been extended to the non-red varieties of corundum. Instead, the reverse happened. Why? One reason appears to be that pure corundum, which is brown or brownish white, has a greater variety of shapes in nature than does red corundum (ruby) or blue corundum (sapphire) – this is called the mineral's *crystal habit*.[13] Both rubies and sapphires have a narrower crystal habit (mainly prisms and double pyramids) than pure corundum. Topaz, on the other hand, does not vary in crystal habit according to its colour.[14] Hence the colour of corundum is correlated more significantly with crystal habit than in the case of topaz. But the mineralogical details are less important than the principles. What speakers choose to do with language – whether to vary the extension of existing terms or introduce new ones and the like – is not the same as, and can come apart from, what they judge to be metaphysically the case. And how language is used is different from what *is* metaphysically the case. Corundum clearly forms a genus of compound. Rubies and sapphires are particularly coloured species of the genus, the colour being caused by the addition of other minerals or elements (chromium for rubies, ilmenite for sapphires). These colours seem to be *properties* of *specific* varieties of corundum. The various colourings of topaz, also a generic compound, vary with the concentration of fluorine. There are species of topaz, indicated by what again look like colour properties rather than mere accidents. In fact, mineralogists and ordinary speakers have, in co-operation, done a pretty good job of carving nature at the joints with the linguistic terms available. There is no specific term for yellow topaz other than 'yellow topaz', but that is good enough. Had speakers chosen to use terms such as 'ruby' and 'topaz' differently, they would have needed to introduce *new* terms, or vary other existing terms, to fill the spaces. So if 'ruby' *had* been extended to all varieties of corundum, another term would have been needed to distinguish the red corundum from the blue and the pure corundum.

Needless to say, artefactual factors have crept in, and one might claim that everything I have said is a 'just-so' story belying the fact that rubies and sapphires are singled out because they are precious whereas pure corundum is not, and yellow topaz has not been singled out by a new name because *all* topaz is precious. I doubt that this is the real explanation underlying the apparently neat mineralogy, but even if it were it would only show the metaphysical truth to be that all topaz is one species, all corundum one species, and all colourings *mere* varieties rather than *specific* varieties of distinct species. In this case the terms 'ruby', 'sapphire', 'yellow topaz', 'pink topaz', and so on, would all be purely varietal terms, none of them denoting distinct species, just as terms such as 'Negroid' and 'Caucasoid' denote not species of humans but *races*, i.e. varieties singled out by pure accidents rather than properties. Again, our mineralogical language, if this were the case, looks adequate to the task of carving reality, but if it were not – say, because 'ruby' had been extended to all varieties of corundum with no new term introduced to denote the red variety – then our language would have been to that extent inadequate, missing out on a clearly delineated variety. We are under no *obligation* to find a term for every species or variety that we come across – again, artefactual reasons might override the need to classify everything – but we should not be lulled into the false confidence that the linguistic incompleteness marks a metaphysical absence. I conclude, then, that LaPorte, for all the interesting and informative aspects of his discussion of these cases, is quite mistaken to reduce our taxonomic practices to a matter of linguistic convention or stipulation.[15]

7.4 Artefacts

The laws of nature, I have argued, are the laws of natures. But not all natures give rise to the same kinds of laws, since it depends on the natures concerned. This is evident in the material sciences (chemistry, biology, physics), but also in the human sciences. There are material laws governing humans in the purely material aspect of their nature (e.g. laws governing human physiological processes), but insofar as humans are not purely material by nature there are no purely material laws of human nature. But human beings are still governed by law, in particular the moral law, which, at least in its fundamental injunctions, is exceptionless. There are also broad laws descriptive of human behaviour, such as 'All humans seek the good' and 'All humans seek the means to achieve their aims', though questions arise as to whether these are so-called ceteris paribus laws and how they should best be formulated. The existence of human freedom prevents there from being laws that describe particular human action, but human nature still gives rise to well-confirmed generalizations and correlations.

Since artefacts have a human dimension to their natures they inherit the indeterminacy inherent in the science of human nature itself. We will not find exceptionless laws governing artefacts *qua* artefacts, except perhaps at a high level of generality: examples might be 'All artefacts are capable of being put to some good use', 'Every artefact is a means to some end', and 'Every artefact potentially pleases someone', though again one might raise the question of whether a ceteris paribus clause is required. Other than that, all we have are well-confirmed generalizations concerning artefacts ('Paintings by Picasso fetch a high price at auction', 'Skyscrapers are found in cities'), as well as the strict laws governing them not *qua* artefacts but *qua* material substances ('Concrete buildings withstand fire better than wooden ones', 'Cakes will not bake at 25°').

As well as not being the object, *qua* artefact, of the material sciences, artefacts are also not substances, since they lack ontological independence. It might *look* like Da Vinci's *Last Supper* would continue to exist were humanity to become extinct tomorrow, but it would not. At least, it would not exist *qua* work of art. All that would exist is the material of the painting, but a part of its essence would have ceased to exist – its relation to what is sometimes called an 'artworld' (e.g. Baker 2000: 44). But wouldn't the painting still be beautiful? It is tempting to reply that this begs the question of whether it would still be a work of art, but the better response is that it would still be beautiful, since a thing needn't be an artefact in order to be beautiful (a sunset, a rainbow). The painting, though no longer an artefact in a people-free world, would still have the intrinsic qualities (such as symmetry, proportion, harmony) of a beautiful thing, and the inherent power, by reason of its subject matter, to evoke an aesthetic response in any humans who might repopulate the world. Further, it would still be true, in the human-free world, that the painting had a history – that it *was* made by a person and so *was* an artefact. But it is not sufficient for the existence of an artefact at a time that it have been created prior to that time. Artefacts have a (human)[16] purpose, and when the possessors of the purpose go, so do the artefacts, since purposes do not exist without people to have them. There would still exist something that *could be* an artefact again, since there could be human purposes again. But while the purposes are absent, so is the artefact.

So what is it that *could* be an artefact again should humans reappear in the people-free world? It is what I will follow Aristotle in calling an *accidental unity* (Ross 1928b: 1015b16ff.).[17] An accidental unity is any group of entities related in some way other than by a common form. Examples include: connected series, such as a series of causally related events or a family tree; natural aggregations, such as heaps and the collection of all the events happening right now; physical systems, such as the weather or a flock of birds; a substance and one or more of its accidents, such as seated Socrates; and artefacts. It is the last two on which I want to concentrate.

Let us call an accidental unity which is a combination of substance and accident an *accidental object*.[18] Seated Socrates is an accidental object: it is the unordered pair of Socrates and his mode of being seated (his seatedness trope). When Socrates sits down, seated Socrates comes into existence.

When Socrates stands up, it ceases to exist. When he sits down again, a *new* seated Socrates comes into existence.[19] It might seem bizarre to posit such objects, but as Brower and Rea (2005) point out, we believe in fists as well as hands, yet a fist is no more than a clenched hand – a hand taken together with its mode of being clenched. It comes into existence when a hand is clenched and goes out of existence when the hand is unclenched. We can count the fists in existence at a time, as well as the hands, and discover that there are more hands than fists. Yet surely every fist just *is* a hand?

Yes and no. A fist is a hand taken with its mode of being clenched, and so is not numerically identical with a hand on its own. The fist has the hand as a part – what we might call an *integral* part, a part necessary for the existence of the whole accidental unity but not identical with that unity. The hand and fist are spatially coincident but not identical. Yet spatial coincidence of material beings is not itself problematic: it depends on what *kinds* of being one is considering (Oderberg 1996). A sphere's accidents of redness and roundness are spatially coincident, yet the accidents are distinct. Two beams of light can be spatially coincident yet distinct. The fist comes into existence after the hand, and so is distinct from it. But doesn't this beg the question by assuming the fist comes into existence, as though it were an object? No, because coming into existence is logically sufficient for something's being an object. (How could anything come into existence and *not* be an object?) But can we say the fist really comes into existence? Well, if the question is whether a fist comes into existence in the same way a hand does, then the answer is obviously no. But there is more than one way for a thing to come into existence. A fist does so by virtue of a hand's becoming clenched. When a hand becomes clenched, a clenched hand comes into existence. But a fist just is a clenched hand: so fists do come into existence.

As for fists and seated Socrates, so for statues and other artefacts that involve the accidental modification of a pre-existing substance, such as (plausibly) paintings, books, certain tools, recordings of music and voice, among others. A statue is the most straightforward case, which is why it is the most often discussed. Consider Michelangelo's *David*, which is a shaped piece of marble. It is an accidental unity of the material substance that is the lump of marble and the accidental form of shape, but unlike seated Socrates or a fist it is also ontologically dependent on an 'artworld' of human purposes. Hence it is doubly not a substance in its own right: it is ontologically dependent and part of its essence is to have an accident as a constituent. Seated Socrates, on the other hand, is not a substance only for the second reason.

So what is the relation between *David* and the lump of marble? Some philosophers insist that it would involve ontological double vision, or improper double counting, to postulate two coinciding material objects. (See, e.g., Noonan 1988; Burke 1992. For a reply to Burke, see Lowe 1995; also 1999a: 198–9.) But it depends on what is meant by 'material object'. Two material substances of the same kind cannot coincide.[20] But why not a substance and the accidental unity to which it is related? If the lump of marble is part of what constitutes *David*, the other part being its shape, why is it improper counting or double vision to postulate two different kinds of material object? It would only be worrisome were this to involve postulating two lumps of matter – but that is no part of what I am claiming.

The relation between the lump and the statue, as I have hinted, is one of constitution, not identity. There is no room to explore the details of what kind of relationship constitution is (for an important account, see Baker 2000), but what it is *not* is any kind of numerical identity. Hence Brower and Rea (2005) are mistaken to think there is a relation of 'accidental sameness' that is a species of numerical sameness not involving identity (see also Rea 1999). For a start, they misinterpret Aristotle when he speaks in the *Topics* of senses of 'sameness' (Ross 1928a: 103a23–32). The most natural reading is that Aristotle recognizes, inter alia, identity statements of the form 'The x that is F is identical with a', where 'a' is a name, 'F' is a predicate term denoting an accident, and the description is used referentially. Hence we invoke numerical identity when we say, 'The man who is seated is Socrates', just as when we say, 'The hand that is clenched is a hand' and 'The lump of marble that is shaped like this [pointing to the shape of *David*] is a lump of marble'. Seemingly odd as it may sound, however, a hand that happens to be clenched is *not* numerically identical with a fist, and the lump that happens to be shaped as *David* (the one actually carved by Michelangelo) is *not* numerically identical with *David*. Rather, the fist is identical with the hand *taken together with* its mode of being clenched. And *David* is identical with the lump *taken together with* its shape. But 'taken together with' must *not* be understood epistemically. A substance taken together with one or more of its accidents exists whether or not anyone takes these things together. When taken together in the objective, conjunctive sense, what we have are accidental unities. And the fact that we do not have ordinary resources in English to mark the distinction between, say, a clenched hand and a hand that happens to be clenched should not be taken to undermine this fundamental ontological distinction – that between a substance that is part of what constitutes an accidental unity and the accidental unity itself, which is the substance *and* the relevant accident.

By contrast, Brower and Rea's relation of 'accidental sameness' entails the bizarre proposition that, although there is exactly one material object that is arranged both statue-wise and lump-wise, the object whose matter is arranged lump-wise is not identical with the object whose matter is arranged statue-wise. They recognize this strange consequence, but insist that every proposed solution to the problem of material constitution is counterintuitive. Yet my proposal is both intuitive and faithful to Aristotle, as long as one accepts the existence of accidental unities in the first place. Nowhere does Aristotle say that seated Socrates (his more common example is musical Coriscus) is one in number[21] with Socrates pure and simple. He does allow identity statements of the form noted above. And he also says that 'in a sense'[22] musical Coriscus is 'one with'[23] Coriscus, because 'one of the parts of the phrase ["musical Coriscus"] is an accident of the other'.[24] And the sense he means, I contend, is the sense of constitution. Where there is seated Socrates, there is only one material substance. But there is also an accidental unity constituted by that substance and one of its modes. Similarly for the statue and for the fist. There is no relation of sameness short of numerical identity. To be sure, there *is* a relation of numerical identity involved: the substance that is identical to Socrates is identical to the substance that partially constitutes seated Socrates; and the substance that is the lump of marble is identical to the substance that partially constitutes the statue. But there is also a relation of constitution: seated Socrates is constituted wholly by Socrates and his mode of being seated; *David* is constituted wholly by the lump of marble and its shape (strictly, by the lump, its shape, and its essential relation to an artworld). 'Accidental sameness', as conceived by Brower and Rea, is not constitution since it is symmetrical whereas constitution is not (which they recognize at the same time as they curiously claim constitution to be a species of sameness without identity!).[25] Nor are they correct to call accidental unities such as seated Socrates, a fist, or a statue 'hylemorphic compounds'.[26] A hylemorphic compound is not any old combination of matter and form, but a substantial union of prime matter and substantial form. To call an accidental unity a hylemorphic compound is to bestow on it a reality on a par with substance that it definitely does not have.

Not every artefact is an accidental object. There are aggregates (such as man-made heaps and collections).[27] There are artefacts which look like special kinds of accidental unity distinct from accidental unities such as seated Socrates – mechanical unities, for instance (watches and other machines). And there is plenty of room for debate about how to classify artefacts. (For instance, is a painting an accidental object or more like a connected series?) What I have argued for here is that no artefact is a substance, some paradigmatic artefacts are accidental objects, accidental objects are a species of accidental unity, and that constitution, rather than a bogus relation of sameness without identity, is what explains the relation of a substance to an artefact.

7.5 Origin and constitution

I noted in Chapter 1 that certain essentialist theses, such as the necessity of origin, cannot be derived from the semantics of rigid designators, or from general modalist appeals to possible worlds, without presupposing substantive metaphysical theses that are no part of such semantics or of possible-worlds theory. It has also been argued that the case for the necessity of origin, when made out as an independent metaphysical position, violates highly plausible propositions concerning mereological variability (Robertson 1998). Further, it has been argued that in order to defend the necessity of origin against counterexamples deriving from variability, the position has to be weakened to the point of encompassing only some limited intuitions about origins (Hawthorne and Gendler 2000). In particular, no two objects *a* and *b* originally made of two hunks of matter *m* and *n* could have been originally made from each other's matter given that *a* and *b* are the only objects originally made from their respective matters (i.e. given that there happen not to be, co-existing with *a* and *b*, two objects *c* and *d* such that, through a process of gradual matter loss from *a* and *b*, *c* and *d* also are originally made of *m* and *n*). Yet it is hard to see why even this must be true. Why couldn't there be two substances that gradually transposed their matter? If they could, why couldn't each have originally been composed of each other's matter?

The point is not so much whether such a scenario is possible, but that we cannot work out whether it is without the metaphysics of real essentialism, in particular the hylemorphism that accounts for the structure of any substance. In order to know how something could have originated, or by what it could originally have been constituted, we need to know *what* it is. For example, aggregations, whether natural or artificial, are defined by their members, so we cannot say that a pile of stones $S_1 \ldots S_n$ could have originally been composed of stones $P_1 \ldots P_n$, given that the pile is nothing more than an aggregation of stones with a certain shape (or range of possible shapes). If the identity of the stones were different (but see the next paragraph for qualification), there would be a numerically distinct pile. If the shape were different (or if it were not within a certain range), again there would be a distinct pile. Since the pile by its nature does not tolerate such changes, and since it is not *change* which determines the issue rather than the composition or the shape, we have to conclude that the pile could not have originated with different stones or shape (or shape outside a certain range) either.

Needless to say, this view skirts around some important questions that I cannot explore here. The most important is just how different the stones and/or shape must be for there to be a distinct pile. This brings in the notorious problem of vagueness, which requires a separate treatment of its own (though I will say a little about it in Chapter 9 in the biological context). But we can at least say with confidence that if enough stones in a pile are changed for others we will have a distinct pile, just as if its shape is sufficiently changed it will cease to exist and be replaced by another pile. (Some will baulk at this latter remark when applied to piles. They might be less aversive were I to speak of heaps.) The pile cannot tolerate just any change of stones or shape, which is enough for us to infer that it could not have originally been composed of just any stones or shape.

How does this square with the idea that aggregates are defined by their members? Although the pile cannot tolerate just any change of stones, since as a certain kind of aggregate it is defined by its members, nevertheless it is not defined by *all* of its members. Yet there is a strong intuition that there is something whose members wholly define it – a mereologically essential collection of stones, such that if even one stone were changed, the collection would cease to exist. I contend that just such an entity is spatio-temporally coincident with the pile. Like the pile, it is an accidental unity. But whereas the pile is best classified as an accidental object – a combination of substances with a certain shape – the mereologically essential collection is a different kind of accidental unity, which we can call simply a collection. Just as more than one accidental object can coincide – such as seated Socrates and musical Socrates – so can different kinds of accidental unity such as an accidental object and a collection.

Nor does it look as though either the collection constitutes the pile or vice versa, since nothing mereologically essential can be composed of something variable, nor can something variable be composed of something essential. But this too is no problem, since musical Socrates and seated Socrates have no relation of constitution between them, even though they share Socrates as a constituent. So, too, the pile and the collection share constituents, namely all of the stones belonging to the collection during such time as the collection exists. All of these thoughts support the intuition that when a child knocks over a pile of stones there is something (the pile) that he has destroyed and something else (the collection) that he has not.[28] Since the collection cannot tolerate the replacement or loss of a single stone, we must conclude that it could not have been originally constituted by stones differing in the identity of even one member.

Substances are different. They are mereologically variable entities, at least at the macroscopic level. The general view of physicists seems to be that mereological change is possible for atomic and subatomic objects as well: ionization, for instance, does not destroy the atom but merely changes its charge. (Perhaps, once we know more about electrons, we will know whether every quark composing an electron is essential to it.) But macroscopic substances are all capable of gaining and losing parts. Since substances have form as their unifying principle, we must look to form in order to judge what variation is compatible with a substance's continuing to exist. And this will be our principal guide to how it might have existed at its origin. For, as a general principle, it is plausible to claim that if a substance S is capable of being F at some time t after it has begun to exist, then it is metaphysically possible for it to have been F at time t_0 of its existence, i.e. at its origin. Here, 'being F' means 'having some accident'; for S could not have belonged to a different genus or species at any time of its existence. (For a challenge to this from cladistics in biology, see Chapter 9.) An exception to this principle is that if the possibility of S's being F at t depends *metaphysically* on its having undergone *change* from not-F to F, then S could not have been F at t_0.

For example, Socrates, who has blue eyes, could have had green eyes, and vice versa. Plato, who has fair skin, could have had dark skin, and vice versa. There is nothing repugnant to the essence of Socrates or Plato such that they could not have been *born* with eye or skin colour different to the ones they actually have at some later time of their existence. Could Socrates have been born *old*? Could he, that is to say, have been born with the matter of a seventy-year-old man? This, I contend, is metaphysically impossible. Although a physical process is metaphysically necessary for Socrates to *change* from having blue eyes to green eyes (as eye colour can indeed sometimes change from infancy to adulthood), miraculous intervention or a spontaneous mutation (if such be possible) could have resulted in his acquiring a new eye colour without any intervening physical process. Such an event would not have been a genuine change of eye colour, as opposed to a mere *replacement*.

By contrast, a physical process is *metaphysically* necessary for the acquisition of an aged state after having had a youthful state. This is because ageing is part of the very essence of organisms, as decay is part of the essence of all material substances, since they are compound objects[29] subject, as far as we know, to universal laws of energy depletion. Divine intervention might *preserve* a material substance from decay and hence from ageing, but it would be contrary to its essence that it should enter a state of decay and decomposition without having undergone, in however short a time, the process of ageing itself. Hence I claim that not even God could produce an aged substance that had not gone through a process of ageing. (This counts against the sceptical hypothesis of Bertrand Russell that the universe could have sprung into existence five minutes ago looking *exactly* like a genuinely old universe (Russell 1921: lecture IX).)[30]

So we can see straightaway that there are limits on what sort of origin a person might have had – and by similar reasoning any other material substance – and that these limits can only be judged by reference to the essence of the substance in question. We cannot simply rely on wholly general principles of origination from hunks of matter such as those espoused by Salmon and Forbes in their defences of the necessity of origin (Salmon 1981: ch. 7; Forbes 1985: ch. 6). This is not only because the premises of their arguments are either false, question-begging, or no more evident than their conclusions, but because their whole procedure does not take essence into account beyond the simple consideration of objects as made of matter. (The same applies to Kripke's gnomic 'proof' of the necessity of origin (Kripke 1980: 114).)

In response to Kripke's famous question, 'How could a person originating from different parents, from a totally different sperm and egg, be *this very woman*?' (Kripke 1980: 113), the real essentialist makes several observations. First, there is a difference between originating from different parents and originating from different gametes, so there are in fact two questions that Kripke poses. The answer to them requires answering the foundational two-part question: Is there something about the *essence* of a human being such that it must have come from the parents/gametes it actually came from? The only thing that might be put forward in support of a 'yes' to either part is the person's individual genotype; for surely this is part of what constitutes a person (at least generically as a kind of animal), and so requires that the person have originated from the parents or gametes capable of producing that genotype. But Socrates's parents, let us suppose, might each have had a genetically identical twin capable of producing genetically identical gametes to the ones from which Socrates proximately originated, in which case why couldn't Socrates have remotely originated from his parents' twins? Similarly, as to the question of the gametes themselves, Socrates's actual parents might have produced genetically identical but numerically distinct gametes from the ones that in fact gave rise to Socrates: so why could he not have originated from these 'twin' gametes?

The defender of the necessity of gamete origin,[31] such as Kripke, might concede both of these possibilities but insist that Socrates could not have come from different parents or gametes if this entailed his having a different individual genotype. As is well known, critics such as Mellor (1977: 80, n.9) and Wiggins (1980: 116, n.22) have answered that we can intelligibly entertain counterfactuals such as 'If JFK hadn't been (born) a Kennedy, he wouldn't have been shot'. But the intelligibility, and indeed the truth, of such counterfactuals does not entail the metaphysical possibility of their antecedents. To see this, consider a non-axiomatic mathematical truth P that is entailed by another truth T and by no other.[32] It is both coherent and true to say, 'If T hadn't been true, then P wouldn't have been true.' Since T is a necessary truth, however, it could not have been false. The reason the counterfactual is true is that its truthmaker is the fact of T's being true and entailing P (and P's being non-axiomatic and not entailed by anything else). In other words, the explanation of P's being true is its being entailed by another mathematical truth, and that explanation can be conveyed by use of the counterfactual, without supposing that T could have been false. Similarly, the explanation for JFK's being shot is (partly) that he was a Kennedy. This can be conveyed by the counterfactual 'If JFK hadn't been (born) a Kennedy he wouldn't have been shot', without supposing it to be possible that JFK might *not* have been (born) a Kennedy.

The metaphysical question is whether a person could have been born of different parents or gametes, where either scenario would entail their having a different genotype. The short answer, from what we know of the relation between genotype and phenotype, is that such a scenario is not possible. The question (posed in general terms earlier) is: Could a person, Socrates for example, have changed genotype? If so, he could have been born with a different genotype. But there is no reason to think he could, and every reason to think he could not, undergo such a change. He could, of course, suffer damage to his genotype through radiation or mutation. Maybe it is metaphysically possible that he could be transformed into another kind of animal with a different genotype – but he would thereby undergo a substantial change and so cease to exist. Everything we know about genotype tells us that even the slightest tinkering produces significant phenotypical changes; a fortiori, a wholesale change of genotype would certainly produce a wholesale change of phenotype, at least as far as physical constitution is concerned. This is of course a major object of empirical research and there is very much we do not know about the relation between genotype and phenotype, but my general point is simply that some kinds of origin are necessary and some are not – it all depends on essence.

Kripke's well-known question as to whether a wooden lectern could have been made of a different block of wood, or even of ice (Kripke 1980: 113), again needs to be treated in the context of a metaphysics of artefacts, along the lines set out earlier in this chapter. As an accidental unity, a lectern is essentially constituted in part by a certain hunk of matter. It could not have been transformed into a block of ice or a different lump of wood without the transformation's being what we might call derivatively substantial. The essence of the lectern depends in part on the essence of the substance constituting it: if that is replaced, so is the lectern. Note, however, that Kripke's question does not reappear at the level of the substance itself that constitutes the artefact: the supplementary question, 'But could this hunk of wood have originally been a block of ice/different hunk of wood?' is nonsensical, and would betray a serious failure to understand the metaphysics of material substances. Of course, Kripke-style questions can be raised about *different* kinds of substances from mere hunks of matter. One could ask, 'Could this oak tree have been originally made of different matter?', and the answer will turn on the metaphysics of living bodies in general and plants in particular. I will not explore the question here.

I will, though, conclude with the more radical proposal that even though a person could not have been born with a different genotype, and hence of different parents or gametes if this entailed that the person had a different original genotype, still the person might have had a radically different origin altogether from the normal human one. I share Lowe's intuition that Socrates might have popped into existence ex nihilo (Lowe 1999a: 152); for reasons to do with causation and explanation I regard it as a necessary truth that Socrates must have had a beginning (see further Oderberg 2002b). But that such a beginning might not have involved any human or animal generation, or even any physical process at all, is coherent and consistent with the essences not only of Socrates but of any material substance. What is it about Socrates's essence that would prevent him from having come into existence by some non-physical, wholly non-natural process, such as by divine fiat? Given the existence of humans, and the expression of their essence in nature through the manifestation of a range of properties, the natural course of biology requires that human beings be born through natural generation. But all of this is consistent with the essence of Socrates being originally actualized by non-natural means. For the essence of Socrates, as for any substance, is nothing more or less than the union of prime matter and substantial form. The substance exists just in case the union is present. *How* the union is produced is another matter altogether, extraneous to the essence. Just as a substance might have been created ex nihilo, so it might have been annihilated by the reduction to nothingness of its matter and form. Note, however: Socrates's physical death just was the *separation* of his matter and form; but whether his death entailed his *annihilation* is another matter, to be discussed in Chapter 10.

8 Life

8.1 The essence of life

One of the most interesting and important topics on which real essentialism can shed light is the question of life. Life is one of the most intriguing and, in many ways, unfathomable phenomena in the universe. What is it to be alive? How can material objects possess life? Is life specifically different from non-life, or, better, are living things specifically different from non-living things? If so, is life wholly explicable in terms of non-life – can the living be explained wholly in terms of the non-living? In this chapter, I want to apply essentialist insights to the question of life. There are many details I will be able only to touch on, and topics that can only be mentioned, many of them requiring full-length discussions of their own. What I hope to do, though, is sketch the essentialist approach to life, and in dealing with some central problems show that essentialism offers a convincing account of what it is to be a living thing, and how the phenomenon of life fits into the overall ontology of the universe.

Since we come to know essences via the properties of things, we come to know life too via the characteristic behaviour of living things. Various features have been singled out by biologists as essential to life, even if they do not always speak in essentialist terms. Three, however, stand out: metabolism or nutrition, growth, and reproduction. Metabolism involves several activities and processes, in particular the synthesis of organic and inorganic material into components, primarily cellular, of the living thing (anabolism); and the degradation or breaking down of organic and inorganic material in the living body for the production of energy, recycling, or excretion (catabolism). Growth occurs when anabolism exceeds catabolism, as a result of which the organism is built up and develops in size, function, and maturity, reaching (in the absence of countervailing factors) a normal state as a mature, properly functioning member of its kind. When catabolism exceeds anabolism the organism declines in various ways, eventually dying as a result of the failure of its metabolic processes to maintain homeostasis, i.e. a stable internal equilibrium. Reproduction is the capacity and tendency of organisms to generate new organisms by their own internal processes. This applies as much to organic substances, whether multicellular or unicellular (the latter reproducing by binary fission), as to cells that are ontologically dependent parts of a substance (such cells reproducing by mitosis).

In some cases, the characterization of a species by a property does not entail that every member of the species possesses the property. Yet this is consistent with the truth that the species is necessarily characterized by the property. This is because the property flows from but is distinct from the essence, and its failure to be possessed will be explicable in terms of abnormality, such as mutation, damage, or interference with the operation of the essence, i.e. with the *nature* of the individual. But in order to assess whether a characteristic is a property or not, we do not have to know in advance *what* the essence of the species is, only that it *has* an essence and that we can investigate its members' functions and operations.

We can see this in the case of reproduction. Not every organism reproduces itself. Not every organism *can* reproduce itself. And there are entire species – usually sterile hybrids – that cannot reproduce themselves. But we know enough about living things in general to know that they have an innate capacity and tendency to reproduce themselves in the absence of counter-vailing factors. Without knowing whether reproduction is a property – the biologist might merely assume it for the sake of investigation – it is possible to find out that hybrids are almost always products of artificial crossing, that sterility is a result of chromosomal abnormality, and that even with normally sterile hybrids fertility can sometimes be restored naturally. (For instance, enzymes can be used to restore fertility to sterile hybrid canola (Canola 2005), and there is a report of the rare observation of fertile mules and hinnies,[1] both of which are nearly always sterile (Rong *et al.* 1988).)

A number of objections might be raised against this view of the reproductive power of organisms, but answering them will help to clarify the essence of life. First, isn't it circular to appeal to mutation, damage, or abnormality in explaining, say, the sterility of hybrids? For surely the essentialist uses 'abnormal' and such terms of hybrids precisely because they cannot reproduce. Hence the insistence that reproduction is a property of life fails: hybrids are classed as abnormal because they cannot reproduce, yet they are thought of by the essentialist as unable to reproduce because they are abnormal. The objection would succeed if we had no independent handle on what the sterility consists in, but we do. Although it is not well understood in detail, one prime reason for hybrid sterility is generally thought to be the differing number of chromosomes possessed by the two species.[2] This prevents the formation of viable gametes (sperm and eggs) by the hybrid offspring. There is a *disruption* to the part of the process of gamete formation called meiosis, whereby chromosome pairing is impossible due to the uneven number of chromosomes. Hence the inability of hybrids to produce viable gametes is understood as an abnormality *independently* of the very fact that they cannot reproduce.[3] (For more on hybrid sterility, see Huskins 1929.) An additional point worth making is that the sterility of some species[4] or individuals does not undermine the idea that reproductive capacity is a property of living things, for the reason that it will not be *qua* living that the species or individual is sterile, but *qua* the species or the individual itself. Hence it is not something about the essence of life by virtue of which some species or individuals are sterile, but about the essence of the species or the accidents of the individual.

A second objection is that even if it were true that reproductive capacity was a property of organisms, caveats included, it would not follow that it was *restricted* to organisms and hence characteristic of them. Why should organic reproduction be considered any different from what happens when an inorganic macroscopic object naturally splits, or when a nucleus undergoes radioactive decay and emits a particle? As regards macroscopic objects, they are incapable of reproducing because they are wholly subject to outside forces that cause them to split, divide, or otherwise disassemble. Rocks just don't reproduce. When a rock falls off a cliff and splits in half it does not produce twins. In organisms, there is an *internal* process that the substance undergoes, or better *implements*, in order to produce offspring. It needs outside energy sources so as to be able to carry out the process, but the process is wholly within it as an individual (asexual reproduction) or within a reproductive pair (sexual reproduction). Reproduction is not something that *happens* to an organism; it is something that it *does*. It is not as though, given enough time, geologists will eventually be able to find the exact mechanism that rocks implement in order to produce offspring. Rocks just can't do that sort of thing.

What about radioactive decay? Isn't this process wholly internal to the decaying particle? Yes, but being internal is only necessary, not sufficient. Radioactive decay is, according to quantum mechanics, spontaneous and in principle unpredictable – it just happens. The nucleus emits, say, a proton; but it does not *do* anything *to itself* or implement any process. And even if radioactive decay were wholly causally determined, there would be no implementation by the nucleus of a process. Things happen to the nucleus – but it does not do anything.

To sharpen what I mean by this, note that in the case of both the rock and the nucleus, what happens to them is precisely that they undergo *decay* or *decomposition*. The falling rock *breaks* in two; the nucleus *destabilizes*. Reproduction, however, is not a process of decay, decomposition, or destabilization, but a *vital* process integral to the functioning organism. But what happens when a unicellular organism apparently spontaneously divides, or a cell of an organism undergoes apparent spontaneous mitosis? For one thing, in the case of organisms mitosis of cellular parts is *regulated* by the organism *for* the integrity and proper functioning of the organism. Cells have to divide so the organism can grow and develop, just as they must also die so the organism can remain healthy. For another, cell division is not a kind of decay or decomposition: the parent cell ceases to exist on division, but this just shows there are more ways of going out of existence than simply decomposing or decaying. When a cell decays or decomposes, it undergoes wholly different processes, called *apoptosis* in the case of programmed death in a multicellular organism, or *necrosis* when any cellular organism suffers acute injury or insult. Further, in the case of binary fission, although predicting when a unicellular organism will undergo it is at present well nigh impossible, this does not mean it is truly spontaneous. Just as in mitosis, we have every reason to think that the organism follows laws of its nature by which: conditions have to be in place for it to reproduce; it prepares to do so by getting itself into the right state; and it implements a process leading to the production of daughter organisms. There is nothing random or in principle unpredictable about this, as far as anyone knows, and even if there were it would still be nothing like the spontaneous emission of a proton by a nucleus, which as I have said *happens* to the nucleus. When the organism reproduces, it *acts*.

The upshot of the considerations I have been raising is that the essence of life is as follows: life is the natural capacity of an object for self-perfective immanent activity. Living things act *for* themselves in order to *perfect* themselves, where by perfection I mean that the entity acts so as to produce, conserve, and repair its proper functioning as the kind of thing it is – not to reach a state of absolute perfection, which is of course impossible for any finite being. Living things, unlike non-living things, exercise *immanent* causation: this is a kind of causation that begins *with* the agent and terminates *in* the agent for the sake *of* the agent. *Transient* causation, on the other hand, is the causation of one thing or event (or state, process, etc.) by another where the effect terminates in the former.[5] All exercises of immanent causation involve transient causal relations as effects and/or instruments. When a person eats food (immanent), she uses transient instrumental causes that are both conscious (placing the food in the mouth, maybe consciously tasting or chewing it, etc.) and unconscious (swallowing, secreting gastric acids, etc.), and there are also transient causal results or effects of the immanent nutritive and eliminative process (expelling waste, perhaps emitting wind!). 'Transient' in this context does not mean 'fleeting' or 'short lived': a transient causal process can be long lasting. What makes it transient is that the process terminates in something other than the cause itself.[6] All living things essentially engage in immanent activity for the sake of their own natures, whether conscious of it or not. It's just the way they are constituted.

Adaptation might be thought of as another property or power of living things, though perhaps it is better to regard it not as a separate property, but rather as a manifestation of the exercise of the other vital powers. For all living things, nutrition, growth, and reproduction are powers, and their exercise manifests the fundamental capacity and tendency of the organism to adapt to its environment (and of course to fail so to adapt when the environment triumphs over its nature). Inorganic objects do not *adapt* to their environment: either they persist in it due to the strength of the forces holding them together outweighing the dissipative forces in the environment, or they degrade and ultimately cease to exist when the latter outweigh the former. They do not adapt themselves – they are either maintained or destroyed. This is one of the reasons why the crystal theory of Graham Cairns-Smith is unconvincing as an account of the origin of life (Cairns-Smith 1990). On his theory, clay crystals formed in the early oceans and, by a process of natural selection working on them, larger and more complex crystals evolved and replicated (through splitting), varying in kind (through irregularities in the crystal structures), and eventually reached a point of size and complexity sufficient for them to synthesize organic molecules, and eventually RNA and DNA, whose initial function was to enhance the structural integrity of the crystals. Eventually, the crystals were subject to a 'genetic takeover': having served as the 'scaffold' on which life formed, the carbon-based, living structures were better able to survive and replicate than the crystals on which they were assembled, which eventually dissolved.

The problem with this account is that, details aside, crystal growth is nothing like the growth that living things undergo. Crystals, like other inorganic substances, grow purely by *accretion* through the play of attractive forces. Once an aggregation of molecules in a supersaturated solution[7] has reached a critical size, it attracts more and more solute molecules and so what is called the proto-crystal begins to grow – and hence to become a crystal – through its own attractive forces. But this is no more like organic growth than apparent adaptation in the inorganic world is like real, organic adaptation. There is nothing wrong with calling crystal accretion 'growth', any more than with calling sediment formation growth or the filling of a reservoir by rainfall growth. But the growth undergone by living beings belongs to their intrinsic, self-perfective tendency, whereby they regulate, enhance, and maintain their proper functioning through the ingestion and assimilation of nutritive material, as well as through other immanent activity (such as physical exertion) that tends to build up the organism. (For further criticisms of Cairns-Smith's theory, see Fry 2000: 126–9; Bedau 1991.)

Growth, adaptation, nutrition, reproduction, and the other vital powers are all manifestations of the *life principle* of organic beings. Like all substances (or parts of substances), powers belonging to the living thing are systematically united by a set of relationships and mutual dependencies that demonstrate unity of operation. The organism is no more a bundle of properties or powers than any other substance. We know the essence of the organism – however incompletely – via its properties and powers, but the essence is not identical to those powers. The essence is the metaphysical principle from which the properties and powers flow, namely the substantial form.[8] In the case of living things, the substantial form has traditionally been called the *soul*, which translates Aristotle's *psūche*. The term 'soul' is now used only in connection with human beings (whether its existence be affirmed or denied), but this is a corruption of Aristotelian metaphysics due mainly to post-Cartesian mechanism, which denied the existence of a special life principle or *psūche* in any living things other than human beings.[9]

It is important to note that the soul of an organism (I will use the term in its broader, traditional sense) is not to be identified with cellular structure, since cells are themselves organisms, even when existing as parts of other organisms. Explaining the essence of life requires that one explain the structure of the cell itself every bit as much as that of an organism that possesses a cellular structure.[10] Hence explaining the essence of any living thing, whether a unicellular or multicellular organic substance, or unicellular or multicellular organic *part* of a substance, requires an appeal to what is common to them all. And this is the life principle, or soul, which informs both the whole organic substance – bacterium, plant, animal, and so on – and every organic part that subserves the whole.

To many, the view that all living beings have a life principle or soul will smack of 'vitalism', though this term has in fact been much abused and it is often not clear what it means in the mouth of a given philosopher or biologist. (LaPorte (2004: 135–42) gives an account of this confusion.) For this reason alone the term should not be used. What the real essentialist holds, however, is the following. All substantial forms are immaterial, just as all universals are immaterial: it makes no sense whatever to ask what colour is made of, or what the form of a rock is made of; and, similarly, it makes no sense to ask what the form of a cat is made of. Nor does it make sense to ask what the form of a *particular* rock or cat is made of, or what a particularized accident, such as the redness of this fire engine, is made of: the physical essence of a thing, i.e. the metaphysical essence as instantiated in a particular substance, is immaterial, as is the mode (or trope) possessed by a substance.

All of this is wholly consistent with the thesis that the form of a cat or rock, or of *this* cat or rock, or colour, or a mode of colour, is wholly explicable in material terms, and hence is wholly dependent on matter for its existence. Further, all forms are *simple* – they are not divisible into parts. When a rock is split in two, a substance ceases to exist and two new substances come into existence, each with its own form. Some lower organisms are no different: many plants can be split into new plants, and it has long been known than the planarian flatworms (phylum *Platyhelminthes*) can be split into many new, complete worms (Alvarado 2004). This is due to the relative homogeneity of the parts of the organism concerned. The more homogeneous, i.e. the greater the similarity of behaviour or function between the parts, the more likely it is that such division is possible. None of this implies, however, that the forms of such beings are *themselves* divisible. On the contrary, it proves that the forms of some beings are not divisible but *multipliable*. Some physical essences, then, are multipliable. But *all* metaphysical essences are as well, because anything universal is capable of having multiple instances. Hence we find multipliability in all metaphysical essences, and in some physical essences – but no divisibility.

Yet this hylemorphic view of form does *not* imply the position, usually taken as a hallmark of 'vitalism', that living things possess an 'immaterial vital principle' which must be invoked in order to explain their behaviour, any more than it implies vitalism about rocks and rivers. LaPorte characterizes vitalism as follows: '[L]iving organisms are powered in a way that nonliving objects like rivers and volcanoes are not, by an immaterial substance, rather than by a particular arrangement of physical and chemical constituents' (LaPorte 2004: 137).[11] And he goes on to quote Medawar and Medawar, who attribute to vitalism the following:

> a flat repudiation of the idea that a living organism's vivacity – its state of being alive – can be explained satisfactorily in terms of its form and composition; that is, in terms of what it is made of and how those constituents interact physically and chemically. Some immaterial vital principle is required in addition.
>
> (Medawar and Medawar 1983: 275–6)

If this is vitalism, the real essentialist wants no part of it. And if this is the only choice available to the metaphysician who eschews physico-chemical reductionism about life, then so much the worse for the anti-reductionist. But like most characterizations born of scientific prejudice and philosophical ignorance of Aristotelian metaphysics, it is a caricature.[12]

Real essentialism holds that essences are all immaterial for the reason just given: forms are not *made* of anything, let alone made of matter. But this is consistent with the existence of forms that are wholly materially dependent, i.e. which can have no existence apart from their present actualization of matter. These forms are *material* according to the sense just given. Although not made of matter, a material form is dependent on matter for its reality. According to traditional terminology, it is wholly *educed* from the potentiality of matter when the substance whose form it is comes into existence, and is *reduced* to the potentiality of matter when the substance ceases to exist.[13] All living things (with one exception, for which see Chapter 10) have substantial forms that depend wholly on their present actualization of matter for their existence. In this sense, they are wholly material beings, and the account of their structure and function is wholly material. It is another thing altogether to hold that this account is wholly physical, or chemical, or some combination of the two. It is the immanent activity of living things that sets them apart altogether from the non-living world and prevents any reductive explanation of their properties and essence in terms that are not explicitly organic and hence the formal object of biological study. Thus life is a *basic* essence and an irreducible category in the material universe. I will return to this later.

8.2 Kinds of organism

First, though, I want to look at the way in which kinds of organism should be characterized at a relatively general level, including the most general.

This process of characterization is primarily a *metaphysical* one, informed by biology. Unfortunately, biological taxonomy, post-Darwin, has been all but evacuated of metaphysical content, and has been explicitly realigned so as to conform to evolutionary phylogenetics. As David Hull puts it, 'The primary goal of taxonomy since Darwin has been to reflect ... successive splittings in a hierarchical classification made up of species, genera, families, and so on' (Hull 1998: 272; see also Ragan 1998). It is one of the themes of this section and section 8.3 that there is an important metaphysical distinction between what things are and where they come from. Essentialists are interested in what things are, wherever they may have come from, though what they are may indeed shed light on their origins and vice versa. As jarring as this may sound to the ears of contemporary systematists (who study the diversity and relationships among organisms with a view to classifying them), it is central to the essentialist classification of what exists, organisms not excluded. The metaphysical study of organisms without empirical information from biology might be empty, but, to continue the Kantian cliché, biology without metaphysics is blind.

Until well into the twentieth century, biologists followed Linnaeus in recognizing two kingdoms of organism, the plants and the animals.[14] As far as it goes, this classification is still held to mark a correct and accepted distinction, but it has been elaborated and complicated by the discovery and analysis of kinds of organism that seem not to fit into either class. This is part of the metaphysical problem of life on which the present section is intended to shed some light. Linnaeus's classification was wholly Aristotelian in inspiration. The vegetative powers of plants are shared by all organisms – nutrition, growth, and reproduction, along with all the adaptive powers that serve these basic functions or otherwise contribute to the proper functioning of the organism. Animals, however, belong to a higher grade of life, possessing specific animal powers – those of sentience, appetition, and locomotion.

Sentience at its most basic is the capacity and tendency for awareness of stimuli. Appetition is the capacity and tendency for seeking after and avoiding stimuli consequent upon awareness of them. Locomotion is the capacity and tendency for self-movement from place to place in fulfilment of appetition. Since sentience is the most basic property, we can define animals as sentient organisms. Plants, as Linnaeus and other biologists observed, have none of these animal powers, only the vegetative ones. We do not observe plants exercising powers of sensation, appetition, and locomotion, but we do observe animals exercising such powers. This is a good a posteriori argument for the distinction between plants and animals, but there is a metaphysical one behind it. In the case of plants, it is a modus tollens. Given that the environment of all living things is a constantly changing mix of beneficial and harmful stimuli – one of the factors regularly appealed to by evolutionary biologists to explain phenomena such as extinctions and the non-ubiquity of perfect adaptations – sentience should guarantee the existence of locomotion, in order that an organism should be equipped to move itself towards sources of beneficial sensations and away from sources of harmful ones. Plants do not have such locomotion. Therefore, they cannot have sentience either. To put the argument more bluntly: what is the point of nature's equipping an organism with sentience but not with the means of moving towards the good stimuli and escaping the bad ones, especially the ones whose sources may destroy the organism?

In the case of animals, the argument is a modus ponens of the reverse entailment. Locomotion should guarantee the existence of a power that gives locomotion its point. What point would there be to an organism's being able to move itself from place to place if it had no power that made such movement useful to it? Again, this would be a potentially destructive situation for the organism, since if it could move without sensing what it had moved to, it could move to a noxious environment and perhaps be destroyed. Yet animals can move themselves from place to place. So they must have a power that makes this useful rather than harmful, and that is sentience – the ability to sense the distinction between good and bad environments.

This sort of argument might be looked at as an inference to the best explanation, and if so it is a strong one. But given the way the world inherently is – a flux of changing environmental conditions – there would seem to be a metaphysical connection between sentience and locomotion: the nature of a non-moving organism *requires* that it lack a power whose possession in the absence of locomotion would certainly destroy such an organism. And the nature of a moving organism requires that it possess a power without which locomotion would be harmful at best, destructive at worst.[15] An objector might retort that the argument presupposes the idea that nature does nothing in vain, which is supposedly a piece of folk biology or metaphysical obscurantism. The objector might appeal to Stephen Jay Gould and Richard Lewontin's concept of a *spandrel*, a non-adaptive by-product of some other genuine adaptation (Gould and Lewontin 1979). But sensation without locomotion, or locomotion without sensation, would not merely be non-adaptive; they would be at least maladaptive and at worst contribute to the death of the organism. It is hard to see how biologists could explain (1) why, if the necessary conjunction of sentience and locomotion is in fact absent, any plant or animal is alive right now or ever was, and (2) how and why an organism could ever be or get into such a state of having one power but not the other.

Still, perhaps we can imagine a world in which sentience could exist without locomotion: one in which an organism was permanently rooted (by nature) in a completely beneficial environment that never ceased to be beneficial.[16] Sentience, on such a scenario, would not be potentially harmful. It might be a mere spandrel. It would certainly be pointless, and the evolutionary biologist would have to explain why the organism possessed sentience at all. But our world is not and has never been like that, nor could it be: my argument is limited to the way natures must be in our world, constituted as it is of material beings essentially subject to change. In other words, my claim is the following: given the evident truth that there exist animals and that they are even minimally adapted to survive and function in their environments, the nature of the material world as a world of beings essentially subject to change is such that the presence of sentience metaphysically guarantees the presence of locomotion.

Maybe a more realistic scenario would be an environment in which sentience was required for detecting stimuli (and perhaps communicating their presence to other organisms), but where locomotion was not necessary since the organisms, acting individually or co-operatively, were sufficiently able to deal with the stimuli by internal adaptation. (See p. 190 on non-motile bacteria and 'quorum sensing'.) In which case my claim would be the more qualified one that sentience entailed locomotion only in those creatures intrinsically unable, either individually or co-operatively, to adapt to stimuli in an immanent way by their own internal, non-locomotive processes. In other cases, sentience might be present yet not conjoined with locomotion so long as the sentient power had a function in the life of the organism on its own or in groups. Still, the sentience would have to be manifested by a range of other, non-locomotive, behaviour.

I want now to look at more specific examples in order to see whether the metaphysical distinction between plants and animals is itself different from, and more insightful than, the current phylogenetic one. First, why should it be *integral* locomotion that requires sentience – isn't the local motion of *parts* sufficient? On this view an organism, if sentient, needs minimally to be capable of moving its parts in avoidance or pursuit of certain stimuli. As a general response, however, the environmental flux in which organisms exist involves threats or benefits not just to parts, but also to wholes. Animals pursue and avoid not merely stimuli that modify their function for good or ill, but also stimuli that kill or that preserve life. Hence we should expect that where local movement of parts is possible, so is locomotion of the whole organism.

Yet plants move their parts in the search for and exercise of nutrition, so doesn't this imply sentience? Plants typically move their roots in search of water; they move towards light (phototaxis); some (such as the Venus fly trap, *Dionaea muscipula*) close their parts upon food; others (such as the Sensitive Plant, *Mimosa pudica*) have leaves that droop and close when touched and reopen after a few minutes. Darwin himself thought plant movement and that in the lower animals were significantly similar, even going so far as to compare the tip of a plant radicle (embryonic root) to the brain of an animal, referring also to the 'transmission of impressions' in plants (Darwin 1880: ch. 12). Nevertheless, apart from the peculiarity of a plant's being able to move its parts as a sensitive response to stimuli but not its whole body (again, this would be highly maladaptive: the plant could do a little in avoidance of noxious stimuli but not the most important thing, viz. *escape*), this sort of plant behaviour looks far more like a mechanical reaction to physical contact or environmental conditions than a genuine, sentient response to stimuli based on awareness. Nyctinastic movement (leaves folding and drooping at night) and seismonastic movement (folding and drooping due to warmth, contact, or agitation) are both explained in terms of a rapid decrease in the internal pressure of cells of the pulvinus (small swelling) at the base of the leaves of the *Mimosa pudica*, causing leaf drooping and contraction (Yamashiro *et al.* 2001). A similar mechanism underlies the behaviour of *Dionaea muscipula* (Hodick and Sievers 1989), with the flow of calcium ions crucial in both cases. Phototaxis is explicable in terms of photoreceptive cells in the plant and chemical reactions consequent upon exposure to light. None of these mechanisms is very well understood, but the point is that although they are mechanical processes involved in immanent activity by the organism, they do not require the postulation of sentience or awareness of stimuli. We can, and biologists often do, call the causes of such behaviour stimuli, but we should not understand the term to imply any kind of awareness on the part of the plant, any more than its sending out its roots in search of water implies an awareness of its environment and a conscious movement towards nutrition.

It might be replied that the pulvinus in plants capable of nyctinastic and seismonastic movement is indeed an organ that responds to stimuli, so why isn't this evidence of sensation? But the pulvinus is a *motor* organ, not a sensory organ, and sensation requires *organs of sense*. Plants as well as animals can have motor organs, which are parts containing cells or structures that cause movement. But a motor organ is not by that very fact a sense organ. Surely, though – to take the objection in the opposite direction – not all animals have sensory organs, and so not all animals have sentience? On the contrary, even the humble bacterium has arrays of receptors that co-operate on exposure to the faintest of stimuli in such a way as to generate internal cellular processes that lead to the bacterium's turning away from or fleeing certain stimuli, or moving towards them. They even *amplify* the faintest of stimuli so that the information can be interpreted and processed. Different stimuli often produce the same response, and the same stimulus often produces different responses. (On sensation in *Thermotoga maritima*, see Park *et al.* 2006.)

Because bacteria are unicellular, they have many different kinds of receptor to sense and interpret the diverse stimuli to which they are exposed. Why is it that the minority of plants that exhibit phototactic, nyctinastic, seismonastic, and related movements have a very small number, no more than a handful, of constant, predictable responses to specific kinds of stimuli? Why can't they do what bacteria do, namely move in response to a massive array of stimuli of diverse kinds in unpredictable ways? They do not exhibit behaviour that we could properly call *flinching*, or *escaping*, or *avoiding* stimuli – bacteria do all of these.

My contention is that it is locomotion of the whole organism that gives evidence of sentience, not a mere reflex in one or other part of an organism that is otherwise rooted to the spot. Moreover, the fact that phototaxis occurs in light-sensitive animals as well as in plants does not show either that plants do have sentience or that those animals lack it. First, even undoubtedly sentient animals such as human beings are phototactic, so phototaxis is no proof of non-sentience. Secondly, the fact is consistent with what I have already claimed, namely that *all* organisms have the vegetative powers, with only the plants having *no more* than those powers. In this case, phototaxis need not be interpreted as anything more than a vegetative activity (at least in some animals), i.e. an immanent activity based on nutritive and tropic (growth-related) power alone, not on sentient power as well – even though in certain kinds of sentient organism, such as us, phototaxis does (usually) involve the sentient power.[17]

A further problem with postulating sentience in the tiny minority of plants displaying nyctinastic, seismonastic, and similar behaviour is precisely that they are a tiny minority. Why should we find such remarkable sentient powers in a handful of plants and nothing similar in the millions upon millions of other species? What is so special about *Mimosa pudica* and its putatively sentient cousins? The only thing that might be suggested is that the species in this small group, unlike all the other plants, are intermediate species – sentient plants on their evolutionary way towards full-fledged animality. If we gave them a few million more years their roots might even become legs. It is not easy to find a systematist who advances such a position.[18]

Surely, it might be objected, it is absurd to claim that bacteria and protozoa (the latter being unicellular eukaryotes, i.e. possessing a cell nucleus) have sentience any more than plants. Yet protozoa have locomotion, and are often classified according to the ways in which they move themselves from place to place, for example using pseudopodia (*Amoeba*), cilia (*Paramecium*) and so on. I will say more about this in a moment. But first consider the more specific objection that we have no reason to regard parasites as locomotive, because they do not need to be: their life-cycle takes place within a wholly hospitable environment and so all they need is the passive power of being moved from place to place. If true, this would conform to my earlier speculation that sentience might not *require* locomotion if the environment were favourable enough. If so, we would have to rely on other evidence of sensory behaviour involving signal processing and interpretation, but the evidence would certainly have been weakened, albeit not sufficiently to rule out sentience altogether.

In fact, as I claimed, the environment of all animals is such that this scenario is probably fanciful; and indeed there is motility (locomotion) even in parasites. The parasite species *Apicomplexans* (called a 'kingdom' in current taxonomy, but remember that I am using 'species' in its primary metaphysical sense) contains parasite species such as *Plasmodium* (the cause of malaria) and *Emeria* (a widespread gut parasite) that move themselves by gliding, twisting, and bending. (On *Emeria* motility, see Upton and Tilley 1992.) Note that motility does not need to be manifested at all stages of the life-cycle for us to be able to attribute locomotion to the organism: few organisms can move themselves around at every stage, and in the case of *Apicomplexans* motility is usually most evident at the zoite stage, e.g. when sporozoites are released from the salivary glands of a *Plasmodium*-carrying mosquito.

Until relatively recently, living things were divided into five kingdoms by most taxonomists: *Animalia*; *Plantae*; *Fungi*; *Protoctista*; *Monera*.[19] The *Protoctista* include the eukaryotic micro-organisms, whether unicellular or multicellular, such as the protozoa, various algae (golden, yellow-green, red), slime moulds (such as *Myxomycota*) and slime nets (*Labyrinthulids*). The *Monera* include the prokaryotes (without a cell nucleus), i.e. the bacteria, which are unicellular though sometimes colony-forming. But since the discovery of *Archaea* by Carl Woese in the 1970s, which used to be classified as bacteria, many systematists have abandoned the five kingdom scheme in favour of his 'three-domain' model: *Archaea*, which inhabit extreme conditions, such as very high temperature or salinity; *Bacteria*, i.e. the prokaryotic micro-organisms previously classified as *Monera*; and *Eukaryota*, i.e. all nucleated organisms from slime moulds to human beings. *Animalia*, *Plantae*, and *Fungi* still exist as kingdoms within the Eukaryotes. (For a good overview, see Tudge 2000: 95–106.) The plants are usually characterized as multicellular, having cell walls containing cellulose, and non-motile, though many systematists regard the category as vague and lacking anything that could be called the essence of the kingdom *Plantae*. The same goes for the animals, where features such as locomotion, sentience, absence of a cell wall, and multicellularity are usually mentioned only for these to be undercut by the common view that this kingdom too is vague, the only essential feature seeming to be the possession of Hox complex genes regulating bodily development. (See Tudge 2000: 181–4, 547.)

It might be thought that current biological taxonomy is far too complex and multifaceted to be accommodated within the basic vegetative/sentient division I discussed earlier. I contend that, despite (or rather because of) the fact that we still know so little about life, and that systematics is clearly in a state of flux, the essentialist should resist the idea that biologists have proven the vegetative/sentient division to be untenable. In particular, the fact that phylogeny (the study of origins) has invaded, and now permeates, morphology (the study of the form and functions of an organism or its species) has led to classifications that from a metaphysical point of view do not represent reality. Hence the fading search for an essence of *Animalia* or *Plantae* and the insistence that *Fungi* are a class apart. It is impossible to canvass all of the issues here, but I will end this section with some further observations that reinforce the idea of distinct life principles in kinds of organism.

First, fungi and plants differ in many ways, such as methods of reproduction and nutrition, but neither have locomotion (Margulis and Sagan 1995: 140–1). From the metaphysical point of view, both have merely vegetative functions and so belong to the same metaphysical species/genus. That fungi do not belong to the kingdom *Plantae* is only a matter of how dissimilarities between the two enable partitioning of the overarching species/genus into lower species, and ultimately into infima species.

Secondly, all motile bacteria and archaea, whatever their relation to the kingdom *Animalia* and whatever their differences from each other, are animals: they can sense their environment and they can move themselves locally towards and away from certain stimuli. From this fundamental viewpoint, it is irrelevant that the archaea might be genetically as different from bacteria as a human being or a tiger is. It is also irrelevant that they are compositionally unique, e.g. in respect of lipids or transfer RNA. In general, they have the same structure as other living things but use wholly different compounds to build them. In terms of overall morphology – which includes, for the essentialist, bodily functions and operations, not just structural characters – they are as much animals as bacteria and as the formal members of the kingdom *Animalia*.

Thirdly, non-motile bacteria (such as the *Cocci*, e.g. *Staphylococcus aureus*) and archaea (e.g. some of the *Crenarchaeota*, which grow and thrive in temperatures near or above boiling) might, at least in some cases, be such that current understanding is unable to determine whether they are genuinely sentient or merely vegetative in their operations. The phenomenon of 'quorum sensing' in some non-motile bacteria (such as species of *Streptomyces* and *Staphylococcus*) suggests that they are aware of their surroundings, though the behaviour is not well understood. Bacteria that exhibit quorum sensing (whether they are motile, as they usually are, or non-motile) apparently sense the population density of other bacteria – usually conspecific, sometimes not – in their environment by signalling to each other, and so are able to co-ordinate behaviour in response to changed environmental conditions. (For instance, *Vibrio cholerae*, the agent of cholera, uses quorum sensing to negotiate the acidic human gut without losing infectivity (Zhu and Mekalanos 2003).) If this is a case of genuine sensation, as it seems, it would confirm the reservations I expressed earlier about stating that sentience entails locomotion in *all* organisms. If the organism has *other* ways than locomotion to achieve an adaptive response to sensed stimuli, such as co-ordination with a critical mass of other organisms through quorum sensing, then we have a sufficient explanation for sentience without locomotion in the particular case. Such a capacity would achieve the same end as locomotion – adaptive response to sensed stimuli. But we would need some such explanation, for the reasons given earlier concerning serious maladaptation (see pp. 185–6). (On quorum sensing, see Fuqua *et al.*1994; Greenberg 1997; Miller and Bassler 2001; March and Bentley 2004.)

Fourthly, the fact that organisms once thought to be plants are actually animals, and vice versa, does nothing to show that the vegetative/sentient distinction is an artificial or vague one of no essentialist import. What are commonly known as algae were all once thought to be plants. In fact the situation is much more complex (Ragan 1998). We know that so-called 'blue-green algae' are colonies of motile *Cyanobacteria*. So-called 'green algae' include the *Ulvophyceae*, such as green seaweed, that are clearly vegetative. The sister group, *Chlorophyceae*, contains motile organisms such as *Chlamydomonas*, as well as non-motile organisms such as *Chlorella*, which are chlorophyll-rich, green, floating spheres. Yet the former is best classed metaphysically as an animal and the latter as a plant, i.e. a purely vegetative organism, whatever their related phylogeny. But modern taxonomy classes them both as plants because they photosynthesize and are thought to be evolutionary ancestors of land plants.

Yet not all plants, even land plants, photosynthesize (e.g. *Monotropa*), let alone the clearly vegetative *Fungi*, which have a wholly different means of nutrition from the *Plantae*. The essentialist should not regard means of nutrition as an important sign of what essence an organism has: that it *does* exercise the nutritive power is a sure sign of its being alive, but the details of how it does so are a matter for empirical observation and more specific classification, not for employment against the distinction between animal and vegetative life. The *Rhodophyta*, or 'red seaweeds', are again clearly vegetative even though they are phylogenetically classified in their own kingdom, far removed from the *Plantae*. On the other hand, the vegetative-seeming slime moulds (*Myxomycota, Acrasiomycota*) are highly animal in their behaviour, though again they are classified well away from the *Animalia*.

The point of these observations (many others could be made) is, first, that the reclassification of organisms that seem clearly to belong to a certain taxon in itself shows nothing about the essences of the organisms other than that we have come to know them better. Secondly, the current mode of phylogenetic classification cuts right across the basic metaphysical distinction between the vegetative and the sentient. As a result of this confusion between essence and origin, or more precisely between formal and efficient causes, current systematics, I contend, is not in a healthy state. (The overview of the algae in Ragan 1998 reinforces this impression.) I will say more about this in Chapter 9.

Fifthly, viruses are, as is well known, a difficult case that it would take many pages to explore. They are generally omitted from the taxonomy of living things (e.g. Tudge 2000: 9) or explicitly asserted to be non-living (Margulis and Sagan 1995: 23–4). Some viruses appear to be motile, using locomotive mechanisms similar to some bacteria (Goldberg 2001). Viruses, however, do not metabolize: they do not take in nutrition, process it, or excrete waste. They do not grow; nor do they maintain homeostasis. As such, they lack even the basic vegetative powers, even though they replicate[20] and exploit (at least in an analogous sense of 'exploit') their host organism.

Hence their motility should not be seen as true locomotion any more than a car has true locomotion; rather, the virus relies on its host organism to supply the energy and material for passive movement (unlike the passive movement of the *Cocci*, which do have vegetative powers; hence there are different ways in which locomotion can be lacking). For these reasons alone, and until further evidence comes to light to undermine the interpretation, they should be regarded not as living things but as 'chemical zombies', to use the epithet of Margulis and Sagan (1995: 24), whose manner of replication is no more suggestive of self-maintaining, self-regulating, immanent activity than is that of a computer virus.[21]

Finally, might not the very idea of sentience in lower organisms such as bacteria, archaea, and protozoans be preposterous? Only if consciousness is equated with self-consciousness and feeling is equated with feeling-like. One of the most baleful effects of post-Cartesian philosophy has been the narrowing of the phenomenon of consciousness to phenomenology, and often to self-consciousness. If a being is conscious, so the standard view goes, there must be something it is like to be that thing. If a being is conscious of something, there must be something it is like to have that conscious experience. And even – for the Cartesian or the philosopher influenced by Cartesian thinking – if a being is conscious it must be at least capable of self-consciousness. Whatever the truth of such ideas in respect of certain kinds of living thing, there is no reason to extend this view of consciousness to everything that has it. When you press your finger against the base of a mercury thermometer, the mercury rises. But the mercury is not *escaping* the heat or *avoiding* it. It does not manifest immanent behaviour, and so can in no way be regarded as conscious (*pace* Chalmers 1996: 293–7).[22] One could, of course, deny the existence of immanent activity altogether and claim that any concept of consciousness worth having, or that is available to us, must make no essential distinction between a thermometer and a bacterium. It is not my purpose to make an explicit defence of the very phenomenon of immanence, and I cannot engage in a full-fledged defence of consciousness as something that transcends physico-chemical explanation. My point is simply that if we grant the existence of immanent activity – and any study of the behaviour of living things demonstrates it – then we must attribute some kind of awareness to even the lowest of non-vegetative organisms, even though they do not (as far as anyone can tell) possess phenomenology, let alone self-consciousness.

I have used terms such as 'sentience' and 'sensation' in characterizing non-vegetative organisms, and it might be thought that such use must imply the attribution of subjective experience, and hence of phenomenology. But it is not clear that it should. There is nothing incomplete, let alone incoherent, in positing the existence of beings that engage in immanent activity, one aspect of which is the registering, processing, interpretation, and use of information, without any corresponding phenomenology. They feel something, but it does not feel *like* anything. They interpret information, and perhaps they have an innate system of computation on natural signs, but they have no language and follow no rules other than those of an inbuilt natural program. They have direct, *de re* knowledge of their environment, but they have no beliefs and form no judgments. They have a primitive mind but no intellect. Their knowledge consists of a causal correlation between natural sign and environment productive of successful (ceteris paribus) immanent reaction to that environment. Perhaps they even misinterpret their environment, and so make mistakes, resulting in unsuccessful adaptation. Why should anything in this repertoire of powers and behaviour require that it feel *like* something for them to register an environmental condition, let alone that it feel like anything to be one of them, or that they have any self-awareness? They might be aware of their own states (and arguably must be, in order to process information) without being aware of themselves as *having* those states. Yet such beings would still be more than chemical zombies, and they would certainly be more than complex thermometers. I submit that every organism rising above the vegetative has at *least* such a repertoire of powers, and as such has a right to be called sentient or aware. As we ascend the scale of living things, phenomenology enters into the picture. At what point, precisely, no one knows. It does not enter into the picture with anything immaterial, and as such must be regarded as a purely material phenomenon in the sense explained earlier (pp. 182–3). But this does not mean it is explicable in physico-chemical terms, any more – or so I argue in section 8.3 – than life itself.

8.3 Against emergence

Biologists and philosophers of biology have had a hard time defining life. Mark Bedau (1996: 334–7) has listed a large number of the defining features, or clusters of features, that have been proposed at one time or another: process; self-reproduction; information storage of self-representation; metabolization; functional interactions with the environment; interdependence of parts; stability under perturbations; the ability to evolve; the capacity for open-ended evolution; purposeful behaviour; autonomous morphogenesis; reproductive invariance; mutability; parts with functions; enormously complex and adaptive organization; composition by a chemically unique set of macromolecules; manifestation of mainly qualitative rather than quantitative phenomena; historically evolved genetic programs; historical connections of common descent; special unpredictability of biological processes.

Some of these features are so vague as either to be meaningless or to apply to everything that exists; some are highly ambiguous; some are possessed by living things but are mere accidents (such as having unique macromolecules); some are false attributions (special unpredictability, at least taken as globally true of all biological processes in all organisms). Many of them, at least under a certain interpretation, are properties of organisms. Metabolization, for one, is a clear property of only the living, when understood as an *immanent* process. Yet positing mere clusters of properties, without appealing to a life principle, is inadequate, as explained earlier. Bedau echoes in this specific case the general metaphysical worry that has been one of the themes of this book, namely what unifies the properties: 'A cluster [of properties] offers no explanation of why that *particular* cluster of properties is a fundamental and ubiquitous natural phenomenon. .... . We want an account of *why* these properties all coexist. Rather than settling this question, the list raises it' (Bedau 1996: 335–6).

What unifies properties in all substances is substantial form. And what unifies the properties of each living thing is its life principle or soul, which, to repeat, is not, except in the case to be discussed in Chapter 10, a 'non-physical substance or force' (Bedau 1996: 334). Bedau posits a life principle as well, what he calls 'supple adaptation'. The term is vague, and his definition of it inherits this vagueness: it is 'an unending capacity to produce novel solutions to unanticipated changes in the problems of surviving, reproducing, or, more generally, flourishing' (Bedau 1996: 338). He thinks the vagueness is a virtue since viruses, for instance, are borderline cases of organisms whose satisfaction of the definition is itself borderline. I have argued that viruses are not alive, but even if this were simply not clear it would be preferable to put the unclarity down to our limited understanding of viruses than to produce a definition that sanctified the vagueness. (Having said that, and though I will say a little about vagueness in Chapter 9, I do not propose to solve the overarching problem of vagueness here.) Vagueness aside, Bedau's 'supple adaptation' will not do as a life principle since it is just another property of living things, manifested in the more determinate properties I have already set down such as nutrition, growth, reproduction, and in the case of animals sentience, appetition, and locomotion, as well as in other exercises of immanent, self-perfective activity. It is the power of self-perfective, immanent activity *itself* that is constitutive of the living thing, not the way it manifests itself in adaptation. We cannot even understand the kind of adaptation distinctive of living things without a prior grasp of immanence, which is shown in Bedau's use of the term 'flourishing'. Living creatures do things *to* themselves *for* themselves, whereas non-living things do not.

What is at once mysterious, and continues to mystify the vast majority of biologists, is just how life is related to physico-chemical composition. Having jettisoned vitalism, understood in the faulty way I have explained, they have since spent decade upon decade trying to explain how life could have emerged from non-life, committed as they are to regarding life as having evolved from non-living matter just as higher species have, they insist, evolved from lower species. Darwin put to one side the question of the origin of life rather than incorporating it into his overall theory of evolution by natural selection (Davies 1999: 46, 61), though he did speculate about the possibility of life's emerging from a 'warm little pond', i.e. a so-called primordial soup. The primordial soup theory still has its adherents, many rallying around the famous Urey-Miller experiments of 1953 in which a mixture of methane, hydrogen, ammonia, and water, subject to an electric spark, yielded amino acids, the building blocks of proteins. The experiments themselves proved nothing about the origin of life, however, since few people think Urey and Miller simulated conditions on the early Earth (said to be around 4.5 billion years ago), and there is no fossil evidence of what kind of primordial soup in fact obtained. Subsequent experiments in the same vein, such as those of Sidney Fox (who generated 'proteinoids' by heating amino acids, their resemblance to real proteins being superficial only), have also come in for sustained criticism. (See further Davies 1999: 63–9; Fry 2000: ch. 7).

The lack of knowledge among biologists of how life emerged from non-life – a model of *abiogenesis* – is manifest in the multiple theories on offer. Some posit (or have posited) proteins first; others cells first; others nucleic acids or specifically RNA first; yet others some combination of one or more of these. Still others, having given up on trying to explain the emergence of life on Earth, have proposed that it originated extraterrestrially. (See Davies 1999 and Fry 2000 for overviews, and Hoyle and Wickramasinghe 1981 for a classic statement.) No one knows how life emerged, say biologists, but emerged it must have, no matter that it be, in the words of Ernst Mayr, a 'near impossibility' (Mayr 1982: 584). As Mayr himself asserts:

> The subject of life's origin is highly complex, but it is no longer the mystery it once was ... In fact, there is no longer any fundamental difficulty in explaining, on the basis of physical and chemical laws, the origin of life from inanimate matter.
>
> (Mayr 1997: 179)

I contend that the insistence upon abiogenesis, even in the face of seemingly insurmountable empirical objections such as those lucidly set out by Davies (1999), has – at least in the present state of knowledge – more of the flavour of a dogma than of a considered position. More importantly, the empirical difficulties reflect a fundamental metaphysical problem with the very idea of life's having emerged from non-life. This is the impossibility of explaining immanent causation in terms of transient causation. If there were such an explanation, then we would have a model of how, in principle, life could have emerged from non-life. Even if we did not know the details, and even if these were forever unavailable due, say, to lack of fossil evidence for the conditions on the early Earth, biologists would still be justified in their confidence in abiogenesis.

There is, however, serious reason to doubt the possibility of such an explanation. The problem is that immanent causation is a fundamentally different *kind* of causation from transient. In immanent causation a being does things to itself for itself. In transient causation a being does things to another being, and even in cases where the being does things to itself, this can be explained without remainder in terms of transient causation among the parts of the thing in question. For instance, we can say truly that a thermostat adjusts the state of its system in response to a change in temperature: this is a kind of self-adjustment. Yet it is wholly explicable in transient terms: the internal thermometer reacts to a change in temperature, which causes the mercury switch (in a simple device) to change position, which causes contact between wires, which creates a circuit that causes an appliance, such as a heater, to turn on. When the temperature reaches a certain level, the switch changes position again, thus breaking the circuit and thereby turning off the appliance. There is nothing left to explain about the working of the thermostat. All the causal mechanisms involved are transient, but because the objects involved in the mechanisms are parts of a larger system, it is correct to say that the thermostat adjusts itself.

In the case of life, the situation is fundamentally different. The organism also adjusts itself via the instrumental, transient causes involved in metabolism, excretion, thermoregulation, and so on, but this all takes place, in a properly (if not perfectly) functioning organism, *for* the organism. It is not merely that the organism is *in control* of the transient causes within it, but that it is in control of them *for its own benefit*. No such thing is true of a thermostat or of any other mechanical device or naturally occurring object. The question is: what has to happen in order to get from mere transient causes to transient causes that take place within the context of immanent causation? The situation parallels the problems of deriving order from chaos and necessity from contingency that I discuss elsewhere (Oderberg forthcoming b). The basic metaphysical idea is that a thing cannot give what it does not have. Chaos could never bestow order without possessing a *power* of bestowing order – but then it would not be true chaos, since chaos has no powers (the 'chaos' in chaos theory is not true chaos but apparent chaos within which mathematicians look for hidden order). Contingency could not give rise to necessity either. It is difficult to begin to see how merely contingent relations can of themselves give rise to necessary ones. What power within contingency could bestow necessity? If it is something that already contains necessity, then necessity has not come from mere contingency. If it does not already contain necessity, then it can only contain more contingency since every being is either necessary or contingent.

Similarly, how could transience give rise to immanence? By what power could merely transient processes give rise to a being that acted immanently? It is hard even to begin to see what such a power could be unless it already contained immanence within it; but in that case we would not have abiogenesis but a manifestation of the law stated in the seventeenth century by William Harvey, discoverer of the circulation of blood, as 'all life comes from life' (*omne vivum ex vivo*); and by Rudolf Virchow, the nineteenth-century founder of cellular pathology, as 'every cell comes from a cell' (*omnis cellula e cellula*).

Put more abstractly, the argument is that fundamental kinds of causation must derive at least in part from the same kinds. The fundamental kinds are: formal (essences); material (material constitution); efficient (transient); final (immanent).[23] To get a formal cause, i.e. an essence of something, you need a prior formal cause, since, to use the Aristotelian jargon, form drives out form. If you want to make water, for example, you need hydrogen and oxygen; hence you need the forms they possess. To get a material cause, i.e. the material components of something, you need prior material components, i.e. a prior material cause. This actually follows from the first point, via the corollaries that there is no form without matter or matter without form: for if you can only get form from form, and there is no form without matter or matter without form, then you can only get matter from matter (albeit in conjunction with form).[24]

To get an efficient cause, you need an efficient cause to produce it, since every efficient cause is itself some combination of form and matter, and you cannot get a combination of form and matter without some other combination of form and matter acting efficiently, or transiently, upon it in order to bring it into existence. (This is simply the principle of causal closure among efficient causes, to which most if not all defenders of abiogenesis would subscribe.) Since this is all true of three of the fundamental kinds of causation, why would it not be true of the fourth, namely that to get final causation you need final causation, i.e. that no combination of merely formal, material, and efficient causes could ever bring about a final cause? If anything, we should expect it to be even more obviously difficult to get final causes from non-final causes, for the reason that final causes are only a small part of the causes operative in the material world, restricted to a very particular kind of thing, viz. the organism. Were it even prima facie possible to get final causes from non-final causes, we should expect to see it happening all the time around us, and yet it does not. That is, in our experience it is only life that gives rise to life, rather than our experience being one of ubiquitous spontaneous abiogenesis.

Note that in objecting to the idea of the emergence of life from non-life I am only referring to emergentism as a theory about a postulated dynamic, diachronic process, not about the synchronic relations between so-called 'lower-level' and 'higher-level' properties. Whether, say, the liquidity of water can be called a higher-level property that is in some sense 'emergent' from hydrogen and oxygen in combination is not my concern. 'Emergentism' is a term of art rather than a theory, used to defend all kinds of positions. I am focusing only on whether there are metaphysical barriers to the possible diachronic emergence of life from non-life. If there are, life is an irreducible phenomenon, by which I mean a phenomenon that lacks, even in principle, an explanation in purely transient terms, in particular in physico-chemical terms.

Furthermore, my point is metaphysical, not epistemological. It is not just that life is theoretically or epistemologically irreducible. Nor is it even that it is ontologically irreducible in the sense that it could have come from non-life but without being identical to anything inorganic, whether by type or token. Rather, it is simply that it could not have been caused by anything inorganic. As to the distinction between metaphysics and epistemology in this context, note that for an emergentist such as Samuel Alexander (1966) life is emergent from purely physico-chemical conditions only in the sense that anything less than a super-intelligent mind armed with knowledge of all those conditions and of the operative physico-chemical laws would be unable to predict the appearance of life from non-living matter. Nevertheless, for him the specific organic qualities of an organism, hence its immanent processes, 'may be exhibited without remainder in physico-chemical terms' (Alexander 1966: 62). But for the epistemological emergentists there is nothing in the *essences* of the living and the non-living which precludes such a prediction.

By contrast, John Stuart Mill's emergentism seems to be metaphysical, since he asserts that 'no mere summing up of the separate actions of [inorganic] elements [in a living thing] will ever amount to the action of the living body itself' (Mill 1886: III.6.i, p. 243). In this Mill is in my view correct, and for the right reason, namely the fundamental distinctness of kind (or lack of 'analogy', in Mill's terminology) between the living and the non-living. There might be good quantum-mechanical reasons why we cannot predict that the interaction of two kinds of atom will produce, say, a liquid. But this does not mean that liquidity is essentially the kind of thing that does not have a complete physico-chemical explanation (though no such complete explanation is yet available). Hence lack of predictability does not entail metaphysical irreducibility. (Predictability, on the other hand, entails reducibility.)

It will be objected that we now know enough about so-called 'self-organizing' systems to be able confidently to assert that life is just another kind of self-organizing system, hence a phenomenon explained wholly by the complexity of the system. There is the work of Stuart Kauffman on autocatalytic systems, whereby a molecule in a primordial soup catalyses chemical reactions that lead to the creation of more of the same kinds of molecule (Kauffman 1993). And there is the work of Ilya Prigogine on self-organizing, non-equilibrium chemical mixtures, or 'dissipative systems' that constantly exchange energy with their environment. These can lead to the appearance of organized structures such as convection cells (Prigogine and Stengers 1984). Interesting and important though this sort of work is, it runs up against a metaphysical roadblock when used to explain the origin of life. Paul Davies points out the specific problem that living things are not self-organizing entities but entities whose existence and function are at least partly determined by a genetic code (see Davies 1999: 120–3 for this and a general critique of the self-organization theory). The question is then thrown back to the familiar one of how any genetic code could have come into existence, and the theory of self-organization exits the stage.

Metaphysically, moreover, the very concept of self-organization is suspect. More precisely, the idea that an entity can organize itself into *existence*, which is what is at issue, is deeply suspicious. For if an entity – any entity – is to organize itself into existence, it has to exist before it can do *any* organizing, let alone organizing its own existence; so it has to exist before it exists, which is absurd. This means that self-organizing systems are really systems that are organized into existence *from without*, as a convection cell is organized into existence by its environment, albeit with apparent spontaneity and unpredictability. Once in existence, there is no conceptual problem with the entity's continually organizing itself through self-regulating, homeostatic, or other mechanisms that involve, say, taking in energy from the environment, utilizing it and expelling waste products. But that it could organize its entry into the world in the *first* place looks like as good a case of metaphysical impossibility as one is likely to get.

A final point: throughout this chapter I have for the most part eschewed the terminology of 'final causes', 'teleology', and the like, preferring to stick to the language of immanent causation. This is partly to avoid confusion and partly because of the inherent preferability of the latter. Immanent causation is a preferable way of talking about the phenomenon of life because teleology and final causation do not of themselves import the notion of *self*-directedness. There can be a goal (or purpose, or final cause) of a thing without that goal being one whose satisfaction does anything *for* the object that acts to satisfy it. Artefacts have purposes that do nothing for them, only for the persons who impose the purposes upon them. Parts of organisms (hearts or other organs, say) have purposes whose satisfaction does something for the wholes of which they are parts rather than for themselves.[25] Hence, whilst teleology or final causation is characteristic of the living world, it is not just any teleology or final causation, but the self-directed kind. As a corollary of this point, conceptual space is thus left open for other kinds of teleology, of a more attenuated nature, that are not self-directed and arguably true even of non-living things. (See further Oderberg forthcoming a).

Further, talk of teleology and final causes can lead to confusion. The former term might be thought to connote some kind of non-natural phenomenon, as in the case of vitalism and immaterial substances. But even though teleology is not explicable in physico-chemical terms, it is still a natural phenomenon that is the proper object of study of disciplines such as biology, physiology, zoology, botany, ethology, their branches and allied disciplines. It is only the partisan of physicalism, or perhaps physico-chemicalism, who equates the idea that life is irreducible to the idea that it is not a fit subject for natural science.

Talk of final causes, on the other hand – the sort of thing that produces in most contemporary biologists and philosophers of biology a David Lewis-style 'incredulous stare' – might be confused with talk of a Final Cause, a supernatural or transcendent cause of the existence of life, since a spooky thing such as a final cause would need an even spookier Final Cause to explain its origin. But the question of how life came about is different from the question of how it did *not* come about. If it is true that life is a basic, irreducible phenomenon with no purely physico-chemical explanation or origin, it does not follow that life was created by some all-powerful (or very, very powerful) being. Maybe it was. Maybe, on the other hand, it has existed forever in an eternal universe. Perhaps it sprang into existence out of nothing once the universe already existed.[26] Or maybe it came into existence with the universe itself, thus necessitating a rethinking of the 'Big Bang' and its products. As far as the present chapter is concerned, there is nothing to choose between these hypotheses. There may be *other* grounds for preferring one over the other, but they will be external to the discussion in which I have been engaged.

9 Species, biological and metaphysical

9.1 Is biological essentialism dead?

Whatever the claims of essentialism in other areas, in biology it has been pronounced dead and buried. The essentialist was already deemed sick when Darwin claimed to be struck by 'how entirely vague and arbitrary is the distinction between species and varieties' (Darwin 1859: 48). Over the next century, the ever-growing doubts about whether anyone can even say what a biological species *is*, let alone identify any, led to the essentialist's ending up on life support at the hands of generations of biologists and philosophers of biology. By the time the theory known as cladism had become virtual orthodoxy, as it did over the decades since the seminal work of Willi Hennig (1966), biological essentialism was deemed beyond recovery. Its death is proclaimed by theorists such as Mayr (2002: 80–90; see also Mayr 1982: 38–9; 1997: 228), Sober (1993: 145–9), Ereshefksy (1992: 187–90), Dupré (1993, 2002), Hull (1965), and the number could be multiplied. This 'anti-essentialist consensus in philosophy of biology' (Okasha 2002: 198) is, as I have already noted, shared by a scientific essentialist such as Ellis, who shuns biological essences in favour of physical and chemical essences because of the 'messiness' of biological kinds.

Yet it is a myth to think that essences will be easier to find in physics or chemistry than in biology. To be sure, there are such essences, as I have argued, but they cannot be known about without, at least in part, invoking the characteristics, necessary and accidental, of macroscopic objects – that is, of substances and other objects that do not belong to the categories of subatomic, atomic, molecular, or elementary particles. In the case of macroscopic substances themselves, such as lumps of metal or samples of liquids or gases, to know their essences requires knowing their characteristic behaviour not just at the atomic/molecular (let us call this the 'micro') level but at the macro level as well. Investigation at the micro level tells us about internal constitution, which is part of essence, but it also tells us about the way the object behaves at the macro level. Hence it is mistaken to say that since we need to investigate all macroscopic objects at the micro level in order to know about them, all there is to essence is at the micro level; for it is precisely in order to know about objects at the macro level that much of our micro-level investigation is conducted.

Further, in the case of micro-level objects themselves, we cannot know about their essences without knowing something about the macro-level actions and reactions they enter into and about the behaviour they cause at the macro level. We cannot know that hydrogen and deuterium are specifically different – whether or not they are counted as species of a common ('hydrogenic') genus – without knowing what sorts of reactions they enter into and features they cause at the macro level, for example that when hydrogen combines (in a 2:1 ratio) with oxygen it forms water but when deuterium does it forms heavy water, and that water and heavy water are specifically different (again, whether or not we count them as species of a common genus). This is not *just* an epistemological or methodological point. The essences of the micro-level objects are partly *characterized* by the fact that the objects' structural, bonding, and similar properties give rise to distinctive macro-level properties. Otherwise, using atomic number, say, to classify the elements would be as useful as classifying them by spatio-temporal location. When we look for essences we look not just for distinctions, but for distinctions that make a difference. And differences at the macro level tell us something important about the distinctions we make at the micro level, e.g. in terms of atomic number.

So it is misguided for the essentialist to think she can escape the macro level, where essences are supposedly 'messy', and take refuge in the clean and tidy essences at the micro level. The macro level will always enter into her judgments of essence at the micro level to *some* extent, usually a large one. But if this point be granted, then the real essentialist will insist that it is also wrongheaded to think the essences of inorganic objects will be more susceptible of identification than the organic entities. Again, the inorganic objects *have* essences, and we can *know* them. It is just that the organic objects – the organisms and their parts – offer us a qualitatively different kind of character, lacked by the non-living, that should in principle make essence even easier to identify – namely the properties associated with immanent causation, as outlined in Chapter 8.

In addition to the unifying role of substantial form as found in inorganic bodies, which in general needs to be understood in terms of shape, structure (both gross and microscopic), composition, attractive and repulsive forces, equilibrium, inertia, and so on, there is in living bodies immanent activity, whereby the organism, as explained in Chapter 8, does things to itself and for itself, such as nutrition, growth, reproduction, appetition, self-maintenance, self-repair, locomotion, and related kinds of behaviour. These are all patent manifestations of unity within the organism: it seeks to maintain its own unity via a suite of capacities dedicated to the preservation, promotion and protection of proper function. Hence if the identification of even *these* sorts of unity-directed properties cannot enable us to get to the essence of a thing, we can have little hope of finding essence in those objects that lack such remarkable and, from the material perspective, peculiar powers. In short, if there are no essences in biology, we are unlikely to find them anywhere else.

Fortunately, however, the interment of biological essentialism is a case of live burial rather than the disposal of a corpse. I will now look at some of the objections that have been raised against biological essentialism, moving on in section 9.2 to anti-essentialism motivated by cladism, then to the particular objection from *vagueness*. I will restrict myself to the most common objections, and in the section on vagueness I will not offer a solution to the general problem, only to that of vagueness as it is alleged to arise in biology. My aim is to show that the essentialist can answer all of the major objections raised by opponents, hence that essentialism in biology is undefeated. In section 9.4 I will say something positive about how species in biology should be conceived along essentialist lines, and why this is the position that biologists and philosophers of biology must adopt if they want to extricate themselves from the confusion in which the so-called 'problem of species' is now mired.

To begin with, there is the usually unspoken objection to biological essentialism that it involves illicit metaphysical (aka 'armchair') biology interfering with the deliverances of the experts who work with the empirical data. As I explained in Chapters 2 and 5, there is no hard and fast division between metaphysical classification and that involved in the (natural and other special) sciences – and this despite the fact that metaphysics and the sciences have different formal objects. Metaphysics is concerned with the structure of reality at the general level, as holding across the sciences and other disciplines. Each science has its own proper object. But metaphysics, having more than a mere 'bookkeeping' role, is explicitly or implicitly present in all the sciences. Metaphysicians and scientists are both looking for the divisions within reality. Hence no biological scheme can conflict with any metaphysical truth, and vice versa, since reality is one. In Porphyrian terms, the lower down the tree one progresses, the more specialized the categories become, having more and more content peculiar to science, with the ever-present metaphysical content fading into the background. But each genuine scientific classification or definition marks a division within reality, and is for this reason alone of interest to the metaphysician. That tigers are essentially different from elephants is a biological fact that also marks an interesting metaphysical distinction, since no part of reality is outside the interest of the metaphysician.

But the metaphysician must tread carefully within the field of a special science, just as the scientist must tread carefully when his metaphysical hat is on (an injunction all too often honoured in the breach by scientists). The Chinese walls that the empiricist tradition has erected between scientists and metaphysicians often makes the crossing of fields all but impossible. Yet it can and must be done, and Chapter 8 gave some indication of how it might be. Biologically informed metaphysics is not armchair biology, and the biologist must be prepared to be brought to book (as well as the converse) when his scientific assertions contradict, even implicitly, the deliverances of metaphysics.

Of the more specific objections to biological essentialism, one concerns what Mayr calls the 'typological' conception of species (Mayr 1959; 1982: 45–7; 2002: 80–1). Part of what Mayr means by this is the idea that species have essences that are constant through time, sharply demarcated, and have 'severe limitations' (Mayr 1982: 260) in possible variation. These points raise issues I will tackle separately, but another aspect of the typological conception seems to be an association with Platonism – hence Mayr's negative references to Pythagoras and Plato (e.g. Mayr 2002: 80) and to 'fixed, unchangeable "ideas"' underlying observed variability (Mayr 1959: 28–9). In fact, most of his points are relevant to real essentialism as well, but he does not distinguish between kinds of essentialism and is at pains (wrongly) to distance Aristotle from essentialist thinking (Mayr 1982: 149–54). But as Denis Walsh reminds the anti-essentialist (Walsh 2006: 431–2), essentialism does not entail Platonism and should do without it. Biology is no exception to the general arguments I gave in Chapter 4 in favour of immanentism. Substances do not copy archetypes in a Platonic 'heaven', and it would be impossible to explain their natures if they did so. Hence, to the extent that the rejection of typological essentialism is a rejection of Platonism, it is irrelevant to the plausibility of real essentialism in biology.

Next, essentialism is held to require the constancy of species across time: '[t]he essence or definition of a class (type) is completely constant; it is the same today as it was on the day of the Creation' (Mayr 2002: 80). I do not propose to enter into exegetical discussion of how to interpret the early chapters of Genesis, but let us suppose, for the sake of argument at least, that there was a moment or period of Creation. This does not imply that every species that existed then exists now: the essentialist believes in extinct species, as does everyone else. Moreover, and whether or not there was a Creation, if essentialism is true then even the extinct species had their essences, and so in that sense every essence or definition is constant: every species is what it is or was what it was. No anti-essentialist argument can be extracted from that. More importantly, as a general principle essentialism is wholly compatible with substantial change, a phenomenon continuously exhibited in the inorganic world. It is an elementary mistake to think that fixed essences exclude substantial change. Hydrogen has an essence but it can still fuse into helium. That an essence is fixed means that nothing that possesses it can cease to possess it without ceasing to exist, and that when something comes to possess it that thing begins to exist. It does not mean that nothing possessing an essence can ever be created, destroyed, or substantially changed into something with a different essence. There is no reason *in principle* why the same could not apply to biological species. This important point has been noted by Sober (1993: 146–7), Okasha (2002: 195–6) and Walsh (2006: 431).

Stamos, however, accuses Sober of being 'deeply mistaken' about this issue (Stamos 2003: 122), citing Rosenberg (1985: 189) to the effect that the essentialist must view evolution as a transmutation not of *individuals* belonging to species, but of the species *themselves* considered as abstract entities; and this latter is incompatible with essentialism about species. It is Stamos and Rosenberg who are mistaken. They are right in implying a dis-analogy between Sober's example of the transmutation of elements and biological evolution, but not all disanalogies are false analogies. In biological evolution no *individual* organism transmutes into anything. What is sup-posed to happen is that mutation in parental gametes gives rise to offspring which, through natural selection, come to form a population belonging to a new species.

Sober's basic point is, however, unaffected. Chemical transformation is an example of one kind of individual's giving rise, through substantial change, to a new kind of individual. Biological evolution also involves an individual of one kind giving rise to an individual of a distinct kind – not through substantial change but through reproductive activity. The processes are dif-ferent, but the outcome is the same. And neither refutes the thesis that each kind is a distinct essence. Moreover, neither essentialism *nor* evolution holds that transmutation between species involves one *kind* changing into another kind where the kind is understood as an abstract entity. Rosenberg is correct that 'the *kind* radium cannot change into the *kind* radon', if such change is supposed to mean something over and above the decay of individual sam-ples of radium into individual samples of radon. But no evolutionist holds that the *kind* reptile changed into the *kind* mammal, if that is supposed to mean more than that individual reptiles gave rise, through reproductive mutation and natural selection (perhaps with intermediate stages), to indi-vidual mammals – with the result that from one kind another arose through biological processes.

The essentialist does not need to be a Platonist to hold that species do not turn into distinct species in any sense beyond the causation of indivi-duals of one species to come into existence by individuals belonging to a different species. Any other sense attached to the notion of species change is barely intelligible, as much as when applied to the idea that triangularity could somehow *change* into sphericity. Neither the essentialist nor the evo-lutionist has such an idea of species change as part of his picture of what happens in biology or anywhere else.

I said that there is no reason *in principle* why substantial change could not apply to biological species. The 'in principle' qualification is important, however. First, I argued in Chapter 8 that there are metaphysical reasons for doubting whether life itself could have emerged from non-living matter. Secondly, I will argue in Chapter 10 that there is a sharp discontinuity between human nature and other natures that casts grave doubt on the idea that human beings could have evolved from anything non-human, *at least* on any current conception of how evolution is supposed to operate. (For a very good defence of this view, though without explicitly endorsing the ontology of human nature that I do in Chapter 10, see O'Hear 1997.) Thirdly, even if essentialism does not exclude the possibility of substantial transformation from one species to another, whether by gradual evolution or sudden change, it is a different question whether this actually *has* happened anywhere on Earth. Of course, the vast majority of theorists are as certain as they can be that it has and that the process was evolutionary rather than revolutionary – though instantaneous speciation (saltationism), for example in the form of polyploidy in some plants, is not wholly out of the running. (For discussion, see Gould 2002: 396–466; Mayr 2002: 104, 200.)

Fourthly, even if essentialism metaphysically allows for evolution or any other kind of substantial transformation, it is a distinct question whether, for plausible physical or chemical reasons, or for reasons to do with what might be called 'bio-engineering' considerations, or for genetic reasons to do with the way mutations operate on an individual or species, or perhaps for some other empirical reason, it is *scientifically possible* for such transformation to occur, at least on our planet. Again, the vast majority of theorists dismiss any such considerations as spurious, but my point is simply that this is a different issue from the metaphysical one.[1] As with the third point, this is not a matter I intend to examine.

Fifthly – and this is a point I will have to lay to one side for reasons more of space than of irrelevance – there may indeed be other metaphysical constraints on what *sorts* of evolution could take place, assuming any has, apart from that related to the origin of life or of human nature. For instance, it is at least worth questioning whether anything sentient could have evolved from anything vegetative, though the reverse is more plausible given that it would involve the *loss* of a higher power, viz. awareness, rather than the *gain* of one from a species that did not have it. (In any case, modern systematics does not posit, as far as one can tell from the necessarily sketchy phylogenetic schemes on offer, any unambiguous evolution from the vegetative to the sentient, though the reverse, e.g. the descent of *Plantae* and *Fungi* from unicellular animals, is generally accepted. Certainly there is no suggestion that any higher animals, such as the vertebrates, evolved from paradigmatic plants!)

It is also worth considering whether any organism with a phenomenological awareness, such as mammals, could have descended from any species lacking phenomenology. The reason is again the general metaphysical one of how a species could bestow what it did not possess, no matter how much its genotype mutated. Evolutionists will reject the very idea that there could be metaphysical obstacles in the way of such a transformation. I cannot take the matter further here, but simply reiterate my main point – that whatever the details, whatever the empirical considerations, and whatever the metaphysical considerations impinging on this or that particular kind of transformation, Mayr is simply wrong to assert that the fixity of species as understood by essentialism excludes any kind of evolution or other substantial transmutation of species. The hedges and qualifications I have raised might carry no weight whatsoever with the biological orthodoxy, but hedges are not brick walls.

Another prominent anti-essentialist argument, emphasized by Mayr, is that Darwinism replaced 'typological thinking' with 'population thinking' (Mayr 1959; 1982: 45–7; 1997: 210–11; 2002: 83). The idea is that individual organisms, and hence their putative essences, play no explanatory role in evolutionary theory. The aim of that theory is to explain biological diversity, but to do this all one needs is an account of the genetic variation in populations, each member of which is unique and not a representative of some essential type. This variation can be encapsulated by general statistical laws that do not refer to the causal powers of individual organisms, so one does not need 'specific knowledge of the individuals themselves' in order to understand evolutionary mechanisms (Morrison 2000: 215). According to Darwin, as Sober explains it, 'the population is an entity, subject to its own forces, and obeying its own laws': the description of individuals is as theoretically irrelevant as describing the motion of an individual molecule in the kinetic theory of gases (Sober 1980: 370).

Without even getting into evolutionary details, the idea that laws or other principles governing population behaviour should float free of the behaviour of individual members of the population concerned is implausible.[2] A psephologist can study the voting behaviour of a population without needing to identify which individual voter cast what vote. But he still has to accumulate data that sum the individual votes. Nor does he need to know anything about the accidental characteristics of voters, for instance whether any of the voters was red haired or over six feet tall. But to make useful interpretations of voting patterns he needs to frame hypotheses about issues that may have influenced individual voters as they considered how to vote. There may be no such entity as the average voter, but, precisely because the notion is a construct or abstraction, useful information about the average voter can only be derived from information about individual votes.

Hence Mayr draws confused conclusions about population behaviour when relating it to individual members (Mayr 1982: 46). A 'mean value' is not necessarily indicative of a 'type', so treating the former as a construct does not entail treating the latter as a construct – but types, or, better, essences, *are* indeed abstractions, as I have already explained at length. They are abstractions from individuals, and their content derives from what is true of individuals; so the latter do not fall out of consideration; rather, they are the building blocks upon which the theoretical edifice of population thinking is based. Further, Mayr is probably right to assert that each individual is unique (genetically and phenotypically),[3] and if he also means accidental variation then knowledge of it is as irrelevant (in most cases) as knowledge of whether the voters have red hair. But this does nothing to undermine the necessity of knowledge about individuals *qua* members of species, i.e. *qua* possessors of a certain essence, any more than it obviates the need to know about how voters behave *qua* voters. The biologist might be able to form hypotheses about populations without identifying which member behaves in which manner, but he still needs to know how individuals behave in order to frame any meaningful hypothesis about what a population is like.

For a population just is a collection of individuals, even though there are facts about populations, summed, averaged, or otherwise derived from facts about individuals, that are not identical to any facts about individuals. Hence it is no surprise that Sober's analogy with the kinetic theory of gases is misleading. The gas laws can be formulated without knowing about, or describing the behaviour of, any individual molecule, but they are quite clearly derived from knowledge about how individual molecules behave: for example, the law expressing the total force of a gas on the wall of its container is derived from a summation over the motions of the individual gas molecules.

As far as biological theory in particular is concerned, Walsh has shown clearly that genetic variation among populations depends on the behaviour of individual organisms, and that knowledge of the former requires knowledge of the latter (Walsh 2006: 435). Genes are not 'disembodied members of populations' but constituents of organisms, and the fate of the genes is tied to the fate of the organisms whose genes they are. Moreover, the process of adaptive evolution is precisely the process whereby populations come to comprise well-adapted organisms. Knowledge of whether a population has evolved requires knowledge of whether adaptive traits have arisen within individual organisms. For evolution to occur, harmful mutations must be sufficiently rare or ineffectual within individuals, and fitness must be fairly constant across genetically similar individuals. Population thinking is simply not possible without individualistic thinking.

Nevertheless, the anti-essentialist goes on to argue, even if individualistic thinking is necessary, this does not mean thinking of the individuals as having essences or belonging to 'types', to use Mayr's term. In any case, there is no such essence because 'biologists do not think that species are defined in terms of phenotypic or genetic similarities' (Sober 1993: 148). In Okasha's words:

> Virtually all philosophers of biology agree that ... species are not individuated by essential characters. ... Empirically, it simply is not true that the groups of organisms that working biologists treat as con-specific share a set of common morphological, physiological or genetic traits which set them off from other species.
>
> (Okasha 2002: 196)

And at the conceptual level, even if there were a set of shared characters, this would not make them essential, '[f]or if a member of the species produced an offspring which lacked one of the characteristics, say because of a mutation, it would very likely be classed as con-specific with its parents'

(Okasha 2002: 197). Walsh puts the point in terms of the plurality of criteria for species membership used by biologists: there is 'no unitary criterion of species membership' because '[a]ny account of biological kinds that is committed to a single criterion of species membership is inconsistent with current scientific practice' (Walsh 2006: 432).

In fact there is a cluster of points in the above, so some disentangling is required. Walsh is right that there are plural species concepts in the work of biologists (and also philosophers of biology). There is the biological species concept, where interbreeding is critical; the ecological species concept, where the crucial role is played by the ecological niche; the phenetic species concept, emphasizing overall similarity; the mate recognition species concept; the cladistic species concept, where genealogy and common descent are decisive; and many other species concepts. There are at least twenty-two according to Mayden (1997), without including the pluralistic species concept itself, i.e. the view that, of the many criteria, all are plausible and defensible (Dupré 1993), and the opposite, eliminativist view, that there *are* no species (Ereshefsky 1999; Mishler 1999). But the mere presence of multiple species concepts, even if all can be given a plausible defence, no more shows that there is no uniquely correct account of species than the presence of multiple plausible concepts of combustion in the seventeenth century was a reason for doubting the existence of a correct account. This is especially the case with a concept such as that of species, which is permeated by metaphysics in a way that a highly empirical concept, such as combustion, is not. If biologists differ in their metaphysical presuppositions they are unlikely to agree about what a species is. In any case, they might all agree one day: a sociological fact about scientific practice does not undermine a metaphysical thesis (or a scientific one, for that matter).

The largely irrelevant appeal to scientific practice[4] needs to be separated from the theoretical resolution of species problems. So, for instance, Sober, elaborating his claim that 'biologists do not think' species are defined in terms of intrinsic similarities (see the quotation on p. 208), goes on to say that '[t]igers are striped and carnivorous, but a mutant tiger that lacked these traits would still be a tiger' (Sober 1993: 148). And Okasha explains that shared characteristics do not make for essential characteristics because if a member of a species produced offspring missing one of the characteristics (due, say, to a mutation) it would still very likely be classified as conspecific with its parents (see the quotation on p. 208). Yet presumably Okasha's rider of 'very likely' is supposed to cover the possibility that Sober states explicitly when he continues: '[b]arring the occurrence of a speciation event, the descendants of tigers are tigers, regardless of the degree to which they resemble their parents' (Sober 1993: 148). Sober then goes on to muddy the waters surrounding this crucial point by linking it to the cladistic conception of species, whereby species are defined as purely historical entities, a practice endorsed by many, perhaps most, biologists. Again, the practice of systematists is irrelevant, and cladism I reserve for section 9.2.

The point about mutation is, however, a separate one, and Sober gives the game away by referring, correctly, to speciation events. For if a mutation, or set of mutations, is sufficiently great and significant – in what way can be left to one side for now – then biologists, even the professedly anti-essentialist ones, will *rightly* assert the existence of a new species. That's just how evolution is supposed to *work*. If the mutation is big enough, a new species comes into existence – which means that the descendant organism will be sufficiently different from its parents to warrant classification as belonging to a distinct kind with its own nature. But some mutations are not big enough to justify this judgment. A stripeless tiger would be such a case. In fact, the 'white tigers' that have occasionally been reported in nature or bred in captivity all have pale or vestigial stripes, and most, including genuine albino tigers, have poor survival rates, are sterile, or otherwise lack good health. We can therefore use our understanding of the nature of organisms in general, and of tigers in particular, to judge that being striped is almost certainly a property of tigers, such that lack of well-defined stripes covering most of the body, and a fortiori of any stripes at all, means the animal is damaged or defective and so suffers an imperfection in its nature. (This does *not* mean, as explained in Chapter 7, that it would fail to be a perfect instance of its kind, since perfect instantiation is a Platonist myth. Lacking a perfection, in the technical sense, means lacking a property, or the full expression of a property, whose possession enables normal functioning or flourishing as a typical member of a kind. More generally, any property is a perfection inasmuch as, being an expression of a thing's essence, it contributes to the demarcation of that thing as a being with a nature, i.e. with a characteristic mode of behaviour.)

In the inorganic world, notions such as flourishing and normal function have only an analogous sense, and so lack of properties usually guarantees lack of essence. A compound that was wholly non-malleable or non-conductive would not be gold. But there is also the possibility of phenomena such as mutilation and adulteration that enable us, analogously to the case of organisms, to speak of an inorganic substance as lacking a property while still having the essence that normally expresses the property – say when impurities in a metal reduce or eliminate its lustre. In the case of living beings, however, the notion of normal function has universal application, and we can use it to clarify how a member of a species can have an essence and yet still fail to express all of the properties that it would normally possess, i.e. if it were functioning properly or flourishing as a typical member of its kind. Sober is, then, right to say that the descendants of tigers are tigers – *barring* the sort of change that would justify a systematist in refusing to place the descendant in the same class as its parents or more remote ancestors. A stripeless tiger would not still be a tiger because it was *descended* from tigers (whatever cladists might say, about which more later), but because there is sufficient understanding of what tigers are to grasp that lacking stripes is, in fact, a defective condition in tigers. And in the abstract, were a genuinely stripeless and healthy tiger biologically possible, this would confirm that having stripes was not after all a property of tigers but an accident – such as race in humans. None of this is inconsistent with essentialism – on the contrary, it *supports* it.

Nevertheless, the anti-essentialist will insist, what *are* the essential characteristics of species? If 'Darwinism leads us to expect variation with respect to all organismic traits', with no criterion for distinguishing the essential from the accidental (Okasha 2002: 197), how can we expect there to be essential characteristics? Yet one only needs to prove the falsity of this assertion in a single case to make the essentialist point; and the essentialist does not have far to look. One does not need to be a professional zoologist to note essential differences between elephants and tigers, birds and fish, bacteria and archaea, toads and bacteria, zebras and monkeys, Bonobos and orangutans, horses and panthers, palm trees and tomato plants, spiders and worms, funnel web spiders and redback spiders, hyenas and gazelles, earthworms and pigs, porcupines and platypuses, and so on ad nauseam, to be convinced that there are, *of course*, essential differences between species. And by 'species' we include not just the infima species, which is what systematists usually mean by species, but all of the species/genera that metaphysics and systematics recognize in the tree of life, however that tree be constructed, e.g. whether as a metaphysical Porphyrian Tree, a Linnaean hierarchy, or a phylogenetic genealogy. For the purpose of making the essentialist point the details are irrelevant, as are the hard cases, the potential vagueness (on which see section 9.3) and the differing species concepts in current use.

Since there *are* essential differences, the question is not *whether* essentialism is true but how, as it were, to carve the biological cake, i.e. how metaphysically informed biology, and biologically informed metaphysics, can most accurately reflect the divisions in nature via taxonomy. The anti-essentialist might reply that the evident demarcation of one species from another does not of itself show that there is something all members of a species must share. Yet this cannot be right, because if elephants, say, are demarcated from zebras, then every individual elephant must be demarcated from every individual zebra, and this must be by virtue of *at least one* property that all elephants must have that zebras lack, and vice versa. In such an obvious case, one does not have far to look. But that it gets more difficult in other cases, especially as one examines putative infima species, is again irrelevant to the principle – it is relevant only to the practice.

But doesn't Darwinism require, for its explanation of organic diversity by natural selection, ubiquitous intra-specific variation (Okasha 2002: 197)? That this is too strong a claim is obvious when we note that it certainly does not postulate variation in, say, a mammalian species with respect to being warm blooded and breathing air with lungs. Nor does it postulate variation in *Panthera tigris* (tigers) with respect to being land-dwelling, in *Rattus rattus* (the Black Rat) with respect to not navigating by echo-location, or in dolphins with respect to having a fusiform (tapered) body. Even the intra-specific variation recognized by Darwinism has its limits.

Yet, it will be rejoindered, the limits do not provide necessary and suffi-cient conditions. The problem harks back to the wrongness of thinking of essences in terms of property clusters. Subject to issues, already mentioned, concerning mutation, defects, abnormality, and the perennial possibility of reclassifying a wide range of putative properties as mere accidents (and vice versa), the systematist has an abundance of necessary characteristic to work with, some of which I have just noted. That they are all rarely if ever listable is simply testament to the fact that essence is not given by properties but by *form*, more precisely substantial form. Properties are indicators of essence, allowing fallible and provisional judgment as to the essence of an organism. Subject to qualification, they can be infallible guides to essence: for instance, if a given organism is not an aquatic creature with a fusiform body, there is no way it can be a dolphin. But given the complexity of even the simplest creature, the list of necessary characteristics will be incredibly large, possibly infinite, i.e. either beyond the technical capacity of systematists to list exhaustively, or perhaps in principle unlistable.

The same goes for sufficient properties: it may be that, for even the apparently simplest organism, listing all of the sufficient characteristics essential to it will be either technically or metaphysically impossible. Yet this is just what we should expect from the very plasticity of animate existence, something Darwinists emphasize again and again. Still, the essentialist sees no cause for concern, since all the systematist should be looking for is not an exhaustive list of necessary and sufficient characteristics, but enough characteristics to enable at least a provisional judgment as to the substantial form of an organism, followed by an accumulation of characteristics to increase the well-foundedness of the judgment.

Moreover, if Walsh (2006) is correct – and he makes a persuasive case – the search for essences is not just a metaphysical presupposition and requirement of systematics in general, but a positive demand of evolu-tionary theory in particular, since only the natures of organisms can explain their adaptive behaviour. For an organism exhibits stability, which is the 'capacity to develop and maintain a well-functioning individual that is typical of its kind'. And this stability is achieved through plasticity, which involves 'highly supple homeostatic responses that compensate for per-turbations and thereby maintain a well-functioning state' (Walsh 2006: 436). The plasticity is manifested in the robustness of regulatory gene networks in finding variable ways of compensating for mutations that challenge the organism's characteristic phenotypic output. It is also manifested in the modularity of an organism's developmental systems, whereby each module, though integrated with the others, is also 'buffered' against perturbations from, and breakdown of, other modules, and so is able to continue to contribute to an organism's normal functioning in the face of such chal-lenges.

Thus the plasticity of organisms in responding to systemic challenge brings with it a mutability that allows for the generation of adaptive novelties: '[t]he conditions that secure the mutability of organisms are the very ones that secure their stability' (Walsh 2006: 437). What makes for adaptive novelty is precisely this phenotypic plasticity, which underwrites novel adaptations, the suppression of harmful mutations, and the constancy of traits across a population. Many evolutionists will suspect Walsh's argument since he sometimes speaks as though every adaptive novelty, including the ones that involve speciation, is a goal-directed response of organisms to a challenge to their proper function. It is, however, not clear that he has to speak like this. When he says that '[t]he accommodation[5] of one part of an organism's phenotype often requires, and elicits, accommodation by others[6] [and in] the process it occasionally produces novel, adaptively advantageous phenotypes' (Walsh 2006: 439), the evolutionist will take Walsh to mean not that every adaptation is a response by the organism to challenges to its stability, but that such responses often result in random genetic mutation that constitutes a speciation event. Moreover, evolution aside, the essentialist will also resile from interpreting every adaptation as Walsh seems to, since it would imply that one kind of response an organism typically makes to systemic challenge is to cease to exist by mutating into a new species with a distinct nature! This would not be a genuine response to perturbation, but an escape from it. Nevertheless, this criticism does not undermine Walsh's main point, which is that without an understanding of an organism's nature it is impossible to grasp the way in which its stability and plasticity are a precondition of adaptive evolution.

On two other scores, however, Walsh's case is mistaken. First, he confusedly attributes two natures to the organism, a 'formal nature', which he defines as 'a goal-directed disposition to produce a viable organism of its kind', and a 'material nature', which consists of 'the causal properties of the developmental system' (Walsh 2006: 428, 441). This is a misunderstanding of hylemorphism, which only ever attributes a *single* nature to an organism or any other substance, that nature being a compound of prime matter and substantial form. The prime matter contributes the pure potentiality of specification as a material substance, and the substantial form contributes that specification. Were an organism to have two natures, this bifurcation would undermine the very unity that Walsh's account explains at length: in what way would there be an 'interactive unity' (Walsh 2006: 441) between the natures, indeed why should there be any at all? Why should they not be constantly at work *against* each other? To reply, 'Because they constitute a unity' would not be to answer the question but to evade it.

Secondly, his dissociation of what he calls 'evolutionary essentialism' from 'taxonomic essentialism' is a mistake. If organisms have natures, as he forcefully argues, then those natures must be repeatable, i.e. they must be shareable between individuals. Hence they must be forms. And if they are amenable to biological investigation they must be identifiable, whether with certainty or only fallibly. To think that organisms have natures but are not *distinguishable* by their natures would be at worst a metaphysical confusion, at best an invitation to 'something we know not what' that is of no use either to metaphysics or to science. What the best taxonomic system *is* is another matter. The Porphyrian Tree, I have argued, is the best metaphysical way of attaining to species essences, and the Linnaean system is just one significant modification of this in biology. Such a system held sway for centuries, well into the twentieth. Variations upon it are still in use. There may be others, and it would not be wise for philosophers to pronounce upon which modification, if any, of the Porphyrian method is most suitable to the demands of biology. But that *something* is needed for systematics to make order out of the multitude of species is a certainty.

9.2 Against the cladistic species concept

Despite the multitude of species concepts, the one that has become virtual orthodoxy among systematists derives from the work of Willi Hennig, and is called the cladistic species concept. Cladism[7] seeks to base all classification explicitly on the phylogenesis of organisms, that is, on their evolutionary relationships as forming a tree whose branches can all be traced back to the common ancestor of every living thing. Taking its cue from Darwin's position that all classification is genealogical, it eschews what it considers to be the subjective, arbitrary, or empirically false species concepts that used to hold sway. Hence cladists (among others) criticize Mayr's biological species concept, based on reproductively isolated populations, for its failing to account for such things as asexually reproducing organisms and natural hybrid fertility, and for confusing cause (speciation) with effect (reproductive isolation) (see, e.g., Ridley 1993: 399–401; Cracraft 1997; Mallet 1995; Mayden 1997: 390–1).[8] They criticize the phenetic species concept, involving classification via the weighted aggregation of similar characteristics (Sneath and Sokal 1973), for being subjective and arbitrary, and for having nothing to do with evolution (Ridley 1993: 386–7; Tudge 2000: 46). Other concepts are also condemned on various grounds. (See also Sober 1993: ch. 6 for a defence of cladism and criticism of competing concepts.[9])

The cladistic species concept was introduced because phylogeneticists consider it to possess important features lacked by the others. It explicitly ties classification to evolution, so developing Darwin's insight. Evolution gives rise to the similarities that really matter as between organisms – the *homologous* characters derived from a common ancestor (such as the five-fingered limb in land vertebrates), not the *homoplastic* characters that appear independently through adaptation to a common way of life (such as body shape in whales and fish). It is wholly objective, since a lineage either exists or it does not: there is only one way in which life has branched out over time. Species are recognized by branching events in a line of descent, which should provide relatively precise (given the time scales involved) spatiotemporal markers for species' coming to and going out of existence. Further, there is no question that advances in phylogenetics, including rapid developments in molecular dating and analysis, have given cladism an impetus that has seen it come almost to dominate current thinking about species.

A highly simplified *cladogram*, or tree structure showing the evolutionary relationships among organisms, is shown in Figure 9.1. The *Reptilia* are not just what biologists and layfolk recognize as reptiles, since the former class includes the birds (*Aves*) and the mammals (*Mammalia*), all of which, along with what we call reptiles, are said to have descended from a primitive amphibian possessing some of what we recognize as reptilian characters. Common sense – which is not, as I will argue, the same as cladistic sense – places birds and mammals in categories separate from each other and from lizards and snakes (belonging to the order *Squamata*) as well as from crocodiles (species *Crocodylidae*) and tortoises and turtles (order *Testudines*). So if we want to equate *Reptilia* with reptiles pure and simple, we need to hive off the birds and mammals and we will be left with a part of the tree that includes the common ancestor of lizards, snakes, tortoises, crocodiles and so on, minus that ancestor's mammalian and avian descendants. Such a grouping, says the cladist, is *paraphyletic* and hence to be shunned at all costs, since it excludes some of the descendants of a common ancestor.[10] The only kosher classifications, for the cladist, are *monophyletic*, and include an ancestor and *all* of its descendants. Hence if we want to speak of reptiles, we should, says the cladist, include birds and mammals, the former having supposedly evolved from dinosaurs via intermediate species such as *Archaeopteryx*, and the latter from another reptilian class, the *Synapsida*, via the class *Therapsida*.

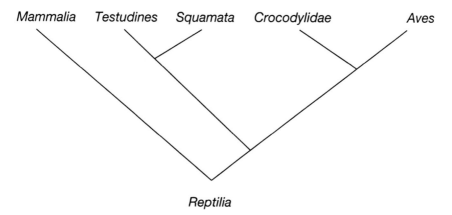

Figure 9.1 A simplified cladogram showing the evolutionary relationships among organisms

Source: Reconstructed from Tudge 2000: 412–15.

The details of cladism are intricate and ramifying, and there are various versions, but there is no space or need to enter into them. I want to consider only the most general, representative aspects of cladism as an approach to taxonomy. The important point is that on a phylogenetic account of species they are to be understood, in the words of Okasha, as 'particular chunks of the genealogical nexus' (Okasha 2002: 200). And this is held to be compatible with essentialism as long as essences are not required to be something intrinsic to their possessors. For belonging to a segment of the phylogenetic tree is a *relational* characteristic: it means being suitably related to a pair of branching or extinction events. Only if an organism descends from an ancestral population that split into distinct lineages (and its descendants became extinct or themselves split into further distinct lineages unless we are interested in the organisms that exist right now) is it to be classified as belonging to a species, namely that population existing diachronically between the two splits or between the split and the extinction. The essence of the species will be historical rather than intrinsic. (As well as Okasha 2002, see Sober 1993: 148.) Hence, it seems, so long as we abandon the notion that essences are intrinsic – whether hidden structure, substantial form, or something else – we can keep our essentialism and be good cladists.

There are, I contend, a number of problems with cladistic classification and its conception of species, as well as with the idea that one can salvage essentialism by making species essences relational rather than intrinsic. The first relates to the 'only if' of the previous paragraph. Mere presence on a chunk of the phylogenetic tree bounded by a pair of splitting events or a splitting and an extinction event (cladists represent these as *nodes* on the tree, so we can call such events *nodal*) is not *sufficient* for conspecificity, whatever its necessity. For suppose there is a splitting into distinct lineages followed by a single extinction event such as a meteorite crash. By cladistic standards no member of one lineage is conspecific with the other, yet they are all bounded by the same nodal events. (Of course, if there are two terminal extinction events or two terminal splitting events, one for each lineage, the members are still not all conspecific, since the lineages are stipulated as being distinct by the cladistic criterion.) What makes them distinct? The fact that the initial split is a *speciation* event. So there must be something else, besides mere genealogy, that secures conspecificity among all and only the members of the same lineage. This is recognized by cladists, but its importance does not seem to be grasped. Ridley concedes that 'the cladistic concept offers no account of what a lineage or a branch point is, whereas the biological and ecological concepts both offer plausible accounts' (Ridley 1993: 402). Hence the cladistic species concept must be supplemented by one or more additional species concepts. (See also Okasha 2002: 201.) In short, the cladistic concept of species cannot define what a species is since it relies on the very concept of speciation.

Ridley's answer (1993: 400–1), endorsed by Okasha (2002: 201), is that the supplemental concept/s, say biological (interbreeding) and ecological (niche occupancy), will delimit the species synchronically, whereas the cladistic concept will delimit it diachronically. Essentialism is not required to see the absurdity of this proposal. There cannot be more than one determinant of a species. In particular, there cannot be one criterion that determines species identity over time and another for species identity at a time. On the *assumption* that the synchronic criterion is biological, it will apply at every time slice of the species' existence, including the beginning – when an interbreeding population comes into existence yet cannot interbreed with its ancestors. But the beginning is precisely the speciation event that marks the first application of the diachronic criterion.

Similarly, the terminal nodal event, whether extinction or further splitting, marks the final application of the diachronic criterion. But that moment – when, say, descendants come into existence that cannot interbreed with their ancestors – will also be the moment at which the synchronic criterion ceases to apply. And at every time slice along the lineage, the biological criterion will delimit the species. But then it *must* also be a diachronic criterion, on the assumption that it is a synchronic one, since it secures the existence and identity of the species at every moment of its existence. The supposed diachronic cladistic criterion drops out of the picture. It remains merely as an historical representation of the way the real species criterion, the one doing the work, applies across space and time. Now, as Ridley (1993: 400–1) and many others argue, the biological species concept contains an arbitrariness that also affects competing criteria such as the ecological and phenetic, not to mention other problems such as those referred to earlier. In particular, the interbreeding relation is non-transitive, whereas species identity is transitive. So in fact it *could* not work as a criterion. My point is simply that if it did work it would have to do so both synchronically and diachronically.[11] None of this, however, vindicates the cladistic concept. If the other concepts fail to do the work required of them, that is a problem for them. There can only be one principle that determines what a species is both at a time and across time.

I have already mentioned the cladistic rejection of paraphyletic classes, i.e. classes that include some but not all of the descendants of a common ancestor. It is worth emphasizing the counterintuitiveness of such a position. It may accord with more classical, Linnaean-style classification to have the bird, crocodiles, mammals, and fish all classed as vertebrates, and indeed I used the vertebrate category in Chapter 5 when defining fish. Cladistics respects such a classification, since the phylogenetic tree shows all these species as descended from a common ancestor, perhaps the Conodonts of the Cambrian period (*c.*500 mya). But it also places crocodiles in the same taxon as birds, which seems absurd. They are both held to descend from *Archosauria* (*c.*250 mya), which to the non-cladistic eye was simply a kind of large lizard, but the cladist focuses on homologies shared by the birds and crocodiles, such as a four-chambered heart and shared teeth and ankle characters. The problem is *not* that the phylogenetic scheme for birds and crocodiles might be wrong: the point is, rather, that even if it is right it entails absurd *classifications* based on traits derived from the most recent common ancestor, rather than on an overall judgment about the actual form and behaviour of the animals. If the latter were allowed, then ancestral traits would sometimes be decisive, i.e. ones passed on from a more remote ancestor – such as being cold blooded and having scales, which is common to lizards and crocodiles. But these are ruled out by the cladist, not because they always yield less similarity – patently they do not – but because if allowed they would cut right across the cladistic scheme of classification. This looks more like a stipulation than a metaphysical or biological requirement.

It follows for the cladist that, no matter how similar two organisms are, if they are not part of the same clade or monophyletic group, i.e. the group that contains the organism's common ancestor and all of its descendants, they do not belong to the same taxon. In particular, if they do not belong to the same evolutionary lineage, then, no matter how similar they may be, they will not belong to the same species (which, for biologists, is usually the metaphysical infima species). This might at first seem innocuous. To use LaPorte's example (LaPorte 2004: 44), the nectar-feeding hummingbird (order *Trochiliformes*) and the nectar-feeding moth (hummingbird hawk moth, *Macroglossum stellatarum*) are similar in some striking ways yet their distinctively similar traits, such as proboscis in the moth and long beak in the bird, and their rapid wingbeat, are examples of convergent evolution, derived from wholly different insect and avian lineages.[12] The cladist would not dream of putting them in the same taxon (let alone species) unless he included whatever was the highly remote and ancient ancestor of insects and birds, and all of its descendants – including elephants, jellyfish, horses, sea urchins, and all the multitude of heterogeneous organisms descended from this primitive ancestor. In no other sense would the hummingbird and the hawk moth belong to the same taxon.

So far, so good. And LaPorte adds that 'the line of hummingbird hawk moths is not a line of birds and cannot become a line of birds', which to the ears of an essentialist also sounds highly plausible. But he then immediately adds, 'no matter how birdlike the line becomes in appearance or even genetic structure' (LaPorte 2004: 44). This thought echoes Sober, who says:

> [I]f we discovered that other planets possess life forms that arose inde-pendently of life on earth, those alien organisms would be placed into new species, *regardless of how closely they resembled terrestrial forms*. Mar-tian tigers would not be tigers, even if they were striped and carnivorous.
>
> (Sober 1993: 148; emphasis added)

Okasha agrees: '[t]wo molecule-for-molecule identical organisms could in principle be members of different species' (Okasha 2002: 201), though he adds that this is true not just on the cladistic concept but on all relational concepts such as the ecological and biological.[13]

This consequence of genealogical classification might refute the ecological species concept; it might also refute the biological;[14] but it reduces the cladistic concept to absurdity. Are we really to believe that if God, or some very powerful being, were to produce a molecule-for-molecule twin of Fido, similar in all respects down to ultrastructure, it would not be a dog? Or that if such a twin were found on Alpha Centauri it would not be a dog – whatever the ecological and other differences between Earth and Alpha Centauri?[15] Unless there are fanciful ectoplasmic or ethereal forces at work, beyond the ken of biology and every other science known to man, Fido and Twin Fido would have the same repertoire of capacities and powers, all the same properties, whether intrinsic or relational, as well as total structural identity. The only thing stopping them from being conspecific, for the cladist, will be their different lines of descent. This looks like the replacement of metaphysics and good science by sheer dogma. As Sneath and Sokal ask, when considering the possible convergent evolution of organisms possessing distinct lines of descent:

> Suppose the convergence had become so absurdly extreme that the two forms are almost indistinguishable and can readily and successfully hybridize: what is the purpose of separating them on grounds of ancestry when in all other attributes they are virtually the same?
>
> (Sneath and Sokal 1973: 48)

Further, cladism suffers from a regress problem. For if classification is by descent, then what about the very first organism, which by definition had no descent? How is it to be classified? It seems the cladist has to insist on some form of descent not merely analogous to, but of the very same kind as, that applying to all descendants of the first organism. What could 'same kind' mean? It could not mean biological generation, since the first organism was not biologically generated. Hence it must mean something like evolution by natural selection, which has doubtful application outside biology. We saw in Chapter 8 that Cairns-Smith's theory of crystal evolution is thought by some to serve as a process for the generation of life, so might it not be sufficiently similar to biological reproduction to count as of the same kind? But then it looks like the cladist has an a priori method for determining the origin of life: since all biological classification must be evolutionary, the first organism *must* have arisen by evolution. So much for competing theories, such as self-organization, that require much experimental testing to see whether they give the truth about life's origins.

In any case, if the origin of life was indeed by a kind of inorganic evolution, the regress does not go away; for how far back does the evolution go? If there is inorganic evolution by natural selection, then cladistics should apply to it at all stages. But then we still need to know how to classify the first inorganic entity capable of evolving by natural selection but not itself a product of evolution. If it has no evolutionary descent then it has no cladistic classification, whatever its constitution as a self-replicating, niche-occupying, begetter of evolving descendants. We are no better off than when looking for a cladistic classification of the first organism. So it looks like the cladist has to believe in the existence of inorganic evolutionary descent at every stage in the past history of the universe. But then the universe cannot be finite in the past, since if it were there would have to be a first inorganic entity that evolved from nothing, and so it would lack a cladistic classification. Hence the universe must be infinite in the past, a temporally infinite process of inorganic evolution by natural selection. Not only does the cladist have a priori means for determining the origin of life, but he can use biology to work out that the universe must have had no beginning. Would that physicists and metaphysicians had such techniques at their disposal.

Another bizarre consequence of cladism is the following (LaPorte 2004: 50–62; Okasha 2002: 205–7). Every taxon above species level is defined as a group of organisms that includes a common ancestor and all of that ancestor's descendants. A species is a lineage originating from an ancestral population and terminating in a speciation event or an extinction. All taxa, including species, are defined in terms of their ancestry – they just *are* chunks of the genealogical tree of life. To be a mammal just is to be descended from a certain ancestral population. To be a tiger also just is to be descended from a particular ancestral population. But tigers are mammals, because they belong to a lineage having descent from the mammalian clade, i.e. from the segment of the tree that has the common mammalian ancestor and all of its descendants. So tigers are essentially mammals because to be a mammal just is to have a certain line of descent, and tigers as a species are defined by their descent, according to cladism. So it looks like some form of essentialism is after all entailed by the cladistic conception.

The problem is that while, for the cladist, every taxon essentially belongs to the higher-level taxa within which it is nested (by a line of evolutionary descent), no *individual* organism essentially belongs to the taxon it actually belongs to. Consider the schematic lineage shown in Figure 9.2. *A*, *B* and *C* are species. At t_1 there is a speciation event, i.e. a splitting of *C* from the *A*–*B* lineage. By cladistic standards, this splitting event means that not only is *C* a different species from *A*, but so is *B*. A simplified example has *A* as a species of the *Eutheria* (the placental mammals), *B* as the tigers (*Panthera tigris*) and *C* as a species of the extinct order *Creodonta*. (The extinction is irrelevant; I have represented them as continuing into the present to make the example more vivid.) Now if the *C*-split had not occurred there would have been no speciation event and so the actual members of *B* would not have been *B*s but *A*s – no matter *how different* the actual *B*s are from the *A*s. Tigger, the tiger at your local zoo, had there been no *Creodonta* and no other split, would have been a member of the Eutherian species from which he descended, even if the latter species, on all morphological and ethological criteria, was *nothing* like Tigger – even if they were as similar as chalk and cheese, as it were. It's not that Tigger would have ceased to exist had there

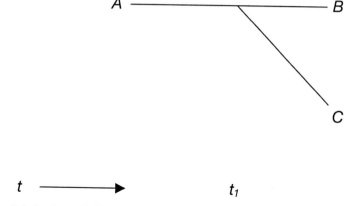

Figure 9.2 A schematic lineage of organisms

been no *C*-split: as LaPorte rightly observes, one can hardly say that 'if some random speciation event occurs in the line of *Homo sapiens* in the next ten minutes in Wyoming, you will cease to exist' (LaPorte 2004: 55). The point is rather that '[w]hether members of *B* belong to species *B* or species *A* depends on whether an accident occurs that ought to have nothing to do with whether those members exist' (2004: 55). And LaPorte cites Kitcher (1989: 200–2) to the effect that 'whether or not a species like *A* becomes extinct at a particular time depends upon whether a side isolate threatening to branch off at that time is wiped out by a cataclysm before achieving species status' (LaPorte 2004: 55). So it is not as though Tigger's essence could have been different, since that is impossible. Rather, Tigger *has* no essence, since his species identity is contingent upon extrinsic events having nothing to do with what Tigger is like as an animal.

Yet this absurd result of cladistics is accepted by LaPorte with equanimity, and taken by Okasha (2002: 205–7) at face value since he upbraids essentialists such as David Wiggins (1980) for failing to take account of 'the species concepts actually at work in biology' (Okasha 2002: 207). The result makes species identity, and hence what an organism *is*, an extrinsic matter, floating free of anything to do with the organism itself – its behaviour, its morphology, its characteristic modes of functioning. As such, the cladistic species concept looks not much more operative than a Platonic Form in explaining what it is about organisms as material substances that makes them what they are and either distinguishes them from each other or marks them out as individuals of a kind.[16]

Yet the situation is even worse when combined with the earlier result that LaPorte notes, namely that, although individual organisms have no essences, the various taxa *are* essentially related to each other via phylogenetic nesting. Hence, although Tigger is not essentially a tiger, all tigers *are* essentially mammals because of their line of descent. But then why not apply the same reasoning at the infraspecific level? Suppose Tigger is a

Sumatran tiger. One hopes the cladist will say that Sumatran tigers are essentially tigers, due to their line of descent from other tigers (though for a hylemorphist descent will have nothing to do with it). But then Tigger must essentially be a tiger after all. Moreover, all tigers are essentially tigers: '*Panthera tigris* = *Panthera tigris*' is a *de re* necessarily true identity statement involving a term rigidly denoting a certain lineage (to borrow from the contemporary essentialists). But if all tigers are essentially tigers and Tigger is a tiger, then Tigger must essentially be a tiger.[17]

Ridley is a little less sanguine about the implications of cladism, for reasons to do with the converse of the argument I gave on p. 220. I said that cladism entails that if the *C*-split had not occurred, *A* and *B* would have been the same species no matter how different they were. The converse is that, given the *C*-split does occur, *A* and *B* will be *different* species no matter how *similar* they are: there may not have been a single genetic or phenotypical (or reproductive or ecological) alteration in the *A–B* line after t_1, yet cladism requires us to call *A* and *B* distinct species. This is no less bizarre than the previous problem. Ridley notes briefly that

> [t]here is no orthodoxy among evolutionary biologists [I take him to mean mainly cladists] about how to treat cases of branching without change .... I would point out, however, that the objections to the cladistic treatment ... are more-or-less phenetically inspired, and lead to the general phenetic difficulties: arbitrary and subjective classification.
>
> (Ridley 1993: 401)

Ridley may be right about pheneticism, but this does not dispose of the problem: one cannot salvage a bad theory by pointing out the weaknesses in another.

As already noted, some cladists try to save some kind of essentialism by claiming that species and higher taxa are historical entities. (Note that all of the taxa are species in the metaphysical sense relative to higher taxa, and generic relative to lower taxa. Species in the biological sense would seem to include only the infima species, but this is unclear in the case of cladism, since what counts metaphysically as an infima species – an extinct species of Eutherian, say, whose members were metaphysically one of a kind on hylemorphic principles – would be generic on cladistic principles if it branched. For the cladist, the only infima species could be the ones existing now – on the terminal points of the phylogenetic tree that had not yet branched.) The very idea of historical essence, however, is misconceived in the case of material substances. Indeed one wonders why, in the absence of cladistic dogma, any biologist would even suppose that the essence of a species could be historical.

The cladist claims, with some force, that the main competing species concepts – biological and ecological – are relational just like the cladistic, so if relational essence is the source of the worry there is nothing special about cladism (Okasha 2002: 201–2). This may be so, but then it merely shows a problem with most modern species theories. (Pheneticism, however, is not relational, though it is less popular.) The properties of species members might in many cases be relational – the power to operate in a certain way in a certain kind of ecological niche, or the power to interbreed with certain other organisms – but these will always be founded upon the intrinsic constitution of the organism, e.g. its reproductive system or its possession of certain kinds of organ (wings, legs, eyes). What *enables* the organism to have certain relational properties is precisely the way it is structured, the way its parts interact, its chemistry, genotype, size, shape, colour, homeostatic mechanisms, nervous system, and so on. All of these intrinsic characteristics are part of the overall *morphology* of the organism, and since morphology is repeatable, organisms sharing a morphology belong to the same species. (More about this in section 9.4.)

One of the themes of this study re-emerges: confusion of essence and property leads to a mistaken understanding of what makes an organism the kind of thing it is. Properties are founded on the essence of a substance and emanate from it, but essence is intrinsic. I noted earlier (Chapter 7) that artefacts have relational essences since they depend for their identity on the existence of minds; but artefacts, as I explained, are not substances. Nor are systems, where the components are all essentially related to one or more other components. Now, leaving aside the issues of whether organisms or anything else depend for their continued existence on the sustaining power of a divine being; whether anything in the universe is designed by an omniscient and omnipotent mind; and whether (as believers in divine creation hold) the first organisms were directly created by a divine act, the fact remains: organisms are not artefacts.[18] The organisms studied by biologists work by their own powers, their own causal capacities, and react to stimuli according to their own intrinsic natures. They have, in other words, their own internal principle of operation, something well explained by Walsh (2006). Biologists who want to analyse the behaviour of *Drosophila* do well not to study human minds, though they may find methodological use in applying principles of design to these insects in order to illuminate features of their structure and function.

The point is that even if organisms *were* designed, whether by God, Martian artistry, or some other power, they were designed *to have an internal principle of operation*, and what the scientist needs to study are those principles of operation. To put the matter slightly paradoxically, if organisms were designed, then they were designed *not* to have relational essences. That there is no real paradox is apparent from the fact that were some super-intelligent scientist able to synthesize an organism from pre-existing organic or inorganic compounds, using a complete knowledge of the physico-chemical and genetic structure and properties of those compounds and an ability to predict the structure and function of the synthesized organism down to the minutest detail, he would not have made anything with a relational essence. Rather, he would have made an organism with its own internal – albeit completely predictable – nature and repertoire of powers and capacities. It might belong to an ecosystem, and ecosystems are an important area of study, but ecosystems are not substances, and to understand an ecosystem the scientist needs to understand the essences of its components. The Gaia Hypothesis of James Lovelock, if taken strictly, holds the entire ecosystem to be one great organism and its components merely ontologically dependent parts. If this were true, no organism would have an intrinsic essence: all essences, apart from the essence of the ecosystem itself, would be relational. But there is no good reason to regard the hypothesis as a true metaphysical picture of how organisms function, and every reason to treat it as no more than a metaphor or a useful heuristic.

To identify essence with descent is, at the more abstract metaphysical level, to confuse formal and efficient causes. A line of evolutionary descent can explain much about why organisms have the features they do: similar structures, organs, function, and so on can often be explained by assuming common descent. And the assumption of common descent can be used to predict similarities – bearing in mind, of course, that speciation events significantly undermine the predictive power of such an assumption. Cladism must be supplemented by other concepts, such as reproductive isolation, in order to make reliable predictions about how much organisms with shared descent are likely to diverge phenetically. But cladism's usefulness need not be in dispute. We can tell a lot about a thing's form and properties by knowing where it came from. But where it came from is not the same as what it is. Bacteria and Archaea aside, biologists hold that all organisms are descended from aquatic, unicellular eukaryotes. Nevertheless, being descended from an aquatic, unicellular eukaryote doesn't make you an aquatic, unicellular eukaryote, even if it explains why you are eukaryotic. Descent gives us the efficient cause of a thing's identity. It does not give us the formal cause, which is the essence – in other words, how the thing *is* in itself. And that individual nature, being repeatable, is not separable from the essence of the kind. Even if an organism with a certain nature is the only one with such a nature that ever has existed or will exist, it is still essentially a member of a kind, albeit a singleton. The separation of individual essence and kind essence, then (as in LaPorte 2004 and Okasha 2002), is as much an illusion as the view that there is such a thing as cladistic essence, however diagnostically, predictively, and explanatorily useful cladism may be in helping us to understand the true essences of organisms.[19] To put the point in a sentence: there is no more reason to base biological taxonomy on genealogical descent than there is to classify the chemical elements according to their line of descent from the Big Bang.[20]

9.3 Vagueness

One of the most prominent arguments for anti-essentialism in biology (as elsewhere) is the argument from vagueness. Since evolution is a gradual process,[21] we should expect to find, and do find, many intermediate or transitional forms between distinct species (where, again, 'species' is used metaphysically to include higher-level taxa). Think of the many intermediate forms from which the modern horse, *Equus*, or the whale (order *Cetacea*), are said to have descended (Mayr 2002: 18–19; MacFadden 1992). The problem for the essentialist is compounded by the intermediate forms existing synchronically, making it hard to distinguish one species from another: think of the finches (family *Fringillidae*) made famous by Darwin (Grant 1986). As Ereshefsky asserts, setting out the anti-essentialist argument from vagueness as found in Hull (1965) and elsewhere:

> The boundaries of species are vague in the same sense that the boundaries between rich and poor, bald and not bald, are vague. There is no precise number of dollars that marks the boundary between rich and poor. Similarly, there is no genetic or phenotypic trait that marks the boundary from one species to the next. Therefore no trait is essential for membership within a species.
>
> (Ereshefsky 1992: 188–9)

Sober, on the other hand, does think that 'essentialism is a doctrine that is compatible with certain sorts of vagueness' (Sober 1993: 148; see also Sober 1980). No scientific concept is absolutely precise, not even in physics, where transmutation between species is both possible and common. As long as the essentialist does not ask for absolute precision and sharp cut-off points, there is enough in speciation to allow biologists to determine when a species comes into or goes out of existence, even if they cannot date the occurrence 'down to the smallest microsecond' (Sober 1993: 148). In particular, since cladogenesis – i.e. branching events on the phylogenetic tree – is the standard model of speciation, there is a means for dating species by dating speciation events (as supplemented by other species concepts such as interbreeding; recall the earlier argument on p. 216). Can the biological essentialist rest content with this position?

The first thing to note is that, leaving aside the many other objections to cladism raised earlier, the point about cladogenesis versus anagenesis (large diachronic variation within a single lineage) again raises its head. For cladists, who rule out speciation by anagenesis, a non-branching lineage remains a single species no matter *how* different the descendants are from their ancestors – even if they occupy radically different niches, cannot interbreed, and are morphologically utterly distinct. Whether this has ever happened in evolutionary time is irrelevant: the point is that it is not a biological impossibility. (For evidence that anagenesis has occurred between *Australopithecus anamensis* and *A. afarensis*, see Kimbel *et al.* 2006; for evidence of anagenesis in island plants, see Stuessy *et al.* 2006; and between the diatoms (a kind of marine plankton, classification still debated) *Stephanodiscus niagarae* and *S. yellowstonensis*, see Theriot *et al.* 2006.)[22]

Hence vagueness is not eliminated if anagenesis is possible. Moreover, even in cladogenesis it may appear vague whether the descendant species are distinct, given for instance that it may take time for reproductive isolation to occur, or for different ecological niches to be occupied. More generally, the stipulative character of cladism rules out even apparent vagueness in respect of species separated by nodal events, no matter how similar they are in other respects. Cladism, then, does not seem to represent a way of dealing with vagueness that is metaphysically satisfying, whatever its biological strengths and weaknesses. Rather, it stipulates vagueness out of existence.

Apparent vagueness in species must be taken seriously as a metaphysical issue, just as in other areas. I do not, however, propose to offer a solution to the problem of vagueness here. It is not even clear whether there is a single solution to all the different sorts of case vagueness can throw up. Or even if there is a single solution, it is not clear whether there is a single *method* for handling vagueness in every area, even though we might be able to enunciate some principles that govern all cases. Vagueness seems to infect everything – accidents, properties, substances, essences, other kinds of being such as collections and aggregates, laws, parts, causes, languages, and so on throughout ontology, language, thought, and reasoning. (For an overview of the issues and various theories on offer, see Williamson 1994; Keefe and Smith 1997.) Vague essences, in particular vague biological species, are just another problem case, though what I propose in dealing with the problem as it appears in biology has possible application to other kinds of vagueness.

To begin with, looking at the problem in advance of biological details, the idea that there could be vague species (whether infima species or higher taxa) seems curious. Note that we must immediately distinguish between epistemic and ontological vagueness. There is nothing strange in the idea that there should be an organism such that our best taxonomic efforts, or the competition of incompatible but current species concepts, should be incapable of determining what species the organism in question belongs to. Ontological vagueness, however, involves the idea that there could be an organism such that *by its very nature* it was incapable of classification as being of one species rather than another. To belong to a species is to have an essence. An essence is a principle of operation, the ontological ground of a thing's behaving and functioning in a characteristic way. So a vague essence would be a nature that was itself not characteristic of one kind of operation rather than another. A substance with a vague essence would be a kind of thing that was no kind of thing in particular.

Yet how could there be such an entity? How could there be a thing that *had* a nature, i.e. that had a characteristic mode of operation, but such that this characteristic mode of operation was not characteristic of anything in particular, or was characteristic of more than one kind of thing? For to have a nature just *is* to be a certain kind of thing and no other, that is, to be demarcated ontologically from all other kinds of thing. To say that a thing has a nature that is not an instance of some essential kind and no other sounds as bizarre as claiming that a person was a father without being the father of anyone in particular, or that a figure had a shape without its being any particular kind of shape. Every actual shape is a particular shape just as every instantiated determinable is a particular determinate. Every instance of a relation is a relation between particular things. Similarly, to have a nature in reality is to have a particular nature. It seems incomprehensible that there could be a thing with a nature, but where that nature was not an actual, concrete, characteristic mode of behaviour and function – and so of itself a particular nature that set it apart from the natures possessed by other things that had a nature at all. In other words, to hold that there could be a vague essence is not merely to assert that a thing could actually *have* an essence that was not the essence of anything in particular, but to assert by implication that there could be a thing that had *no* essence. Hence to assert the existence of vague essence is to deny the existence of essence altogether in the thing whose vague essence it is supposed to be. If the thing is of no kind in particular, it is of no kind at all.

The believer in vague essence is, it seems, really committed to denying essentialism altogether. I will not recapitulate the essentialist arguments I have already given, or the objections to anti-essentialism. But the friend of vague essence might agree that the very idea of vague essence is incoherent, insisting that all she means by this paradoxical notion is that vagueness precludes essentialism and that this is sufficient reason not to be an essentialist. Might there not be an organism such that it had no essence precisely because it was ontologically indeterminate what essence it had? And don't the transitional and intermediate forms identified by biologists prove this to be so?

One reason for resisting the suggestion is that we are left in a quandary with respect to the vast majority of organisms for which there does not appear to be any such indeterminacy. Moreover, that there must be *some* determinate species is knowable a priori, given that there are any indeterminate ones. For if there are indeterminate species – in particular, where the indeterminacy is supposedly a case of intermediacy or transitionality – there must be determinate ones relative to which the indeterminacy is measured. This applies generally to all sorts of vagueness. If there is a putatively vague colour – a colour such that it is indeterminate which colour it is – this is because there are non-vague colours relative to which the vagueness of the colour in question is measured. It appears vague whether, say, colour C is pink or purple. And if it is vague whether a person with N hairs on his head arranged in a certain way is bald, that is because there is such a thing as determinate baldness and non-baldness. That is precisely how the sorites arguments are generated. Indeed it is arguably the case that *all* examples of vagueness require the existence of non-vague cases on the same dimension of characterization, whether the vagueness is presumed to be ontological or epistemic. Biological vagueness puts this fact into relief because the vague cases are intermediate or transitional, and so must be identified as vague by reference to non-vague exemplars.

If this is so, then what do we say about the non-vague species? If we say they are really vague too, this destroys the possibility of identifying vagueness at all: if nothing is determinate, how can we plausibly say that anything is indeterminate? But if everything is neither determinate nor indeterminate, we end up in absurdity. So we must say that the apparently determinate cases really are determinate if we want to hold to the vague cases' really being vague. The question then arises: given that there are determinate species, why should there be any indeterminate ones at all? In the case of diachronic identity, where vagueness puzzles also arise, we can ask: given that there are times in the career of a persisting object where boundaries determinately do *not* exist, why should there be any times where the boundaries are indeterminate? In previous work (Oderberg 1993: 166) I framed the question in terms of knowability: if we can know where a persisting object's temporal boundaries are not, why can't we know, at least in principle, where they are?

I will return to knowability later, but my point here is that the question has ontological, not merely epistemic, force. In the case of identity through time, the question is what it is about persistents such that they can have determinate non-boundaries – it is determinate that when I remove a tiny sliver of wood from my desk it does not cease to exist – but can also have indeterminate boundaries, such that it is metaphysically indeterminate when the object does cease to exist. I claimed in Chapter 5 that identity over time is ungrounded, i.e. unanalysable in terms that do not presuppose the very notion that we seek to analyse. But I also explained that identity is tied to the nature of the persistent as given by substantial form (as opposed to individuation, which is tied primarily to matter). But the principle of identity, which is form, should be the same for the boundaries as well as the non-boundaries. That is, the principle of identity governing where the temporal limits of a persistent are not must be the same as that governing where the limits are. There can only be one governing principle of identity for an object; if there are two, what would they be?

Since the governing principle – form – provides determinate non-limits, what is it about a persistent such that form also provides the limits but these are *not* determinate?[23] One could embrace a bizarre kind of nihilism, according to which *even* the non-limits are vague: it is *never* determinate whether an object continues to exist. But there is nothing to recommend that other than the insistence that persistents have vague temporal boundaries, the recognition that there can only be one governing principle of diachronic identity, and the suspicion of a clash between that principle's yielding determinate non-boundaries and vague boundaries. Better, I submit, either to revisit the idea that there are vague boundaries or to explain how it can be – what it is about the nature of a persisting object – that it can have vague boundaries and non-vague non-boundaries.

I cannot take the issue of diachronic identity further here, but use it only as a way of making the same point about species. There are endless examples of determinate species, i.e. species whose members are determinately members. We might not be able to say everything there is about a humble member of *Canis lupus* (the wolf species)[24] that makes it what it is, we may not have a complete grasp of its nature, but we recognize it when we see it. It has a nature such that there are endless determinate members of its kind. Yet if there are vague boundaries to this species, as given by intermediate or transitional species, what is it about the nature of the wolf that allows this to be so? One common answer will be the pheneticist one that species are determined by their characteristics, and these come in clusters. The more features present, the more determinate it is that we have a member of *C. lupus*. When few or none are present, as in the *Vulpes* genus (fox) or the *Giraffa camelopardalis* (giraffe), it is determinate that the creature is not a member of *C. lupus*. When quite a few are present, as in *C. latrans* (coyote), it is indeterminate. But pheneticism, whilst entailing the possibility of vagueness, mistakes characteristics for essence, treating an organism as a bundle of characters. For reasons I have already given, as well as the trenchant criticisms of pheneticism by cladists and supporters of other species concepts, we cannot use it to underwrite metaphysical vagueness.

Other species concepts also bring their indeterminacies with them, and cladists claim the advantage of relative precision in their phylogenetic account. Problems with cladism aside, though, it is simply unclear how a single nature can be such as to enable both determinate and indeterminate membership of a species. The essence of an organism is its form, but either a form is present or it is not; it is not clear what vague possession of a form would even amount to. No change of *degree* in a thing can change its membership of a kind: as the old Scholastic maxim goes, *plus et minus non mutat speciem*. If all variation were a matter of degree, there would be no substantial variation and everything would belong either to the same species or to no species at all. Yet we know there are distinct species and we know there is substantial change. This has to be underwritten by form, since form is the only metaphysical principle that is not susceptible of degree and at the same time unifies the characteristics of a thing to yield a single member of a species. If it can yield metaphysical indeterminacy, we need to know by virtue of what it can do so, and this is elusive. If there is some other principle of species membership that can yield both indeterminacy in some cases and determinacy in others, we need to know not just what it is and why it can do so, but that it also satisfies the desiderata of essence. No such principle is forthcoming.

If we are hylemorphists, as I have argued we should be, then we should expect ontological determinacy in species membership. But this is quite compatible with epistemic indeterminacy. It may be that the best efforts of taxonomists are unable to place an organism in one category rather than another, but this will be a matter of lack of knowledge or lack of techniques sufficient to solve the problem. The friend of vagueness will retort that this is strong evidence of an underlying ontological indeterminacy, and that therefore there must be something wrong with the hylemorphic account of essence. I concede that it may not be metaphysically satisfying to reply to the taxonomist faced with vagueness that he simply does not know enough about the natures he is examining, but that he should take it on metaphysical faith that there *is* an answer to his worries, even if he will never find it, and even if no answer will be available no matter how much biology our finite minds engage in. But such concerns can be allayed if there is a *method* for resolving vague cases, even if it does not always yield certainty. If there is a procedure the taxonomist can use that respects metaphysical determinacy and handles vague cases, then the fact that our finite minds cannot be guaranteed certainty in all cases will be no more cause for concern than the fact that we will never uncover all the answers about the workings of the physical world, we will never know everything about chemistry, and we will not even come to an end in discovering all the properties of water. If a usable and useful procedure is available, this will soften the blow of being told by the metaphysician that the taxonomist must take it on faith, if he will not go through the reasoning, that form is determinate.

There is no room here to go through the details of such a method, but the essentialist has one and I will sketch it briefly. It is founded on the following rule: *when in doubt, divide*. Recall that in Chapter 5 I defended the principle of disjointness for the Porphyrian Tree, following Thomason (1969): for any kinds K_1 and K_2, if they have a greatest lower bound (a highest lower kind), it will be either K_1 or K_2; hence there can be no cross-classification. Of the possibility of cross-classification, Thomason has this to say:

> It sometimes happens that things are discovered which can lay claim to membership in sorts supposed to be disjoint: for instance, microbes which appear to be both animal and vegetable. I would prefer to regard such anomalous cases as not falling under the original scheme – e.g., as *neither* animal nor vegetable – thus preserving the principle [of disjointness].
>
> (Thomason 1969: 98)

I think this remark of Thomason's contains a crucial insight that should be used to handle vague cases. The method based on it can be called the *method of partition*. According to this procedure, when the taxonomist is faced with an indeterminate case, being unable on best inquiry to classify organism O as belonging to species S_1 or S_2 (or some other species), he should simply classify it as belonging to a new species S_n, and only reclassify it as belonging to an already-recognized species if further inquiry makes postulation of the new species unnecessary.

Thomason's own example, of an organism that lays claim to being both animal and vegetable and so should be classified as neither, is not a felicitous one, for reasons I gave in Chapter 8. There I suggested that there was no kind in between animal and vegetative, hence that all organisms can ultimately be classified as one or the other (bearing in mind that human beings, as rational animals, are not *just* animal). But that is a different argument and does not impinge upon the general point being made here. If there were no conceptual bar to postulating a kind of organism in between animal and vegetative, the method of partition would license it. For that method has nothing to say about what species we should recognize, only that we should recognize as many species as necessary to handle indeterminate cases. In addition, the method does not say we should handle a vague case by *conjoining* candidate species – by, that is, saying of organism *O* whose membership of species S_1 or S_2 is vague that it is an S_1–S_2. For this would involve either illegitimate cross-classification or related metaphysical implausibility. Still, there is another sense in which we can *speak* of conjoining species in such a way as not to say anything different from *disjoining* them.

To explain, consider the famous case of *Archaeopteryx*, generally held to be a transitional species in between reptiles and birds.[25] The general consensus is that it is something in between a reptile and a bird, but there are students of the existing fossil specimens who are convinced *Archaeopteryx* is a bird, others that it is a reptile, and yet others that the fossils are a forgery. (For a good overview, see Chambers 2002. I will leave aside the forgery hypothesis.) The creature has avian features, such as a furcula (wishbone), opposable hallux (big toe) and, most important of all, feathered wings allowing flight.[26] But it also has reptilian features, such as the absence of a horn-covered maxilla (i.e. no bill), unfused trunk vertebrae (unlike birds), a reptilian brain shape, and a reptilian attachment of neck to skull (from the rear, whereas in birds it is from below).[27]

Now if we plausibly take *Archaeopteryx* as a typical case of indeterminacy as between reptiles and birds, the method of partition recommends placing it into a different species – neither reptile nor bird. Ontological vagueness is ruled out for the reasons I have given: *Archeopteryx* has *some* nature of other, *some* unified principle of structure, function, and behaviour. But to say that it is a reptile-bird in the sense of being *both* a reptile *and* a bird is metaphysically repugnant: these are two distinct forms, two distinct modes of being for the organisms belonging to these categories. According to the principle of the unicity of substantial form (see Chapter 4.2), no substance can have more than one substantial form: the principle whereby it has one property is the principle whereby it has all properties. So *Archaeopteryx* cannot have both an avian substantial form and a reptilian one. Hence it must have neither, given that there is no overwhelming reason to place it in either class. The taxonomist could still call it a reptile-bird, but only in the sense according to which 'reptile-bird' would be a mere notational variant of 'neither reptile nor bird'. More accurately, since most species are neither reptile nor bird, when we call *Archaeopteryx* neither reptile nor bird this is a shorthand for 'neither reptile nor bird, but the possessor of a unique form similar to both in properties', and we can of course spell this out in more detail according to how much we know of the morphology of *Archaeopteryx*.

As with so many classifications, as I explained when discussing the Porphyrian Tree in Chapter 5, property descriptions are the markers by which taxonomy indicates the possession of a certain substantial form; they are a kind of placeholder for a term that encapsulates the genus or specific difference of the substance in question. Current taxonomic practice, heavily influence by cladistics, simply places *Archaeopteryx* in one of the eight known subclasses of the class *Aves*, which includes all the feathered, but not necessarily flying, creatures (modulo feathered dinosaurs; see note 26). A simple Porphyrian binomial classification, far more a starting point than a final classification, would begin with the idea that *Archaeopteryx* is a bird-like animal with reptilian properties, where both genus and difference could be spelled out in great detail.

Why not a reptile-like creature with avian properties? A pheneticist might answer that having feathered wings capable of flight deserves a higher numerical weighting in the phenetic cluster than any of the reptilian properties, and there is something right about this. But the real essentialist does not identify essence with phenetic clusters. What she is interested in is the overall structure, function, and behaviour of the creature in question. This is *not* the same as overall phenetic similarity, since pheneticism, at least as current practice seems to suggest, assigns significance to characters primarily in a statistical and quantitative fashion, but without appealing to a unifying essence as the way of determining the weightings of the empirical data (Sneath and Sokal 1973: 9, 421). At the risk of oversimplifying, phenetic characters are observed and weighted by statistical methods such as degree of dependent variation between them: a character C_1 might be found to vary in a population in a linear way with character C_2 but not with C_3. It might then be judged that C_1 and C_2 are more significant in the population than C_3, which may vary randomly, perhaps being absent altogether in some cases. Pheneticists can then build up a 'phenetic distance statistic' which groups a certain set of organisms together as varying by less from the number measured by the statistic than does another set of organisms. The first set of organisms will then be defined as belonging to a species distinct from the second. (See Ridley 1993: 360–4, 386–7; for the details, see Sneath and Sokal 1973.)

Pheneticism can be seen as an attempt to improve on the older morphological species concept by the use of quantitative methods and avoidance of reference to 'ideal types'. As Ridley points out, in his extensive criticism of pheneticism, either morphological types lurk in the background as the unspoken reference point for phenetic measures, or there is no objective basis for preferring one measure over another (Ridley 1993: 387). He is correct in his accusation that pheneticism needs morphological types to underpin its phenetic measures, but wrong to assume that such types must be 'ideal', along the lines of the 'typological essentialism' reviled by Mayr.

To do so is to make the usual mistake of conflating essentialism with its Platonic variety. As I argued in Chapter 4, real essentialism does not employ Platonic types or Forms (with a capital F) to underwrite classification by essence. There is no such thing as the ideal bird, or the ideal reptile, or the ideal exemplar of *Archaeopteryx*. There are paradigmatic members, typical members, normal members, and the like, where the qualifiers are explicated in terms of the range of properties that members of the species possess, the way organisms behave, how they exercise their powers, and so on.

But there is no need to, and every reason not to, posit an 'ideal type' to which members of the species must conform. The very concept is doubtfully coherent. What would it *be* to constitute an ideal member of a species? How well would an archaeopteryx have to fly? How many feathers would it have to possess? There is no non-arbitrary answer to such questions. All the morphologist can do is look for normal ranges of structure and function, such as kinds of flight (in the case of *Archaeopteryx*, it was probably a weak but stable flapper), feather size, shape, and distribution (very much like those of modern birds), overall body plan, limb construction, making unavoidably risky inferences from these as to habits, and looking to all the other characteristics that go to make up an organism with a definite, unified principle of operation.

The metaphysically informed morphologist has yet other conceptual tools to hand. For instance, since all organisms have nutritive properties but only animals have locomotive properties (or so I argued in Chapter 8), there is a clear reason for considering flight to be more important in classifying *Archaeopteryx* than, say, the lack of a bill. The former goes to locomotion, the latter to nutrition.[28] On this way of looking at things, being able to fly is more important for classification, more closely related to essence, to put it loosely, than what kind of structure an organism uses to feed. But that doesn't mean *Archaeopteryx* should be classified with all other flying animals, even generically; on this the morphologist can agree with the phylogeneticist and the pheneticist. Rather, it should be classified along with the species to which it is morphologically most similar. Having feathered flight might then put it in a genus, with its reptilian properties going to the specific difference – and this irrespective of its evolutionary descent. Its phylogeny will be a useful tool in diagnosing or predicting morphology, but no more than that. Pheneticism, for its part, must rely on this way of thinking if there is to be a 'sound philosophic basis' for classification, as Ridley puts it (Ridley 1993: 387). The more it does so, however, the more it falls back on the older morphological concept and the more quantitative measures fade into the background.

Consider also *Ambulocetus natans*, widely held to be the transitional species demonstrating the otherwise unlikely evolution of whales from land-dwelling mammals. It was amphibious, possessing hindlimbs and being able move about on land. It almost certainly lacked a blowhole, breathing instead through nostrils like land mammals. But it was well adapted to aquatic movement, and its ear structure and teeth were more similar to those of whales than of land mammals. (For more details, see Berta 1994.) Is this a case of vagueness? It is in the sense that we do not know nearly enough about *Ambulocetus*, based on the meagre fossil evidence, to say exactly how it behaved and what its overall morphology was like. Berta (1994: 180) briefly dismisses a phenetic definition of whales and similar forms on the ground of arbitrariness: for instance, lack of hindlimbs is an unhelpful marker of whales, since the extinct *Archaeoceti* possessed them yet they are regarded as a species of whale since they were aquatic. But singling out a character, or even a cluster of characters, is problematic from the start. Mere possession or lack of a hindlimb is insignificant when divorced from morphology. Locomotion being part of the essence of an animal, it is not only the kind of limb an animal possesses that matters for classification, but what it does with that limb.

If the archaeocetes really were all aquatic, and their morphology was otherwise very similar to modern whales, we have good reason for regarding them as whales on solid essentialist grounds, without having to resort to phylogeny other than as a diagnostic tool as opposed to a principle of classification. Given that *Ambulocetus* was amphibious, this in itself is a reason for distinguishing it from the whales and from the land mammals. The method of partition recommends the positing of a new species whenever there are grounds to do so. The essentialist grounds are morphological, and these are sufficient for a defeasible judgment that *Ambulocetus* does not prove metaphysical vagueness in the essence of whales or land mammals. All it proves is that there is a kind of animal that is like both but essentially neither.

It is not possible to go into the detail required to show anything more than an outline of the method of partition in action. What I have proposed is a methodology that should allay any suspicion that the vagueness of biological species is anything more than epistemic. The method of partition may have application to other kinds of vagueness as well. If we follow the maxim 'When in doubt, divide', we should be able to see that, in at least some cases, belief in metaphysical vagueness is no more than a projection onto the world of our incomplete grasp of essence, and that this incomplete grasp is itself a function of finite minds operating on partial evidence.

9.4 A plea for morphology

I have argued that anti-essentialism in the debate over biological species is a flawed position. If anything has an essence, organisms do. But the explanation of species essences requires substantial forms: nothing less than these can do the job essentialism demands, of explaining the distinctive and characteristic behaviour of organisms in a way that marks them off one from another according to their repeatable natures. Hence, contrary to the view of Walsh (2006), an essentialism of natures does entail taxonomic essentialism. As long as we are not misled by the plurality of species concepts employed by biologists or by the equation of taxonomic essentialism with a Platonist typological essentialism, we have no reason to separate essence and taxonomy and every reason to keep them together. Moreover, a binomial taxonomic method that seeks the genus and then pins down the specific difference, according to Porphyrian principles, is still the most reasonable way of proceeding to classify organisms, and in fact persists in use among biologists, even among all but the most extreme cladists. (For an example of such extremism, see Mishler 1999.) Mayr states that Aristotle himself rejected the method of dichotomous division (Mayr 1982: 151), but what Aristotle was doing was rejecting the method as exemplified in the divisions with which he was familiar. The Porphyrian method came later.[29]

What ties individual natures and taxonomy together is the study of substantial forms. In other words, it is *morphology* – literally, the study of form – that metaphysically underpins the way in which biologists should approach the study of living things. Morphology in biology is just one aspect of real essentialism, which is about morphology everywhere and in everything. Living things are no exception to a hylemorphic ontology, so if hylemorphism is true generally it will be true specifically. Hence biologists should not think that a plea for morphology in biology is something special and disconnected from the essentialist's overriding plea for morphology in the study of all of reality.

Yet surely morphology in biology is dead, along with the essentialism that goes with it? In fact, as have seen, morphology creeps into virtually every major way in which species are identified in contemporary systematics. It finds its way into ecological tests, reproductive criteria, cladistic analysis, genetic identification, mate recognition, and more. But it is nearly always treated as what Mayden (1997) calls a 'secondary species concept', an operational adjunct to something more fundamental, one that aids in sharpening systematic analysis without serving as the primary test by which species are recognized. Morphology is, however, the basis of all recognition and classification. I end this chapter with some remarks that build on what I have already said in direct or indirect defence of morphology throughout the preceding discussion. A fuller treatment is for another occasion.

Mayden quotes some statements of what the morphological species concept amounts to. Reviewing them, as well as Mayden's own evaluation, will help to sharpen the focus on what morphology is and is not. For example, according to Cronquist, '[s]pecies are the smallest groups that are consistently and persistently distinct, and distinguishable by ordinary means' (Cronquist 1978: 15). We need not spend long on this, because it is barely a definition, let alone a morphological one. First, it ignores species that are higher taxa, whereas morphology is about species at all levels, not just the infima species. We cannot begin to identify the infima species without recognizing the higher levels of classification. Secondly, 'consistently and persistently' is both vague and irrelevant. Thirdly, 'ordinary means' is also a vague tip of the hat to common sense. No mention is made of form, and common sense needs this more than it needs an account of what is 'ordinary'.

According to Shull, '[s]pecies may be defined as the easily recognized kinds of organisms, and in the case of macroscopic plants and animals their recognition should rest on simple gross observation such as any intelligent person can make with the aid only, let us say, of a good hand-lens' (Shull 1923: 221). Again, irrelevancies abound. One wonders whether the *Archaea*, for one, would meet this definition. The tools of identification are irrelevant, as is the ease or difficulty of identification. Gross observation is very important in morphology, but it does not mean, say, simple observation of shape, anatomy, or body plan, though these are all important factors to consider. Gross observation just is the indirect observation of form via properties, which is a *holistic* practice involving an overall identification of the characteristic structure and function of the organism in question. Ecological, ethological, reproductive, recognitional, as well as anatomical, physiological, genetic and other criteria must be pooled together to arrive at an overall morphology for an organism. There might not be a straight empirical test for essence (see Chapter 3), but the fact that accidents do occur in clusters provides empirical evidence for arriving at an *intellectual* – not an empirical – judgment that an organism has a certain morphology that distinguishes it from other, perhaps very similar, kinds of organism. The presence or absence of one accident often causes the presence or absence of others, and a variation in one often causes a variation in others in ways that significantly affect structure or function. All of this helps to ground a morphological judgment.

So why not replace morphology with some version of a cluster theory? Indeed this is what we find in Boyd (1999) and Wilson (1999b), in which they seek to revive biological essentialism in the guise of 'homeostatic property clusters' (HPCs). An HPC is a cluster of properties such that no one or more of them *must* be possessed by an individual to which the term 'species' applies, but *some* of which properties must. The properties are homeostatic 'in that there are mechanisms that cause their systematic coinstantiation or clustering' (Wilson 1999b: 197). As far as species go, they are defined by HPCs consisting of 'morphological, genetic, ecological, genealogical, and reproductive features'. The cluster 'tends to be possessed by any organism that is a member of a given species', but none of them is a 'traditionally defined essential property' and 'no proper subset of them is a species essence'. No property is more basic than any of the others, and so they do not form a 'strict ontological hierarchy' (Wilson 1999b: 199). Possession of every member of the HPC is sufficient for membership of a given species, but possession of only one of a disjunction of subsets of the HPC is necessary.

The HPC theory looks like another version of the bundle theory of essence, and to this extent it suffers from the general weaknesses outlined in Chapters 4 and 7 and elsewhere throughout this book. In particular, homeostatic clusters must be unified by a metaphysical principle in order to yield an essence. The mere presence of causal interactions between different accidents of an organism does not guarantee that any of them belong to its essence and so qualify as genuine properties. For instance, it might be the case that if the height of a certain animal were to vary it would not be able to obtain certain sorts of food. There might be a solid causal relation between such accidents. Yet they might be no more than *mere* accidents rather than properties indicative of essence, since an animal might belong to its species without having to have that particular height or the particular capacity, to acquire a kind of food, which co-varies with height. There might actually *be* other such conspecific animals that have a smaller height than the target animal and so are unable to obtain the same kinds of food; but their conspecificity is not undermined for that.

Connected to this is the obvious question of just which disjunction of homeostatic properties an organism must possess in order to be conspecific with another organism; in other words, what is 'enough' of the properties that must be possessed? The response of both Boyd (1999: 143–4) and Wilson (1999b: 201) is that this is an a posteriori matter, and also that its indeterminacy simply reflects the continuities in nature. I have already argued against indeterminacy. And as for its being an a posteriori matter, this is of no assistance unless the investigator making the a posteriori judgment is *herself* guided by a principle. Wilson does not even allow some homeostatic properties to be more basic than others, though Boyd does (Boyd 1999: 144), but Boyd says, again, that relative importance is an a posteriori matter. Yet how can the investigator know which properties are more important than which? Morphology gives the answer, because all properties, whether homeostatic or not, are referred back to the unified way in which an organism functions given its structure. The contrast by Boyd, Wilson, and others between morphological features, on the one hand, and ecological, reproductive, genetic, and other features, on the other, betrays their thinking of morphology in terms only of something like shape, body plan, anatomy, or such like. Form is none of these, but it encompasses them all as well as the features with which morphology is mistakenly contrasted. The investigator has to be guided by the following question when studying causally interacting clusters of characteristics: 'Is there a distinctive structure and function in this organism which differentiates it substantially from the comparators I am using as a point of reference?'

Mayden cites this definition from Regan which, for all its generality, comes close to embodying the principle guiding an answer to the question just posed: '[a] species is a community, or a number of related communities, whose distinctive morphological characters are, in the opinion of a competent systematist, sufficiently definite to entitle it, or them, to a specific name' (Regan 1926: 75). The competence of the systematist, however, must be assessed not just empirically but philosophically. If the systematist treats morphological characters incorrectly, for example as equally significant, as floating free of a unifying substantial form, or in a limited way as only associated with, say, shape or body plan, he will fall into taxonomic error. Unfortunately, most discussions of morphology abound in such mistakes. The application of morphology to species is not for the taxonomist only, or for the ethologist or geneticist, or for any particular biological or zoological specialism. Nor is it for the metaphysician. It is for the metaphysically informed scientist competent in all of the fields required for morphological analysis.

What Mayden himself has to say about the morphological concept of species is illuminating. First, he concedes that it 'is probably considered the most sensible and commonly used method of species definition by taxonomists, general biologists, and laypersons alike' (Mayden 1997: 402). And this despite the overwhelming influence of cladistics. Secondly, he says that in the case of allopatric populations (those separated by a geographical barrier) information about reproductive isolation is usually unavailable, so morphological distinctiveness is only a 'surrogate to lineage independence' (Mayden 1997: 403). But this is a false contrast: morphology *includes* reproductive behaviour, as well as mate recognition, communal behaviour (such as herding) and every other kind of function or operation. If I come across two populations of *Canis lupus familiaris* isolated by an ocean, and one consists of St Bernards and the other of Dachshunds, and I don't know much about dogs, I might be inclined to count them as belonging to different species. If morphology is just about body shape, then it will often not get the taxonomist very far. But once I find out that, at least with some artificial assistance, Dachshunds and St Bernards can interbreed, probably with fertile offspring, I have very good if defeasible evidence that they are conspecific (defeasible because fertile hybrids occasionally occur). Once I find out more about the way they interact with each other, the way they behave towards humans, their anatomy, physiology, genotype, habits and instincts, reaction to non-canines, and so on, I can come to a very strong conclusion that the St Bernard and the Dachshund are both varieties of domestic dog. The example might be homely, but the principle is not.

Further, Mayden says that morphology 'bridges a decided gap' between sexual and asexual species – an important advantage over other concepts. But he goes on to assert that the morphological distinctiveness must be 'heritable and representative of lineage independence' (Mayden 1997: 403). Yet why should it be heritable if, as evolutionists hold, a mutation in an asexually reproducing organism could result in a morphologically distinct species? And lineage independence is not what morphology represents, but the reverse: the former is indicative of the latter.

The 'only real problem' with the morphological concept, Mayden further concedes, is that the possibility of sibling species, cryptic species, or plesiomorphic morphologies, means the morphologist will 'underestimate biological diversity' by counting as conspecific what are in fact lineage-independent species that merely 'appear similar'. The problem is not real. A plesiomorphy is an ancestral character shared by divergent taxa – examples are the five-digit limb or the possession of a backbone, shared by most or all land mammals. If the morphologist were only concerned with plesiomorphies he would have a classification problem. But plesiomorphy is not all there is to morphology. Derived characters, specialized to different species, are also part of the overall morphological analysis and provide many of the differentiae used to distinguish species. Similarly, sibling species, which look very much alike but are reproductively isolated or otherwise genetically distinguishable, would only be a problem if they were morphologically identical. The various species of bird known as the flycatcher (*Empidonax*), for example, sometimes look very alike, but they are not wholly indistinguishable to the trained eye. Even if they were, their different birdcalls enable them to tell each other apart. Birdcall is as much a part of morphology as colour or shape. So is reproductive isolation itself, and genetic variation, though in the latter case one would expect such variation to show up in some kind of structural or behavioural difference. (On sibling species, see Mayr 2002: 182–3. 'Cryptic species', I should add, is just another term for 'sibling species'. Being cryptic refers to their similarity; siblinghood refers to their being in fact distinct species. Hence Mayden is making one point by using these terms, not two.)

Mayden does raise another 'potential problem', namely that there is

> the inherent tendency to require an arbitrary level of morphological divergence. By employing such a criterion the researcher assumes that all morphological traits, especially those traditionally employed in a taxon, evolve at a constant rate of divergence. This is an unjustified assumption and is falsified by the observation that even within a taxonomic group morphological divergence is largely random.
>
> (Mayden 1997: 403)

It is not clear what the potential problem is. The morphologist need make no assumption about rates of evolution. All that matters is that conspecific organisms have the same morphology relative to the level of classification in question. All mammals are metaphysically conspecific (i.e. are in a metaphysical species, albeit not an infima species – what biologists usually mean by 'species') inasmuch as they share a mammalian morphology. Whatever the randomness of mutation, there is nothing random about being in the same taxon due to shared morphology. A mutation that throws up a morphologically distinct organism by that very fact throws up something belonging to a different taxon, whatever the process involved. Mayden's objection is obscure at worst, irrelevant at best.

Finally, despite his meagre criticisms, Mayden concludes that the morphological concept is 'fatally flawed as a primary concept' of species, finishing his evaluation with the usual refrain that morphology 'does not allow the researcher to treat species as historical entities forming lineages'. To this he adds the confused remark that 'the definition of every species will necessarily change as the essential attributes of a species at t_1 will be different from t_2 through descent' (Mayden 1997: 403). The definition of a species does not change. If the essence is different, the species is different, whether the change is diachronic (descent) or synchronic (variation at a time). Historical descent is important for diagnosing species identity, and species do exist over time, so in this sense they are historical entities just like any other substance. But they are not *defined* by their lineage, and as such are decidedly *not* historical entities.

In sum, morphology has far more going for it – properly understood – than biologists and philosophers of biology acknowledge, even the ones who grudgingly concede its commonsensical approach and general usefulness, whether on its own or as an adjunct to some more 'primary' concept. The search for such a primary concept, with morphology out of the picture, has proven somewhat elusive. With morphology in the picture, we have a concept that ties biology to metaphysics. Any other usable concept of species turns out to be the handmaid of morphology, not the other way around.

10 The person

10.1 The essence of personhood

The clash between classification by descent and classification by essence might be thought relatively insignificant in the overall scheme of things. What does is matter whether organisms, let alone inanimate objects, have essences? And if they do, what does it matter that the essences should be identified with evolutionary lineages – in particular with lineages in between speciation events (for species) or with monophyletic groups containing the most recent common ancestor and all its descendants (for higher taxa)? Of what overriding importance is the decision to classify according to one principle rather than another?

The fact that science should be in harmony with metaphysics, and that metaphysics demands a certain way of looking at classification, is important enough. But in this chapter I want to focus on a more limited, and in many ways more important, topic. That topic is *us*. For the correct metaphysics of classification by essence has profound implications for our conception of ourselves as human beings. These implications were already recognized by Darwin and have been trumpeted by evolutionists ever since, from T.H. Huxley in Darwin's time to Richard Dawkins in our own. In other words, evolution was from its beginning as a formal theory (rather than loose speculation) permeated by a philosophical view of things, a view famously summed up in the words of the palaeontologist George Gaylord Simpson: '[t]he meaning of evolution is that man is the result of a purposeless and materialistic process that did not have him in mind' (Simpson 1967: 345). And again:

> [Darwin] gave an answer to the tremendous question that so deeply concerns ... What is Man? [He] answered this question to the effect that man is a natural product of the universe; ... man is an animal, a vertebrate, a mammal, and a primate. ... By bringing man into the evolutionary picture, Darwin finally took the last step in our emancipation and finally made our world rational.
>
> (Simpson 1959: 271–2)

Most evolutionists, however (including Simpson), go on to recognize something 'special' about human beings, whether it be that we are moral beings, or self-conscious, or responsible, or of unique intelligence or problem-solving capacity, and so on. In all of this they are right, but such features are all aspects of man's fundamental rationality. Man is, as Aristotle said, a rational animal.[1] And possessing rationality looks like something metaphysically of a different order from what characterizes the other animals. (The intelligence of some primates does not, I believe, amount to rationality, at least not in the sense in which I will explain it. I do not have space to explore that here.) In other words, the rationality of human beings seems to call for a special classification. Yet looking at humans according to standard phylogeny, we do not seem to occupy a distinctive place in the scheme of things. Phylogenetics has given extra impetus to the Darwinian idea that we are but another product, among millions, of naturalistic evolutionary processes that did not have us in mind. As Colin Tudge puts it – and his remarks are worth quoting in full:

> To be sure, Darwin's idea of evolution has overtaken the eighteenth-century, anti-Enlightenment conceit of special creation; but well into the twentieth century many biologists instinctively felt that human beings represent the culmination of evolution, and that our species is not simply the centre of evolutionary unfolding but is in effect the point of it: indeed, to a large extent, biologists merely substituted the word 'evolution' for 'creation' in an otherwise traditional account of how life came into being. But in the late twentieth century we can see that our contribution to the genealogical tree of life is as peripheral and minuscule as that of Earth to the Universe. The tree as we see it now is truly vast. Since life first began on Earth, it has probably produced hundreds or even thousands of billions of twigs, where each twig is a species; and *Homo sapiens* is just one of them. Furthermore, and more significantly, the tree has at least three great boughs [*Archaea*, *Bacteria* and *Eukaryota*], and each bough has many branches, and our twig is part of just one of them. In short, our species has been as comprehensively peripheralized by biology as it has by cosmology; and the biological discipline that has brought about this shift is that of systematics, which I take to be classification based on phylogeny.
>
> (Tudge 2000: 95)

The passage implicitly refers to the Copernican Revolution; the passages before it explicitly do so. Tudge is here representing the mainstream view of modern taxonomy: just as Copernicus overthrew the view that our world was metaphysically unique in the cosmos, so Darwin destroyed forever our view of ourselves as unique in that world. We are, so Tudge and the phylogeneticists contend, no more important than the smallest – albeit perhaps shiniest – fruit hanging off the remotest spur among a thicket of branches in an enormous tree. It is hard to know the extent to which phylogeneticists are in part *motivated* by a desire to dethrone man from his singular position among living beings. Maybe this is just a happy outcome of an otherwise objective and scientifically rigorous reconfiguration of taxonomical method. I argued in Chapter 9 that phylogenetic classification, particularly in the form of cladism, suffers from a number of flaws, one of the most important being its confusion of efficient with formal causes. Whatever the *origin* an organism may have, what it *is* according to its substantial form is something distinct. Human beings are no exception. Whatever our origin in the tree of life, we are whatever our essence is (the true law of identity, as stated in Chapter 5.1). And our essence is what constitutes us *intrinsically*, even if, as per necessity of origin, we may have some properties restrictive of the kinds of origin we could have had (see Chapter 7.5). Hence, even if the human species came into existence by descent along the lines shown in Figure 5.4, its metaphysical classification will be something altogether different.

Having said that, does what we are restrict the *kind* of evolutionary origin we could have had? Does it preclude an evolutionary origin at all? I am not going to examine these questions here, at least not directly. The limits inherent in evolutionary explanations of human nature have been forcefully argued by O'Hear (1997), among others, and to canvass the issues would require a whole other discussion. In this, the final chapter, I am going to confine my analysis to a strictly essentialist examination, on hylemorphic terms, of what the human being is. I will not say anything about whether any of the other hominids that have existed are or are not 'one of us'. (For overviews, see Klein 1999; Bilsborough 1992; Reader 1988.) Interesting as the question is, it is irrelevant to the argument I will present: if any of them were rational, they were of our species; if none were, they were of different species. Nevertheless, given what I will try to show about the ontology of human nature, it is certainly hard to see, on either biological or metaphysical grounds, how we could have come into existence purely by descent with modification, whether according to the lineage in Chapter 5.2 or otherwise. More generally, the position I will defend seems straightforwardly incompatible with any purely *naturalistic* origin of the human essence. But if what I have to say about human nature is correct, that is a problem for evolutionary theory in general and for naturalism in particular, not for the theory of human nature. Maybe the evolutionary account will need radical modification. Maybe it will need to be abandoned as a theory of human origins. Maybe it will need to recognize phenomena that cannot be explained in its own terms. These are issues that I will put aside for another day.

10.2 Hylemorphic dualism

It is one thing to say that the essence of the human being is to be a rational animal. It is another to explain just what that involves and why it is so radically distinct from the other essences that exist in our spatio-temporal world. The position I am going to defend is a kind of dualism, but very much unlike the standard dualistic theories that represent the current minority view in the philosophy of mind and the theory of personal identity. It is also quite distinct from what passes for dualism in the usual textbook expositions.

Despite the fact that it continues to have followers, and that it can be said to have enjoyed something of a micro-revival in recent years, dualism persists in being more the object of ridicule than of serious rational engagement. It is held by the vast majority of philosophers to be false, mysterious, bizarre, obscurantist, or unintelligible. Its adherents are assumed to be biased, scientifically ill informed, motivated by prior theological dogma, cursed by metaphysical anachronism, and/or to have taken leave of their senses. Dualists who otherwise appear relatively sane in their philosophical writings are often treated with a certain benign, quasi-parental indulgence.[2]

The 'dualism problem', as one might call it – the problem of the odd place of dualism as no more than an intellectual curiosity in current debate, its adherents characterized as 'swimming against the tide'[3] – is complicated by the fact that when it comes to attempts to describe and then, predictably, refute dualism it is almost without exception the Cartesian form that takes centre-stage. There is as well a respectable place for property dualism,[4] the theory that, although the mind is material, mental *properties* such as consciousness are not reducible to material properties such as states of the brain. Event dualism has also begun to attract attention (e.g. Pietroski 2000), this being the view that the correct distinction is between mental *events*, such as thoughts, and the physical events, such as brain processes, to which the former are irreducible.

Still, Cartesian dualism has clear and unassailable pride of place as the whipping post on which dualists are ritualistically flailed. The idea that the mind is a separate, immaterial substance in its own right, with only a contingent relation to the body it inhabits, is said to raise a host of problems. How could such an entity interact causally with a physical body? Exactly what sort of relationship does this spiritual substance have to a body? What are the identity conditions for such a substance, and how in the end can such an obscure kind of thing explain anything about human mental life?

I will not defend Cartesian dualism in this chapter. Nor will I tackle the thorny question of mind–body interaction, though the position I set out has deep implications for how we should answer it. Instead, I will lay out a case for the sort of dualism that gets little attention and that, if any form of dualism is defensible, is by far the best candidate. Hylemorphism being the general metaphysical theory for which I have argued throughout this book, the correct account of the human being – better, the human *person* – is also a form of hylemorphism. Hence the obvious name for it is *hylemorphic dualism* – the dualism of Aristotle and the Aristotelians, most notably Aquinas and the Thomists. It has lagged behind the other dualisms as far as the number and prominence of its contemporary defenders are concerned, though there are signs of renewed interest and serious intellectual attention.[5]

The central claims of hylemorphic dualism begin with two theses that will by now be familiar: (1) all substances are compounds of matter and form; (2) the form is *substantial* since it actualizes matter and gives the substance its very essence and identity. Now follow theses (3) the human person, being a substance, is also a compound of matter and substantial form; (4) since a person is defined as an individual substance of a rational nature, the substantial form of the person is the rational nature of that person; (5) the exercise of rationality, however, is an essentially immaterial operation; (6) hence human nature itself is essentially immaterial; (7) but since it is immaterial, it does not depend for its existence on being united to matter; (8) so a person is capable of existing, by means of his rational nature, which is traditionally called the soul, independently of the existence of his body; (9) hence human beings are immortal – but their identity and individuality does require that they be united to a body at some time in their existence. I have already defended (1) and (2), so will only say a little about them. The defence of (3)–(9) will be the main burden of this chapter.

10.3 Consciousness, psychology, and the person

Before going on to defend theses (3)–(9), however, I want to say a little about the nature of current debate about what a person is. This debate has, in my view, been skewed in recent years by the thought that *if* there is a residual puzzle that has not yet been solved by the twentieth century's onslaught of materialism, naturalism, and physicalism, it must be the problem of *consciousness*. As Chalmers (1996) summed up the so-called 'hard problem', if there really is something that materialists cannot successfully grapple with, it is the phenomenology of conscious experience, the felt quality of our interaction with the world. Everything else about the mind, according to Chalmers, can be captured within a physicalistic functionalist model. To be sure, there is still the problem of explaining how to *identify* the correct functional analysis of human psychological operation, but that there is one, and that it is at least in principle realizable in inorganic systems such as computer models, is something already taught to us by cognitive science.

This bifurcation of the question of the nature of the mind, and hence the nature of the person – into a question about human cognition on the one hand and a separate question about the special 'problem of consciousness' on the other – and then the subsequent focus on the 'problem of consciousness' as *the* outstanding conceptual issue in the quest for a total naturalistic theory is, I submit, quite mistaken. I do not deny that there is indeed a 'problem of consciousness', and that many of the central claims of the non-reductionists, including so-called 'naturalistic dualists' such as Chalmers, are correct: principally, that there is no explanation of the subjective nature of conscious experience in physicalistic terms. What I do deny, however, is that this is a problem affecting only the phenomenology of conscious experience rather than one concerning the psychological in general. For it is at least plausible to claim that there is also a *phenomenology of psychology* as much as of conscious experience, and the typical responses to such a claim look, as they do in respect of conscious experience, to be question-begging.

By a phenomenology of psychology I mean simply the 'what it is like' of ordinary psychological operations such as judging, reasoning, and calculating. There is, I submit, even 'something that it is like' to calculate that 2 + 2 = 4. It may not be qualitatively identical for all people, but then neither is the taste of strawberry ice cream exactly the same for all people. Moreover, one might suppose this whilst at the same time noting that our similar physiological structures imply that the individual experiences for each kind of act should be highly similar. They would contain a certain phenomenological core, and the class of such experiences would be such that its members were all more similar to each other, all things being equal, than they were to any experience involved in a different mental act, state, or process.[6]

It might be objected that the phenomenology of calculating that 2 + 2 = 4, if there were such a thing, would hardly be different from that attending the calculation that 4 + 4 = 8, thus reducing the idea to absurdity – a distinction without a difference. Yet this would be as misplaced as denying the distinct phenomenologies of seeing reddish yellow and seeing yellowish red because they are so similar. That there are such phenomenological differences in calculation is not something for which there is non-introspective proof any more than there is for the standard kinds of qualia to which non-reductionists (such as Jackson and Chalmers) draw attention. (For a useful list, see Chalmers 1996: 6–11.) Yet introspection does, I believe, make apparent the qualitative character of calculation, a character easily heightened by comparing, say, the experience of doing algebra with that of doing calculus. Again, there is a conscious experience of performing a piece of deductive reasoning that differs from that attending the judgment of a single proposition. I cannot offer here a taxonomy of such experiences, or anything like a catalogue of dimensions of similarity such as can be done, to some degree, for the usual perceptual experiences on which the debate always settles. All I propose for consideration is that there is a phenomenology of psychology, whatever the details.

It will not do to respond (as would most defenders of the idea that artificial intelligence captures the essence of human cognition) that, since computers can do arithmetic and by their very nature have no conscious experience, it must be the case that what I claim to exist for human beings is an illusion. For the response assumes that what we do and what computers do when they calculate that 2 + 2 = 4 is the same in the first place. As a matter of scientific sociology, for what it is worth, no one has the faintest idea of what *humans* do when they do arithmetic – specifically, what goes on in the brain when even the simplest of calculations is carried out. Hence, as one would expect, there is no agreement on what physical system best models what we do.[7] But the logical point is that one may not assume that what humans and computers do is fundamentally the same; rather, this is a proposition that has to be proved. Moreover, the phenomenological evidence in the human case is so strong that we have an a priori reason for thinking that *whatever* physical model is proposed it will not capture what we do. One could, of course, seek to show that some physical model captures what we do *if* one took there to be no problem concerning the reduction of conscious experience in the first place. But this is a claim that dualists of all stripes deny, so minimizing the problem will gain no traction. Nor, again, is it of any force to claim that since humans can perform unconscious calculation, such an activity can have no phenomenology. For the question is not about what we can do when unconscious. Similarly, if unconscious perception were a genuine phenomenon (a matter of dispute: see, e.g., Merikle and Reingold 1998), this would not disprove the existence of subjective experience during conscious perception. So one cannot neutralize the claim that there is a phenomenology of psychological activity by appealing to unconscious kinds of the same or similar activity.

Is it not a pretty exotic if not irrelevant claim that there is a problem of consciousness for psychology as much as for sensory experience? Yet it is important for present purposes, since it highlights the error involved in trying to understand the human essence by corralling consciousness into a corner of the mind, particularly that corner associated with the mind's lowest function, namely perception. It is no more than a perpetuation of the Cartesian error of identifying the soul with awareness. It positively invites a dichotomizing of the human being into a conscious self plus the physical add-ons. For the Cartesian dualist, this means identifying the person with the soul. For the reductionist, reacting in a perfectly understandable way to the ontological split, it means doing away with the Cartesian soul as a piece of obscure metaphysical baggage and reducing the person to some collection or other of physical states of whatever complexity.[8] Dualists must resist both errors, and they can only do so by insisting on the essential unity of the person. To point to the fact that human psychology is shot through with phenomenology is but one way of emphasizing that unity; and it is that unity which is at the heart of hylemorphic dualism.

It would be wrong to deny that either phenomenology or consciousness in general is relevant to the problem of explaining the essence of the person: any plausible theory must, for example, account for a person's sense of self as an enduring entity, his capacity for higher-order conscious states, and his awareness of himself as a being endowed with freedom and responsibility. What I am denying, however, is that the problem of the human essence is primarily one about phenomenology or consciousness. Rather, it is about human psychology, where this means the specific mental operations of the human being.

10.4 Form, body, and soul

I follow the classic definition of Boethius (480–524 AD): a person is defined as an individual substance of a rational nature.[9] The human person[10] is a certain kind of individual rational substance – a rational animal. The substantial form of the person – her nature – just is the person's rational animality, the genus being animality and the difference being rationality; it is also called the person's *soul*. Anyone who objects to the term 'soul' as metaphysically or theologically loaded can simply use the term 'rational animal nature' or 'rational nature' (where the latter implicitly includes animality) wherever 'soul' will appear in what follows. It is now necessary to understand exactly *of what* the soul is the form.

First, as argued in Chapter 4.2, each substance has only one substantial form. This form permeates the entire substance and is therefore the principle of all of its proper activities. Secondly, as argued in Chapter 4.3, the form actualizes pure potentiality, i.e. prime matter. As applied to persons, the situation is this. A person, like any other substance, is actualized by a substantial form. This substantial form is the principle by virtue of which the person is a person, and that means the principle of life, of consciousness, and of rationality. These are all one principle since the doctrine of unicity applies as much to persons as to any other substance. The fact that persons are also sentient and alive does not mean that there are three forms – the form of life, the form of sentience, and the form of rationality. For what could this mean? There are not three distinct substances – the organism, the animal, and the rational creature – any more than there is a single person with three essences. There is but one substance with one essence – a person who is living and sentient and rational. What gives the *person* life is precisely what makes the *person* sentient, and what makes him sentient is just what makes him rational, even though canine sentience, by contrast, does not involve canine rationality. The reverse also holds: for instance, what makes the *person* rational is also what makes him organic, since the sort of rationality persons have essentially involves the use of sensation, and sensation requires life. There may be kinds of rationality that do not require sensation (such as God's), but they are irrelevant to consideration of the human person.

The person, then, like any substantial kind of thing, is an essential unity manifesting a multiplicity of operations: one nature, many manifestations of that nature. The nature is called by hylemorphists the soul, the term having been traditionally used for all living things as denoting their principle of animate operation – even plants – but now restricted to human beings. Why not say that the soul is the form of the body, just as the hylemorphist says that the person is a union of body and soul? As explained in Chapter 4.3, there is nothing wrong with speaking this way, as long as we are not misled. The soul is not the form of the body as a spherical shape is the shape of a lump of bronze. Rather, it is like a father's being the father of his child, or this shade of crimson's being the shade of this red patch. In the latter case, there are not two accidental forms – red and crimson – co-existing where the single colour patch is. What makes the patch crimson is by that very fact what makes it a shade of red rather than of some other colour. Of course, if we analyse colour in terms of wavelengths, or hue and saturation and so on, it is true that what makes the patch red is not what makes it crimson, since a patch can have the physical characteristics by virtue of which it is red without having the characteristics by virtue of which it is crimson. But the crimson accident is not an add-on to the redness accident, as though the patch were first red, then crimson, in some temporal sequence or order of existence. Rather, the patch has a determinate shade of red: it is at one and the same time determinably red and determinately crimson. Its redness is an abstraction from its crimsonness.

Similarly, the person is not first a body (with hands, feet, a brain, etc.) and then a union of body and soul, whether we construe this as a temporal sequence or an order of existence – as though it were 'primarily' or 'fundamentally' a body, and 'secondarily' or 'additionally' a combination of body and soul. The principle whereby Fred has hands, feet, and a brain is the same principle as that whereby he is rational – a single form actualizing pure potentiality. His having a body – in particular an animal body – is *generically* true of him; it puts him in the genus *animal*, and so his being an animal is an abstraction from his being a person. Similarly, his being rational is his specific difference, and so is also an abstraction from his being a person. Genus and difference are both abstractions from a single essence. Once we grasp this way of understanding essence, we can speak of a person as a union of soul and body, indeed as having two physical component to their essence, where 'physical' means, in the traditional sense, 'of the nature (*physis*) of the thing'. By nature, a person is a thing with a body, and that body is animated by rationality, down to its fingers and toes (which does *not* mean Fred has rational toes!).

Possible objections will be: what if humans, as evolution tells us, evolved from non-human ancestors? Doesn't that mean humans have a body first and a soul second? Isn't a human just an ape with a soul? The reply is that *if* the current account of human descent is correct, the first human will *not* have come into existence first as an ape, only to have rationality 'zapped' into it at some early stage of its existence. Not even the most diehard evolutionist believes that. The first human to have the first rational thought (à la the Eureka moment in the film *2001*) would not have been an ape that got lucky via a bolt of lightning, but an animal that, from the beginning of its existence, was empowered (due to a mutation in the gametes of its parents) to think and act rationally.

A related objection is that rationality is first true of individual human beings at some time *after* they come into existence. Aren't there humans first, and don't they become rational some time later? Such is the view of *personists* in bioethics, who separate humanity from personhood, treating the latter as a phase of human existence much like being an adolescent or middle-aged. Interestingly, the personist view of human beings is in some ways similar to the Scholastic view, held by Aquinas among others (following Aristotle), of 'delayed ensoulment', whereby the rational soul was thought to come into existence at least forty days after conception.[11] The Scholastic view (incorrect but a natural one for them to have held, given their limited knowledge of the process of fertilization and embryological development) gives no support, however, to the view that hylomorphism is at least *compatible* with the thought that rationality is a metaphysical add-on to a pre-existing human body. For this was not their position; rather, they thought that what existed immediately prior to rational ensoulment (itself an act of God) was an animal that was sufficiently materially complex to be turned, by *substantial transformation*, into a body made human by the infusion of a rational soul. Hence the Scholastic view gives no weight to the idea that the soul is the form of a pre-existing *human* body; on the contrary, they come into existence at exactly the same time, the latter by virtue of the former. (For a good overview of Aquinas's position and clarification of common misinterpretations, see Haldane and Lee 2003a, 2003b, criticizing the views of Robert Pasnau; see Pasnau 2003 for a reply.)

The personist agrees that the advent of personhood is a delayed event in the generative process, but according to him the event does not involve a substantial change, only an accidental one: a pre-existing human being takes on rationality at a certain stage of, say, brain development. This view is in conflict with the idea that personhood and humanity cannot come apart *vis-à-vis* the human person. For it confuses the *exercise* of rational thought with the *power* of rational thought. A creature can have the power to do *X* without having the *use* or exercise of the power, say because it is not at the right developmental stage. Rationality is built into the human embryo from the moment it comes into existence: all it needs is maturation before it can use that power. (I cannot discuss the issue in detail here. See Oderberg 2000: ch. 1 for more.)

10.5 Soul, intellect, and immateriality

In what sense, then, is hylomorphism a kind of dualism? The hylemorphic theory is dualistic with respect to the analysis of *all* material substances without exception, since it holds that they are all composites of primordial matter and substantial form. When it comes to persons, however, the theory has a special account. The soul of Fido, for instance, is wholly material in the sense of being wholly materially dependent for its operation. In other words, all of Fido's organic and mental functions are material inasmuch as they have an analysis in wholly material (though not necessarily physico-chemical) terms. The soul of a person, on the other hand, is wholly immaterial, the argument for this being that a person has at least some mental operations that are not wholly explicable in material terms – and we can deduce what a thing's nature is from the way it necessarily acts or behaves. If, however, some such operations are not wholly materially explicable, the soul itself cannot be anything other than wholly immaterial because there is no sense in postulating a soul that is a mixture of the material and the immaterial.[12]

To take the last point first, if the soul were a mixture of the material and immaterial it would be subject to contrary properties: *qua* material it would have spatio-temporal properties, *qua* immaterial it would not; *qua* material it would have material parts, *qua* immaterial it would not; *qua* material it would be divisible, *qua* immaterial it would not. (See also *De Anima* III.4; Ross 1931: 429a25.) Although very much imperfect, the analogy with abstract objects is useful: the colour red, for instance, though wholly dependent on material tokenings for its existence, is in its own nature an immaterial, abstract object, not a mixture of the material and the immaterial. Its very immateriality is what allows it to be wholly instantiated in more than one place at one time, which is not possible for material objects. But if it is true of immaterial objects wholly dependent on material instantiation that they are not a mixture of the material and the immaterial, how much more will it be true of immaterial objects that are not wholly materially dependent? (We will see this lack of dependence in section 10.6.) Note also that this point does not exclude the following. (1) The *person*, being a *compound* of matter and form, is a compound of the material and the immaterial. In this sense one can speak loosely of the person's being a 'mixture' of the material and the immaterial. The soul, however, does not have parts and so is not itself a compound object (I will assume rather than argue for this point): so it would really possess contradictory properties only were it to be both material and immaterial, which it is not. (2) The soul, although immaterial in itself, can be described as having a certain essential relation to matter, in that its complete operation requires embodiment. Again, however, this does not mean that the soul has contradictory properties.

Now if the soul is immaterial, it follows that human nature is immaterial, since the soul of a person just is that person's nature. This can be defended via the concept of a hierarchy of capacities. Although one might baulk at the idea of such a hierarchy, in fact the idea is easily explained by saying that F-type capacities are superior to G-type capacities just in case the former entail the latter but not vice versa. It follows that sentience is superior to nutrition because sentient operations require nutritive ones but not vice versa – we have abundant examples of this. Hence the nature of an object that has sentience and nutrition as capacities is sentient, and by implication nutritive, but not merely nutritive. In other words, the nature of a thing is defined in terms of its highest capacities. (See further Chapter 8.) Human rationality is superior to both human sentience and human nutrition according to the definition given, so human nature is defined in terms of the rational capacity. But if the rational capacity is immaterial, it follows that human nature, i.e. the substantial form of the human person, is immaterial. (This does not imply that nutrition, say, is an immaterial process, only that human nature, being essentially immaterial, contains a *power* of nutrition that can exist apart from any embodiment. But in the absence of the requisite material conditions – embodiment and objects upon which to act – that power cannot be exercised.)

There are various ways of establishing the immateriality of human reason, or the human intellect, and consciousness does play a large role in some of them (see, e.g., Moreland and Rae 2000). But as I have already suggested, an excessive focus on consciousness is liable to distort the debate about human nature; it is also deleterious to our very conception of it. Instead, hylemorphists take their primary cue from Aristotle, who asserts that the intellect has no bodily organ.[13] In other words, intellectual activity, i.e. the forming of ideas or concepts, the making of judgments, and logical reasoning (as all grounded in fundamental intellectual powers),[14] is an essentially immaterial process, i.e. intrinsically independent of matter, however much it may be *extrinsically* dependent on matter for its normal operations in the human being.[15] The Aristotelian position, it must be emphasized, is not that hylemorphism *of itself* entails the immateriality of the intellect, but that within the hylemorphic conception, considering the *specific function* of the human person, the intellect must be immaterial. The central theses of hylemorphism in general, then, tell us in what manner and to what extent the human person is immaterial, as I will explain in section 10.5 and following.

The reason for the truth of the proposition that the intellect is immaterial is that there is a *fundamental ontological mismatch* between the proper objects of intellectual activity just mentioned and any kind of potential physical embodiment of them: we might call this the *embodiment problem*, but looked at in a slightly narrower way, in cognitive-scientific terms, it might be called the *location* or *storage* problem. Concepts, propositions, and arguments are abstract; potential material loci for these items are concrete.[16] The former are unextended; the latter are extended.[17] The former are universal; the latter are particular. Nothing that is abstract, unextended, and universal – and it is hard to see how anything abstract could be other than unextended and universal – could be embodied, located, or stored in anything concrete, extended, and particular. Therefore the proper objects of intellectual activity can have no material embodiment or locus.

To complicate the problem even more for the materialist, consider those concepts that are not only universal, unextended, and abstract, but also semantically simple. Suppose, per impossibile, that the materialist could overcome the problem of the first three features of concepts, adding that those that are semantically complex, such as the concept of a *black dog*, had their locus in the brain spatially distributed in a way that mirrored their complexity. Thus, suppose the concept *black* had location A, the concept *dog* had location B, and some kind of structural relation between A and B constituted the relation between these concepts as elements of the unified concept of a *black dog*. (Whether it is even right to analyse complex concepts in this way is another matter that cannot be discussed here.) Now what about simple concepts such as the concept of *unity*, or of *being*, or of *identity*? Such concepts do not admit of analysis into semantic parts, though it is possible to explicate the notions contextually, illustrate them, and so on. They are, nevertheless, semantically simple. So there is not even a prospect of finding a material locus for such concepts, assuming all the other difficulties could be overcome, unless the putative locus is materially simple, in the sense of being material and yet metaphysically indivisible.

Yet the very idea of a material metaphysical simple makes no sense. If a material object were simple it would be unextended – but then in what sense would it be material? An extensionless point is not a something but a nothing, and so cannot be a locus for concepts, which are something. Further, extensionless points cannot have any constitutive relation to the extended, which is why Aristotle was adamant that the infinite divisibility of space is only potential, not actual. Suppose, however, we could make sense of the idea of a material metaphysical simple – could it be the candidate locus for simple concepts? Well, are we to postulate a simple located in the brain? If so, is it the same simple that embodies all simple concepts? It would have to be if we were to postulate a single mind having those concepts. But it is hard to make sense of the idea of multiple simple concepts in one materially simple location – about as hard as making sense of many dimensionless points located at one dimensionless point. Yet if we proposed multiple material loci, we would have to account for the mental unity by which one mind has many concepts. All of this without yet integrating into our account complex concepts, like that of a *black dog*, given the existence of materially simple loci. We do not want to give complex concepts simple loci – how could that be possible? Yet if there were a non-simple location for such concepts, in the way suggested above, for example, how again could we account for mental unity given that the simple concepts had simple locations? All in all, the existence of simple concepts merely aggravates the already immense difficulty of smoothing over the fundamental mismatch between concepts and their putative material embodiment.

Needless to say, one of the fundamental problems of cognitive science, in its ubiquitously materialistic contemporary guise, has been to explain the storage of concepts. Yet most of the research is either beside the point insofar as it attempts to solve the embodiment problem, or else yields precious little knowledge. For example, one recent paper notes: 'A common feature of all concrete objects is their physical form [note the use of the term "form," which in the context of the paper means something more than shape]. Evidence is accumulating that suggests that all object categories elicit distinct patterns of neural activity in regions that mediate perception of object form (the ventral occipitotemporal cortex)' (Martin and Chao 2001: 195). The authors go on to describe how functional brain-imaging techniques show that representations of different object categories are located in discrete cortical regions that are 'distributed and overlapping', embedded in a 'lumpy feature-space'. To be sure, functional imaging may well reveal *correlations* between certain intellectual activities and certain cortical activities: for the hylemorphic dualist such correlations are only to be expected, since persons as embodied beings require corporeal activity in order to interact with the world. Persons are not pure spirits capable of immediate intellectual apprehension or action upon the environment (assuming such things to exist for the purpose of contrast). Nevertheless, the substantial form is what directs and controls corporeal activity, whether by acting upon physical inputs or producing physical outputs.[18]

The authors go on, prudently, to say:

> Clearly, it would be difficult, as well as unwise, to argue that there is a 'chair area' in the brain. There are simply too many categories, and too little neural space to accommodate discrete, category-specific modules for every category. In fact, there is no limit on the number of object categories.
>
> (Martin and Chao 2001: 196)

Indeed, this latter observation points again to the ontological mismatch between concepts and their putative material embodiment. The intellect is capable of grasping a potential infinity of concepts, but no corporeal organ can harbour a potential infinity of anything.[19] In particular, the intellect is distinguished by this feature: that it can grasp a potentially infinite number of *categories* of concepts, and within each category a potentially infinite number of exemplars. In other words, there is no limit to the number of kinds of thing the intellect can recognize, and no limit to the number of examples of each kind which it can grasp. By contrast, the eye or ear, for instance, can only receive colours and sounds, respectively; and within each kind of sense datum they can only receive a limited number of examples – hence we cannot naturally see certain colours or hear certain sounds. The very physical finiteness of the organs of sight and hearing means they are bounded with respect to what kinds of information they can take in. This is patently not so for the intellect – and it does *not* exclude the fact that the intellect, being finite in its own way, cannot discover certain things. There is a difference between the intellect's not being able to reach certain truths by its own operation and its suffering an intrinsic *material* limitation on the kind of information it can take in. The absence of the latter, again, is consistent with its being *extrinsically* limited in respect of the physical information it can take in: for example not having the concept of a colour that is beyond the visual spectrum available to the eye. But if the sort of limitation I have been talking about applies to the eye and the ear, it must apply to *any* proposed organ for embodying concepts. The features of the eye and ear that make them singularly unsuitable for intellectual operation apply equally to the brain, the nervous system, or any other proposed material locus. It is the very materiality of such a locus that would prevent it from embodying the proper objects of intellectual activity.

If researchers into functional imaging have shown anything, then, it is merely that category-specific object recognition is correlated with activity in certain distinct, if highly diffuse and non-discrete, regions in the brain. But this sort of research, as interesting and as potentially useful for brain-damaged patients as it might be, goes no way to even beginning to provide a theoretical or empirical foundation for the idea that concepts, judgments, and inferences themselves have a physical location.

There are, of course, many kinds of challenge that might be levelled against the defence I have given of the immateriality of the intellect. You might level a Rylean-style charge of illegitimate reification against the very idea of concepts as things.[20] You might object that an appeal to immateriality to solve the embodiment problem is a classic case of *obscurum per obscurius*. You might deny that there are concepts in any meaningful sense at all and claim that there are only distinct, particular acts of representation. There is no space here to canvass these and other objections. But the general reply should be emphasized, namely that a refusal to reify concepts means an inability to explain fundamental semantic and logical phenomena: not merely the fact that the concept of a *black dog* is a function of the concept of *black* and the concept of *dog*, but that the *concept-possessor* understands this, which is more than saying he can *recognize* a black dog only if he can recognize black things and dogs. Rather, it means that if he has those concepts he can *see* how one is derived from the others. Mutatis mutandis for judgments and inferences. And if a person *grasps* a certain concept, and if that concept is an object (*pace* Frege's worries about the concept horse),[21] then the person grasps an object. Since this is a mental act, his mind must take hold of something, and if it takes hold of a thing then that thing must make a kind of contact with it. This means, since there is no other plausible way of understanding it, that the concept must somehow be in its possessor's mind. But if a concept is not the sort of thing that can be physically inside the possessor's brain, his mind cannot be his brain, and moreover must be immaterial since only an immaterial thing can be suited to laying hold of the concept.

10.6 Soul, identity, and material dependence

What, then, of the complex relationship between the soul, the person, and the matter the soul informs to produce the person? The first thing to note is that the soul is not the person.[22] The person is the human being, the substantial compound of matter and form. A person is an individual substance of a rational nature, but the soul is not such a substance – for it *is* the rational nature, not a substance *with* a rational nature. Hence the fundamental flaw in the Cartesian conception of the person is the illegitimate identification of the person with the soul, taking them to be one and the same substance. It might with good reason be said that Descartes, having given up on the notion of substantial form[23] yet eager to preserve personal immortality, had nowhere else to go. Yet the mistake is basic, and leads to so many of the problems that have dogged Cartesian dualism ever since.

Next, given the unicity of substantial form, one cannot take there to be separate, lower orders of soul or nature in the human person. Growth, nutrition, reproduction, sentience, perception: all of the operations of the organism belong to the unique human nature of the person. A human being is an essential unity, not a plurality. Some of those operations, however, depend essentially on matter – such as reproduction and sensation – and others, such as the operations of the intellect, as I have argued, do not. But if the person is not to be broken down into a plurality, how do we reconcile the partial dependence and partial independence of matter that we find in human nature? We have to say something like the following. The person, being essentially embodied, depends for its existence and identity on embodiment, as also for some of its operations. Whether it exists at all depends upon its having a human nature individualized in matter; and *which* person it is depends on which material individualization it is. Again, this is not proposed as an analysis of identity in other terms, but as an account of the *causes* of that identity.

To say, however, that the person is existence- and identity-dependent on its embodiment does not entail that all of its parts depend for their existence on being united in the embodied person. As an imperfect analogy, we observe that a broom cannot exist without a brush but the brush can exist without the broom to which it belonged. That is, it is not a universal truth that if an F cannot exist without a certain part P, then P cannot exist without F: it depends on the kind of thing one is talking about. In the case of non-rational animals, we can say that the animal cannot exist without its soul, but neither can the soul exist without embodiment in the animal since all of the animal soul's operations are wholly material, not rising beyond sensation and perception of the concrete particular. On the other hand, since some of the operations of the intellectual soul are not material, it can exist without its embodiment in matter. The principle at work here is the following: x can exist without y if and only if x can operate without y. The first half is that if x can exist without y, then x can operate without y: if x exists without y, then x's nature is actualized without y; but if x's nature is actualized, then x possesses the very operations given to it by its nature, and so can operate according to that nature without y. x might operate in an imperfect way because of the lack of y, but its essential nature and the functions proper to that essential nature will not in themselves be destroyed. Fido can exist without his tail, so he can function without his tail even though the lack of a tail impairs that function. But he cannot exist without a head, and so cannot function without a head.

The second half of the biconditional says that if x can operate without y, then x can exist without y. If x can operate without y, albeit perhaps imperfectly, then x must have a nature that can be actual without y's being actual. But for x to be actual is for x to exist, and for y not to be actual is for *y* not to exist. So *x* can exist without *y*. I can function without ten fingers; so I can exist without ten fingers. I might not be able to hold a baseball bat without ten fingers, but holding a baseball bat – indeed being able to hold anything – is not essential to my functioning as a human being. By contrast, I cannot function (at least in the material world) without a heart (or without something that fulfils the role of a heart); hence I cannot exist (in the material world) without a heart (or something that fulfils that role). Whether or not the biconditional is true for any *x* and *y* or only for material substances, the hylemorphist only needs it to be true for living things in order to make his point about human souls as opposed to other souls. Since the human soul can operate without matter, it can exist without matter. It might exist in an imperfect state, since it could not, for instance, perform acts of sensation that require material stimuli and the formation of mental images, but it can still exist apart from matter.[24]

Although the soul of the person is not existence-dependent upon matter, in the way I have claimed – it does not require material embodiment to exist – it is implausible to deny that its existence depends upon matter in the following sense: that it must be embodied at *some* time during its existence. This is a weaker form of existence-dependence, and it follows from the fact that the human soul just *is* the rational nature of an individual substance belonging to a certain *species*. Human persons just are embodied creatures, and so not only must their souls be 'attached' to their bodies – at least at *some* time in their history – for them to exist, but their souls, in order to be *souls of persons*, i.e. in order to be what they are, must also be at some time the *forms* of bodies. This means that the idea of a human person disembodied throughout its history is incoherent. Such a being might be a disembodied person, but it would not be a disembodied *human* person because human persons are just not that kind of thing. In which case, if the human soul has a disembodied existence, that existence can only be made possible by its once having been the form of a body.[25] Further, it is also *identity-dependent* on its once having been the form of a body.[26] In other words, to be the particular soul that it is, it must once have been the form of a particular body making a particular individual substance of a rational nature; just as, in its embodied state, the soul's identity depends on whose, i.e. which person's, soul it is.[27] In short, the principle of individuation for persons must be *cross-temporal*.[28]

As far as identity goes, I have already argued (Chapter 5.5) that form is the bearer of the identity of a substance, in the sense that it is the primary part of the substance responsible for its being the substance it is over time. The soul, as the form of the body, is therefore also the bearer of personal identity. From the subjective point of view, when I reflect upon my own identity as a person it is my soul that exercises that intellectual operation, recognizing itself as the bearer of my identity as a person. This does not mean that the first-person pronoun is ambiguous, only that it refers to me as a person by means of referring to that person's chief part, which is the soul;

just as, when I say 'I am in pain' after I stub my toe, 'I' refers to me as a person by means of one of my parts, in this case my toe: I am in pain because my toe is in pain. (I take the primary reference of the first-person pronoun, as used by me, to be myself as a person; but I would say, tentatively, that the reference to my soul (in the case of thought) or my toe (when I stub it) is a kind of secondary or *instrumental* reference.)

In the disembodied state, I continue to exist; that is, the person that is me persists despite my physical *death* – which is the separation of my form from my matter – even though one of my constituents, namely my body, does not. What this means, then, is that my death results in the person that I am *continuing to exist as my chief part*, namely the part by virtue of which I am specifically different from any other kind of animal. When the body my soul informs ceases to exist, as surely it does at some time, the person I am dies but does not thereby cease to exist; hence death and cessation of existence, for entities like us, are not the same event.[29] I persist both *as a person* and as the form that once was the form of the body that was a part of that person. My soul is the bearer of my identity as a person, but I am not, and was never, nor will ever be, strictly numerically identical with my soul.[30] Another imperfect analogy helps to make the point. Suppose it were technically possible to reduce my organic existence to that of a bodiless head.[31] Then I would exist *as* a head, but I would not be numerically identical *with* a head any more than I would have been numerically identical with my whole body. There would be no reason to affirm one and deny the other, yet affirmation of both would violate the transitivity of identity. And yet in *some* sense I would be a head: perhaps we can say that I would be *constituted* by a head, as I was once constituted by a whole body. (Let us leave aside the soul for the moment – the point is supposed to be graspable by materialists as well.) Although the concept of constitution is not well understood, I think that the best way of interpreting it in this context is to say that my existing as a head just means my being reduced to one of my parts, my existing in a radically mutilated state – just as I might, through a terrible accident, be reduced to a legless torso without being numerically identical to a legless torso.

Finally, the consequences for personal responsibility must be something like the following. If persons die when their souls leave their bodies – though they do not cease to exist, unlike the case of other substances whose form and matter are separated – can any sense be made of a soul's bearing any responsibility for the acts of the whole person of which it once was a constituent? To pursue the gory analogy of the bodiless head, there does not appear to be anything repugnant to reason in the idea that a person existing solely as a head should be punished for crimes committed while the head was connected to a body (mutatis mutandis for a person existing as a legless torso). Yet perhaps intuitions differ strongly on this question.

I think we can accommodate any divergence by considering generally whether sense can be made of the idea that a part of an *F* can be held responsible for the acts of a whole *F.* To see that such an idea is not only coherent but has real-world application, consider the case of a corporation (a legal and moral person) whose chief executive is held responsible for that corporation's illegal actions. Considering the corporation as a kind of aggregate or collection, and its directors as constituent parts of that collection, we can see that the chief executive as a part of the corporation can be held responsible for the latter's transactions, as can the directors in general.[32] It is true but irrelevant that the courts have traditionally been reluctant to impute such responsibility in a blanket fashion, their reluctance being motivated not by metaphysics but by a recognition of the disincentive such blanket responsibility would be to anyone thinking of becoming a director, let alone CEO, of a corporation.

All we need to see is that it is coherent to suggest that a part might be held responsible for the action of the whole – moreover that not any part will do, but only that part (or those parts) which are, as it were, in the driver's seat. The soul, if it is part of the person at all, certainly is in the driver's seat; so if any part of the person can be held responsible, it must be the soul. But since, as I argued, the person I am continues to exist *as* a soul (even though I am not numerically identical *with* a soul), it must be me who is responsible precisely for what I did when my soul informed a certain body.[33] But doesn't this imply a twofold responsibility, and hence a twofold punishment or reward (if there be such after death)? No, because the soul is held responsible solely by virtue of its being the chief part whereby *I*, the person, did whatever I did that incurred responsibility. As Aquinas puts it, I am rewarded or punished 'in the soul' for what I did when my soul informed my body. To return to the example of my being reduced to a bodiless head, if it is true to say that the head suffers a punishment, it does not do so *qua head*, but *qua* the part that now constitutes *me*. If there is to be any punishment at all of bodiless me, the only way it can be carried out is *by* punishing my head.

10.7 Conclusion

My aim in this chapter has been to set out the main lines of the much neglected hylemorphic theory of the person, and of the dualism that is at its heart. It has not been possible to canvass the many questions and objections that may be raised. If I have shown nothing more than that the theory is worthy of far more serious attention than it has commonly been given – my hope for the entire book – then that will be enough. I do, however, want to conclude with a general observation. The theory that I am not strictly identical with my soul, hence that soul and person are distinct, the person having an essential connection to its body as well as its soul, seems more strange to dualist ears than it should.

This is partly to do with the 'problem of personal identity', as it has come to be known. A problem with a relatively recent currency (due to Locke), it is more fitted to a metaphysical viewpoint that at the very least takes the ideas of disembodied existence and of the immateriality of the soul to be at best highly problematic, at worst not even worth a place in the conceptual landscape on which the problem is grappled with. More strongly, I would venture to say that the problem of personal identity is a problem made for materialists – at least those materialists who take seriously the peculiar ontological status of the mental, the existence of free will and rational agency, and perhaps even the possibility of a future life. The contemporary dualist reaction to materialism, however, has tended to be one of recoiling from the idea of any essential connection between body and soul, and hence between person and both. This has led in turn to making the apparently 'obvious' move (for the dualist) of identifying person with soul, or at least of regarding person and soul as having an exclusive essential relationship.

For the hylemorphic dualist, on the other hand, the acceptance of a genuinely immaterial element in the human essence means a greater flexibility in trying to comprehend just how human persons persist. The concept of form can be pushed heavily into service, as can the idea of the person as a compound substance, in this respect just like a material substance – namely, a substance composed of matter and form. Nevertheless, the hylemorphic dualist must avoid the disastrous fall into Cartesianism or Platonism, both of which diminish the role of the body in personhood. Once the soul is united to a body, it is the form of that body for all time, even after that body has ceased to exist. Its identity after death – and hence the identity of the person that is reduced to it – depends on its having once informed certain matter. The soul must always have a retrospective character, one that looks back on what choices it made when it actualized that matter, and hence on what the person did of which it was once the chief part. (Again, think of the chief executive who, long after his corporation's demise, is forever tarred with the brush of responsibility for those decisions *he* took – and hence that his corporation took – when he was its chief constituent.)

The soul has, as it were, the indelible stamp of personhood, and due to its very nature as an actualizing principle of matter it has an essential tendency or direction toward the full flowering of its capacities in matter. Whether it may also look forward to a *reunion* of itself with matter is, however, beyond the scope of philosophy to answer.

Notes

1 Contemporary essentialism and real essentialism

1 For useful surveys, see Divers (2002); Girle (2003).
2 Noting personal communication from Lewis.
3 If it is a relation at all: see Chapter 5, note 1.
4 I use 'Leibniz's Law' here only for the Indiscernibility of Identicals.
5 That is, one has to grasp that a certain property (necessary self-identity) applies to a thing before one can grasp that the very same property (necessary identity) also applies to it.
6 I have heard some philosophers deny categorically that Leibniz's Law is a species of the Law of Non-Contradiction, but I have not heard a good reason for the denial and contend that anyone who attends to just what Leibniz's Law is *saying* cannot fail to see that this is so. See further Oderberg (2004b): 691.
7 That is to say, it is a virtual part of his essence that he is *at least* a material object, which is all I need to make the point. It is another question whether he is *only* a material object.
8 To be an entity of some sort or other is just to be a being. I do not, though, think that *being* is a genus, i.e. an ontological category of the same logical sort as, say, *substance*. For more on this, see Chapter 5.3.
9 Perhaps necessary distinctness can be said to apply across the board to all entities, in which case Socrates's necessary distinctness from the Eiffel Tower is also a feature of him insofar as he is an entity of some kind or other. But some might object that it does not apply across the board inasmuch as asserting the necessary distinctness of, say, the set of prime numbers from Socrates would be a category mistake; hence my restriction to material objects. In any case, whatever one's view of category mistakes, all I need to make the point is the fact that there is a suitably general characterization of Socrates such that necessary distinctness is part of his essence as formally stated at that general level. If this is the case, as I think it is, then being necessarily distinct from the Eiffel Tower is virtually part of Socrates's essence.
10 Although I cannot go into details, the sense of logical presupposition I am using here takes it to be a species of entailment, according to which the thing entailed is implicit in the thing that entails. In this sense the thing entailed can be taken to be a necessary condition of the thing that entails. Such a sense excludes the thought that 'p v q' is either implicit in the content of 'p' or a necessary condition of its truth, even though the former is entailed by the latter.
11 This does *not* mean he is virtually a material object. He is *actually* one, but being a material object is not part of his formally stated essence as rational animal, which comprises the lowest genus and the specific difference (about which much more later).

12 Or, if one wants to get more general, as an entity of some sort or other. See note 8.
13 Note: sometimes I use the term 'property' in a loose sense to cover any characteristic or feature of a thing, prescinding from whether it is essential to it. Sometimes I use the term in a context where it is clear I mean something essential to the thing. Later on (in Chapter 7 in particular) I give the term a more technical meaning, restricting it to features that are essential but not *part* of a thing's essence and explicating it in terms of essence. Until then, I will mostly use terms such as 'feature', 'characteristic', and 'quality' when speaking wholly generally rather than about essence in particular, but loose uses of the term 'property' will occasionally appear. Context should make it clear in what sense I am using the term.
14 I am talking only about the natural numbers.
15 For representative passages giving Aristotle's approach to numbers, see Aristotle's *Metaphysics* XIII (M): 3 in Ross (1928b): 1077b17–30; 1078a2–8; 1078a21–6.
16 If all light disappeared tomorrow there would no longer be any colour. But this does not mean objects are not coloured in the dark, because being in the dark just means not being currently illuminated. Light still exists.
17 I use scare quotes because the normal meaning of 'miracle' just implies something resulting from direct divine causation, so by definition God could not cause something to come into existence wholly uncaused.
18 Husserl 1970: 252.
19 For more on constitution, see Wiggins (1980: 30ff.); and for an extended discussion (not without its problems), see Baker (2000).
20 http://www.wordreference.com/definition/water (accessed 27 April 2006).
21 Encyclopaedia Britannica 2006 Ultimate Reference Suite DVD (accessed 27 April 2006).
22 There is plenty of debate as to whether the multiple realizability argument against reductionism has any force. It was made popular by Fodor in 'Special Sciences' (Fodor 1974) but has come in for criticism, a recent example being the work of Jones (2004), who sees no problem with disjunctive laws and kinds at the lower level to which higher level types are reduced. Jones, however, fails to give attention to the *heterogeneity* point concerning disjunctive physical realizers of higher-level types. Perhaps there are *some* disjunctive physical (or other) laws and kinds, but it does not follow that there *must* be one for every multiply realizable higher-level type if the only conceivable realizers are sufficiently heterogeneous, which in fields such as economics (Fodor's favourite example) is egregiously the case. Jones also claims that, even if there is no lower-level law, it does not matter since we can proceed on a disjunct-by-disjunct basis to effect a reduction using bridge principles for each case, which is all the reductionist needs. The problem here, apart from the fact that the proposal is more in the form of an IOU than a proof, is that for all we know it is disjunctions all the way down – that the problem may reappear at every level at which a token reduction is supposedly available.
23 The lump of marble partly constituting the statue does itself have an essence that is partly microstructural. But it does not follow that the *statue* has an essence that is microstructural. For more both on artefacts and on the role of microstructure in essence, see especially Chapter 7.
24 I am not endorsing this latter point: it's just that if it were true it would be irrelevant to the statement of realism. (The kind of case that may count in its favour: I wince at the first touch of the dentist's drill, thinking it hurts, and quickly realize that I'm not actually feeling anything, or that the pushing sensation I do feel is not after all painful.)
25 See Ross (1928b: 1030a). No one is quite sure why Aristotle used the imperfect in *to ti ēn einai* – literally 'the being what it was'. The Romans struggled over it and ended up with the term *essentia*.

26 To be accurate, this statement needs qualification. What I am talking about are only objects that fall into species and genera, as will be explained in Chapter 5. There are objects, in particular God, that are logically not multipliable. But that is because God is not in a species or genus, and this is because it is of the nature of the divine being to be metaphysically unique. For St Thomas Aquinas's argument for the metaphysical uniqueness of God, see Aquinas (1955: ch. 42, pp. 158–64). For a contemporary argument, see Hoffman and Rosenkrantz (2002: 166–8).

27 I am restricting myself, as I do throughout the book, to essence as it appears in the material world. My account will not carry over literally to cases such as God or disembodied spirits. I will occasionally say a little about such entities, but the general real essentialist position is that we need to give an *analogical* account of their essences, which extends and is compatible with the approach taken to the world of the material. Elements of such an account will be found in Chapters 5.3, 5.4, 6.1, and 6.2.

28 I will desist from continually placing 'scientific' in scare quotes both for easiness on the eye and, more importantly, because to keep using them might give the impression that I think scientific essentialism is pseudo-scientific. It is not that it is pseudo-scientific, but that it is not an accurate account of the way the world is, for all the correct aspects of the theory. On the more traditional use of the term 'science' (*scientia* = knowledge), this flaw does make it unscientific. The temptation to keep the scare quotes, however, comes from the unmerited monopoly Ellis claims for 'scientific', as though real essentialism of the kind I defend does not deserve the title.

2 Some varieties of anti-essentialism

1 Although I mention only Locke in what follows, the anti-Aristotelian, anti-essentialist revolt in the post-Scholastic period goes back to Hobbes, Bacon and various philosophers of lesser prominence. For an example of Hobbes's attack on 'the entities and essences of Aristotle', accompanied by numerous misunderstandings of just what real essences are (as well of other traditional doctrines), see the penultimate chapter of *Leviathan* (Hobbes 1991: ch. 46, pp. 458–74, 465 for the quotation in the text here), whose title makes his position clear: 'Of Darkness from Vain Philosophy and Fabulous Traditions'.

2 At least on one reading, Kant is making a similar objection in respect of Cartesian souls: see the Third Paralogism in the *Critique of Pure Reason* (Kant (1933: 341–4, A362–6).

3 In the medieval Scholastic terminology, *agere sequitur esse*.

4 For more on the critique of bare particulars, see Mertz (2001), and the subsequent discussion in Moreland and Pickavance (2003); Mertz (2003).

5 For a good discussion of relations such as instantiation, which he calls 'formal ontological relations', see Lowe (2006: ch. 3). Lowe is also at pains to emphasize that the instances of universals are not the objects possessing the qualities that the universals are identical with in their concrete manifestation, but the modes or particularized qualities themselves. In this I think he is almost certainly correct. (I follow Lowe in reverting to the more traditional terminology of modes rather than tropes.)

6 What if you see a green thing but to you it looks blue – have you observed greenness? This sort of case is not problematic, since if it is possible to see a green thing whilst not seeing it *as* green, then by parity of reasoning one can see greenness without seeing it *as* greenness. If this is thought objectionable, then the essentialist can claim that if you do not see a green thing as green you do not see a *green* thing at all and so do not see greenness at all. The former interpretation seems more plausible.

7 Again, I am not concerned with whether the definition is strictly accurate, though it is the one agreed upon by most current icthyologists.

8 Although this definition is correct, and I will refer to it often throughout the book, this does not exclude its being made more precise or detailed, supplemented by biological and psychological specificity.

9 I leave aside convoluted questions about whether one can observe a mind directly. In the broad, non-technical sense, I take it that one can do so: one can observe *that* Jack has a mind by observing his rational behaviour; and in doing so one observes his mind as well as one observes most things.

10 This supports the univocality interpretation of 'triangle', but we should not conclude that ancient geometers themselves actually *meant* by 'triangle' what the univocality interpretation holds, namely that 'triangle' means 'closed, three-sided, rectilinear figure'. The ancient geometers thought Euclidean triangles were only a genus, not a species of triangle, hence for them 'triangle' almost certainly had the more restricted Euclidean meaning. So a hypothetical conversation about triangles between an ancient and a modern geometer would have been at cross-purposes. The univocality interpretation, however, indicates that modern geometers considered non-Euclidean triangles to be sufficiently similar to Euclidean ones to be called, still, triangles, hence that *Euclidean triangle* was a species of a triangle as well as a genus. LaPorte would have it that the decision whether to call non-Euclidean triangles *triangles* was a mere stipulation. Yet the decision was not merely one about what to *call* certain polygons, but how to *classify* them, and mathematicians evidently reached the plausible decision that the space in which a polygon is constructed is not essential to it and can be separated from primary features such as rectilinearity – where rectilinearity is understood in Euclidean terms (as the shortest distance between two points) even by modern mathematicians.

11 In Chapter 9.1 I assert: 'That an essence is fixed means that nothing that possesses it can cease to possess it without ceasing to exist, and that when something comes to possess it that thing begins to exist'. Elliott Sober has objected in correspondence that a thing can cease to possess the essence of bachelorhood without ceasing to exist. I reply that it is this mistaken way of thinking that leads to Quine's paradox in the first place. The mistake is generated in part by equivocation over an expression such as 'possess the essence of bachelorhood'. Bachelorhood is a universal – specifically, it is an *accident*. And every accident has its essence (see Chapter 7). The essence of bachelorhood is to be a certain kind of relation between a man and certain social institutions. But when a man is a bachelor *he* does not possess an essence over and above his human essence; he possesses an accident that *itself* has an essence. *He* does not acquire essential features by virtue of his bachelorhood, even though bachelorhood *itself* has essential features.

12 David Lewis is arguably a kind of relative essentialist, basing his essentialism on counterpart theory: see Lewis (1983b, esp. section III). Note that in Postscript C he acknowledges that he is 'by no means offering a wholehearted defense of "Aristotelian essentialism"', adding that the vagueness of the counterpart relation means that 'almost anything goes. The true-hearted essentialist might well think me a false friend, a Quinean sceptic in essentialist's clothing' (1983b: 42). For criticism of his so-called essentialism, see Forbes (1986: 22–6).

13 The number of planets used to be nine, but in an attempt to keep up with the vagaries of astronomy, and in deference to the recent decision of the International Astronomical Union to downgrade Pluto, I have changed Quine's example from nine to eight.

14 Under pressure from critics, though, he moves around between various possible diagnoses of the problem.

15 See Smullyan (1948: 31–7).

16 To see more explicitly how we can avoid resort to analysis in terms of first-order logic, the point I am making can be illustrated by employment of the Traditional Formal Logic (Term Functor Logic, or TFL) developed by Fred Sommers (1982), and as modified for numerical quantification by Lorne Szabolcsi. 'Eight planets exist' can be rendered as 'Eight things are planets', which can then be paraphrased into 'Exactly eight things are planets'. Numerical term logic allows us to turn this into 'More than seven but no more than eight things are planets', which, using the formalism of TFL supplemented by numerical terms, gives us +[+ 7 T + P] + [−8T − P]. No matter how we plausibly render '8 is necessarily greater than 7' using TFL, the two propositions will not give us 'The number of planets is necessarily greater than 7'. (On numerical term logic, see Murphree (1998). Szabolcsi's work is as yet unpublished. For more detail, see also Pfeifer and Kleiter (n.d.).) I am grateful to George Englebretsen for discussion of this topic.

17 Founder of Cynicism, companion of Socrates and later an opponent of Plato; *c.*446–366 BC.

18 Literally *ōieto euēthōs*, 'thought simply/stupidly'.

19 I will leave out the 'etc.', but note that we need only use abbreviated and incomplete definitions for present purposes.

20 For instance paddlefish.

21 Aristotle and the Scholastics typically use examples such as 'seated Socrates' and 'white man'.

22 Popper misinterprets Aristotle's other reference to Antisthenes on essence (in *Metaphysics* 1043b24), even more seriously than he does the reference at 1024b32 (Popper 1966: 300). He claims Aristotle *agrees* with his own criticism of essence, since the former cites Antisthenes with approval, who (in Popper's words, interpreting what Aristotle says about Antisthenes) 'attacked essentialist definitions as useless, as *merely substituting a long story for a short one*; and it shows further that Antisthenes very wisely admitted that, although it is useless to *define*, it is possible to describe or to *explain* a thing by referring to the similarity it bears to a thing already known, or, if it is composite, by explaining what its parts are' (emphasis Popper's). This, says Popper, Aristotle agrees with, only to 'wander off' the subject later by bringing in genus and species, and matter and form.

This reading is mistaken. For Antisthenes's criticism is levelled at *Platonism*, and Aristotle agrees with him only insofar as he has Plato's theory of essence as his target. According to Plato, essence is given by form only, and form is an immaterial thing subsisting apart from matter. As such it would have to be simple. But simple things are incapable of definition, since a definition breaks an object down into something that is determined by something else – for the Aristotelian, genus as determined by specific difference (speaking abstractly), and matter as determined by form (speaking concretely). Hence, for the Platonist, whatever is proposed as a definition could not really define anything, but could only be an account of what something is like – in Aristotle's example, that silver is like tin. But the Platonist cannot say what silver *is* essentially, since the essence of silver is an indefinable form. Aristotle explicitly contrasts Platonism with his own theory of essence as complex, and it is curious that Popper does not notice this. For a clear and correct interpretation of Aristotle, see St Thomas Aquinas's *Commentary* on the *Metaphysics*, Book 8, Lesson 3 (Aquinas 1995: 564–8).

23 The term 'natural kind' is far too vague and misleading to be of much use in essentialist thinking. Plenty of contemporary philosophers would say they believe in natural kinds but not in essences, and there are various ways (e.g. evolutionary) of describing kinds as natural without committing oneself to their being unified essentially. Only by giving the term a much stricter definition could we equate it with 'essential kind'. Still, contemporary essentialists typically use the term 'natural kind' in a way that means nothing more or less than 'essential kind'.

24 Not to be confused with anything transcendental in the Kantian sense.
25 There is much more to the definition of substance than this, and I will canvass some of the issues in Chapter 4.4. But the traditional conception of substance given here is accurate and sufficient for our purposes.
26 There are all sorts of questions about what any explanation, let alone an ultimate one, consists in. My point is solely that if we think ultimate explanation is impossible *because* there can be no most general explanation, then the thought is unjustified.
27 Jesper Juul provides an amusing and instructive example concerning 'food': see http://www.jesperjuul.net/ludologist/?p=115 (accessed 22 May 2006).
28 I discuss some of the essential features of art, in a fairly popular way, in Oderberg (2004a).
29 Wittgenstein, of course, has a technical meaning for 'grammar', covering all usage that contributes to sense, but the point still applies.
30 A Wittgensteinian might reply that our conceptual scheme (what the spectacles metaphorically represent) might not determine *truth*, i.e. what there is, but it does determine what *makes sense* (what we *can* see through the spectacles). In reply, I claim that our conceptual scheme is not the determinant of sense any more than of truth. True, conceptual confusions tautologically show up in our misuse of concepts, but the logical basis of such confusions is not the misuse of concepts but the nature of reality. The reason that it is confused to say the number 7 is yellow stems from the natures of number and of colour, and hence from the metaphysical possibility or otherwise of certain kinds of predicate applying to certain kinds of thing.
31 This should not be taken as an endorsement of Putnam's overall semantic theory. I am simply extracting the most plausible and general part of his account and using it to explain essentialist methodology. As far as semantics goes, it is not the primary concern of metaphysics. (See Chapter 1 and, further, Chapter 3.5.)
32 As we will see in Chapter 10, both of these claims are false, though each points to a truth about the human essence.
33 Where philosophy is mentioned, not specifically metaphysics.

3 The reality and knowability of essence

1 Here, of course, I am referring to tokens, not types.
2 Here I use the term 'property' in the loose, contemporary sense. Rationality is, strictly speaking, not a property but a specific difference – a distinction that will be explained throughout the book, especially in Chapters 5 and 7.
3 They are traditionally called properties or *propria*, but also *proper accidents*, *necessary accidents* (as in Gorman 2005) and *necessary properties*. I will generally use the unqualified term 'property', but equivalent terms such as those just mentioned will appear from time to time, as well as terms such as 'essential feature' and 'essential property', since these highlight the important connection between properties and essence. A property is no part of a thing's essence, but it is not merely necessary – it *flows* from, is *explained by* and is a *consequence of* the thing's essence.
4 For a brief but good discussion of what he calls 'constitutive essence', see Fine (1995a: 56–8). He contrasts it with what he calls 'consequential essence' and explicitly draws the analogy with essence and properties (or *propria*). His use of logical consequence, however, is worrying, since we do not want to count being a man-or-a-mouse as a property of Socrates even though it logically follows from his being essentially a man. This does not seem to bother Fine. Gorman (2005: 280–1) makes the same point.
5 The case could be made with reference to various parts of the anatomy, but modesty prevents my going down that route.

6 In the context of this discussion I follow Elder in using the term 'property' in the loose, contemporary sense equivalent to 'quality' or 'feature'. As explained earlier, and as I will do for most of the book, I will normally reserve the term 'property' to mean, in the strict sense, necessary accident, i.e. quality, feature, characteristic, or other modification that flows from a thing's essence and is necessary to things of that kind because of their essence.

7 Again, construing 'property' loosely, as does Elder.

8 'Ratio humana essentias rerum quasi venatur' (quoted in Coffey 1914: 76).

9 Leave aside violation of the Third Law of Thermodynamics for the purposes of the argument.

10 Putnam eschews 'species/genera' terminology, whereas the essentialist avoids 'natural kind' talk as far too vague. See Chapter 2, note 23.

11 This is an expansion and interpretation of Hugh Mellor's brief remarks. I am grateful to him for confirming (in personal correspondence) that my interpretation is correct.

12 If you don't like angels then choose your favourite disembodied minds.

13 In Chapter 5 the relations between genera and species will be spelled out in detail.

4 The structure of essence

1 6th–5th centuries BC.

2 The same sentiments are of course found in Spinoza. For Aristotle's response in the *Physics* to Parmenides, see Ross (1930: 191a24ff.).

3 From the Greek *hylē* (matter) and *morphē* (form).

4 Even though the form may exist without *present individuation* by matter, about which more in Chapter 10.

5 Descartes says this about substantial forms:

> For they were not introduced by philosophers for any other reason than that by them an explanation might be given for the proper actions of natural things, of which the form is to be the principle and root, as was said in an earlier thesis. But clearly no explanation can be given by these substantial forms for any natural action, since their defenders admit that they are occult and that they do not understand them themselves. For if they say that some action proceeds from a substantial form, it is as if they said that it proceeds from something they do not understand; which explains nothing.
> (Descartes's letter to Regius, January 1642, in Adam and Tannery
> 1899: 506)

He also says that 'the prophets and apostles, and others who composed the sacred scriptures at the dictation of the Holy Ghost, never considered these philosophical entities, clearly unknown outside the Schools', and that substantial forms are 'nowhere, we think, clearly mentioned in Holy Scripture' (Descartes's letter to Regius, January 1642, in Adam and Tannery 1899: 502). Although Descartes is here responding directly to the charge by the Calvinist theologian Voetius that the former's denial of substantial forms is inconsistent with Scripture, the context suggests that he is more than happy to sound triumphant about there being no clear biblical mention of them, as though this lent positive support to his denial. Contrary to popular parody, however, Scholastic method hardly takes reference in Holy Writ to be a criterion for the acceptability of a philosophical concept.

6 As a matter of historical fact, it would have been all but impossible for students of philosophy such as Locke and Hume, given the era in which they were edu-

cated, to have been given a correct instruction in Aristotelian and Scholastic metaphysics. This was no strict fault on their part.

7 Note that the problem Elder raises is not that of vagueness, which he proposes to solve degree-theoretically. I say more about vagueness in biology, with only a gesture towards the more general problem, in Chapter 9.3.

8 In fact their analysis does *not* count cotton glued to a heavy object as a mereological compound, despite what they say, since their proposal requires a relation of 'connectedness' between the parts of the compound, where one can trace a path from one part to the other via a series of 'joinings' defined in terms of dynamic equilibrium. Since there is no join, in the technical sense, across the thread and the heavy object at the point at which they are glued, any more than there is a join between the whole thread and the heavy object, there is in fact no finite series of joinings such that the thread and heavy object form a mereological compound on their analysis. Lest this be thought only to help their case by discounting what common sense tells us is not a genuine piece of matter, note that one could easily change the example. On their analysis, a caravan firmly attached to a car yields a mereological compound. Yet even if we can make sense of the very idea of counting material objects (if we can't, so much the worse for their whole project), it would be bizarre to answer, when questioned as to how many large objects one was looking at, 'Three – the car, the caravan and the car + caravan'.

9 It was famously defended by Aquinas, but denied by Avicebron (Ibn Gabirol), Avicenna (Ibn Sina), Averoes (Ibn Rushd), Albert the Great, and Duns Scotus, among others. For a historical account of the debate, see Callus (1961).

10 The writers are not themselves (at least overt) hylemorphists, it should be noted. See, e.g., Hoffman and Rosenkrantz (1997) (at least for lumps of matter conceived as mereologically variable, which is how we standardly consider them); Merricks (2001); van Inwagen (1990).

11 We can safely leave aside such transient phenomena as the continued growing of hair and nails post-mortem.

12 A sortal term, here 'dog', tells us what sort of thing – in the most liberal sense – an object is. A phase sortal is a sortal term applying to a thing that goes through a temporary stage or phase denoted by the term; e.g. 'teenager' is a phase sortal under which human beings fall. A *substance* sortal, on the other hand, is such that an object that falls under it *must* fall under it or else cease to exist altogether, e.g. 'human' for human beings.

13 Not even cryo-preservation can delay the onset of all forms of disintegration, which is why it will be of doubtful use to those who have been so preserved.

14 Note that this does *not* imply, absurdly, that Fido's nose is a dog, only that Fido's nose is nothing other than a canine one. The canine form is not partially present in the nose – it is wholly present but it informs the nose and every other part according to its own exigencies *qua* canine form. The way a substantial form informs the parts of, say, a dog is thus not essentially different from the way an accidental form such as whiteness informs the parts of a white object: a white object has white parts, a canine substance has canine parts. The difference lies in the relative heterogeneity of the parts, which depends on the forms themselves. Organisms generally have sharply differentiated parts, whereas colour is relatively homogeneous. See also Aquinas (1956: ch. 72, pp. 213–15).

15 The same point applies to such phenomena as the transplantation of foreign DNA or cells into another species. Fido may have had mouse cells inserted into him by an experimenter, but if those cells really do enter into the dog's very make-up, taking their operative place within the genome, they have no substantial identity of their own any more than they did in the body of the mouse from which they were taken. Outside any creature – sitting, say, on a Petri dish – the

cells are substances in their own right, but when yoked to the nature of the creature into which they are inserted their existence is virtual, not substantial. Contrast the case of parasitism, where the parasite inside the organism retains its substantial identity because, however closely it may interact with and depend upon the functioning of its host, it does not enter into the very nature of that host, it does not become part of what *informs* that host or determines its specific identity.

16 To be clear on what my denial amounts to: I recognise that physicists currently believe there to be 'elementary particles', i.e. particles with no structure and no parts, in particular leptons and quarks. But I regard it as a metaphysical, rather than a physical, truth that no spatially extended object can be essentially elementary and hence indivisible. So I take it that strict metaphysical atomism is false a priori. Leaving aside the raised eyebrows such a philosophical claim might cause given the supposed empirical evidence to the contrary, note that what physicists *actually* hold is that if quarks (for instance) have a structure it must be smaller than 10^{-16} cm, but measurements cannot yet reach that far. Further, if it turned out that quarks *did* have a structure, they would, as physicists quite rightly admit, no longer merit the name elementary. What this shows is (1) that there is at least no law of nature, as currently understood, that prevents quarks from having structure and hence parts and (2) that merely calling a particle elementary does not mean that it really is so. It is, then, unjustified to claim that my denial of the existence of elementary particles has simply been proven false by physics.

17 This is a different though related sense of 'virtual' from that used in Chapter 1.2. There, a virtual part of an essence is what is not part of the explicit statement of the essence but what that essence logically presupposes. Here, the virtual existence of a part in a whole logically presupposes the whole of which the part is a constituent, so the presupposition is the reverse. Note that I take the ontological dependence of the part on the whole to entail a kind of logical presupposition (with logic construed in a broad sense, not tied to a formal system such as first-order logic). What is common to both cases is the idea that when something is related virtually to something else it is in some sense contained in, and dependent upon, that other thing. Fido's being an animal is contained in, and dependent upon, Fido's being a dog. The quark's nature within the living body is contained in, and dependent upon, the nature of that body.

18 Joel Katzav has drawn my attention to the similar position adopted by A.N. Whitehead (see Whitehead 1926: 98–9 and the pages leading up to these). He says:

> Thus an electron within a living body is different [quaere substantially?] from an electron outside it, by reason of the plan of the body. . . . But the principle of modification is perfectly general throughout nature, and represents no property peculiar to living bodies.
>
> (Whitehead 1926: 99)

This appears to be wholly in accord with the Scholastic doctrine, at least if 'different' is taken to mean 'substantially different'.

19 *De Anima*, II.1, 412b4; my translation. See also Ross (1931): 'the first grade of actuality of a natural organized body'. The Greek is: 'entelecheia hē prōtē sōmatos physikou organikou'.

20 In the case of local change, of course, it may be the other relatum which does the moving; but the object with respect to which it moves still bears distinct relational accidents. For the sake of simplicity I am here only concerned with intrinsic change, and hence, for example, with local change by an object by virtue of its own intrinsic motion.

21 Consisting of two protons and two neutrons, i.e. the nucleus of helium.

22 Why not say that the water contains actual oxygen which boils at 100 degrees when present in water? But then we would have to assume that actual water contained actual oxygen, and that both were boiling at 100 degrees. Yet this is as scientifically inaccurate as it is metaphysically implausible. When water boils, the weak hydrogen bonds between the water molecules break. The water molecules themselves remain intact when the water moves from its liquid to its gaseous state. There is no boiling of oxygen, the most basic empirical proof of which is that there is no liquid oxygen present (or gaseous oxygen post-boiling). At a more basic level, however, there are in water no actual oxygen molecules (or atoms) because of the electron sharing between the valence shells surrounding the hydrogen and oxygen nuclei. In any case, the idea that boiling water contains two actual substances each boiling at the same temperature is of dubious coherence. The virtual/actual distinction makes far more sense of the empirical phenomena. (I am indebted to Catherine Kolf for assistance with this point.)

23 More on the term 'virtual'. Recall I have used it in a sense that involves entailment, so that being an animal is, for example, virtually a part of the human essence. There are various senses of 'virtual', but one can also use entailment here in a qualified sense: being water entails being composed of hydrogen and oxygen. But what must be grasped is that being *actually* composed of hydrogen and oxygen does not entail being composed of *actual* hydrogen and *actual* oxygen, as opposed to *potential* hydrogen and oxygen, i.e. being composed of particles that retain some of the potencies of those elements, and can be reconstituted into them.

24 Note that I am not talking about subjects generally, some of which are non-substances and which still possess tropes (e.g. events are subjects of properties but are not substances). The discussion is restricted to substances, and this is sufficient to show the flaws in trope theory.

25 Not that Lowe is a hylemorphist, I should add, since he denies prime matter and identifies a substance with its substantial form. (See Lowe 1999a: 194–8, where he also treats statues as substances, contrary to my view of artefacts in Chapter 7.)

26 For related proposals on defining substance in terms of some kind of ontological independence, see Chisholm (1994); Fine (1995b); Hoffman and Rosenkrantz (1994; 1997).

27 I say that they *exist* in the mind rather than that they are merely conceived of in the mind as abstract, because this real existence is required for the possibility of knowledge. I cannot pursue that topic here.

28 It might be thought that exemplary causes are a category of cause additional to the four Aristotelian causes of material, efficient, formal, and final. I regard them, rather (though with some hesitation), as a species of final cause.

5 Essence and identity

1 Talk of self-identity as a relation may already be a step too far. Fred Sommers has argued persuasively that the very idea of identity as a relation is an artefact of modern predicate logic and can be dispensed with in his system of traditional formal logic that develops Aristotelian syllogistic. (See further Sommers 1969; 1982: ch. 6.) If so, the contemporary statement of the 'law of identity' as something like 'Everything is identical with itself' is not even an etiolated version of the true law of identity; rather, it is an illusion. (And of course Wittgenstein famously rejected the identity relation in the *Tractatus*.)

2 Lowe has, however, informed me (personal correspondence) that he has since changed his thinking, and now denies that a thing is to be identified with its essence since essences are not entities. See also Lowe (forthcoming a).

3 In an earlier work (Oderberg 1986) I argue against the view that things in themselves can be deduced from the thesis that different perceivers are endowed with
different perceptual apparatus.
4 George Schlesinger (in conversation) suggested that *child* might be disjunctive: a
child is either a boy or a girl. But in this case one wants to say that a child is
simply the offspring of a human, and this is a non-disjunctive essence which must
be manifested by one of two contingent genders (contingent, that is, to the
essence instantiated by them).
5 The conditions in which water exists are also a factor, but are not relevant to
Twin Earth thoughts. One cannot refute the claim that the properties of water
are fixed by its molecular structure by imagining a world in which water's boiling
point at ground level is wholly different to its boiling point at ground level on
Earth because of different atmospheric conditions.
6 For instance, lead is non-ferromagnetic but is not a d-block metal; iron, of
course, is ferromagnetic but also a d-block metal.
7 For the locus classicus in Porphyry, see his *Isagoge* (Introduction to Aristotle's
Categories) in Barnes (2003); Barnes has a few brief remarks on the Tree at pp.
109–10. For a typical nineteenth-century logician's account, see Venn (1889: 312–17).
8 Pasnau says this as a gloss on a passage in Aquinas (1920d: I.76.3 ad 4, pp. 38–9)
in which Aquinas is defending the doctrine of the unicity of substantial form, for
which I argued in Chapter 4. Aquinas is saying that one cannot deduce a real, as
opposed to a merely a conceptual, distinction between genus and species in an
individual substance from its logical classification according to these categories.
He is *not* asserting that genus and species do not reflect a real distinction per se,
that objects do not fall objectively under species–genus classifications that reflect
the real structure of their essences. His point is that species and genus are in no
way really separable in the individual substance, which has only one form from
which we can abstract the generic and specific constitution of the individual.
9 I presume this is what Ragan has in mind when he says of Linnaeus that 'his
genera, unlike Porphyry's, could contain multiple species' (Ragan 1998: 3). The
Porphyrian Tree allows multiple species within a genus, though it filters all but
one out of the classification by using the dichotomous method. The rest figure
implicitly within the complement.
10 Actually, Thomason does not mention either *summum genus* or *infima species*,
and it is unclear whether by the empty element he means the individuals, since
nothing is a member of these, or the lowest species themselves, which by definition contain no species. The lack of clarity is of little consequence, however, since
necessarily nothing is among the individuals if nothing is contained in their species. Whether his overall account applies to the Tree is not something I can
explore here.
  Ellis cites a counterexample to disjointness in chemical kinds (Ellis 2001: 56): the
kinds *cupric compounds* and *sulphates* have a common member, copper sulphate,
but neither is a species of the other. I find this unconvincing. *Cupric compound* does
not belong on any Tree since *compound* is not the proximate genus of anything
that is in fact a copper compound. The proximate genera include the ones falling
under *non-element* such as those mentioned in note iii to Figure 5.2, of which
sulphate is the proximate genus of copper sulphate. The proximate genera for
other copper compounds will occur on other parts of the Tree, for instance under
the *non-metals* for copper alloys. There is no lack of perspicuity in this classification, since all copper compounds anywhere on the Tree can be referred back to
the species *copper* for an understanding of what they specifically are. Ellis's error
is due to his failure to take account of proximate genera in taxonomy.
  Wiggins finds in Thomason's account 'real promise' (Wiggins 1980: 202) but
then goes on to oppose the method of dichotomous division, citing an example

of the need for cross-classification in linguistics. He is right that the method of division at least implicitly precludes cross-classification: no category F divides any category G that is not both on the same path of the Tree and higher than F. But Wiggins's example does not work. He cites as falling under the consonants both the unvoiced (p,s) and the continuants (s,z), under both of which fall the sibilants. (He doesn't say what the sibilants are, but he means s, inter alia.) But his scheme of classification does not correspond to actual phoneme classification, according to which s (in English) is the unvoiced alveolar fricative. Using the divisions *voiced/unvoiced*, *alveolar/non-alveolar*, and *fricative/non-fricative*, we can classify all of the consonants of English without cross-classification. And this is just what phoneticists do.

The Tree requires us to proceed downwards from the most general to the most specific, and whilst it might be relatively easy in zoology, say, it will be less easy the more the classificatory scheme has conventional or artefactual elements. Phoneticists do not usually use a tree structure but a multidimensional grid-like classification. (For the details, see Clark and Yallop 1995: ch. 4.) However, since the unvoiced consonants are more numerous than either the alveolars or the fricatives, and on the assumption that we want to define, say, s, we should probably have these highest in the Tree under *consonant*. Alveolars and fricatives are equinumerous, so we can choose which category to have next. Hence we could define s as the alveolar fricative unvoiced consonant, or as the fricative alveolar unvoiced consonant. On the other hand, it is plausible to rank certain dimensions of classification as higher than others in terms of what might be called *structural* generality rather than mere numerosity. It is at least arguable that place of articulation (where in the mouth) is structurally more general than manner (the way the parts of the mouth are shaped etc.) and manner is structurally more general than voicing. If so, we should perhaps define s as the unvoiced fricative alveolar consonant.

A further point: Wiggins cites John Wallace's definition of *infima species* as follows: 'An *infima species* is a natural kind predicate K_1 such that, for any other natural kind predicate K_2, either every K_1 is a K_2 or no K_1 is a K_2' (Wiggins 1980: 202, citing Wallace's unpublished 1964 PhD thesis 'Philosophical Grammar'). Now Wiggins is sympathetic to *infima species* (Wiggins 1980: 117–18), but he fails to recognize that Wallace's definition is inadequate because of the imprecise term 'natural kind'. The precise thing to say is that within a given scheme of classification the infima species are such that, for every other genus or species, every member of the former falls under the latter or none does. If we mixed schemes, say substance and accident, we would end up classifying *man* as not an infima species because, for example, some men are white and some are not. Yet colours are natural kinds as well, only natural kinds of *accident*. Hence we have to say that man is an infima species because, as a kind of substance, he is such that, for every other kind of substance, either every man falls under it or none does. Similarly, within the classification of accidents according to colour, the infima species are such that, for every kind of colour, either every member of the former falls under the latter or none does. Hence every particular whiteness falls under *white* and under *colour*, but none falls under *black*. Particular whitenesses form an infima species. But aren't there essential differences between particular shades of white? I would argue that these are best regarded as necessary accidents of particular modes of whiteness, rather than specific differences constituting new categories of colour. This is because the particular shade of whiteness of a thing is explained as a determination of its whiteness, a way in which whiteness manifests itself in the particular white thing. Its being a particular shade of white is entailed by its being white at all, even though which particular shade it has is not so explained, any more than what kind of sense of humour a person has is not explained by her being a person, though that she has a capacity for humour at all is so explained. It is doubtful that one can give a wholly non-phenomenological account of why it is that shades of a colour do not constitute new species of colour.

11 I have tried to minimize the use of italics for biologically recognized species/ genera, for ease on the eye, though they will sometimes appear.

12 Historical properties will of course enter into the definition of essentially historical entities such as genealogies themselves, or perhaps kinds of artefact whose purpose is historically defined, such as certain customs.

13 Based on mitochondrial DNA evidence.

14 For a lengthy analysis of holes, see Casati and Varzi (1994). This is not to say that they would necessarily endorse my description in the main text.

15 Where 'transcendental' has nothing to do with Kant.

16 See, e.g., St Albert the Great (as expounded by J.M.G. Hackett in Gracia 1994: 97–9 and references therein); Aquinas (1920a: I.11.3, *resp.*, p. 116). See also Gracia (1983).

17 The left conjunct is included since my examination is confined to material individuals. It does not apply to immaterial substances such as God, who is not a species of anything, and disembodied spirits such as angels, which are famously (and correctly, I believe) held by Aquinas to be *identical* with their own singleton species rather than plural members *of* a species; hence no two angels are of the same species. See further Aquinas (1920c: I.50.4, pp. 13–14).

18 For a contemporary defence of haecceities, see Rosenkrantz (1993). He takes a haecceity to be an identity-involving property – *being identical with x*, for some individual *x*. But he rejects the idea that this involves the relation of identity and the individual *x* as constituents. Hence the obvious circularity objection, on his view, has no bite. Without going into the details of Rosenkrantz's account, I note simply that the more one tries to avoid circularity by denying what seems obvious – that *being identical with x* involves both identity and *x* as constituents – the more obscure haecceities become, and indeed for Rosenkrantz not only are many of them ungraspable by us, they are also incapable of being grasped even by God. But since an omniscient being can by definition know everything it is logically possible to know, and there is no apparent reason why some haecceities should be logically impossible to know if others can be known, the unknowability of some looks like a limitation on God's omniscience. Moreover, given that *we* know individuals when we see them, it is strange that we should be able to know this, i.e. to grasp individuality, without knowing in all cases that by virtue of which individuality holds. Hoffman and Rosenkrantz (2002: 124ff.) define omniscience in such a way that universal knowledge of haecceities is excluded, but only because it is built into the definition that the objects of an omniscient being's knowledge must be graspable in the first place. But this begs the very question at issue, namely why some haecceities should be ungraspable by an omniscient being, given that others are capable of being grasped. The tension is thus not eliminated.

19 Wiggins (1980: *passim.*, esp. ch. 1).

20 The translation, which is more accurate than that of Ross (1931), is taken from Harper (1879: 235), from whose important work much of the present outline is derived (with modifications).

21 I have left out the scare quotes around 'particular thing' in the translation; the Latin is 'hoc aliquid'.

22 This is what we owe to Suarez. See Gracia, 'Francis Suarez', in Gracia (1994: 475–510), and references therein; also Harper (1879: 238ff.).

23 Joseph Owens admirably emphasizes the neglected role of form in individuation: see his 'Thomas Aquinas' in Gracia (1994: 175–81).

24 Following Harper (1879: 247ff.).
25 'Individuum autem est quod est in se indistinctum, ab aliis vero distinctum' (Aquinas 1920b: I.29.4, p. 35). Needless to say, 'indistinct' does not have its current meaning, but means 'having the character of an undivided unity'.
26 See Owens in Gracia (1994: 182–3 and references), for St Thomas's espousal of this position. A cursory glance at the work of Thomists (e.g. John of St Thomas, and latterly Harper) shows that indeterminate quantity is accepted as the designation of individuating matter.
27 I did not consider whether substances of different kinds can coincide in space and time, but the general considerations advanced here lend obvious support to the idea that they cannot; which does not mean distinct *material objects* cannot coincide; only that if they did at least one of them would not be a substance. This I hold to be true of artefacts, such as a bronze statue and the lump of bronze constituting it.
28 Of course a miraculous intervention could reinstate a corrupted substance, but even then its essential principles (matter and form) would have to have survived the period of non-existence, which they do in the case of man. (See further Chapter 10.)
29 As do Gracia and Kronen in Gracia (1994: 526).
30 Other authors to cast doubt in one way or another on the idea of finding a non-question-begging criterion of identity include Jubien (1996), Merricks (1998), and Rea (1998).
31 For extensive criticism, see Oderberg (1993); also Chisholm (1976: Appendix A); Rea (1998); Lowe (1999a: 114–18).
32 On both of which, see Oderberg (2004b). The 'problem of temporary intrinsics' derives from Lewis (1986: 202–5), though it is traceable to Kant.
33 Oderberg (1993: esp. ch. 2).
34 This does not require treating statues as substances, i.e. it is consistent with regarding them as ontologically dependent entities. (See further Chapter 7.4.) For more on coincidence, see Lowe (1995), replying to Burke (1992).
35 Despite what is often proposed to philosophy undergraduates, however, human beings do not turn over all of their cells during their adult life. Most neurons and muscle cells are not replaced. A girl is born with all the egg cells she will ever have, all in an arrested stage of cell division. Then, after puberty, ordinarily just one cell each month finishes its process of cell division to produce the released egg. Some organisms have fixed numbers of cells: the lobster has exactly nine nerve cells in its cardiac ganglion that are fixed for life; the adult roundworm *Caenorhabditis elegans* has exactly 959 somatic cells (not counting sperm and eggs) which are never replaced. Much of the physical material forming our cells is replaced, though. Even the mineral in our bones is constantly being turned over. The DNA is a prominent exception. Although there are some attempts to correct errors in the sequence which may accumulate with time, once a DNA molecule is produced it stays unchanged until the cell divides or dies. When the cell divides, one of the old strands ends up in each new cell unchanged. That one strand may go unchanged through many cell divisions until the cell it happens to reside in dies. Another structure not replaced is the lens of the eye. Damage to these cells or to the proteins in them tend to accumulate so that our vision is constantly deteriorating. (Thanks to Richard Norman, Emeritus Professor of Biology at the University of Michigan, Dearborn, for this information.)

6 Essence and existence

1 Those defending the (merely) notional or logical difference include, famously, Suarez (C16th–17th), but also Alexander of Hales (C13th), Aureolus, (C14th),

Durandus (C14th), and Gabriel Biel (C15th). It was also defended by Averroes (C12th) and is latterly defended by Harper (1879: 106ff.). Those defending the real distinction are primarily St Thomas Aquinas and his many followers (see, e.g., Aquinas 1956: ch. 52, pp. 152–5), but also St Albert the Great (C13th). For a modern defence, see Coffey (1914: 101ff.).

2 The translation is mine, though Ross's version brings out the distinction even more starkly: 'what human nature is and the fact that man exists are not the same thing'.

3 In the Fourth Set of Objections to the *Meditations*; see Cottingham *et al.* (1984: 140–3).

4 As both sides of the debate affirm.

5 I leave aside contemporary attempts to resurrect the Ontological Argument, such as Alvin Plantinga's, which rely on the mere possibility of God's existing supposedly to demonstrate His actual existence. See Plantinga (1974: ch. X) and criticism in Oppy (1995).

6 An objection to the Ontological Argument is sometimes put in terms of a distinction between nominal and real definitions – one cannot get from a nominal definition of God to a real one. It is not clear that the objection is a good one, and in any case it is not the objection I am raising here. One can have a real definition of something, even something which if it existed would exist of necessity, without being compelled *thereby* to admit its existence, even if the thing really *does* exist.

7 Fine says that 'what drives us to submit the property of being a man to the conditional analysis is the belief that it is impossible for something to be a man without existing' (Fine 1994a: 7). But this confuses necessary and sufficient conditions. It seems that Fine should have said the reverse: the conditional criterion is driven by the belief that if Socrates exists, then he is a man. But this leads to the absurdity that if he exists he is an existent man, and so by the modal criterion is essentially an existent man, so he exists essentially. ('But how can Socrates be essentially an existent man without also being essentially existent?' (Fine 1994a: 8).)

8 As already argued in respect of diachronic identity in Chapter 5. Note that one does not *define* identity by stating its logical properties (reflexivity, etc.).

9 Kant uses the word 'being' (*sein*), but it is clear he means existence rather than being as I have used it (see Chapter 5).

10 The theory applies also to other domains, such as that of fiction: the world is not titan-ish, but the domain of Greek mythology is.

11 I leave aside for now the issue of miraculous interventions and divine causal action, as well as issues surrounding the origin of the human soul. For more on the latter, see Chapter 10.

12 I put to one side questions concerning the supposed singularity of the 'Big Bang', where the laws apparently break down. This particular issue is not relevant to the general argument.

13 Again, let us omit questions concerning the divine purpose a creator might have in bringing one kind of universe into existence rather than another.

14 Leave aside the problem for the combinatorialist concerning the possibility of what existed at the beginning of the universe, which by definition could not be a recombination of anything actual.

15 If there is nothing, then there are no propositions and no facts, hence no proposition *that there is nothing* and no fact that there is nothing. Nothing is the *absence* of everything, facts and propositions included.

16 The point here is that, following Lowe (1999a: 226), we need a particular *and its kind* in order to generate the infinite series of natural numbers. The number 1 will be the kind containing the singleton set of the particular, 2 will be the kind containing the set containing both the single particular and the kind the singleton

member belongs to, 3 will be the kind containing the set containing these last two as well as the set containing them, and so on.

17 See Aquinas (1920a: I.25.1, pp. 345–7).

18 Although Lowe uses the standard term 'dispositions', I will use 'powers', as this is what he appears to mean.

19 As Lowe correctly points out, that a power characterizes a kind does not entail that every member of the kind has the power (Lowe 2006: 126).

20 Although Lowe's theory as set out in (2006) does not account for accidental powers, in (1989) he presents a theory of dispositional predication that at least implicitly deals with accidental powers in terms of a conditional analysis (Lowe 1989: ch. 10). (I engage in some reconstruction, with the assistance of personal correspondence from Lowe, for whose comments I am grateful.) The basic idea is that we first account for essential powers via an unconditional law of the form 'Ks have P', for some kind K and some power P. An accidental power P_a belongs to a member of K only if 'Ks have P_a' is not a law. We then introduce a characteristic F such that it is not necessary that Ks are F, but some K has F: K has F accidentally, in essentialist terminology. Now, if these conditions hold, and if it is also a conditional law governing Ks that Ks have P_a if they are F, then we can say truly that the K in question has P_a accidentally: P_a will be an accidental power of the K. For some cases, though, we have to add a third condition to the effect that the K also has some other accidental characteristic G that prevents it from manifesting P_a. It will then be the case that if it is a conditional law governing Ks that Ks have P_a if they are F and G, then P_a will be an accidental power of the K. The presence or absence of a prevention clause marks, roughly, the distinction between what might be called *manifesting* a power and *actualizing* a power.

This analysis looks plausible in, say, the case of the dispositionally square rubber eraser that is occurrently trapezoid when subjected to distorting forces (Lowe 2006: 124–5). For 'F' we might choose something like 'is cut from a sheet of rubber by four cuts made at right angles to each other'. For 'P_a' we might choose 'is able to adopt a square shape'. For 'G' we can choose 'is subjected to distorting forces'. Some individual piece of rubber R might be such that it is F and G. Since it is not an unconditional law governing pieces of rubber as a kind that they have P_a, but it is a conditional law governing the kind that if Rs are F and G then they have P_a, we can say that the individual piece of rubber has P_a accidentally. Here, the idea is that the piece of rubber only has the accidental power of adopting a square shape when it is prevented from doing so. When it does so it fully actualizes that power and the power is no longer present. It returns when distorting forces are again applied. (Why it is capable of returning is due to more fundamental, essential powers of the matter constituting the rubber.)

In the case of the mere manifestation of a power, such as when a person runs (she doesn't lose the power of running by running), no prevention clause is needed and so on Lowe's account the possession of the accidental power of running will be explained in terms of a conditional law along the lines of 'Humans have the power to run if they have two normally functioning legs, are capable of standing upright, etc.'

One problem with this analysis is that there simply might not be any candidates for F or G. Fred has a hypnotic power, and he has it accidentally, but there may be no other characteristic of him upon which possession of the power is conditional: it might just be a brute power. Maybe it was given to him by God, or he was struck by lightning. It might not be a *law* governing humans that if they are struck by lightning they acquire a hypnotic power – even if it were the case that we could account for the power in terms of some genetic mutation caused by the lightning – since there might still be some randomness involved, for example as to whether the mutation gives rise to the power. Or if there is no genuine randomness in nature, being miraculously endowed with the power would certainly take it outside the realm of law. Further, there is no obvious candidate for *G*, such as would parallel the subjection of the eraser to distorting forces. Fred might in no way be prevented from manifesting the power: he just has it and might choose never to use it. In fact whether he chooses to use it or not is irrelevant: he has the power whatever else he may do. So it is hard to see what conditional law would be involved that could account for possession of the power.

Finally, it is crucial to Lowe's analysis that *F* and *G* should themselves not be powers, since otherwise he would be defining accidental powers in terms of themselves. Thus *F* and *G* must be occurrent characteristics, to use his terminology. Yet it might be powers all the way down. A thing might have an accidental power P_a solely by virtue of having some other accidental power Q_a, and Q_a by virtue of another power S_a, and so on with nothing occurrent that conditions any of the powers. The explanation may terminate in a brute accidental power. So not only might Fred have the hypnotic power as a brute fact, but he also might have it by virtue of his accidental power to capture people's gaze for an inordinately long time, and this because of his extraordinary accidental power of concentration. Then, even if we could find some *G* equivalent to the occurrent condition of being subject to distorting forces as applied to the eraser, and even though it would be a law that humans who are *G* and have an extraordinary power of concentration will be able to hypnotize others, we will not have obtained an analysis of what it is to have an accidental power pure and simple, since we can only do so in terms that make reference to other accidental powers. I conclude that Lowe's proposal, though not obviously a non-starter, is beset with significant difficulties. (For further recent discussion by Lowe, see his forthcoming b).

21 Whence the verb 'to tantalize'.

22 It is likely that Molnar's misinterpretation of Aquinas in his (2003: 126) is due to his use of Clark (1988) which (at least at p. 122, where the extract is from the *Summa Theologica* I.2.3) is less a translation than a free rendering. For a proper translation, where expressions such as 'capable of existing', absent in Aquinas, make way for the accurate 'potentiality', 'act', and so on, see Aquinas (1920a: 24).

23 One confusion is that Martin goes on to claim that mathematical properties are in pure act (1993: 185), which shows he does not really understand what pure act is. As suggested in my account of numbers, mathematical objects are abstractions from particulars. As such, they are delimited by the very particulars from which they are abstracted. These particulars either contain potentiality or are ontologically dependent on things that contain potentiality. Hence mathematical objects have what might be called a derived potency: it is because of this that they are distinct, determinate things with their distinct and often incompatible properties. These properties, too – such as the primeness of the number 7 – have a potentiality derived from the objects of which they are properties. So they cannot be pure actualities. To say otherwise is to conflate necessity with actuality, which is what I suspect to be at the heart of Martin's confusion here. The number 7 cannot be anything other than prime, but both the number 7 and primeness itself would not exist in a world without particulars. This is explained by the potentiality of the latter.

24 The distinction between active and passive powers is often traced back to Locke (especially Locke 1975: II.xxi.2, p. 234). But note that Locke would have received this doctrine as part of his highly attenuated Scholastic education. It is a doctrine wholly rooted in the Scholastic tradition and deriving from Aristotle, as seen in

his distinction between action and passion in the *Categories* and between the active and passive intellect in the *De Anima*.

25 Construed broadly to cover any form of self-nourishment.

26 Construed broadly to cover any form of metabolization of nutrients.

27 Putting it in modal talk: from '$(x)(x$ is $K \rightarrow$ Nec $(x$ is $F))$' and '$(x)(x$ is $K \rightarrow$ Nec $(x$ is $G))$' it does not follow that '$(x)($Nec $(x$ is $F \rightarrow x$ is $G))$'.

28 Just as from p and q one can deduce $p \rightarrow q$. In any case, it might be logically valid to argue thus but it does not explain the connection between the premises, as the paradoxes of material implication and entailment show.

29 Are they false in worlds where the particles concerned do not exist? Some might contend that they are vacuously true, but this is resisted by real essentialists, who are immanentists about universals. If, as the real essentialist contends, the laws are abstractions from particular behaviour, they depend for their obtaining on the existence of the particulars from which they are abstracted. Without the particulars there are no essences, hence nothing by virtue of which the laws obtain. That is why the real essentialist should hold that the laws of nature, if metaphysically necessary, are so in the sense that they are true in all worlds in which the essences which they are about exist, and in other worlds there are no such laws (not that they are *false*).

30 By which I mean metaphysically necessary, unless I indicate otherwise.

31 I leave aside whether this postulate is true (some physicists contending that the speed of light has varied over time), and assume it for the sake of argument.

32 Fundamental in the sense of belonging to the most basic physics – not physically simple, let alone metaphysically so.

33 Part of Coulomb's Law governing the electrostatic forces between charged particles, and hence between the atomic constituents of salt and water molecules. See further Bird (2001).

34 The other factors being the magnitude of the charges and the distance between them.

35 I say 'perhaps' since it is not clear whether *all* kinds of organism would have to be subject to the same laws of growth and decay.

36 With antecedents in Leibniz and Euler. Instantiations of it were known to the Greeks, for example in the case of reflection of light.

37 Joseph Louis Lagrange (1736–1813).

38 Alternatively, perhaps substantivalism about space and time is true, and what makes the PLA true is a property of space and time. Also, Katzav's (2005) rejoinder to Ellis ignores what Ellis (2005) says about global kinds, and so misses Ellis's point. Katzav adds that the PLA is contingent, hence not a law by Ellis's lights anyway. But this does not help Katzav. One immediate response is that the essentialist might distinguish between conceivability and possibility: we might be able to conceive of an object's having had a non-minimal quantity of action, but this does not make it possible (Bird 2004: 15).

More importantly, even if the PLA were indeed metaphysically contingent, it would play no part in the essentialist derivation of laws from the essential powers of objects. Rather, the PLA would be just another accidental regularity, albeit a highly general one, that could be abstracted from the accidental characteristics of all objects. As I noted earlier, not all powers of an object are essential to it – certainly the dispositional essentialist should not say otherwise – and so the fact that an object's accidental powers involved its acting according to the PLA would be wholly consistent with essentialism. Hence Katzav's remark that 'the PLA presupposes that which dispositions an object possesses is a contingent matter, and therefore that dispositions neither flow from, nor are part of, objects' essences' (Katzav 2005: 94) is irrelevant to the essentialist position. It is also inaccurate, since the PLA does not determine *every* power an object has. (It does not determine the human power of bipedal motion, for example, even if human motion is only ever in accord with the PLA. Nor does it determine the power of coloured objects to reflect light, even if the trajectory of the light they reflect is in accord with the PLA.) Or, if it does, Katzav has offered no argument to show this. Finally, Katzav claims that the PLA is incompatible with dispositionalism (leaving aside dispositional essentialism) because '[t]he dispositionalist assumes that the dispositions of objects alone are the ultimate explanatory ground for events. However, if we accept the PLA, we accept that there is an additional ground, and hence explanation, for why the objects that make up physical systems possess the dispositions they possess' (Katzav 2004: 212). The dispositionalist will respond that this is simply question-begging. The PLA will not be an *additional* ground beyond an object's intrinsic properties and explanatory of its dispositions. For behaviour in accord with the PLA will be just another disposition, albeit a high-level one.

7 Aspects of essence

1 I leave aside questions concerning inverted spectra, alleged relativity of perception, and so on.

2 We can make further divisions within each category, but there is no room for that here. Aristotle can be consulted for some of these.

3 As indicated in Chapter 6, the closest I can get to giving any meaning to 'categorical' as opposed to 'dispositional' is in terms of the distinction between act and potency.

4 There will be disagreement over whether a property such as charge is wholly a power. But, as I suggested in Chapter 6, even fundamental particles are actualities and their powers are shaped by actualities – they cannot be pure potentiality. Hence the determinateness of quantity found in mass, charge, energy and so on.

5 It is the need to think of powers in this dual way – as actualities but in a secondary sense – that is, I think, at the heart of what Aristotle says about what has come to be known as 'second potentiality' and 'first actuality', in *De Anima* II.5 (see Ross 1931: 417a).

6 From which it does not follow (contra Mellor 1974, 1982) that there is no distinction between the 'dispositional' and the 'categorical', or between potentiality and actuality (as I interpret it). See also Mumford (1998: 67–73) and Molnar (2003: ch. 11).

7 For Aquinas's defence of the coherence of transubstantiation, which adds more detail to the topic than the bare bones I have provided, see Aquinas (1923: III.75–7, pp. 262–327). For contemporary defences, see Anscombe (1981) and Dummett (1987).

8 At least on the most natural and plausible reading of Gorman (2005).

9 I am grateful to Michael Gorman for reminding me of this Porphyrian point, and for extensive and very helpful comments on this section. On the difference between necessary characterization and universal possession, see Chapter 8.1.

10 There are ways in which an explanatory relation might still be thought to hold, for example by treating the quark structure and the possession of a single proton as properties and maintaining some sort of property dualism, supplemented perhaps by a neutral monism about the substance possessing the properties. The deeper essence, then, would be whatever it was about the neutral substance that determined the existence of the distinct properties. Since I find property dualism either obfuscatory or implicitly reductionistic, I leave it to one side.

11 In biology, swans are a genus (*Cygnus*), but metaphysical genera and species are not identical to biological genera and species. Essentialist taxonomy, it will be recalled, counts kinds other than the highest and lowest – that is, the inter-

mediate kinds – as either species or genera relative to their place in the taxonomic tree. From a taxonomic point of view, then, swans are also a species, and indeed there may well be a physiological case for counting them as a species even if the biological species of swan cannot interbreed. I say more about this topic in Chapter 9.

12 The full account will make reference to more than chemical structure, but also macroscopic features specifying the form of the substance, e.g. as resinous, a milky sap when derived from the opium poppy (*Papaver somniferum*), capable of existing in other states, and so on.

13 The use of 'habit' here has a distinctly Aristotelian air, though what mineralogists call crystal habit would strictly come under the category of quality, relating as it does to shape, which is a kind of quality for Aristotle. (See Ross 1928a: 10a10.)

14 See Farndon (2006): 160–1, 215.

15 I leave it to the reader to apply the considerations I have raised to the case of water. All I will say is that LaPorte (2004: 103–10) is, in my view, wrong to hold that there is no fact of the matter about whether deuterium oxide (so-called 'heavy water') is properly called 'water', that 'we could go either way' (LaPorte 2004: 109, referring even to the thought that a putative variety of H_2O that went pink and fluffy 'might' with propriety be called 'water').

Putnam is wholly confused and confusing in his discussion of water and XYZ by persistently referring to 'different kinds of "water"' (Putnam 1975a: 241), as though the use of scare quotes somehow clarified the issue. LaPorte is right that micro-structure is not everything, even in the case of water. But having the composition H_2O is indeed the specific difference of water. D_2O differs so radically from H_2O in its properties – e.g. its toxicity to animals, its freezing point, its temperature of maximum density – that it cannot be regarded as just another variety of water. Hence its chemical structure as a variety of H_2O (deuterium being hydrogen with a neutron in the nucleus) is not all there is to its essence. (Though it could with justice be insisted that the extra neutron sure makes a difference, whatever deuterium's status as an isotope of hydrogen.)

LaPorte thinks that 'if D_2O were *not* water there would be trouble for the view that water = H_2O' (LaPorte 2004: 189). I have already indicated that 'Water = H_2O' is barely intelligible (see Chapter 1), but, that aside, if D_2O were not water, as I contend, there would be no problem at all for the view that water is essentially composed of H_2O. All it means is that the 'H' denotes not generic hydrogen but what LaPorte calls (following common terminology) 'protium', i.e. non-isotopic hydrogen. That we do not actually call water something like 'diprotium monoxide' hardly matters, since we already mark the distinction by using 'H' and 'D'. That scientists use the term 'water' for both compounds testifies only to their similar (but not identical) chemical structure, and matters no more metaphysically than that 'ice' is used for solid-sate CO_2 (dry ice) as well as for frozen water. The fact that we mark the distinction with 'H' and 'D' indicates the common, and correct, thought that heavy water is no more a species of water than vinegar is a species of wine (even though water and heavy water are both oxides of hydrogen and wine and vinegar are both fermentations of fruit).

16 I leave aside what look like artefacts created by animals, such as tools, nests, traps, etc. I regard these only as artefacts in an attenuated sense.

17 *To hen kata sumbebēkos* = 'the one according to accident.'

18 Gareth Matthews (1982) calls them 'kooky objects'. They are the examples of accidental unity on which Aristotle concentrates.

19 Although Aristotle is not clear about this, the accidental object must be a substance and a mode rather than a universal. The pair of Socrates and the universal of seatedness exists just so long as Socrates does and someone is seated, even if Socrates himself is not seated.

20 What about substances of different kinds? An incomplete substance, i.e. prime matter or substantial form, coincides with another incomplete substance of a different kind, namely substantial form and prime matter respectively. And both coincide with the compound substance, which is of a different kind from either, being complete. Are there more common or garden cases, such as an iron ball and the lump of iron (partly) constituting it? The more you think about such a case – think also of a ball of wax – the more it looks like a case of accidental unity, constituted in part by the underlying material substance, viz. the lump of iron or of wax. Balls of wax are, it seems, more like fists than like hands.

21 *Hen arithmōi* (*Topics* 103a32).

22 *Tropon tina* (*Metaphysics* 1015b23–4).

23 *Hen*.

24 Ross (1928b: 1015b24–5).

25 They also deny that accidental sameness is relative identity.

26 I take the liberty of altering their spelling of 'hylemorphic' by changing the 'o' to an 'e'.

27 Not considering the relational accidents which might relate the members of certain aggregates. An aggregate taken together with the geometrical arrangement of its members, for instance, is a kind of accidental unity.

28 Again, I leave aside the question of whether the members of a collection must also possess some degree of mutual proximity in space and time.

29 I leave aside for now the question of material metaphysical simples, on which see Chapter 10.5.

30 Some children are born with the rare genetic disease known as progeria, by which they have many of the characteristics of an old person and age more rapidly than normal people. But they are not born old, nor are they conceived old: rather, they begin ageing more rapidly than normal in the womb and are born with those characteristics of an aged person which result from that process. This case shows that what is really of metaphysical interest is not how people are born, but how they are conceived. Children with progeria do not begin their existence as old people.

31 That is, the necessity of originating from the gametes from which an individual in fact originates.

32 To be more precise, P is not entailed by any other truth not itself entailed by T and by nothing else. (A recursive specification will make the scenario perfectly precise.)

8 Life

1 A mule is the product of a male donkey and a mare; a hinny is the product of a female donkey and a stallion. For chromosomal reasons among others, hinnies are rarer than mules.

2 Needless to say, I am speaking here only of interspecific hybrids.

3 Nor does the existence of heterosis, or hybrid vigour, count against the abnormality of hybrid sterility. The hybrid might, due to the genetic diversity of its parents, have physical virtues going beyond either of them, but they would not somehow 'cancel out' the abnormality of being unable to reproduce.

4 Where by 'species' I here mean any species falling under the broad metaphysical species *living thing*. This will include typical biological species as well as any recognized by real essentialism, whether also recognized as such by biologists or not. For more on biological species and their relation to metaphysical species, see Chapter 9.

5 A useful discussion of immanent and transient causation is Chisholm (1982), but note that he emphasizes human agency as the paradigm of immanent causation

without extending it explicitly to causation by other biological agents, and without underscoring the nature of the process as one beginning with and terminating in the agent. A good discussion of immanent causation in Aristotle's natural teleology is that by Cooper (1982).

6 Of course there are complexities that would need spelling out in a longer treatment. When I throw a ball at a window I engage in both immanent and transient causation. Transiently, I break the window: the causal process begins with me and terminates in the window. Immanently, I exercise free will: I do something for some reason that belongs to me and so the transient process is an instrument to the fulfilling of my purpose, satisfaction of my desire, and so on. All of which, note, is not only compatible with altruistic behaviour but presupposed by it. When I help a person in need because they are in need, I transiently do something for them, but immanently perfect my own nature by conforming to morality – even if I am not thinking about this at the time. Altruism does not even make sense if this basic self-perfection is not presupposed in the action. When I act immorally, I still act immanently, though I do not perfect but rather damage myself as a moral agent by not conforming to the demands of morality.

7 Where the solution contains more of the solute material than it would normally have, i.e. when saturated. In saturation, the solvent has dissolved all of the material it can and any more will appear in solid form. When supersaturated, the amount of solute is more than when the solution is saturated, and so the extra amount tends to be precipitated or crystallized.

8 On the medieval debate about whether there is a real distinction between a substance and its powers, and further explanation of why there must be such a distinction (with special reference to human nature and human powers), see Coffey 1914: 246–52, 300–5.

9 Though we see the legacy of the Aristotelian viewpoint in words such as 'animal' and 'animated' (from the Latin *anima* = *psūche*).

10 A cell does not have a cellular structure in anything more than a tautological sense. Its structure consists of the components of the cell and their relationships, just as the structure of a multicellular organism consists of its components, which are themselves cells, and their relationships.

11 In fact this is one aspect of vitalism that he mentions, and which he calls 'substantial vitalism'. The other, 'chemical vitalism', is that only a living organism can synthesize organic chemicals. The latter is both experimentally false and of no philosophical relevance to the present discussion.

12 The use and abuse of the term 'vitalism' in order to stigmatize those who do not accept physico-chemical reductionism about life can be seen in philosophers such as Paul Churchland and Daniel Dennett. Churchland, in the context of a discussion of reductive materialism about the mind, characterizes vitalism as an 'empty shell', a mere 'denial of the materialism it opposed' in the face of the 'almost uninterrupted stream of successes' achieved by the physico-chemical analysis of life (Churchland (1979: 109–10). Putting to one side Churchland's evident ignorance of the difficulties scientists continue to face in providing a physico-chemical theory of life and its origin, one should note his conflation of materialism with physico-chemical reductionism. One of my central claims is that life does not require any immaterial principle, by which I mean a principle that is not wholly dependent on and explicable in terms of matter; but that it still escapes physico-chemical reduction. Again, Churchland speaks of seventeenth-century vitalism as holding there to be a 'vital spirit' animating all living things (Churchland 2000: 511–12). Whilst this may be true of much of the vitalist thinking at that time (due in large part to the corruption of Aristotelianism as then taught in many places), Churchland's implication is that this is the only alternative to physico-chemical reductionism. (His putting of a bizarre anti-vitalist argument

from self-refutation in the mouth of the vitalist compounds the ridicule but does not betray any real grasp of the vitalist's issue with the reductionist.)

Dennett (1991): 281 makes the same sort of confusion as Churchland, though in an even more simplistic fashion: the 'vitalist' is heard to deny that a cat is really alive even though it has apparently been demonstrated to be no more than DNA, proteins, and so on. The demonstration is taken for granted – though what it is supposed to be a demonstration *of* is unclear. The nonsensical denial has not been made by any vitalist, as one would hope. The key thought in vitalism that has any force – that whatever a living thing is, it cannot be just physics and chemistry – is not even mentioned in passing. And Dennett asserts that either human beings are 'made of robots' or else vitalism is true, meaning that we contain an 'extra, secret ingredient' (Dennett 1995: 206). Taken as a general claim about life, as Dennett assumes it should be, the assertion is a false dichotomy – moreover, one containing disjuncts of doubtful coherence. (The case of humans is a special one, and I discuss it in Chapter 10.)

13 For a useful discussion of this, see Bobik 1998: 231–41, commenting on Aquinas's *De Mixtione Elementorum*.

14 By 'organism' I henceforth mean organic substances as opposed to their parts, unless I specify otherwise. It is the substantial organisms that come first in the order of classification and explanation: the cellular and other parts are explained in terms of how they subserve the substance.

15 Might this be too strong? Mightn't an individual organism that was non-sentient but had locomotion 'get lucky' by moving randomly from harmful to beneficial environments? Even if this unlikely scenario were to be true of a single organism, it is virtually impossible to see how a whole *species* could get lucky in this way, and what we are concerned with is how the nature of a species must be constituted given the kind of world that exists. (I am grateful to Fiona Woollard for raising this point.)

16 Consider the fanciful 'Weather Watchers' scenario of Strawson (1994: ch. 9). My claim is limited to one about the natures of things in this world. Strawson's scenario of rooted, perfectly passive organisms that nevertheless have beliefs, desires, and other mental states, if coherent – and it is not undoubtedly so – does not take into account whether such creatures could exist in the necessarily changing world that is our own. It does not seem to me that they could last for more than a very short time. For theirs would be a world of perpetual frustration and disillusionment, leading inevitably to psychological disintegration. By 'exist' in this context, then, I don't mean mere persistence for a time, but flourishing according to a thing's nature. The Weather Watchers, I suggest, could not remotely flourish in our world, any more than other creatures endowed with sentience but lacking locomotion – barring the possible exceptions mentioned in the discussion on pp. 185–6. I admit, though, that my interpretation of the Weather Watchers' likely plight in our world is highly speculative – as speculative as Strawson's original though experiment.

17 There is, however, evidence that some plants exposed to a pathogen appear to use methyl salicylate as an airborne signal that activates disease resistance in neighbouring plants (Shulaev *et al.* 1997). If my interpretation is correct, as outlined on pp. 187–8, this would not be an example of plant sentience but an immanent vegetative power that happens to assist neighbouring plants without needing to be understood as conscious signalling. If it were more than this, we should wonder why the plants concerned do not display the highly diverse and flexible signalling of which even the *Cocci* bacteria such as *Staphylococcus aureus* are capable. A sentient plant would be expected to communicate with other plants in all sorts of situations, including the range of pathogenic situations to which plants are regularly exposed. In any case, the interpretation of methyl salicylate

emission in plants requires much more study before we can draw firmer conclusions about what exactly is happening.

18 For a quirky survey of some of the (often bizarre) literature defending plant consciousness, see Nagel (1997). She does not, however, address the philosophical issues discussed in this section.

19 My use of italics will be unavoidably inconsistent due to the inconsistency of their use by biologists themselves. In general, however, I will try to keep them to a minimum, reserving them mainly for taxa with Latin names.

20 Note that by replication I do not mean reproduction. The contrast is illustrated by comparing the replication of viruses with reproduction by intracellular parasites, both of which need a host cell in order to produce copies or descendants of themselves. Virus replication involves the copying by the host cell of viral DNA, resulting in many, possibly thousands, of copies of the invading virus. Parasite reproduction, by contrast, involves the parasite's undergoing mitotic cell division within the host cell, harnessing the energy and material of the host cell in order to reproduce. In viral replication, the virus does not use any energy and does not metabolize; rather, having invaded the host cell, it is the *latter* which requires material and energy in order to copy the foreign viral DNA which it mistakenly takes to be part of its own genome. The status of viruses is a matter of ongoing debate, so I take the contrast only to be strong but inconclusive evidence of a difference. Of course, talk of 'invasion' and such like might suggest the virus is carrying on its own immanent activity. All things considered, though, I regard this as no more than a metaphor. Virus replication, to continue metaphorically, is more like a genetic version of photocopying than genuine biological reproduction. The paper does not put itself into the copier – outside forces do that. And it is not the paper that expends energy in being copied – it is the copier that expends the energy.

21 I am grateful to Dr Alan Cann, of the Department of Microbiology at the University of Leicester, for helpful discussion and information about some of the issues in this section. This does not imply that he shares my interpretation of the empirical data.

22 Dennett (1998: 327) thinks a thermostat has beliefs and desires but is not conscious. This is tendentious, however, since having beliefs and desires presupposes some level of awareness; since thermostats are not aware of anything, they cannot have beliefs, desires, or any mental states. Whilst awareness, such as that possessed by a bacterium, does not entail consciousness of the sort possessed by, say, a human being or even a higher mammal, it does constitute sentience as I have defined it, and hence consciousness. Dennett's view of thermostats is typical of the contemporary conflation of consciousness with phenomenology.

Note also that Chalmers countenances the idea of 'protophenomenal properties' (Chalmers 1996: 298), properties which need not be accompanied by phenomenal ones but from which the latter, when they are present, are constituted. He suggests these might be instantiated in a 'simple system' such as a thermostat, but this is bizarre for reasons I have already indicated, on the assumption that such properties involve any kind of awareness. That certain animals lacking phenomenology might have them, though, is tantamount to making the distinction, as I have, between consciousness as sentience and consciousness as phenomenological awareness.

23 Final causation and immanent causation overlap but are not quite the same (see the end of this chapter (p. 199) and Oderberg (fothcoming a) for more). But immanent causation is the paradigm of final causation, and for present purposes that is enough. Moreover, all cases of final causation have to be understood within the context of immanent causation.

24 Suppose you want matter. But there is no matter without form, so to get matter you must get form. But you cannot get form without form. And there is no form without matter. So to get matter you must have matter.

25 The heart also carries out self-repairing and self-maintaining activities, just as any living entity does things for itself. The point is that it also has purposes that are not for its benefit but for that of the organism that has the heart. Moreover, its own self-directed purposes are wholly derivative from the purposes whose satisfaction does something for the organism of which it is a part.

26 Note that springing into existence out of nothing is not a kind of *emergence*, so the emergentist should not want to agree with such a proposal. Moreover, the principle that nothing can give what it does not have does not preclude something's springing into existence from nothing, since that principle is about what things can give to other things – and nothing is not a thing. We need to appeal to a different principle if we want to argue against the idea that anything – life included – could have sprung into existence from nothing.

9 Species, biological and metaphysical

1 By this I mean that the scientific issue of whether evolution is possible depends on empirical facts about the world we live in, as well as metaphysical truths about the essences of things that are needed to provide the *conditions* for evolution to take place. And these issues are separate from whether essentialism about the organisms *themselves* allows for evolution.

2 An aspect of population thinking that I will not examine is whether it commits us to thinking of species not as kinds but as *individuals* scattered through space and time. This is a prominent view strongly advocated by Hull and by Ghiselin (see the papers by them in Ereshefsky 1992). There are sound philosophical reasons (let alone biological) for rejecting such a view, and a number of them are set out by LaPorte (2004: 9–14). The most he concludes, however, is that Hull and Ghiselin have not shown that species *are* individuals, rather than that anything in their argument implies they *cannot* be. There is no space to pursue the stronger claim here, but I will note that from the fact that every species is associated with a population it does not follow that the species *is* the population, let alone that populations are individuals. Kinds and individuals have radically different properties, and parthood and instantiation are radically different relations.

3 I leave aside suppositions about the genotypes of identical twins and so on.

4 I say 'largely' because the fact that scientists disagree about how to define or explain their key concepts can be evidence, maybe strong evidence, of the fact that the data they are dealing with does not lend itself to straightforward interpretation, that there are multiple complexities not easily resolved, and so on. Such disagreement calls for sensitivities in interpretation and evaluation of empirical information by any theorist trying to explain the concept in question; hence it is methodologically relevant. That this applies to the species concept is something the essentialist can happily accept.

5 He means 'accommodation' in the intransitive sense of part of an organism's phenotype becoming accommodated to its environment.

6 He means, by 'accommodation by others', the becoming accommodated to their environment on the part of other elements of the organism's phenotype.

7 From the Greek *klados* = branch.

8 Ridley and Cracraft are cladists; Mallet and Mayden are not, but give typical criticisms appealed to also by cladists.

9 Sober is not dogmatic about there being a single correct species concept (Sober 1993: 158), but his sympathies lie in the cladistic direction.

10 Tudge, however, advances reasons for continuing to speak of the *Reptilia*, minus birds and mammals, as a genuine taxon in its own right (Tudge 2000: 407–8). Heretical as such thinking is to cladism, it seems that his vestigial essentialism admirably forces its way to the surface at this point.

11 To reiterate: by saying that the diachronic cladistic criterion drops out of the picture I am not thereby saying that the biological concept, for instance, *would* provide an acceptable criterion, since interbreeding is non-transitive. My point is simply that the cladistic criterion is not doing any work. So consider the sort of case discussed by LaPorte (2004: 59–61) of a species S_0 that splits at t into equal halves. By t_1 the branches have diverged sufficiently that on, say, the biological criterion they are not conspecific since their members cannot interbreed; they are now species S_1 and S_2. However, there has been too little diachronic change to prevent potential interbreeding between the members of either branch and the members of the ancestral species S_0. What are we to say about species identity? LaPorte uses splitting scenarios such as this to make some anti-essentialist points, which I consider shortly when discussing such cases in more detail. For present purposes, though, note that this is a counterexample to the biological criterion, due to non-transitivity. But it does not follow that the cladistic criterion is doing any work, as shown by the problems inherent in using it to decide whether the split at t is a speciation event or not. If we are to decide whether S_1 and S_2 are of different species we will need to apply a non-cladistic criterion, whether it be biological, ecological, or something else. If we want to know whether, before t_1, the branches are conspecific, again we will have to use some non-genealogical criterion. To determine whether either or both branches are conspecific with S_0, the same again applies. Merely to denominate the split at t a 'speciation event' is arbitrary. To call it a 'split' in the first place is empty. What kind of a split is it: ecological, recognitional, morphological?

12 LaPorte makes them sound far more similar than they are. Early naturalists would often confuse them in flight, as would hunters, but it doesn't take a zoologist to see from inspecting static specimens of them that their similarity is highly limited and superficial, as one would expect. See Warrick *et al.* (2005), who remark, rather unsurprisingly: '[h]ummingbird hovering approaches that of insects, yet remains distinct because of effects resulting from an inherently dissimilar – avian – body plan' (Warrick *et al.* 2005: 1094).

13 One might think also of Donald Davidson's 'Swampman' thought experiment (Davidson 2001). Here, a lightning bolt produces a 'physical replica' of Davidson after he has died. The underdescription of the scenario makes it difficult to know exactly what Swampman is supposed to be like, but Davidson's point is that the lack of a proper causal history would prevent it from having certain of the mental states (such as memories) Davidson himself had, and so from being numerically identical to Davidson. But he does not directly address whether Swampman would be *human*. (He finds it hard to see how it would have any thoughts at all, but presumably it could begin to *acquire* them.) The cladistic thought is different, and more extreme: it is that even with a normal evolutionary cause, and even assuming that the twin of a certain organism was molecularly and behaviourally identical (it didn't merely *seem* to have memories, it actually had them, even if they were not the same as the memories of the other organism), it would not be of the same *species* as that organism if they did not share a most recent common ancestor.

14 Suitably understood, though, the biological concept would not be obviously refuted. Molecular twins might not be able to interbreed, e.g. if they are both male, but sexual organisms that are similar in all respects but for sex must be able to interbreed.

15 My view is shared, at least implicitly, by Mallet (1995), though on genetic grounds. But the view is decidedly in the minority among biologists and philosophers of biology.

16 The cladistic view of species identity for individual organisms is therefore akin to the theory of extrinsic numerical identity (the 'best candidate' or 'closest con-

tinuer' theory) for individuals as expounded most famously by Nozick (1981) for persons (see also Garrett 1985 for Ship of Theseus cases). I discuss extrinsicness elsewhere (Oderberg 1993: 156–63), arguing that it cannot be ruled out at least for some artefacts, even if it has no bite in respect of persons. It is hard to see why any other organisms should be treated differently from persons in this regard. But if *which* organism something is does not look like an extrinsic matter, how could *what* it is in the first place be extrinsic?

17 LaPorte has broached the objection (in correspondence; it is not his considered opinion, however, but is worth mentioning) that 'whiteness = whiteness' is also a *de re* necessary truth, but it does not follow that all white things are essentially white. True enough, but it is not to the point and shows why, as Lowe has argued, the instances of universals such as whiteness are not white things but individual whitenesses, i.e. modes or tropes (see Chapter 2, note 5). And these are essentially what they are. Assuming *Panthera tigris* is a rigid designator of a species, its instances will be the individuals who are members of that species. Hence they will essentially be members of that species by the same reasoning that applies to whiteness.

Another example of LaPorte's (in correspondence) is 'food': 'food = food' is a *de re* necessary truth, but not all food items are essentially food. My reply is that 'food' should be taken in one of two ways, neither of which undermines my argument. It could be taken to denote an accident rather than a kind of substance, i.e. the accident of having nutritional value for at least one organism (or perhaps species). To say that something is food would, then, be to say that it had this accident. My response would then be exactly the same as for 'whiteness'. Or 'food' could be taken to denote, rather than a substance, a kind of *artefact*, i.e. a kind of thing that is ontologically dependent on certain purposes, tendencies, uses and so on that at least one organism or species of organism possesses in respect of referents of the term. (Clearly the account would have to be complicated in terms of something's being food for one organism/species but not for another, etc.) On the second proposal, then, 'food' would denote accidental unities of lumps of matter and their nutritive characteristics (see Chapter 7.4). Again, it would follow that food items were essentially food.

18 Note here the difference between what I am claiming about organisms and the view associated with what has come to be known as 'intelligent design' (ID) theory. ID theorists tend to treat organisms (apart from humans) as divinely made machines that can be understood according to the principles of human engineering and other technology. And they consider the complexity of such organisms to be largely if not wholly quantifiable and subject to empirical testing. I argued in Chapter 3 that there is no empirical test for essence. Moreover, as should be patent from hylemorphism, essence is not quantifiable (except, of course, for purely quantitative entities themselves), though the mathematical properties of things tell us something about their essences (at the most basic, that a thing is either material or an abstraction from matter). To deny that organisms are artefacts is not to reject the claim that they are in some way products of a divine creative act. It is to deny that they can be understood just as we understand artefacts. Hence, however the divine creative act should be interpreted (to the extent it can be interpreted at all), it should not be as a mere piece of super-powerful engineering. (For a brief critique of ID theory from a hylemorphic viewpoint, see Machuga 2002: 161–6.)

19 Just how useful is a matter of dispute. For criticism, see Sneath and Sokal (1973: 40–52) and elsewhere in their book.

20 Or whatever first physical event marked the beginning of the universe.

21 It is, of course, inaccurate to say without qualification that it is gradual. There are plenty of examples of more sudden changes, the Cambrian explosion for one.

But gradualness appears to be found often and in many places. The less the gradualness, the less bite the objection from vagueness has.

22 The extent to which examples such as these count as evidence for biologists depends on the species concept they employ. I count them as evidential because of their various connections to morphology, which I defend in section 9.4 as the ground of species essence. I am grateful to Edward Theriot of the School of Biological Sciences at the University of Texas at Austin for discussion of the *Stephanodiscus* case.

23 It might be thought that the non-limits are themselves indeterminate given the existence of cases where the limits are indeterminate, since vagueness about the limits is also vagueness about the non-limits. This is true, but it does not undermine my point. My point is that there are determinate cases where an object is within the boundaries beyond which it does not exist. If I remove a sliver the desk determinately still exists, as it does when I remove another sliver. The non-limits appear to be vague *only when* the limits do, i.e. when we consider cases where it is not clear that the object has gone out of existence. (Does my desk cease to exist after I remove a large chunk of some kind, or after a billion slivers have been removed, etc.?) When pertinent questions concerning the boundary are not involved, i.e. when we are well within it, the non-boundary is determinate. That is all I mean by saying that the non-limits are determinate.

24 This includes the domestic dog, *Canis lupus familiaris*, which is considered a subspecies.

25 I ignore cladistic qualms about the paraphyletic reptile taxon, and use 'reptile' according the common meaning, which includes also primitive forms such as the dinosaurs. I also treat *Archaeopteryx* as a single species, despite occasional worries over whether the extant fossils are members of a common genus only.

26 Feathered dinosaurs more primitive than *Archaeopteryx* have apparently been discovered (Qiang *et al.* 1998), but they were probably unable to fly. Phylogenetically, they would not be classed with birds even if they *were* able to fly, since they do not share a common ancestor with them. Leaving aside cladistic issues, they are characterized morphologically as belonging to the *Maniraptora* and hence as clearly reptilian.

27 For a classic study of the morphology of *Archaeopteryx*, see Ostrom (1976).

28 They have other functions than purely locomotive or nutritive, of course, but these are derivative.

29 The passage Mayr is referring to is in *On the Parts of Animals* (642b5–644a11; Loeb 1937: 78–93). Here Aristotle criticizes various ways in which the dichotomous method is used. For instance, Aristotle rightly points out (643b17–24) that successive divisions should use differentiae that are relevant to, i.e. a pertinent division of, the preceding differentiae. When we divide the organisms into the sentient and the non-sentient, and then the sentient into the rational and the non-rational, the difference of rationality is pertinent to the higher division of sentience, because it specifies a *kind* of sentience – rational consciousness or rational awareness. To divide sentience into, say, bipedal and non-bipedal would be foreign to the higher specification. (Aristotle's example involves feathered/featherless and white/black.)

Again (644a5–9), he criticizes the use of a differentia such as *two-footed* to specify human beings, since obviously being two-footed does not capture the essence of man. Hence, if we are to proceed as the dichotomists of his time did, we would need to add a multiplicity of differentiae to the definition of the human being, which contradicts dichotomous division. But this only goes to show that the dichotomies with which Aristotle was familiar were woefully inadequate through being insensitive to essence. He asserts that 'we cannot get at the ultimate specific forms of the animal ... by bifurcate division. If we could, the number of ultimate differentiae would equal the number of ultimate animal forms' (643a15–20). Although the passage is obscure, he seems to mean that we do not necessarily get a new species for each difference: a single difference can differentiate more than one species, say if they belong to distinct genera. (Being an egg layer might differentiate species in distinct genera, for instance.)

If this is what he means, he makes a correct point and indicates a general moral: there is no way that the method of dichotomy can provide a simultaneous classification of all the animal forms, let alone the infima species. All it does is classify each species, one at a time, by a filtering method that gets down to the genus and specific difference. To represent all of these genus/difference combinations at the same time is at least in principle possible (despite the technical difficulties involved in representing at one time the millions of extant species, let alone the extinct ones). But such a representation would not show at one and the same time each process of bifurcate division; indeed it is hard to see how it would be anything more than a *list* of all the genera and species, with the difference given for each. Repetition would be ubiquitous. Hence my scepticism about being able to achieve a *taxonomic tree* of all living things at once. A phylogenetic one is in principle possible and many incomplete examples exist (e.g. Tudge 2000), but such a tree is genealogical only (see my criticisms of cladism in section 9.3).

Moreover, Mayr's interpretation of Aristotle is further weakened because the passage from 643b29–644a11 has been 'corrupted by confusing interpolations' (Loeb 1937: 92), making its construal even more difficult. Finally, even a cursory glance at *Metaphysics* 1037b28–1038a35 (Ross 1928b) shows that Aristotle believes in definition by dichotomous division. It is clear from this passage and from works such as the *Categories* and the *Topics* that Aristotle is committed to this approach, hence to binomial classification, and therefore that the Porphyrian method merely builds on what he says. But that method is not one for the simultaneous classification of all things at once.

10 The person

1 In fact he never makes this exact statement, though it is implicit in his writings. The closest he gets is when he hypothesizes in the *Protrepticus* or *Exhortation to Philosophy*, a work of which only fragments remain:

> If, therefore, man is a simple noncomposite living being, and if his being and essence are determined in accordance with reason and intelligence, then he has no other function or ordination than the attainment of the most exact truth which is the truth about reality.
>
> (Aristotle, in Chroust 1964: 26–7)

Aristotle is here arguing that if man is a simple being, i.e. identified with a soul, then rationality is his essence since it is the essence of the soul. He goes on to say that even if man is a complex animal composed of body and soul, the soul is the most excellent part and so man would still be essentially rational. In either case his essence is to be a rational animal.

2 Here, in no special order, are some typical examples illustrating the claims of this paragraph, nearly all in the context of discussions of Cartesian dualism or property dualism: (1) For Braddon-Mitchell and Jackson (1996: 8), dualism is akin to explaining lightning in terms of Thor's anger, and hence is fundamentally primitive and pre-scientific; (2) For McGinn, to believe in dualism is to believe in 'supernatural entities or divine interventions' (McGinn 1989: 350), the attribution being clearly pejorative; (3) For Patricia Churchland, 'the concept of a non-physical

soul looks increasingly like an outdated theoretical curiosity' (Churchland 2002: 173); (4) Cummins (1989: 2) gives a one-page caricature, and a highly inaccurate and misleading one at that, of the sort of position defended in this chapter, which involves putting the word 'form' in upper-case letters rather than seeking to explain just what form is supposed to be: 'Mind-stuff inFORMed', etc.; (5) needless to say, Gilbert Ryle's (1949) vivid metaphor of the 'ghost in the machine' has helped to stifle serious debate for decades; (6) Daniel Dennett, for instance, refers approvingly to Ryle's having 'danced quite a jig on the corpse of Cartesian dualism' (Dennett 1987: 214); (7) Armstrong describes Cartesian dualism as 'curiously formal and empty' (Armstrong 1968: 23). These and countless other examples are not meant to imply that the critics do not always offer arguments, of varying degrees of insight, against dualism in its several forms; but in general the opposition tends toward the curt, the dismissive, and the incredulous.

3 To use Campbell's (1993) term in his discussion of Foster (1991).

4 Mainly associated with Nagel: see Nagel (1974); also Jackson (1982, 1986). David Chalmers's so-called 'naturalistic dualism' (Chalmers 1996) looks also like a kind of property dualism, identifying mental properties with irreducibly non-physical properties, but these are wholly material in the broad sense and governed by unknown laws of natural science.

5 Defenders of hylemorphic dualism, though not under that name, include Haldane (1994, 1999); Moreland and Rae (2000); Machuga (2002); Feser (2005). None of them sets out and defends all of the theses I do, and my case is in no way based on theirs. Also, they differ among themselves on various points, and I disagree with a number of theses one or more of them defend. The case I set out in this chapter draws heavily on Oderberg (2005a).

6 It seems that Meinong also held to a phenomenology of judgment (Meinong 1905). I am grateful to Barry Smith for drawing this to my attention.

7 For an idea of the vast difference between kinds of physical models of cognition that currently have supporters, see van Gelder (1995).

8 In speaking of the Cartesian position, I recognize that Descartes does not always appear to adhere to the position traditionally attributed to him. In the *Treatise on Man* (1664) he speaks of the human being as 'composed of soul and body' ('composé ... d'une âme et d'un corps'; Alquié 1963: 379) whilst at the same time attempting what looks like a purely mechanistic explanation of human action. (See also *The Principles of Philosophy* IV: #189, where in the French (1647; Alquié 1973: 503–4) he simply speaks of the union between soul and body, but in the original Latin (1644) he uses the Scholastic 'informare' – the soul informs the body.) When I speak of the Cartesian view, then, I am referring to the view traditionally ascribed to him, which is also the position that most clearly emerges from the central works published during his life.

9 'Persona est naturae rationalis individua substantia': Boethius, *Liber de persona et duabus naturis contra Eutychen et Nestorium, ad Joannem Diaconum Ecclesiae Romanae*: c. iii (*Patrologia Latina* 64: 1343c–d).

10 I will use 'person' and 'human person' interchangeably unless stated otherwise. This is not meant to derogate from the possibility and existence of essentially disembodied persons such as God or other beings. If there are such entities, the human person is a just a species of person. If there are not, the person just *is* the human person.

11 Which the Scholastics, following Aristotle, understood as involving a combination of male semen and female matter, such as menstrual blood.

12 A word of explanation is in order. Lest it be thought that hylemorphic dualism commits itself to a self-contradictory position concerning the immateriality of what are purely material objects such as tables and chairs, or dogs and cats, it

must be emphasized that the theory is not one only about universals but about particulars as well. As abstract objects, universals such as *chairness* and *felinity*, and even *humanity*, are immaterial; they are essences construed metaphysically (see Chapter 6.1). If it is correct to say that universals are wholly present wherever and whenever they are instantiated (correctly interpreted – see Chapter 4.5), we are compelled to assign to universals a kind of spatio-temporal location that must still be compatible with their essential immateriality.

Their immateriality, however, does not entail that they can exist without their instances. On the Aristotelian view of universals, the ceasing to exist of, say, all the green things means the ceasing to exist of the universal *greenness*, even though *greenness*, *qua* abstract object, is immaterial. Of course *greenness* continues to exist even if this particular tree is destroyed, as long as there are other green things; but the total absence of green things entails the absence of *greenness*. Hence we cannot deduce from the facts that a universal *F* is an immaterial entity and that *F* is instantiated in some particular object, that *F* can survive the destruction of that object (for it might be the only instance of *F*).

Even more important for present purposes, however, is the point that every particular instance of a universal is distinct from the universal itself: the hunger of Felix is a *mode* (trope) of hunger. Property instances are *concrete* entities, not abstract ones, and as such are not essentially immaterial, even construed metaphysically. (To call tropes 'abstract particulars', as trope theorists do (e.g. Campbell 1990), should be taken to reflect not their immateriality but their being *abstractions* from the substances in which they inhere.)

So one cannot read off from hylemorphic dualism the view that an individual instance of some universal is immaterial if the universal is (and hence the absurd conclusion that every substance is immaterial) by appealing to the fact that – in the case of substance – the instance possesses a substantial form. As possessed by a substance, the substantial form is *particular*, not universal, and *concrete*, not abstract. If it is immaterial, it will not be because it instantiates an immaterial universal, e.g. *human nature* or *felinity*, but rather because there is something *about* the instances of the relevant universal such that they themselves are properly to be regarded as immaterial. In the human case, this is the idea that the human intellect is immaterial in its essential operations, hence that the *physical* essence of the human being is immaterial.

13 *On the Generation of Animals* II.3, 736b28, Loeb (1943): 171: 'for bodily activity [*somatikē energeia*] has nothing in common with the activity of reason [*nous*]' (my translation); see also *De Anima* II.1, Ross (1931): 413a6; and *De Anima* III.4, Ross (1931): 429a25.

14 Hence Stephen Stich (1999) doubly misconstrues what the traditional definition of man as a rational animal amounts to. First, he interprets rationality purely in terms of logical reasoning, rather than in terms of the basic intellectual operations (in particular abstraction) that give rise to the powers of logical reasoning, idea formation, and judgment making. Secondly, he supposes that the ubiquity of certain kinds of reasoning error in the population threatens the definition. Yet the fact that human beings *can* (let alone *do*) reason correctly in most cases (even some cases will do) suffices to prove the point about the human intellect. Reasoning errors no more undermine the conception of man as a rational animal than does memory failure or low IQ. All they show is that we humans have finite minds and make plenty of mistakes.

15 Extrinsic dependence is a kind of non-essential dependence. For example, certain kinds of plant depend extrinsically, hence non-essentially, on the presence of soil for their nutrition, since they can be grown hydroponically. But they depend intrinsically, hence essentially, on the presence of certain nutrients that they normally receive from soil but can receive via other routes.

16 The point here is not one about *instantiation*, since the instantiation of the abstract by the concrete is a commonplace (which is not to say that it is easily understood) that reveals nothing special about the human mind. Human beings and human minds do not instantiate concepts, they possess and store them. The ontological problem, then, is how an abstract object such as a concept, with all its sui generis properties, could ever be stored in or possessed by a concrete object such as a brain.

17 The thought here is that concepts are not even *categorially capable* of embodiment due to a lack of extension, the lack being not merely a privation, such as when a concept happens not to have a possessor, but an intrinsic incapability of possession, as in the case of a number's not being red. Looked at this way, it is arguably straight nonsense to claim that a concept is either extended or unextended; but this supports my point equally well, since it does make sense (and is true) to say that a brain is extended – and so the ontological mismatch is preserved. (Thanks to Fred Sommers for emphasizing this point to me.)

18 I leave to one side the difficult issues surrounding causation and the conservation of energy, for exploration at a later time. It may be that conservation laws simply do not apply when mental activity is involved; or it may be that conservation does apply, but that the soul never creates new energy, and instead merely *regulates* the distribution of conserved energy already present.

19 One does not need to resort to exotic arguments to prove that the mind can grasp a potential infinity of concepts: one need only refer to the possibility of iteration or of grasping, say, a potentially infinite conjunction. Noam Chomsky's emphasis on 'linguistic creativity' is relevant here.

20 See Ryle (1949) for a sustained attack on what he saw as the illegitimate practice of taking the mind to be an entity or substance of some kind, rather than as a concept denoting various kinds of behaviour. In attacking the supposed conceptual mistake of making a thing out of what is not a thing Ryle was, of course, heavily influenced by Wittgenstein.

21 Due to the distinctive features of Frege's semantic and syntactic theory, an expression such as 'the concept horse' ought to refer to an object – namely the concept of a *horse*. But since he radically distinguishes between concept and object (objects, such as the horse Dobbin, *satisfy* concepts, such as the concept ' ... is fast'), how could one and the same thing be both a concept and an object? (See Frege 1952.) I suspect that this paradox in Frege is genuine, and take it to count against his rigid distinction between concept and object.

22 Aquinas (1920d: I.75.4, pp. 11–12). Hence Machuga, though a hylemorphist, is wrong to insist that 'we are a soul' (Machuga 2002: 16). For another view contrary to the thesis that persons are not souls, though not couched in 'soul' terminology, see Lowe (1999c: 8–9), where he identifies the individual concrete substance with its own substantial form, suggesting later that perhaps persons are examples of matterless substances, i.e. forms without matter (Lowe 1999c: 21). But it is not clear from his discussion why the two must be identified. For if, using his example and assumptions, the form of a statue is the property of its particular *being a statue of such-and-such a shape* (a view that my analysis in Chapter 7.4 implies to be not quite correct, since statues are accidental unities of which the accidental form is but a component), and if the individual statue itself is an instance of the substantial kind *statue of such-and-such a shape* (though again, as I argue in Chapter 7.4, artefacts are not substances), then the form as property and the statue as concrete substance are not one and the same. The statue would be a compound of matter and form (however one wishes to construe matter, and it should be noted that Lowe eschews prime matter in favour of proximate matter such as *the lump of bronze*), and it is this compound that would be the instance of the kind. The form remains only a part of that compound, its

very individuality being given by the matter with which it is united (though, again, Lowe rejects the idea of matter as the principle of individuation). On my analysis of artefacts in Chapter 7.4, again the statue would not be identical with its form, since the form is only a component of an accidental unity, and it is this unity to which the statue is identical. Hence Lowe's account is incorrect both on its own terms and in terms of my own account of artefacts. And if false for artefacts, it will be no more true for persons or other genuine substances.

23 See Chapter 4, note 5.

24 The idea that form can exist without matter might seem repugnant to the very Aristotelian conception of substance that I have been defending throughout this book. But it is not; nor is it to be confused with Platonism about universals, which is of course repugnant to Aristotelianism. For an interesting recent defence of form without matter that seeks to stay faithful to both the *Categories* and the *Metaphysics*, see Lowe 1999c; but see note 22 above.

25 What about the possibility of a soul's having begun to exist in a disembodied state, with its existence and identity being dependent not on its having once been the form of a body, but on its becoming *at a future date* the form of a body? This depends on whether one can make sense of the idea of backwards material causation – the idea that x exists at t_1 because of the matter to which x will be united at t_2 ($t_1 < t_2$). There are of course epistemological problems with the idea of identifying something on the basis of its future matter, but perhaps there is no straightforward metaphysical problem if the future is at least knowable in principle, say to an omniscient mind.

26 For more on the concepts of identity-dependence and existence-dependence, see Lowe (1999a: ch. 6; 2005).

27 Robinson sums up this position succinctly, in answer to the Aristotelian question of 'why and how a soul should be – in this life at least – tied to a particular body as a substantial unity': 'the soul is the form of the body, for the individualized identity of a form depends necessarily on the matter in which it is individualized, so there can be no worry about how it comes to belong to this body' (Robinson 1991: 225–6).

28 Note that this is a distinct principle from Armstrong's cross-temporal principle of instantiation for universals (Armstrong 1978a: 113; 1978b: 9–10; 1989a: 75–6). It is possible to accept my principle without accepting Armstrong's (and I do), since my principle entails only that for the universal of (human) *personhood* to be instantiated at some time, the instance existing at that time – a particular person – must, if not embodied at that time, have been embodied at some prior time. It does not follow that there can be a universal of *personhood* at some time without a particular person existing at that same time, as Armstrong's principle allows. Indeed I deny that a universal can exist at a time without having an instance at that time. Conversely, one can accept Armstrong's principle without accepting mine: a Cartesian dualist can hold that *personhood* is instantiated even without there being a present instance whilst denying that the required past instance was ever embodied. (In fact, Armstrong's principle is unrestricted across time, allowing even future instances to be sufficient for the present existence of a universal, thus making the principle even more implausible.) To anticipate slightly, note also: I hold that when a disembodied soul exists at a time, the person whose soul it is exists at that time. But the extra requirement of necessary past embodiment prevents any collapse into Cartesianism.

29 Just as the soul, being intrinsically independent of matter for its existence, does not cease to exist via separation from a material body, so by parity of reasoning it would seem that the soul cannot come into existence merely by virtue of the coming into existence of a material body. In other words, neither the soul's generation nor its corruption depends on matter. As Aristotle puts it in *On the*

Generation of Animals (II.3, 736b20, Loeb 1943: 169), the rational soul is unique in having to come 'from outside'. It requires further argument, be it philosophical or theological, to determine whether 'from outside' entails pre-existence (Plato) or immediate creation (Christianity). But if the general point is right, evolution of the human species by any mode of descent currently recognized by biologists is highly questionable.

30 Although the overwhelming textual evidence from Aquinas is that this is exactly what he believes, there is also a particularly tricky sentence from his *Commentary on 1 Corinthians*, referred to by Finnis (2005: 254) to which attention should be drawn. In his commentary at 15.2 on ch. 15, verses 13ff. ('If there be no resurrection of the dead, then Christ is not risen again ... if the dead not rise again, your faith is in vain', etc.), Aquinas says: 'My soul is not me [anima mea non est ego]; and so even if my soul should attain salvation in another life, still neither I nor any man would have attained it'. This looks as though he is denying that the person survives death and asserting that only the soul does so. Read in context, however – both the context at hand and that of all his other remarks on the subject (including those referred to in this chapter) – I do not think that this is what he has in mind. Immediately prior to the quoted assertion, he points out that the soul is a part of the man, and not the whole man (*totus homo*). So by going on to say that the man does not achieve salvation after death, he implicitly means this of the *whole* man, and this is correct, since the person after death is deprived of his body. Moreover, since he is commenting on St Paul's claim that without the resurrection of the dead faith is in vain, and explains that man has a natural desire for his salvation (*naturaliter desiderat salutem sui ipsius*), he must be taken to be pointing out that what a person desires is the salvation of his whole self, body and soul – not of himself in some reduced or impoverished way, as a mere part, viz., the soul. Hence the sort of salvation ultimately desired, which prevents faith from being in vain, is that represented by Christ's resurrection, to wit that of the entire person, body and soul, in his fullness. (For the Latin text of Aquinas's commentary, see the *Corpus Thomisticum* at http://www.corpusthomisticum.org/c1v.html (accessed 6 September 2006), but note that this portion of the commentary is a transcription of Aquinas's lectures by a student or some other person, without the benefit of Aquinas's own revision of the text.)

31 Gruesome as it may sound, patents have already been taken out on just such a procedure (see US Patent no. 4666425).

32 Aquinas himself uses the analogy of governor and state to support the idea that what the person does can be imputed to the soul (Aquinas 1920d: I.75.4 ad 1, p. 12). The soul then, according to him, can after a fashion be called the man (= the person), though it is not strictly identical with the man. Which is compatible with the proposition that the man (= person) continues to exist *as* a soul, i.e. in a radically mutilated form.

33 Having said that each man is an individual person, Aquinas goes on to explain that the 'particular judgment' due to him 'is that to which he will be subjected after death, when he will receive according as he hath done in the body (2 Corinthians 5:10), not indeed entirely but only in part since he will receive not in the body but only in the soul' (Aquinas 1935: III.88.1 ad 1, p. 12).

Bibliography

Adam, C. and Tannery, P. (eds) (1899) *Oeuvres de Descartes III: Correspondence*, Paris: Cerf.

Adams, R.M. (1974) 'Theories of Actuality', *Noûs* 8: 211–31. (Reprinted in Loux, M. (ed.) (1979) *The Possible and the Actual*, Ithaca, NY: Cornell University Press.)

Alexander, S. (1966) *Space, Time, and Deity: The Gifford Lectures at Glasgow 1916–18*, vol. II, London: Macmillan. (Orig. pub. 1920.)

Alquié, F. (ed.) (1963) *Descartes: Oeuvres Philosophiques, Tome I*, Paris: Garnier.

—— (1973) *Descartes: Oeuvres Philosophiques, Tome III*, Paris: Garnier.

Alston, W. (1979) 'Yes, Virginia, There Is a Real World', *Proceedings and Addresses of the American Philosophical Association* 52: 779–808.

Alvarado, A.S. (2004) 'Planarians', *Current Biology* 14: R737–8.

Anscombe, G.E.M. (1981) 'On Transubstantiation', in *The Collected Works of G.E.M. Anscombe, Volume III: Ethics, Religion and Politics*, Oxford: Blackwell.

—— (2005) 'Human Essence' [lecture given in 1988], in Geach, M. and Gormally, L. (eds) *Human Life, Action and Ethics: Essays by G.E.M. Anscombe*, Exeter: Imprint Academic.

Aquinas, St Thomas (1920a) *Summa Theologica, Part 1, QQ.I–XXVI*, vol. 1 of *The 'Summa Theologica' of St Thomas Aquinas, literally translated by the Fathers of the English Dominican Province*, London: Burns, Oates and Washbourne.

—— (1920b) *Summa Theologica, Part 1, QQ.XXVII–XLIX*, vol. 2 of *The 'Summa Theologica' of St Thomas Aquinas, literally translated by the Fathers of the English Dominican Province*, London: Burns, Oates and Washbourne.

—— (1920c) *Summa Theologica, Part 1, QQ.L–LXXIV*, vol. 3 of *The 'Summa Theologica' of St Thomas Aquinas, literally translated by the Fathers of the English Dominican Province*, London: Burns, Oates and Washbourne.

—— (1920d) *Summa Theologica, Part 1, QQ.LXXV–CII*, vol. 4 of *The 'Summa Theologica' of St Thomas Aquinas, literally translated by the Fathers of the English Dominican Province*, London: Burns, Oates and Washbourne.

—— (1923) *Summa Theologica, Part 3, QQ.LX–LXXXIII*, vol. 17 of *The 'Summa Theologica' of St Thomas Aquinas, literally translated by the Fathers of the English Dominican Province*, London: Burns, Oates and Washbourne.

—— (1935) *Summa Theologica, Part 3 (Supplement), QQ.LXXXVII–XCIX*, vol. 21 of *The 'Summa Theologica' of St Thomas Aquinas, literally translated by the Fathers of the English Dominican Province*, London: Burns, Oates and Washbourne.

—— (1955) *Summa Contra Gentiles, Book 1: God*, book 1 of *On the Truth of the Catholic Faith (Summa Contra Gentiles)*, trans. A.C. Pegis, Garden City, NY: Image Books/Doubleday & Company, Inc.

—— (1956) *Summa Contra Gentiles, Book 2: Creation*, book 2 of *On the Truth of the Catholic Faith* (*Summa Contra Gentiles*), trans. J.F. Anderson, Garden City, NY: Image Books/Doubleday & Company, Inc.

—— (1994) *Commentary on Aristotle's De Anima*, trans. K. Foster, O.P., and S. Humphries, O.P., Notre Dame, IN: Dumb Ox Books. (Orig. pub. 1951.)

—— (1995) *Commentary on Aristotle's Metaphysics*, trans. J.P. Rowan, Notre Dame, IN: Dumb Ox Books. (Orig. pub. 1961.)

Armstrong, D.M. (1968) *A Materialist Theory of the Mind*, London: Routledge and Kegan Paul.

—— (1978a) *Nominalism and Realism: Universals and Scientific Realism, Vol. I*, Cambridge: Cambridge University Press.

—— (1978b) *A Theory of Universals: Universals and Scientific Realism, Vol. II*, Cambridge: Cambridge University Press.

—— (1983) *What is a Law of Nature?*, Cambridge: Cambridge University Press.

—— (1989a) *Universals: An Opinionated Introduction*, Boulder, CO: Westview Press.

—— (1989b) *A Combinatorial Theory of Possibility*, Cambridge: Cambridge University Press.

—— (1997) *A World of States of Affairs*, Cambridge: Cambridge University Press.

Bacon, J. (1995) *Universals and Property Instances: The Alphabet of Being*, Oxford: Blackwell.

Bacon, J., Campbell, K., and Reinhardt, L. (eds) (1993) *Ontology, Causality and Mind: Essays in Honour of D.M. Armstrong*, Cambridge: Cambridge University Press.

Baker, L.R. (2000), *Persons and Bodies: A Constitution View*, Cambridge: Cambridge University Press.

Ball, P. (1999) H_2O: *A Biography of Water*, London: Phoenix.

Barnes, J. (ed.) (2003) *Porphyry: Introduction*, Oxford: Clarendon Press.

Barrett, R. and Gibson, R. (eds) (1990) *Perspectives on Quine*, Oxford: Blackwell.

Bedau, M. (1991) 'Can Biological Teleology Be Naturalized?', *The Journal of Philosophy* 88: 647–55.

—— (1996) 'The Nature of Life', in Boden, M.A. (ed.) *The Philosophy of Artificial Life*, Oxford: Oxford University Press.

Benacerraf, P. (1965) 'What Numbers Could Not Be', *Philosophical Review* 74: 47–73.

Bennett, M.R. and Hacker, P.M.S. (2003) *Philosophical Foundations of Neuroscience*, Oxford: Blackwell.

Berta, A. (1994) 'What Is a Whale?', *Science* 263: 180–1.

Bilsborough, A. (1992) *Human Evolution*, London: Blackie Academic and Professional.

Bird, A. (1998) 'Dispositions and Antidotes', *Philosophical Quarterly* 48: 227–34.

—— (2001) 'Necessarily, Salt Dissolves in Water', *Analysis* 61: 267–74.

—— (2002) 'On Whether Some Laws Are Necessary', *Analysis* 62: 257–70.

—— (2004) 'The Dispositionalist Conception of Laws', *Foundations of Science* 152: 1–18.

Black, M. (1952) 'The Identity of Indiscernibles', *Mind* 61: 153–64.

Bobik, J. (1965) *Aquinas on Being and Essence: A Translation and Interpretation*, Notre Dame, IN: University of Notre Dame Press.

—— (1998) *Aquinas on Matter and Form and the Elements*, Notre Dame, IN: University of Notre Dame Press.

Boyd, R. (1999) 'Homeostasis, Species, and Higher Taxa', in Wilson (1999a): 141–85

Braddon-Mitchell, D. and Jackson, F. (1996) *Philosophy of Mind and Cognition*, Oxford: Blackwell.

Brower, J.E. and Rea, M.C. (2005) 'Material Constitution and the Trinity', *Faith and Philosophy* 22: 487–505.

Burke, M.B. (1992) 'Copper Statues and Pieces of Copper', *Analysis* 52: 12–17.

Butler, J. (1914) *Fifteen Sermons Preached at the Rolls Chapel and a Dissertation on the Nature of Virtue*, ed. W.R. Matthews, London: George Bell and Sons.

Cairns-Smith, A.G. (1990) *Seven Clues to the Origin of Life*, Cambridge: Cambridge University Press. (Orig. pub. 1985.)

Callus, D. (1961) 'The Origins of the Problem of the Unity of Form', in Weisheipl, J. (ed.) *The Dignity of Science: Studies in the Philosophy of Science Presented to William Humbert Kane, O.P.*, Washington, DC: The Thomist Press.

Campbell, K. (1990) *Abstract Particulars*, Oxford: Blackwell.

—— (1993) 'Swimming against the Tide', *Inquiry* 36: 161–77.

Canola (2005) 'Growing Canola: Hybrids and Synthetics', *Canola Council of Canada*, http://www.canola-council.org/hybridssyntheticcanola.aspx (accessed 1 August 2006).

Carroll, J.W. (1994) *Laws of Nature*, Cambridge: Cambridge University Press.

Casati, R. and Varzi, A.C. (1994) *Holes and Other Superficialities*, Cambridge, MA: Bradford Books/MIT Press.

Chalmers, D. (1996) *The Conscious Mind*, Oxford: Oxford University Press.

Chambers, P. (2002) *Bones of Contention: The Archaeopteryx Scandals*, London: John Murray.

Chisholm, R. (1976) *Person and Object*, La Salle: Open Court.

—— (1982) 'Human Freedom and the Self' [lecture given in 1964], in Watson, G. (ed.) *Free Will*, Oxford: Oxford University Press.

—— (1994) 'Ontologically Dependent Entities', *Philosophy and Phenomenological Research* 54: 499–507.

Chroust, A.-H. (1964) *Aristotle: Protrepticus, A Reconstruction*, Notre Dame, IN: University of Notre Dame Press.

Churchland, P.M. (1979) *Scientific Realism and the Plasticity of Mind*, Cambridge: Cambridge University Press.

—— (2000) 'Eliminative Materialism and the Propositional Attitudes', in Cummins, R. and Cummins, D.D. (eds) *Minds, Brains, and Computers: The Foundations of Cognitive Science – An Anthology*, Oxford: Blackwell. (Orig. pub. in *The Journal of Philosophy* 78 (1981): 67–90.)

Churchland, P. (2002) *Brain-wise: Studies in Neurophilosophy*, Cambridge, MA: Bradford Books/MIT Press.

Claridge, M.F., Dawah, H.A., and Wilson, M.R. (eds) (1997) *Species: The Units of Biodiversity*, London: Chapman and Hall.

Clark, J. and Yallop, C. (1995) *An Introduction to Phonetics and Phonology*, 2nd edn, Oxford: Blackwell.

Clark, M.T. (ed.) (1988) *An Aquinas Reader: Selections from the Writings of Thomas Aquinas*, New York: Fordham University Press.

Coffey, P. (1914) *Ontology*, London: Longmans, Green and Co.

Cooper, J. (1982) 'Aristotle on Natural Teleology', in Schofield, M. and Nussbaum, M.C. (eds) *Language and Logos: Studies in Ancient Greek Philosophy Presented to G.E.L. Owen*, Cambridge: Cambridge University Press.

Cottingham, J., Stoothoff, R., and Murdoch, D. (eds) (1984) *The Philosophical Writings of Descartes, Volume II*, Cambridge: Cambridge University Press.

Cracraft, J. (1997) 'Species Concepts in Systematics and Conservation Biology – An Ornithological Viewpoint', in Claridge *et al.* (1997): 325–39.

Cronquist, A. (1978) 'Once Again, What Is a Species?', in Knutson, L.V. (ed.) *Biosystematics in Agriculture*, Montclair, NJ: Allenheld Osmun.

Cummins, R. (1989) *Meaning and Mental Representation*, Cambridge, MA: Bradford Books/MIT Press.

Daly, C. (1994) 'Tropes', *Proceedings of the Aristotelian Society* 94: 253–61. (Reprinted in Mellor, D.H. and Oliver, A. (eds) *Properties*, Oxford: Oxford University Press, 1997.)

Darwin, C. (1859) *On the Origin of Species*, London: John Murray.

—— (1880) *The Power of Movement in Plants*, London: John Murray.

Davidson, D. (2001) 'Knowing One's Own Mind', in his *Subjective, Intersubjective, Objective*, Oxford: Oxford University Press. (Orig. pub. in *Proceedings of the American Philosophical Association* 60 (1987): 441–58.)

Davies, P. (1999) *The Origin of Life*, London: Penguin.

Dennett, D. (1987) *The Intentional Stance*, Cambridge, MA: Bradford Books/MIT Press.

—— (1991) *Consciousness Explained*, London: Penguin.

—— (1995) *Darwin's Dangerous Idea: Evolution and the Meanings of Life*, London: Penguin.

—— (1998) *Brainchildren: Essays on Designing Minds*, Cambridge, MA: Bradford Books/MIT Press.

Divers, J. (2002) *Possible Worlds*, London: Routledge.

Drewery, A. (2005) 'Essentialism and the Necessity of the Laws of Nature', *Synthese* 144: 381–96.

Dummett, M. (1981) *Frege: Philosophy of Language*, 2nd edn, London: Duckworth.

—— (1987) 'The Intelligibility of Eucharistic Doctrine', in Abraham, W.J. and Holzer, S.W. (eds) *The Rationality of Religious Belief: Essays in Honour of Basil Mitchell*, Oxford: Clarendon Press.

Dupré, J. (1993) *The Disorder of Things*, Cambridge, MA: Harvard University Press.

—— (2002) *Humans and Other Animals*, Oxford: Oxford University Press.

Elder, C.L. (2004) *Real Natures and Familiar Objects*, Cambridge, MA: Bradford Books/MIT Press.

—— (2005) 'Undercutting the Idea of Carving Reality', *Southern Journal of Philosophy* 43: 41–59.

Ellis, B. (2001) *Scientific Essentialism*, Cambridge: Cambridge University Press.

—— (2005) 'Katzav on the Limitations of Dispositionalism', *Analysis* 65: 90–2.

Ellis, B. and Lierse, C. (1994) 'Dispositional Essentialism', *Australasian Journal of Philosophy* 72: 27–45.

Ereshefsky, M. (ed.) (1992) *The Units of Evolution: Essays on the Nature of Species*, Cambridge, MA: Bradford Books/MIT Press.

—— (1999) 'Species and the Linnaean Hierarchy', in Wilson (1999a): 285–305.

Farndon, J. (2006) *The Practical Encyclopedia of Rocks and Minerals*, London: Lorenz Books.

Fee, J. (1941) 'Maupertuis, and the Principle of Least Action', *The Scientific Monthly* 52: 496–503.

Feser, E. (2005) 'Personal Identity and Self-Ownership', in Paul, Miller, and Paul (2005): 100–25.

Fine, K. (1994a) 'Essence and Modality', *Philosophical Perspectives* 8, Atascadero, CA: Ridgeview Publishing Company.

—— (1994b) 'A Puzzle Concerning Matter and Form', in Scaltsas, T., Charles, D. and Gill, M.L. (eds) *Unity, Identity and Explanation in Aristotle's Metaphysics*, Oxford: Clarendon Press.

—— (1995a) 'Senses of Essence', in Sinnott-Armstrong, W. (ed.) *Modality, Morality, and Belief: Essays in Honor of Ruth Barcan Marcus*, Cambridge: Cambridge University Press.

—— (1995b) 'Ontological Dependence', *Proceedings of the Aristotelian Society* 95: 269–90.

Finnis, J.M. (2005) ' "The Thing I Am": Personal Identity in Aquinas and Shakespeare', in Paul, Miller, and Paul (2005): 250–82.

Fodor, J. (1974) 'Special Sciences', *Synthese* 28: 77–115.

Forbes, G. (1985) *The Metaphysics of Modality*, Oxford: Clarendon Press.

—— (1986) 'In Defense of Absolute Essentialism', in French, Uehling, and Wettstein (1986): 3–31.

Foster, J. (1991) *The Immaterial Self: A Defence of the Cartesian Dualist Conception of Mind*, London: Routledge.

Frege, G. (1952) 'On Concept and Object', in Geach, P. and Black, M. (eds) *Translations from the Philosophical Writings of Gottlob Frege*, Oxford: Blackwell. (Orig. pub. 1892 as 'Über Begriff und Gegenstand'.)

French, P.A., Uehling, T.E., and Wettstein, H.K. (eds) (1986) *Midwest Studies in Philosophy XI: Studies in Essentialism*, Minneapolis, MN: University of Minnesota Press.

Fry, I. (2000): *The Emergence of Life on Earth: A Historical and Scientific Overview*, London: Free Association Books.

Fuqua, W.C., Winans, S.C., and Greenberg, E.P. (1994) 'Quorum Sensing in Bacteria: The LuxR-LuxI Family of Cell Density-Responsive Transcriptional Regulators', *Journal of Bacteriology* 176: 269–75.

Garrett, B. (1985) 'Noonan, "Best Candidate" Theories and the Ship of Theseus', *Analysis* 45: 212–15.

Girle, R. (2003) *Possible Worlds*, Chesham: Acumen.

Goldberg, M.B. (2001) 'Actin-Based Motility of Intracellular Microbial Pathogens', *Microbiology and Molecular Biology Review*: 65: 595–626.

Gorman, M. (2005) 'The Essential and the Accidental', *Ratio* 18: 276–89.

Gould, S.J. (2002) *The Structure of Evolutionary Theory*, Cambridge, MA: Harvard University Press, 2002.

Gould, S.J. and Lewontin, R.C. (1979) 'The Spandrels of San Marco and the Panglossian Paradigm: A Critique of the Adaptationist Programme', *Proceedings of the Royal Society of London, Series B: Biological Sciences* 205: 581–98.

Gracia, J.J.E. (1983) 'Individuals as Instances', *Review of Metaphysics* 37: 39–59.

—— (ed.) (1994) *Individuation in Scholasticism, the Later Middle Ages, and the Counter-Reformation, 1150–1650*, Albany, NY: State University of New York Press.

Grant, E. (ed.) (1974) *A Sourcebook in Medieval Science*, Cambridge, MA: Harvard University Press.

Grant, P.R. (1986) *Ecology and Evolution of Darwin's Finches*, Princeton, NJ: Princeton University Press.

Greenberg, E.P. (1997) 'Quorum Sensing in Gram-Negative Bacteria', *American Society for Microbiology News* 63: 371–7.

Gunderson, K. (ed.) (1975) *Language, Mind, and Knowledge: Minnesota Studies in the Philosophy of Science, Vol. VII*, Minneapolis, MN: University of Minnesota Press.

Hacker, P.M.S. (1987) *Appearance and Reality*, Oxford: Blackwell.

—— (1990) *Wittgenstein: Meaning and Mind*, vol. 3 of *An Analytical Commentary on the Philosophical Investigations*, Oxford: Blackwell.

—— (2007) *Human Nature: The Categorial Framework*, Oxford: Blackwell.

Haldane, J. (1994) 'Analytical Philosophy and the Nature of Mind: Time for Another Rebirth?', in Warner, R. and Szubka, T. (eds) *The Mind–Body Problem: A Guide to the Current Debate*, Oxford: Blackwell.

—— (1999) 'A Return to Form in the Philosophy of Mind', in Oderberg (1999): 40–64.

—— (ed.) (2002) *Mind, Metaphysics, and Value in the Thomistic and Analytical Traditions*, Notre Dame, IN: University of Notre Dame Press.

Haldane, J. and Lee, P. (2003a) 'Aquinas on Human Ensoulment, Abortion and the Value of Life', *Philosophy* 78: 255–78.

—— (2003b) 'Rational Souls and the Beginning of Life (A Reply to Robert Pasnau)', *Philosophy* 78: 532–40.

Hallett, Garth L. (1991) *Essentialism: A Wittgensteinian Critique*, Albany, NY: State University of New York Press.

Harper, T., S.J. (1879) *The Metaphysics of the School*, vol. 1, London: Macmillan & Co.

Hawthorne, J. and Gendler, T.S. (2000) 'Origin Essentialism: The Arguments Reconsidered', *Mind* 109: 285–98.

Heil, J. (2003) *From an Ontological Point of View*, Oxford: Clarendon Press.

Heller, M. (1990) *The Ontology of Physical Objects: Four-Dimensional Hunks of Matter*, Cambridge: Cambridge University Press.

Hennig, W. (1966) *Phylogenetic Systematics*, Urbana, IL: University of Illinois Press. (Orig. pub. in 1950 as *Grundzüge einer Theorie der Phylogenetischen Systematik*.)

Hirsch, E. (1988) 'Rules for a Good Language', *The Journal of Philosophy* 85: 694–717.

—— (1993) *Dividing Reality*, Oxford: Oxford University Press.

Hobbes, T. (1991) *Leviathan*, ed. R. Tuck, Cambridge: Cambridge University Press. (Orig. pub. 1651.)

Hodick, D. and Sievers, A. (1989) 'On the Mechanism of Closure of Venus Flytrap (*Dionaea muscipula* Ellis)', *Planta* 179: 32–42.

Hoffman, J. and Rosenkrantz, G.S. (1994) *Substance among Other Categories*, Cambridge: Cambridge University Press.

—— (1997) *Substance: Its Nature and Existence*, London: Routledge.

—— (1999) 'On the Unity of Compound Things: Living and Non-Living', in Oderberg (1999): 76–102.

—— (2002) *The Divine Attributes*, Oxford: Blackwell.

Hoyle, F. and Wickramasinghe C. (1981) *Evolution from Space: A Theory of Cosmic Creationism*, London: Dent.

Hughes, C. (1997) 'Aquinas on Continuity and Identity', *Medieval Philosophy and Theology* 6: 93–108.

Hull, D.L. (1965) 'The Effect of Essentialism on Taxonomy: 2000 Years of Stasis', *British Journal for the Philosophy of Science* 15: 314–26, 16: 1–18. (Reprinted in Ereshefsky (1992): 199–225.)

—— (1998) 'Taxonomy', in Craig, E. (ed.) *The Routledge Encyclopedia of Philosophy*, London: Routledge.

Hume, D. (1978) *A Treatise of Human Nature*, ed. L.A. Selby-Bigge and P.H. Nidditch, Oxford: Clarendon Press.

Huskins, C.L. (1929) 'Criteria of Hybridity', *Science* 69: 399–400.

Husserl, E. (1970) *Logical Investigations*, vol. 1, trans J.N. Findlay from the 2nd German edn (1913), London: Routledge and Kegan Paul. (Orig. pub. 1900.)

Jackson, F. (1982) 'Epiphenomenal Qualia', *The Philosophical Quarterly* 32: 127–36. (Reprinted in Chalmers, D. (ed.) (2002) *Philosophy of Mind: Classical and Contemporary Readings*, Oxford: Oxford University Press.)

—— (1986) 'What Mary Didn't Know', *The Journal of Philosophy* 83: 291–5.

—— (1996) *From Metaphysics to Ethics: A Defence of Conceptual Analysis*, Oxford: Clarendon Press.

Johansson, I. (1989) *Ontological Investigations: An Inquiry into the Categories of Nature, Man and Society*, London: Routledge.

Jones, T.E. (2004) 'Special Sciences: Still a Flawed Argument after All These Years', *Cognitive Science* 28: 409–32.

Jubien, M. (1996) 'The Myth of Identity Conditions', in Tomberlin, J.E. (ed.) *Philosophical Perspectives 10: Metaphysics*, Oxford: Blackwell.

Juul, J. (2003) 'The Game, the Player, the World: Looking for a Heart of Gameness', in Copier, M. and Raessens, J. (eds) *Level Up: Digital Games Research Conference Proceedings*, Utrecht: University of Utrecht, 30–45. Available at http://www.jesperjuul.net/text/gameplayerworld (accessed 9 October 2006).

Kant, I. (1933) *Critique of Pure Reason*, trans. N. Kemp Smith, London: Macmillan. (Orig. pub. 1781, 1st edn; 1787, 2nd edn).

Kaplan, D. (1979) 'Transworld Heirlines', in Loux (1979): 88–109.

Katzav, J. (2004) 'Dispositions and the Principle of Least Action', *Analysis* 64: 206–14.

—— (2005) 'Ellis on the Limitations of Dispositionalism', *Analysis* 65: 92–4.

Kauffman, S.A. (1993) *The Origins of Order: Self-Organization and Selection in Evolution*, New York: Oxford University Press.

Keefe, R. and Smith, P. (eds) (1997) *Vagueness: A Reader*, Cambridge, MA: Bradford Books/MIT Press.

Kiefer, H.E. and Munitz, M.K. (eds) (1970) *Language, Belief, and Metaphysics*, Albany, NY: State University of New York Press.

Kimbel, W.H., Lockwood, C.A., Ward, C.V., Leakey, M.G., Rak, Y., Johanson, D.C. (2006) 'Was *Australopithecus anamensis* Ancestral to *A. afarensis*? A Case of Anagenesis in the Hominin Fossil Record', *Journal of Human Evolution* 51: 134–52.

Kitcher, P. (1989) 'Some Puzzles about Species', in Ruse, M. (ed.) *What the Philosophy of Biology Is: Essays Dedicated to David Hull*, Boston, MA: Kluwer.

Klein, R.G. (1999) *The Human Career: Human Biological and Cultural Origins*, 2nd edn, Chicago, IL: University of Chicago Press.

Klima, G. (2002) 'Contemporary "Essentialism" vs. Aristotelian Essentialism', in Haldane (2002): 175–94.

Kripke, S. (1971) 'Identity and Necessity', in Munitz (1971): 135–64. (Reprinted in Schwartz (1977): 66–101.)

—— (1980) *Naming and Necessity*, Oxford: Blackwell.

LaPorte, J. (2004) *Natural Kinds and Conceptual Change*, Cambridge: Cambridge University Press.

Leibniz, G.W. (1998) *Philosophical Texts*, trans. and ed. Woolhouse, R.S. and Francks, R., Oxford: Oxford University Press.

Lewis, D. (1983a) *Philosophical Papers I*, New York: Oxford University Press.

—— (1983b) 'Counterpart Theory and Quantified Modal Logic', in Lewis (1983a): 26–39.

—— (1986) *On the Plurality of Worlds*, Oxford: Blackwell.

Locke, J. (1975) *An Essay Concerning Human Understanding*, ed. P.H. Nidditch, Oxford: Clarendon Press. (Orig. pub. 1689.)

Loeb (1937) *Aristotle: Parts of Animals*, trans. A.L. Peck, Loeb Classical Library, Cambridge, MA: Harvard University Press.

—— (1943) *Aristotle: Generation of Animals*, trans. A.L. Peck, Loeb Classical Library, Cambridge, MA: Harvard University Press.

Loux, M. (ed.) (1979) *The Possible and the Actual*, Ithaca, NY: Cornell University Press.

Lowe, E.J. (1989) *Kinds of Being*, Oxford: Blackwell.

—— (1995) 'Coinciding Objects: In Defence of the "Standard Account"', *Analysis* 55: 171–8.

—— (1999a) *The Possibility of Metaphysics: Substance, Identity, and Time*, Oxford: Clarendon Press.

—— (1999b) 'Abstraction, Properties, and Immanent Realism', in Rockmore, T. (ed.) *Proceedings of the Twentieth World Congress of Philosophy, Vol. 2: Metaphysics*, Bowling Green, OH: Philosophy Documentation Center.

—— (1999c) 'Form without Matter', in Oderberg (1999): 1–21.

—— (2005) 'Ontological Dependence', *The Stanford Encyclopedia of Philosophy (Summer 2005 Edition)*, ed. Edward N. Zalta. Available at http://plato.stanford.edu/archives/sum2005/entries/dependence-ontological/ (accessed 8 June 2006).

—— (2006) *The Four-Category Ontology: A Metaphysical Foundation for Natural Science*, Oxford: Clarendon Press.

—— (forthcoming a) 'Metaphysics as the Science of Essence'.

—— (forthcoming b) 'Modes of Exemplification'.

MacFadden, B.J. (1992) *Fossil Horses: Systematics, Paleobiology, and Evolution of the Family Equidae*, Cambridge: Cambridge University Press.

Machuga, R. (2002) *In Defense of the Soul: What It Means to Be Human*, Grand Rapids, MI: Brazos Press.

Mackie, J.L. (1976) *Problems from Locke*, Oxford: Clarendon Press.

Mallet, J. (1995) 'A Species Definition for the Modern Synthesis', *Trends in Ecology and Evolution* 10: 294–9.

March, J.C. and Bentley, W.E. (2004) 'Quorum Sensing and Bacterial Cross-Talk in Biotechnology', *Current Opinion in Biotechnology* 15: 495–502.

Marcus, R.B. (1993) 'A Backward Look at Quine's Animadversions on Modalities', in her *Modalities: Philosophical Essays*, New York: Oxford University Press: 215–32. (Orig. pub. in Barrett and Gibson (1990): 230–43.)

Margulis, L. and Sagan, D. (1995) *What Is Life?*, London: Weidenfeld and Nicolson.

Martin, A. and Chao, L.L. (2001) 'Semantic Memory and the Brain: Structure and Processes', *Current Opinion in Neurobiology* 11: 194–201.

Martin, C.B. (1993) 'Power for Realists', in Bacon, Campbell, and Reinhardt (1993): 175–86.

—— (1994) 'Dispositions and Conditionals', *The Philosophical Quarterly* 44: 1–8.

Matthews, G.B. (1982) 'Accidental Unities', in Schofield, M. and Nussbaum, M.C. (eds) *Language and Logos: Studies in Ancient Greek Philosophy Presented to G.E.L. Owen*, Cambridge: Cambridge University Press, 223–40.

Mayden, R.L. (1997) 'A Hierarchy of Species Concepts: The Denouement in the Saga of the Species Problem', in Claridge *et al.* (1997): 381–424.

Mayr, E. (1959) 'Typological Versus Population Thinking', in Meggers, B.J. (ed.) *Evolution and Anthropology: A Centennial Appraisal*, Washington, DC: Anthropological Society of Washington, 409–12.

—— (1982) *The Growth of Biological Thought: Diversity, Evolution, and Inheritance*, Cambridge, MA: Harvard University Press.

—— (1997) *This Is Biology: The Science of the Living World*, Cambridge, MA; Harvard University Press.

—— (2002) *What Evolution Is*, London: Phoenix.

McGinn, C. (1989) 'Can We Solve the Mind–Body Problem?', *Mind* 98: 349–66. (Reprinted in Warner, R. and Szubka, T. (eds) (1994) *The Mind–Body Problem: A Guide to the Current Debate*, Oxford: Blackwell.)

McKeon, R. (2001) *The Basic Works of Aristotle*, New York: The Modern Library.

Medawar, P.B. and Medawar, J.S. (1983) *Aristotle to Zoos: A Philosophical Dictionary of Biology*, Cambridge, MA: Harvard University Press.

Meinong, A. (1905) 'Über Urteilsgefühle: Was Sie Sind und Was Sie Nicht Sind' [On Judgement Feelings: What They Are and What They Are Not], *Archiv für die Gesammte Psychologie* 6: 22–58.

Mellor, D.H. (1974) 'In Defense of Dispositions', *The Philosophical Review* 83: 157–81.

—— (1977) 'Natural Kinds', in Pessin and Goldberg (1996): 69–80. (Orig. pub. in *British Journal for the Philosophy of Science* 28 (1977): 299–312. Also reprinted in Mellor, D.H. (1991) *Matters of Metaphysics*, Cambridge: Cambridge University Press.)

—— (1982) 'Counting Corners Correctly', *Analysis* 42: 96–7.

Merikle, P.M. and Reingold, E.M. (1998) 'On Demonstrating Unconscious Perception: Comment on Draine and Greenwald', *Journal of Experimental Psychology: General* 127: 304–10.

Merricks, T. (1998) 'There Are No Criteria of Identity over Time', *Noûs* 32: 106–24.

—— (2001) *Objects and Persons*, Oxford: Oxford University Press.

Mertz, D.W. (1996) *Moderate Realism and Its Logic*, New Haven, CT: Yale University Press.

—— (2001) 'Individuation and Instance Ontology', *Australasian Journal of Philosophy* 79: 45–61.

—— (2003) 'A Response to Moreland and Pickavance', *Australasian Journal of Philosophy* 81: 14–20.

Mill, J.S. (1886) *A System of Logic*, 8th edn, London: Longmans, Green, and Company. (Reprinted by Kessinger Publishing (n.d.).)

Miller, M.B. and Bassler, B.L. (2001) 'Quorum Sensing in Bacteria', *Annual Review of Microbiology* 55: 165–99.

Mishler, B.D. (1999) 'Getting Rid of Species?', in Wilson (1999a): 307–15.

Molnar, G. (2003) *Powers: A Study in Metaphysics*, ed. S. Mumford, Oxford: Oxford University Press.

Moreland, J.P. and Pickavance, T. (2003) 'Bare Particulars and Individuation: Reply to Mertz', *Australasian Journal of Philosophy* 81: 1–13.

Moreland, J.P. and Rae, S.B. (2000) *Body and Soul: Human Nature and the Crisis in Ethics*, Downers Grove, IL: InterVarsity Press.

Morrison, M. (2000) *Unifying Scientific Theories: Physical Concepts and Mathematical Structures*, Cambridge: Cambridge University Press.

Mumford, S. (1996) 'Conditionals, Functional Essences and Martin on Dispositions', *The Philosophical Quarterly* 46: 86–92.

—— (1998) *Dispositions*, Oxford: Oxford University Press.

—— (2004) *Laws in Nature*, London: Routledge.

Munitz, M. (ed.) (1971) *Identity and Individuation*, New York: New York University Press.

Murphree, W.A. (1998) 'Numerical Term Logic', *Notre Dame Journal of Formal Logic*: 346–62.

Nagel, A.H.M. (1997) 'Are Plants Conscious?', *Journal of Consciousness Studies* 4: 215–30.

Nagel, T. (1974) 'What Is It Like to Be a Bat?', *The Philosophical Review* 83: 435–50.

Noonan, H. (1988) 'A Reply to Lowe on Ships and Structures', *Analysis* 48: 221–3.

Nozick, R. (1981) *Philosophical Explanations*, Cambridge, MA: Belknap Press.

Oderberg, D.S. (1986) 'Perceptual Relativism', *Philosophia* 16: 1–9.

—— (1993) *The Metaphysics of Identity over Time*, London: Macmillan/Palgrave.

—— (1996) 'Coincidence under a Sortal', *The Philosophical Review*: 105: 145–71.

—— (ed.) (1999) *Form and Matter: Themes in Contemporary Metaphysics*, Oxford: Blackwell.

—— (2000) *Applied Ethics: A Non-Consequentialist Approach*, Oxford: Blackwell.

—— (2001) 'How to Win Essence Back from Essentialists', *Philosophical Writings* 18 (Autumn): 27–45. Available at www.rdg.ac.uk/dsoderberg.

—— (2002a) 'Hylomorphism and Individuation', in Haldane (2002): 125–42.

—— (2002b) 'Traversal of the Infinite, the "Big Bang" and the Kalam Cosmological Argument', *Philosophia Christi* 4: 305–36.

—— (2004a) 'Perennial Philosophy's Theory of Art', *Quadrant* (January–February): 68–74. Available at www.rdg.ac.uk/dsoderberg.

—— (2004b) 'Temporal Parts and the Possibility of Change', *Philosophy and Phenomenological Research* 69: 686–708.

—— (2005a) 'Hylemorphic Dualism', in Paul, Miller, and Paul (2005): 70–99.

—— (ed.) (2005b) *The Old New Logic: Essays on the Philosophy of Fred Sommers*, Cambridge, MA: Bradford Books/MIT Press.

—— (2005c) 'Predicate Logic and Bare Particulars', in Oderberg (2005b): 183–210.

—— (2006) 'Instantaneous Change Without Instants', in Paterson, C. and Pugh, M.S. (eds) *Analytical Thomism: Traditions in Dialogue*, Aldershot: Ashgate.

—— (forthcoming a) 'Teleology: Inorganic and Organic', in González, A.M. (ed.) *Contemporary Perspectives on Natural Law*, Aldershot: Ashgate.

—— (forthcoming b) 'The Metaphysical Foundations of Natural Law', in Zaborowski, H. (ed.) *Natural Law and Contemporary Society*, Washington, DC: Catholic University of America Press.

O'Hear, A. (1997) *Beyond Evolution: Human Nature and the Limits of Evolutionary Explanation*, Oxford: Clarendon Press.

Okasha, S. (2002) 'Darwinian Metaphysics: Species and the Question of Essentialism', *Synthese* 131: 191–213.

O'Leary-Hawthorne, J. and Cortens, A. (1995) 'Towards Ontological Nihilism', *Philosophical Studies* 79: 143–65.

Oppy, G. (1995) *Ontological Arguments and Belief in God*, New York: Cambridge University Press.

Orenstein, A. (2002) *W. V. Quine*, Chesham: Acumen.

Ostrom, J. H (1976) 'Archaeopteryx and the Origin of Birds', *Biological Journal of the Linnean Society* 8: 91–182.

Park, S-Y., Borbat, P.P., Gonzalez-Bonet, G., Bhatnagar, J., Pollard, A.M., Freed, J.H., Bilwes, A.M., Crane, B.R. (2006) 'Reconstruction of the Chemotaxis Receptor-Kinase Assembly', *Nature Structural and Molecular Biology* 13: 400–7.

Pasnau, R. (2003) 'Souls and the Beginning of Life (A Reply to Haldane and Lee)', *Philosophy* 78: 521–31.

—— (forthcoming) 'Abstract Truth in Thomas Aquinas', in Lagerlund, H. (ed.) *Representation and Objects of Thought in Medieval Philosophy*, Aldershot: Ashgate.

Paul, E.F., Miller, F.D., and Paul, J. (eds) (2005) *Personal Identity*, Cambridge: Cambridge University Press. (Orig. pub. as *Social Philosophy and Policy* 22 (2005).)

Pessin, A. and Goldberg, S. (eds) (1996) *The Twin Earth Chronicles: Twenty Years of Reflection on Hilary Putnam's 'The Meaning of "Meaning"'*, Armonk, NY: M.E. Sharpe.

Pfeifer, N. and Kleiter, G.D. (n.d.) 'Syllogistic Reasoning with Intermediate Quantifiers'. Available at http://www.users.sbg.ac.at/~pfeifern/pdf/cogsci05.pdf (accessed 17 May 2006).

Pietroski, P. (2000) *Causing Actions*, Oxford: Oxford University Press.

Plantinga, A. (1970) 'World and Essence', *Philosophical Review* 79: 461–92.

—— (1974) *The Nature of Necessity*, Oxford: Clarendon Press.

Popper, K.R. (1966) *The Open Society and Its Enemies, Vol. II: The High Tide of Prophecy*, 5th edn, London: Routledge and Kegan Paul.

—— (1972) *Conjectures and Refutations*, 4th edn, London: Routledge and Kegan Paul.

—— (1979) *Objective Knowledge*, rev. edn, Oxford: Clarendon Press.

Prigogine, I. and Stengers, I. (1984) *Order out of Chaos: Man's New Dialogue with Nature*, New York: Bantam.

Putnam, H. (1970) 'Is Semantics Possible?', in Putnam (1975b): 139–52. (Originally in Kiefer and Munitz (1970): 50–63; reprinted in Schwartz (1977): 102–18.)

—— (1973) 'Meaning and Reference', in Schwartz (1977): 119–32. (Originally in *The Journal of Philosophy* 70: 699–711.)

—— (1975a) 'The Meaning of "Meaning"', in Putnam (1975b): 215–71. (Originally in Gunderson (1975): 131–93.)

—— (1975b) *Mind, Language, and Reality: Philosophical Papers, Vol. 2*, Cambridge: Cambridge University Press.

Qiang J., Currie, P.J., Norell, M.A., and Shu-an J. (1998) 'Two Feathered Dinosaurs from Northeastern China', *Nature* 393: 753–61.

Quine, W.V. (1943) 'Notes on Existence and Necessity', *The Journal of Philosophy* 40: 113–27.

—— (1960) *Word and Object*, Cambridge, MA: MIT Press.

—— (1969) 'Natural Kinds', in Schwartz (1977): 155–75. (Also in Quine, W.V. (1969) *Ontological Relativity and Other Essays*, New York: Columbia University Press. Orig. pub. in N. Rescher (ed.) (1969) *Essays in Honor of Carl G. Hempel*, Dordrecht: Reidel.)

—— (1990) *Quiddities*, London: Penguin.

Ragan, M. (1998) 'On the Delineation and Higher-Level Classification of Algae', *European Journal of Phycology* 33: 1–15.

Rea, M.C. (1998) 'Temporal Parts Unmotivated', *The Philosophical Review* 107: 225–60.

—— (1999) 'Sameness without Identity: An Aristotelian Solution to the Problem of Material Solution', in Oderberg (1999): 103–15.

Reader, J. (1988) *Missing Links: The Hunt for Earliest Man*, London: Penguin.

Regan, C.T. (1926) 'Organic Evolution', in *Report of the British Association for the Advancement of Science, 1925*: 75–86.

Ridley, M. (1993) *Evolution*, Oxford: Blackwell.

Robertson, T. (1998) 'Possibilities and the Arguments for Origin Essentialism', *Mind* 107: 729–49.

Robinson, H. (1991) 'Form and the Immateriality of the Intellect from Aristotle to Aquinas', in Blumenthal, H. and Robinson, H. (eds) *Aristotle and the Later Tradition*

(Oxford Studies in Ancient Philosophy, ed. Julia Annas), Oxford: Clarendon Press; supp. vol.: 207–26.

Rong, R., Chandley, A.C., Song, J., McBeath, D., Tan, P.P., Bai, Q., Speed, R.M. (1988) 'A Fertile Mule and Hinny in China', *Cytogenetics and Cell Genetics* 47: 134–9.

Rosen, G. (1990) 'Modal Fictionalism', *Mind* 99: 327–54.

Rosenberg, A. (1985) *The Structure of Biological Science*, Cambridge: Cambridge University Press.

Rosenkrantz, G.S. (1993) *Haecceity: An Ontological Essay*, Dordrecht: Kluwer.

Ross, J.F. (1989) 'The Crash of Modal Metaphysics', *Review of Metaphysics* 43: 251–79.

Ross, W.D. (ed.) (1928a) *Aristotle: Categories et al.*, Oxford: Clarendon Press. (Vol. I of *The Works of Aristotle.*)

—— (1928b) *Aristotle: Metaphysics*, 2nd ed., Oxford: Clarendon Press. (Vol. VIII of *The Works of Aristotle.*)

—— (1930) *Aristotle: Physics*, Oxford: Clarendon Press. (Vol. II of *The Works of Aristotle.*)

—— (1931) *Aristotle: De Anima*, Oxford: Clarendon Press. (Vol. III of *The Works of Aristotle.*)

Russell, B. (1921) *The Analysis of Mind*, London: George Allen and Unwin.

Ryle, G. (1949) *The Concept of Mind*, London: Hutchinson.

Salmon, N. (1979) 'How Not to Derive Essentialism from the Theory of Reference', *The Journal of Philosophy* 76: 703–25.

—— (1981) *Reference and Essence*, Oxford: Blackwell.

Schwartz, S.P. (ed.) (1977) *Naming, Necessity, and Natural Kinds*, Ithaca, NY: Cornell University Press.

Searle, J. (1991) *Minds, Brains, and Science*, London: Penguin. (Orig. pub. 1984.)

Shalkowski, S. (1994) 'The Ontological Ground of Alethic Modality', *The Philosophical Review* 103: 669–88.

Shoemaker, S. (1969) 'Time Without Change', *The Journal of Philosophy* 66: 363–81.

Shulaev, V., Silverman, P., and Raskin, I. (1997) 'Airborne Signalling by Methyl Salicylate in Plant Pathogen Resistance', *Nature* 385: 718–21.

Shull, G.H. (1923) 'The Species Concept from the Point of View of a Geneticist', *American Journal of Botany* 10: 221–8.

Sidelle, A. (1989) *Necessity, Essence, and Individuation: A Defense of Conventionalism*, Ithaca, NY: Cornell University Press.

Sider, T. (2001) *Four-Dimensionalism: An Ontology of Persistence and Time*, Oxford: Clarendon Press.

Simons, P.M. (1994) 'Particulars in Particular Clothing: Three Trope Theories of Substance', *Philosophy and Phenomenological Research* 54: 553–75.

—— (1999) 'Farewell to Substance: A Differentiated Leave-taking', in Oderberg (1999): 22–39.

Simpson, G.G. (1959) 'Darwin Led Us into this Modern World', *The Humanist* 5: 267–75.

—— (1967) *The Meaning of Evolution*, New Haven, CT: Yale University Press.

Sinnott-Armstrong, W. (ed.) (1995) *Modality, Morality, and Belief: Essays in Honor of Ruth Barcan Marcus*, Cambridge: Cambridge University Press.

Smith, Q. and Craig, W.L. (1993) *Theism, Atheism, and Big Bang Cosmology*, Oxford: Clarendon Press.

Smullyan, A.F. (1948) 'Modality and Description', *The Journal of Symbolic Logic* 13: 31–7.

Sneath, P.H.A. and Sokal, R.R. (1973) *Numerical Taxonomy: The Principles and Practice of Numerical Classification*, San Francisco, CA: W.H. Freeman and Co.

Sober, E. (1980) 'Evolution, Population Thinking, and Essentialism', *Philosophy of Science* 47: 350–83. (Reprinted in Ereshefsky (1992).)

—— (1993) *Philosophy of Biology*, Oxford: Oxford University Press.

Sommers, F.T. (1969) 'Do We Need Identity?', *The Journal of Philosophy* 66: 499–504.

—— (1982) *The Logic of Natural Language*, Oxford: Clarendon Press.

—— (1997) 'Putnam's Born-Again Realism', *The Journal of Philosophy* 94: 453–71.

—— (2005) 'Comments and Replies', in Oderberg (2005b): 211–31.

Stalnaker, R. (1976) 'Possible Worlds', *Noûs* 10: 65–75. (Reprinted in Loux (1979).)

Sterelny, K. (1983) 'Natural Kind Terms', in Pessin and Goldberg (1996): 98–114. (Orig. pub. in *Pacific Philosophical Quarterly* 64 (1983): 110–25.)

Stich, S. (1999) 'Is Man a Rational Animal?', in Kolak, D. (ed.) *Questioning Matters: An Introduction to Philosophical Inquiry*, Mountain View, CA: Mayfield Publishing Co.

Stamos, D.N. (2003) *The Species Problem: Biological Species, Ontology, and the Metaphysics of Biology*, Lanham, MD: Lexington Books.

Stout, G.F. (1921) 'The Nature of Universals and Propositions', in Landesman, C. (ed.) (1971) *The Problem of Universals*, New York: Basic Books. (Orig. pub. in *Proceedings of the British Academy* X (1921–2): 157–72.)

Strawson, G. (1994) *Mental Reality*, Cambridge, MA: Bradford Books/MIT Press.

Stuessy, T.F., Jakubowsky, G., Gómez, R.S., Pfosser, M., Schlüter, P.M., Fer, T., Sun, B.-Y., and Kato, H. (2006) 'Anagenetic Evolution in Island Plants', *Journal of Biogeography* 33: 1259–65.

Theriot, E.C., Fritz, S.C., Whitlock, C. and Conley, D.J. (2006) 'Late Quaternary Rapid Morphological Evolution of an Endemic Diatom in Yellowstone Lake, Wyoming', *Paleobiology* 32: 38–54.

Thomason, R.H. (1969) 'Species, Determinates and Natural Kinds', *Noûs* 3: 95–101.

Tudge, C. (2000) *The Variety of Life: A Survey and a Celebration of all the Creatures That Have Ever Lived*, Oxford: Oxford University Press.

Upton, S.J. and Tilley, M. (1992) 'Effect of Select Media Supplements on Motility and Development of *Eimeria nieschulzi* in Vitro', *The Journal of Parasitology* 78: 329–33.

van Gelder, T. (1995) 'What Might Cognition Be, if Not Computation?', *The Journal of Philosophy* 92: 345–81.

van Inwagen, P. (1990) *Material Beings*, Ithaca, NY: Cornell University Press.

Venn, J. (1889) *The Principles of Empirical or Inductive Logic*, London: Macmillan and Co. (Reprinted 2005 by Elibron Classics.)

Walsh, D. (2006) 'Evolutionary Essentialism', *British Journal for the Philosophy of Science* 57: 425–48.

Warrick, D., Tobalske, B.W., and Powers, D.R. (2005) 'Aerodynamics of the Hovering Hummingbird', *Nature* 435: 1094–7.

Whitehead, A.N. (1926) *Science and the Modern World*, Cambridge: Cambridge University Press.

Wiggins, D. (1980) *Sameness and Substance*, Oxford: Blackwell. (Rev. edn, *Sameness and Substance Renewed*, Cambridge: Cambridge University Press, 2001.)

Williams, D.C. (1953) 'The Elements of Being', *Review of Metaphysics* 7: 3–18, 171–92.

Williamson, T. (1994) *Vagueness*, London: Routledge.

Wilson, R.A. (ed.) (1999a) *Species: New Interdisciplinary Essays*, Cambridge, MA: Bradford Books/MIT Press.

—— (1999b) 'Realism, Essence, and Kind: Resuscitating Species Essentialism?', in Wilson (1999a): 187–207.

Wittgenstein, L. (1958) *Philosophical Investigations*, Oxford: Blackwell.

Woods, J. (1967) 'On Species and Determinates', *Noûs* 1: 243–54.

Wuellner, B., S.J. (1956) *Dictionary of Scholastic Philosophy*, Milwaukee, WI: Bruce Publishing Company.

Yamashiro, S., Kameyama, K., Kanzawa, N., Tamiya, T., Mabuchi, I., and Tsuchiya, T. (2001) 'The Gelsolin/Fragmin Family Protein Identified in the Higher Plant *Mimosa pudica*', *The Journal of Biochemistry* 130: 243–9.

Zemach, E. (1976) 'Putnam's Theory on the Reference of Substance Terms', in Pessin and Goldberg (1996): 60–8. (Orig. pub. in *The Journal of Philosophy* 73 (1976): 116–27.)

Zhu, J. and Mekalanos, J.J. (2003) 'Quorum Sensing-Dependent Biofilms Enhance Colonization in *Vibrio cholerae*', *Developmental Cell* 5: 647–56.

Index

Printed in the United States
150140LV00002B/47/P

9 780415 323642